Grendon and the Emergence of Forensic Therapeutic Communities

Developments in Research and Practice

Edited by
Richard Shuker and Elizabeth Sullivan

D1795665

(W)WILEY-BLACKWELL

A John Wiley & Sons, Ltd., Publication

This edition first published 2010
© 2010 John Wiley & Sons Ltd.

Wiley-Blackwell is an imprint of John Wiley & Sons, formed by the merger of Wiley's global Scientific, Technical, and Medical business with Blackwell Publishing.

Registered Office
John Wiley & Sons Ltd, The Atrium, Southern Gate, Chichester, West Sussex, PO19 8SQ, UK

Editorial Offices
The Atrium, Southern Gate, Chichester, West Sussex, PO19 8SQ, UK
9600 Garsington Road, Oxford, OX4 2DQ, UK

350 Main Street, Malden, MA 02148-5020, USA

For details of our global editorial offices, for customer services, and for information about how to apply for permission to reuse the copyright material in this book please see our website at www.wiley.com/wiley-blackwell.

Library of Congress Cataloging-in-Publication Data

Grendon and the emergence of forensic therapeutic communities : developments in research and practice / edited by Elizabeth Sullivan, Richard Shuker.
        p. ; cm.
    Includes bibliographical references and index.
        ISBN 978-0-470-99055-1 (hardback)
1. HM Prison Grendon.   2. Prisoners–Mental health services–England.   3. Therapeutic communities-England.   I. Sullivan, Elizabeth. II. Shuker, Richard.
    [DNLM: 1. HM Prison Grendon.   2. Prisons–history–England.   3. Antisocial Personality Disorder–therapy–England.   4. Community Mental Health Services–organization & administration-England.   5. Criminal Psychology–methods–England.   6. History, 20th Century–England.   7. Prisoners–psychology–England.   8. Therapeutic Community–England.   WA 305 FE5 G826 2010]
    RC451.4.P68G753   2010
    362.2'20942557–dc22

                                                                2009053122

A catalogue record for this book is available from the British Library.

Set in 10.5 on 13 Minion by Toppan Best-set Premedia Limited
Printed in Singapore by Markono Print Media Pte Ltd.

1   2010

Grendon and the Emergence of Forensic Therapeutic Communities

Contents

About the Editors

Richard Shuker is a Chartered Forensic Psychologist and Head of Psychology and Research at HMP Grendon. He has managed cognitive behavioural programmes within adult and young offender prisons and is lead clinician on the assessment unit at Grendon. His special interest is in needs assessment and treatment of high-risk offenders. He is series editor for the book series *Issues in Forensic Psychology* and has publications in the areas of therapeutic communities, risk assessment, and treatment readiness and outcome.

Email address: richard.shuker@hmps.gsi.gov.uk

Elizabeth Sullivan gained her first degree in psychology with the Open University and her PhD in social psychology from Royal Holloway, University of London. Her doctoral thesis was on coping with threatened identities. Elizabeth is a Fellow of the Higher Education Academy (FHEA) and a Chartered Scientist (CSci). She was Senior Research Officer at HMP Grendon between 2004 and 2007, during which time she developed a research strategy for Grendon expanding the qualitative research agenda. Her work included guest editorships with Richard Shuker of *Issues in Forensic Practice* and the *Prison Service Journal,* and winning BPS funding for organising a series of seminars on Readiness for Treatment. Elizabeth worked closely with prisoners on research-related activities resulting in conference presentations and publications. Prior to her time at Grendon, Elizabeth was Senior Research Fellow & Senior Lecturer in Social Work at De Montfort University. Currently Elizabeth is Senior Lecturer in Social Work at the University of Bedfordshire and also serves as a non-executive director on the board of Bedfordshire and Luton NHS Partnership Mental Health Trust.

Email address: elizabeth.sullivan@beds.ac.uk

Contributing Authors

Geraldine Akerman is a senior forensic psychologist working at HMP Grendon. She is a Chartered Forensic Psychologist, Chartered Scientist and Associate Fellow of the British Psychological Society. In addition Geraldine is an associate member of the divisions of Counselling Psychology, and Positive and Coaching Psychology and she has been employed by the Prison Service since January 1999. She has worked with perpetrators of sexual offences since November 1999 and is trained to work with life-sentenced prisoners. Geraldine has published papers relating to developing a behaviour checklist, measuring community mindedness in a therapeutic community, developing empathy with men who have committed offences via the internet, applying the 'Good Lives' model to men who have committed sexual offences, and devising a fantasy modification programme to run in a therapeutic community. Geraldine is currently Co-Editor of *Forensic Update* and is studying for a PhD at Birmingham University in the area of devising a measure of sexual interest in male offenders.

Email address: Geraldine.akerman01@hmps.gsi.gov.uk

Peter Bennett studied South Asian history and social anthropology at the School of Oriental and African Studies, University of London. He went on to carry out two years' fieldwork in central India for his PhD, publishing a book and numerous articles on caste and sect. He joined the Prison Service as an officer at Birmingham in 1983, followed by positions as governor grade at Everthorpe, Hull, Moorland and Headquarters. He has been Governor in charge at Nottingham and Wellingborough and latterly at Grendon Therapeutic Community Prison and Springhill Open Prison. He has been chair of the Perrie Lectures Committee and is a director of the Koestler Trust and a director of the Newbridge Foundation.

Email address: Peter.bennett02@hmps.gsi.gov.uk

Michael Brookes is currently Director of Therapeutic Communities at HMP Grendon and Visiting Professor to Birmingham City University. He is a Consultant Chartered Forensic Psychologist. Michael started working in secure settings as a group worker at Glenthorne Youth Treatment Centre in Birmingham before joining the Prison Service in 1985 at HMP Gartree. From this base he also provided a psychological service to HMPs Ashwell, Leicester and Stocken. In 1991 Michael transferred to the East Midlands area where he was involved in creating the first area psychology team. He also managed directly the psychology teams at HMPs Lincoln and Lindholme. Upon transferring to Headquarters in 1997 Michael became Head of the Psychology Liaison Unit and also of the HR Planning and HR Strategy teams. In his current appointment Michael has responsibility for the delivery of therapy within HMP Grendon's unique custodial therapeutic community environment where psychological treatment is the central and pivotal regime activity.

Email address: michael.brookes02@hmps.gsi.gov.uk

David J. Cooke is a Consultant Forensic Clinical Psychologist and former head of the Forensic Clinical Psychology service in Glasgow. He is the Professor of Forensic Clinical Psychology at Glasgow Caledonian University and a Visiting Professor in the Faculty of Psychology at the University of Bergen in Norway. He was privileged to be the psychologist for the Barlinnie Special Unit for ten years. He undertakes research on psychopathic disorder and violence and is interested in the clinical application of this research to risk assessment. He served on the Maclean Committee on serious violent and sexual offenders. He is the author of over 150 scientific books, monographs, chapters and research papers. He has provided workshops on violence risk assessment and the assessment of psychopathy in the UK, Europe, North America, New Zealand, Iran and the Caribbean. He is a Fellow of the British Psychological Society and the Royal Society of Edinburgh: he was awarded the Senior Award for Outstanding Lifetime Contribution to Forensic Psychology from the Division of Forensic Psychology of the British Psychological Society in 2006. He is President of the European Association of Psychology and Law.

Email address: djcooke@rgardens.vianw.co.uk

Eric Cullen is a retired Consultant Forensic Psychologist. Previously he was Head of Psychology at Grendon Underwood, Lead Consultant for

Dovegate Therapeutic Community in Staffordshire and honorary Senior Research Fellow at the University of Birmingham. Eric is also an Associate Fellow of the British Psychology Society and was a magistrate. Currently, he is a member of the Correctional Services Accreditation Panel (CSAP) for the Ministry of Justice. Eric is author or editor of three books, six chapters and numerous articles, especially on democratic therapeutic communities for offenders.

Email address: erriccullen@tiscali.co.uk

Judith de Boer-van Schaik obtained a degree in sociology and methods of social research at the University of Leiden (The Netherlands). She had several functions at the Ministries of Health and Justice and in 1995 she was appointed Head of the Department for Forensic Psychiatry (TBS hospitals) of the Ministry of Justice, then in 2001 appointed Staff Director of the Van der Hoeven Clinic in Utrecht. In 2004 she was detached as a lecturer at the DSPD unit in Broadmoor and in 2007 was project manager for the community-based DSPD project in Liverpool.

Email address: jud.boer@compaqnet.nl

Frans Derks obtained a degree in psychology of religion at the Radboud University in Nijmegen (The Netherlands) and has worked since 1990 as a research psychologist and policy advisor at the Van der Hoeven Clinic in Utrecht.

Email address: fch.derks@hoevenkliniek.nl

Martin J. Fisher is a Chartered Psychologist, an Associate Fellow of the British Psychology Society, a Chartered Scientist and a Registered Forensic Psychologist. He currently works as Consultant Forensic Psychologist in the Public Sector Bids Unit of NOMS. In addition he is involved in the broader development of Psychological Services within the NOMS organisation. He is a member of GAP and GRAG and a member of the NRC review team for prison-based research applications. Having spent 15 years working in Prison Service establishments and a further six years working as an Area Psychologist for the Prison Service in the South East of England, Martin has a broad range of experience of consultancy, research and clinically orientated work in custodial, community and health settings. Martin is currently the CPD lead for the Division of Forensic Psychology and leads on responses to Government consultations for the Division. He has published academically in the fields of risk assessment, hostage incident profiling and organisational change. He is an Honorary Forensic Psychologist with Hampshire Partnership NHS Foundation Trust, and is a visiting lecturer in Forensic Psychology at Portsmouth University.

Email address: martin.fisher@hmps.gsi.gov.uk

David Holman is a senior lecturer at the Institute of Work Psychology, University of Sheffield. His primary research interests are emotion and well-being at work and job design, and his current research focuses on interpersonal affect regulation (as part of an ESRC-funded project on Emotion Regulation of Others and Self), performance monitoring in call centres, and job redesign in call centres. David has published extensively in leading international journals and is the co-editor of several books.

Email address: D.Holman@sheffield.ac.uk

Carol Ireland is a Chartered Psychologist, Forensic Psychologist and Chartered Scientist. She also works at the University of Central Lancashire, where she is the Director of Studies for the MSc in Forensic Psychology. At the university she also leads on the post-graduate qualifications for the Child Exploitation Online Protection Agency (CEOP) and post-graduate qualifications in crisis communications. She also supervises MSc and PhD students in their research, and is well versed in this area. She also works for Mersey Care NHS Trust, at Ashworth High Secure Hospital, where she is lead for group sex offender therapies and crisis (hostage) negotiation. Carol manages her own consultancy firm, Bowland Psychological Services, delivering expert witness reports, training and consultancy. Having spent five years working in prisons she is well versed in the challenges of delivering applied research. She has over 35 publications, including research-based journal articles as well as books and book chapters on broader aspects of forensic psychology concerned with consultancy and crisis (hostage) negotiation, and sexual offending. She also sat on Research Governance for six years as part of an NHS Trust. She is currently Chair of the British Psychological Societies Division of Forensic Psychology.

Email address: caireland@uclan.ac.uk

Jinnie Jefferies is a counselling psychologist and UKCP registered psychodrama psychotherapist. She is presently Head of Psychodrama at HMP Grendon and trainer for staff working in forensic therapeutic communities. She has pioneered training in Greece, Ireland and London and has written widely on psychodrama, in particular its use with personality disorders and forensic patients. Over the past decade she has made several television programmes using psychodrama and action methods and has recently been presented with a major award by the Butler Trust for her psychodrama work with long-term and lifer prisoners at HMP Grendon.

Email address: Jinnie.jefferies@hmps.gsi.gov.uk

Douglas S. Lipton has served as Director of Research and member of the board of directors for the US National Development and Research Institutes, as well as Deputy Director for the New York Division of Substance Misuse Services in charge of state drug abuse research. He has researched and published extensively on therapeutic communities interventions for substance misusers and has evaluated drug abuse control and treatment programmes around the world for the United Nations.

Email address: douglipton@nyc.rr.com

James McManus is a clinical psychologist working with a community mental health team in Manchester. He studied for his first degree in psychology at the University of Manchester before specialising in clinical psychology and completing the doctoral course at the University of Oxford. He has worked in the NHS for the last ten years and has experience of therapeutic work with a range of client groups, including experience of working in psychology departments in medium and high security settings.

Email address: j.mcmanus@nhs.net

Alan Miller has been working in the field of child and adult forensic psychology since 1999 and has experience of working with psychologically challenging individuals since 1981. He has been a social services care manager with learning disabled adults and prior to this was Senior Group Worker in a therapeutic community for children and adolescents. He is currently Consultant Forensic Psychologist for the St Luke's Hospital Group in the South East of England and Wales. Recently Alan has been involved with the development of services for adults with autism spectrum disorders in the independent hospital sector. Prior to this he was a Therapy Manager at HMP Dovegate Therapeutic Community. Alan serves on the Board of Assessors in Forensic Psychology. Previous publications include the ASET accredited course Understanding and Managing Anger and 'What Happens after Therapy?' in *Dynamic Security and the Therapeutic Community* (ed. Parker, 2006). He also has experience as a university visiting lecturer in psychology. Alan is an Associate Fellow of the British Psychological Society and a Fellow of the Royal Society of Medicine.

Email address: alanmiller@btinternet.com

Michelle Newberry is Research Officer at Grendon Therapeutic Community Prison. She holds a BSc, MRes and PhD in Psychology and is a Chartered Psychologist. Her experience includes working with adults with personality disorders and schizophrenia as well as individuals with learning disabilities, head injuries and dementia. Michelle has taught psychology at different universities and has conducted a wide variety of research in the field of forensic psychology. At HMP Grendon she has researched topics such as interpersonal relating and offence typology, changes in prisoners' relating styles following treatment, associations between psychopathy and blame attribution, and personality profiles and risk of reoffending.

Email address: Michelle.Newberry@hmps.gsi.gov.uk

Margaret Newton first joined the staff of Grendon Prison as a psychologist shortly after its opening in 1962, when she was involved in both clinical work and research. Outcome research has been an enduring concern: starting with the first year's cohort, she carried out a series of follow-up studies of residents during Grendon's first decade. Returning to Grendon in the 1990s, her research included a major reconviction study and she has published work on different aspects of outcome and on Grendon's performance as a prison. She has now retired from the prison service.

Contact through Psychology Unit, Grendon.

Karen Niven is a research associate at the Institute of Work Psychology, University of Sheffield. Her research focuses on emotion and well-being in organisations. Karen is particularly interested in looking at the ways in which organisation members deliberately try to influence their own emotions and the emotions of those around them. She is currently working on a large ESRC grant concerning Emotion Regulation of Others and Self.

Email address: K.Niven@sheffield.ac.uk

Lorna A. Rhodes is Professor of Anthropology at the University of Washington, where she teaches medical anthropology, the anthropology of institutions, and ethnographic research methods. She is the author of *Emptying Beds: The Work of an Emergency Psychiatric Unit* (University of California Press, 1991) and *Total Confinement: Madness and Reason in the Maximum Security Prison* (University of California Press, 2004). She has also published a number of articles about supermax prisons, including 'Changing the subject: conversation in supermax' (*Cultural Anthropology*, 2005), and 'Supermax as a technology of punishment' (*Social Research*, 2007). Lorna was medical anthropology editor of *Social Science and Medicine* from 1989 to 1993 and currently serves on several editorial boards, including *Medical Anthropology* and the *Howard Journal of Criminal Justice*.

Email address: lrhodes@u.washington.edu

Adrienne Rivlin holds a BA in Philosophy, Politics and Economics and an MPhil in Sociology, both from the University of Oxford. Having won a

Department of Health PhD studentship, Adrienne is currently completing research at the Department of Psychiatry, University of Oxford, for her doctoral thesis on the risk factors for suicide in prisoners. Her research interests include suicide and self-harm and prisons research. Recent publications include Rivlin, A. (2007) 'Self-harm and suicide at Grendon Therapeutic Community Prison'; Marzano *et al.* (2009) 'Interviewing survivors of near-lethal self-harm: a novel approach for investigating suicide amongst prisoners'.

Email address: adrienne.rivlin@psych.ox.ac.uk

Guy Shefer holds an MPhil and is currently studying for a PhD in criminology at the Institute of Criminology, University of Cambridge. He also holds an LLM from Duke University School of Law. In his PhD he explores various aspects of culture transformation and prisoner–staff relationships in different models of prison-based TCs.

Email address: gs316@cam.ac.uk

John Shine is a Consultant Forensic Psychologist working for the East London and the City Mental Health NHS Trust. He has worked as a forensic psychologist for over 25 years in prison, probation and forensic mental health settings, including HMP Grendon and HM Inspectorate of Probation. He has a longstanding interest in the assessment and treatment of psychopathy and personality disordered offenders and was a former member of the NHS Forensic R&D Expert Advisory Committee. He has published articles in over a dozen academic journals on a wide range of subjects in the field of forensic psychology and has edited two books. He is a co-author of the recent Professional Practice Board Report by the British Psychological Society: *Understanding Personality Disorder*.

Email address: John.Shine@eastlondon.nhs.uk

Alisa Stevens is a lecturer in Criminal Justice Studies at the University of Kent. For her DPhil in Law (Centre for Criminology, University of Oxford), she researched residents' experiences of the democratic therapeutic communities at HMPs Gartree, Grendon, and Send. Alisa argued that 'the TC way' can enable people to reconstruct their identity, transform their self-concept, and embrace a desistance-focused future. Alisa's other research and teaching interests include penology and the correctional services, desistance and rehabilitation, theories of crime, and qualitative research methods.

Email address: a.stevens@kent.ac.uk

Peter Totterdell holds a research chair at the Institute of Work Psychology, University of Sheffield. His research is aimed at understanding and elucidating the processes that influence the well-being and effectiveness of people at work. He is currently principal investigator on a large ESRC grant concerning Emotion Regulation of Others and Self, which involves a collaboration between investigators from a range of psychological disciplines based at five UK universities.

Email address: P.Totterdell@sheffield.ac.uk

Bill Wylie is an art therapist, artist, writer and researcher. He is Head of Art Therapy at HMP Grendon Therapeutic Community Prison, and has worked in varied therapeutic settings throughout Britain, including Rampton High Secure Hospital where he held an honorary research post and gained an MSc in art therapy with reference to personality disorder. He has researched, published and presented nationally and internationally. A member of the advisory board of the Society of Indian Philosophy and Religion at Elon University and an invited tutor in art therapy at Goldsmiths College, he devised – and for many years presented – an introductory course on art therapy at Glamorgan University Summer School. He is an advisor to the Personality Disorder KUF MSc Programme. His particular interests are in ethics and aesthetics as expressions of the transcendent function of mind; he has contributed to the discourse on the nature of consciousness in India and participated in an ecological conference at Elon University, North Carolina. The concept of transformation – the development of self-awareness and authenticity – underpins the therapeutic process that he employs in his work at HMP Grendon.

Email address: Bill.wylie@hmps.gsi.gov.uk

Foreword

I was honoured to be asked to write the introduction to this book, a book that highlights the sustained contribution that Grendon has made to our understanding of the role therapeutic communities (TCs) have in effective interventions with offenders. For ten years I was privileged to serve as the psychologist for the Barlinnie Special Unit: a unit based on the principles of therapeutic communities, a unit which one of the contributors to this volume described as '(in)famous' (Stevens, chapter 1) and others have described as being 'porridge with cream' (Cooke, 1989, 1997). Professionally, working in that unit was a formative experience; the opportunity to review this volume has allowed me to reflect on progress in the field over the last two decades, in general, and in particular, to reflect on the contribution of Grendon.

One of the many strengths of this volume is that, rather than merely focusing on the rather sterile approaches based on recidivism outcome studies, it explores the processes that underpin complex institutions through a multifaceted lens. Accounts of Grendon are provided based on ethnographic, phenomenological, participant observation, social analytic as well as the more usual outcome approach. The result is a rounded view of process that provides an in-depth understanding of prison regimes. There can be little doubt that the cognitive-behavioural revolution has paid major dividends in terms of offender treatment, but with its hegemony has come the loss of other perspectives – perspectives that can add valuable insights into effective interventions with offenders. This book provides such a perspective.

This is a book for practitioners and those interested in creative approaches to the management of prisoners. It embraces explanation beyond the individual and highlights the importance of institutional context as a driver of prisoner behaviour. The TC approach provides a respectful and supportive context; it is a flexible approach, which allows the embracing of the best of new developments. This is well illustrated in this volume in the discussion of various cognitive behavioural approaches, the Good Lives model and Livesley's integrative treatment approach for those with personality disorder.

The volume provides both historical and international perspectives. The excellent chapter by Stevens (chapter 1) provides both a clear historical account and an analysis of the processes though which TCs may be effective. I enjoyed her description of regular community meetings dealing with issues 'both the mundane and the substantial'. Her account makes it clear that TCs remain a rare approach with only 5 out of 140 prisons in England and Wales adopting the approach, and none in Scotland.

The historical perspective is continued in the thoughtful and analytic chapter provided by Douglas Lipton (chapter 4). Lipton focuses on practice in the US. He distinguishes between the hierarchical TC more typical of services in the US (frequently for those with substance misuse disorders) and the demographic TCs more typical of the UK. His careful analysis of outcome studies pertaining to Grendon suggests that there is a 'dose effect' with individuals having to have completed 18 months of treatment for a reduction in recidivism to be more likely. This should not be a surprise given the complexity of the psychological and social changes required to effect meaningful change. There can be other benefits: he cites both the TC at Glen Parva and the Barlinnie Special Unit as demonstrating dramatic reductions in prisoner-on-staff assaults; tellingly he notes that in the US, correctional staff compete to be assigned to TC prisons because of the reduced likelihood of assault.

I was heartened and intrigued to discover that TC approaches are not merely part of the history of corrections but that new and innovative TCs have been implemented in recent years. Cullen and Miller (chapter 2) describe the development and implementation of the Dovegate Unit, a 200-bedded unit set up in a private sector prison in 2002. The authors indicate that an overarching concept was that the unit should be construed as a different way of living – not just a treatment process. One implication of this is that other approaches to treatment, for example cognitive skills, are not viewed as antagonistic but can be delivered in a supportive environment. The authors provide a balanced evaluation of the challenges and the successes of the Dovegate unit since its implementation.

Another recent and innovative approach is described by John Shine (chapter 5). He shows the TC concept can evolve in that he enshrines Livesley's framework for an integrated treatment model of personality disorder within the broader TC philosophy. This approach ensures that clients are contained in a social environment – which is both rich and safe – and which facilitates experimentation with new ways of interacting with others.

Other chapters demonstrate how the TC approach can be used to embrace other theoretical models in a creative synergy. Michael Brookes (chapter 6) discusses how the principles of the Good Lives Model have been integrated into the philosophy at Grendon. Shuker (chapter 7) discusses how risk management can be enhanced; the TC framework provides a mechanism by which to engage prisoners deemed to be high risk, and provides processes by which to address the manifold interpersonal, affective and behavioural difficulties that underpin high-risk behaviours. Critically, TCs provide an arena in which the effective evaluation of change may take place.

A valuable and compelling international account of a TC is provided by Judith de Boer-van Schaik and Frans Derks (chapter 3) in their description of the venerable service provided by the Van der Hoeven Clinic in Utrecht. A key theme highlighted is the importance of processes designed to allow inmates to take responsibility for their own lives through the development of new skills and new social networks. Responsibility is one of the key ingredients of effective TCs. The chapter reports an impressive reduction in reoffending given the nature of the population contained in the clinic.

As noted earlier one of the strengths of the volume is the diversity of perspectives brought to bear and the ability to integrate a range of interventions that go beyond the merely cognitive. It highlights the eclecticism of approaches that can be embraced within the broader philosophy of the TC model. Bill Wylie (chapter 9) describes the application of art therapy approaches – I was particularly intrigued by his account given the significant role that art played in the Barlinnie Special Unit (Carrell & Laing, 1982). He argues that art is a powerful means by which unconscious feelings can be brought to consciousness; he provides an exploration of the meaning of imagery created by men engaged in art therapy at Grendon. Similarly, Jinnie Jefferies (chapter 8) describes the use of psychodrama as a powerful method for exploring destructive patterns of feelings and interpersonal style that so frequently characterise this population. She describes how psychodrama can be used to explore life experiences, but crucially, how psychodrama can be used to experience novel ways of relating to others.

In a series of chapters, research – applying diverse methods – focuses on diverse aspects of Grendon. Fisher, Ireland and Sullivan (chapter 20) explore the challenges of implementing research in a prison environment. Rhodes (chapter 12) uses ethnographic methods to examine how Grendon fits within the wider context of 'normal' prison environments and explores the constant tensions that any 'special' approach to prisoner management will have with mainstream approaches. The author suggests that the TC approach helps obviate the harm done by traditional institutional practice.

An important voice – not often heard – is that of the inmates. Sullivan (chapter 11) discusses the experience of the 'service user'; this is not tokenism but genuinely informative. She emphasises the importance of treatment readiness, and the challenges confronting new members of the community being thrust into an environment where the psyche is exposed. The leavers interviewed comment positively on their gains in self-esteem and persistence brought about, in part, from a supportive environment. Shefer (chapter 15) describes the use of staff and prisoner surveys to explore the quality of life in Grendon. While views are generally positive the reality is that all incarceration brings with it the pains of confinement. In Grendon prisoners focus on the need to confront and deal with past misdemeanours – staff do not construe it as an easy billet either. Continuing the theme of quality of life, Rivlin (chapter 16) explores the comparatively low rates of suicidal and parasuicidal behaviour in Grendon; she attributes the low rate to enhanced contact with family members, the engagement with meaningful activities, supportive staff–inmate relationships, a reduced incidence of bullying and enhanced self-esteem. McManus (chapter 13) explores the staff experience using ethnographic methods and identifies the risk to staff of vicarious traumatisation consequent on listening to prisoners' narratives. He emphasises the importance of self-care skills for staff. Akerman (chapter 10) explores the particular challenges of engaging with sexual offenders within a TC setting. For example, the need to develop subtle and sensitive approaches to therapeutic alliance in order to facilitate disclosure of deviant ideation, as well as the need to maintain staff cohesion and avoid splitting.

Two chapters try to disentangle some of the key ingredients for an effective TC. Niven, Holman and Totterdell (chapter 14) describe the ways in which emotional influence can be used to regulate the affective response of others. Shuker and Newberry (chapter 18) examine the impact of improving individuals' interpersonal behaviour and how it is possible to use the processes of TCs to bring about more adaptive interpersonal behaviour. The particular problems of ethnic minorities in TCs are considered by Newberry (chapter 19). She indicates that ethnic minorities are frequently under-represented in TCs and explores attempts to increase recruitment, the perception that TC approaches may conflict with traditional conceptual frameworks, and the need to support staff to become more culturally aware.

In conclusion, this volume makes clear that TCs are alive and well in Grendon and beyond, they are not just alive but are making a contribution within institutions for offenders and providing valuable information about the impact of institutional life on offenders. There is a danger that TCs will remain a niche approach in 'special' units for 'special' prisoners, while the reality is that the lessons learned in these institutions provide lessons for effective practice in the wider penal context, giving respect and giving responsibility – rather than infantilising – produces effective prison management (Cooke *et al.*, 2008).

David J Cooke

References

Carrell, C. & Laing, J. (1982). *The Special Unit Barlinnie Prison: Its education through its art*. Glasgow: Third Eye Centre.

Cooke, D. J. (1989). Containing violent prisoners: an analysis of the Barlinnie Special Unit. *British Journal of Criminology, 29*, 129–143.

Cooke, D. J. (1997). The Barlinnie Special Unit: the rise and fall of a therapeutic experiment. In E. Cullen *et al.* (Eds) *Therapeutic Communities for Offenders* (pp. 101–120). London: Wiley.

Cooke, D. J. *et al.* (2008). Casting light on prison violence: Evaluating the impact of situational risk factors. *Criminal Justice and Behavior, 35*, 1065–1078.

Acknowledgements

We would like to thank Liz Warner for all her help in assisting with the preparation of this book.

Part I

Developments in Therapeutic Communities

Introduction

In September 2002 I was appointed Governor of Grendon, a prison I had long admired and yet had never anticipated having a part to play in its therapeutic tradition. However, in spite of my enthusiasm and the reassurances of many colleagues that I was well suited to the position, my early experiences were fraught with tension and conflict.

I have described elsewhere how I soon began to feel like an interloper sent to erode further Grendon's therapeutic core (Bennett, 2007). My role quickly became one of a broker, straddling the two very different worlds of Grendon and the Prison Service, or the 'system' as many Grendonites referred to it (Bennett, 2006, pp. 137–138). On the one hand, the Governor was seen to represent the 'system' with its managerial culture of performance management, audits and cognitive skills programmes, while on the other hand, I was expected to support a therapeutic community regime, many of whose participants retained a deep sense of suspicion of the wider Service and some of whom believed that Grendon's very survival as the only prison devoted entirely to therapy was at stake.

Conflicts were endemic and unhealthy, particularly those acted out between therapy and operations, between those who saw themselves primarily as being tasked with ensuring the security of a category B prison and those who sought to preserve a safe environment for the practice of therapy based on principles of openness, trust, challenge and individual

Grendon and the Emergence of Forensic Therapeutic Communities: Developments in Research and Practice
Edited by Richard Shuker and Elizabeth Sullivan
© 2010 John Wiley & Sons, Ltd.

responsibility. Getting the balance right is crucial if Grendon is to be effective as a therapeutic community prison.

Looking back at my own part in this drama, I can see that the timing of my arrival was far from auspicious. Grendon was undergoing one of its periodic bouts of insecurity brought on by the new managerialism and popularity of cognitive skills programmes. Moreover, the escape of three prisoners a year earlier, with its inevitable traumatic aftermath, only served to exacerbate the mood of isolation, vulnerability and suspicion. It did not help that Grendon lacked clear strategic direction within the Service as a referral option for long-term offenders with complex needs.

I mention this low point in Grendon's recent history because it provided reason for reflection and an impetus for moving forward. Along with senior therapists and operational managers, including Michael Brookes, the newly appointed Director of Therapeutic Communities, who was commissioned to undertake a Grendon Review, we set about reconciling destructive internal conflict. We also recognised the need to incorporate mainstream developments in risk assessment, public protection, offender management, audits and performance targets while yet preserving intact the traditional therapeutic core. I have no doubt that the widely acknowledged success of Grendon over recent years lies partly in its achievement of mainstream performance targets and partly in the accreditation of its therapeutic regime, the latter being decisive in reasserting its reputation as an official therapeutic intervention.

We also pursued vigorously the promotion of Grendon not only to attract those men who might derive greatest benefit from therapy, but also to demonstrate Grendon's continuing and increasing relevance in a changing custodial world.

Like our predecessors, who had wrestled with similar issues, we were convinced that good research was essential in proving Grendon's worth as a rehabilitative regime. Indeed, Grendon has a long and impressive body of research and the prison has no difficulty in attracting applicants. But from the outset, I have contested that the published research has been overly narrow in scope. For one thing, there is an urgent need for an overarching review of existing research in order to identify significant themes. For another, the available body of research is restricted; much is highly statistical and focuses primarily on reconviction outcomes. There are of course notable exceptions, including the excellent monograph by Genders and Player (1995); many of the issues covered by them have continuing resonance.

I am not suggesting that reconviction studies are unimportant; far from it, reconviction rates remain one of the most important measures of rehabilitation and we are bound to seek the best ways of achieving the best reconviction outcomes. But there is so much more to Grendon that is relevant and positive in terms of reforming prisoners and prison reform that statistical reconviction studies fail sufficiently to encompass.

Grendon is a prison widely acknowledged for its excellent prisoner–staff relationships, for its low levels of violence, drug use and resort to the use of force. It has no segregation unit and for a prison holding many men labelled potentially difficult and disruptive, it has remarkably few serious incidents.

As might be expected in a therapeutic context where men are constantly challenged, emotions often run high. Nevertheless, the prison feels exceptionally safe. How Grendon works, how all these positive outcomes are achieved, deserve our serious attention and are legitimate areas of enquiry for a range of disciplines. It is precisely for these reasons that I commend the editors of this book for broadening the approach as well as the focus of research in order to present a comprehensive view of this unique prison.

I have explained the background to how and why this volume was conceived. But what of its wider relevance?

One of the most frequently asked questions by visitors to Grendon is 'why not more Grendons?' If Grendon is an exceptionally safe and humane prison, which also happens to be highly effective in the rehabilitation of serious offenders, then surely it is worthy of replication? I have my stock answers. There are a few therapeutic communities in mainstream prisons, notably Dovegate in Staffordshire, originally described as the 'Grendon of the North.'

Moreover, group therapy Grendon-style is not suitable for all offenders. Participation is voluntary and research suggests that therapy is more effective for those who have at least eighteen months to spend in a community.

But I am becoming increasingly confident that there are many more prisoners who could benefit from a Grendon-style regime, as indeed there are many aspects of the humane and rehabilitative regime at Grendon which could be transported to, or developed in, other prisons and which the research in this volume brings to the fore.

Peter Bennett

References

Bennett, P. (2006). Governing a humane prison. In Jones, D. (Ed.) *Humane Prisons*. Oxford: Radcliffe Publishing Ltd.

Bennett, P. (2007). Governing Grendon's therapeutic communities: the big spin. In Parker, M. (Ed.) *Dynamic Security: The Democratic Therapeutic Community in Prison*. London: Jessica Kingsley.

Genders, E. & Player, E. (1995). *Grendon: A Study of a Therapeutic Prison*. Oxford: Clarendon Press.

Chapter 1

Introducing Forensic Democratic Therapeutic Communities

Alisa Stevens

Introduction

Of the 140 prisons in England and Wales, just five currently offer a vision of 'offender management' based upon the principles and aims of the democratic therapeutic community (TC). Grendon – a category B (medium secure) establishment for up to 235 men – is the first, largest, and still the only dedicated TC prison, but has been joined in its penologically distinctive quest by TC units within the 'mainstream' men's prisons of Gartree, Dovegate (both category B) and Blundeston (category C), and at Send, a closed women's prison.

Democratic therapeutic communities, whether located in their traditional mental health, or more recently developed custodial, settings, offer a consciously designed, predominantly residential social environment and programme of treatment intended to help their members understand and, as far as possible, lessen or overcome their social, psychological, and emotional problems. It is the community as a collective and collaborative entity that is the primary therapeutic instrument (Roberts, 1997a), within which psychodynamic therapy – which emphasises the processes of change and personal development – is employed to unearth and 'work through' the (often unconscious) motivations and learned maladaptive protective

Grendon and the Emergence of Forensic Therapeutic Communities: Developments in Research and Practice
Edited by Richard Shuker and Elizabeth Sullivan
© 2010 John Wiley & Sons, Ltd.

behaviours that result from formative experiences, particularly those acquired during a traumatic or abusive childhood (Malan, 1979). This potent combination of dynamic interaction between the individual, his peer community, and psychodynamic therapy encourages gradual accumulation of self-knowledge and insight which ultimately allows for profound and permanent personal change. Within prisons, this means that the community – the residents (the preferred TC term for inmates) *and* prison staff – work together to move from historical exploration and understanding towards a reduction in problematic behaviours and attitudes and hence ultimately, a non-offending future.

Psychiatric Origins

The origins of the TC treatment modality are generally attributed to the creation of specialist units – at Mill Hill, and more particularly, Northfield psychiatric military hospital – to treat traumatised World War II combat veterans presenting with acute dissociative and hysterical disorders. Keenly aware of the punitive and disabling mistreatment of Great War shell-shocked soldiers, and inspired by an emerging body of social scientific literature on small group processes and interpersonal relations (notably, Adler, 1924; Freud, 1922; and Mead, 1934), a handful of psychoanalytically-orientated psychiatrists considered the contemporary hegemonic 'medical model', as practised in secure psychiatric hospitals, to be systemically incapable of treating traumatised military personnel either effectively or humanely (Whiteley, 2004). In these 'total institutions', authoritarian, paternalistic professionals preoccupied themselves with the maintenance of control, hierarchy, and routine and slavish adherence to a myriad of, often bizarre, bureaucratic rules (Belknap, 1956; Caudill, 1958; Goffman, 1961; Stanton & Schwartz, 1954); whilst their deferential patients internalised an apathetic and pliant 'sick role' (Parsons, 1951) devoid of autonomy and individuality. By contrast, these TC pioneers hypothesised that this damaging and dependency-prone social environment only exacerbated in traumatised persons their tendency towards neurosis and personality disorder and that a more tolerant and empowering milieu might therefore relieve their symptoms of distress. Accordingly, they incrementally engineered a genuine revolution in psychiatric social relations by renouncing both the oppressive culture of the secure hospital and the traditional psychoanalytic dyad of 'expert' therapist and 'grateful' patient, in favour of a flexible, egalitarian organisational structure and collaborative, group-based interaction (Manning, 1976).

The initial, modest attempt at establishing a democratic TC occurred in the unlikely setting of a temporarily converted public school at Mill Hill, north London, to which psychiatric patients from the Maudsley Hospital were evacuated in 1940. In charge of a psychosomatic unit conducting physiological research into the aetiology of effort syndrome (or neuro-circulatory asthenia, characterised by breathlessness, chest pain, giddiness, and persistent fatigue), the psychiatrist Maxwell Jones decided to share the research findings with his patients through regular didactic lectures. He soon realised, however, that the patients understood more, and their morale and self-esteem consequently improved, if he involved them in interactive group discussion by which each member contributed to the 'social learning' of the community. These small discussion groups began to affect the social structure of the ward, encouraging a flattened hierarchy and, in turn, greater sociological contextualising of the challenges treatment posed for both patients and staff (Jones, 1952, 1968; Whiteley, 2004).

Wilfred Bion, meanwhile, was appointed director of the Training Wing of Birmingham's Northfield military psychiatric hospital and charged with rehabilitating men who, although psychologically disturbed, were considered capable of returning to military service (Whiteley, 2004). Together with his colleague John Rickman, Bion decided to confront the patients' unruly and disruptive behaviour by re-defining disciplinary problems, in suitably combative terms, as the 'common enemy'. For six weeks in 1943, they introduced discussion groups and communal activities, designed to replace the fractured social bonds of war with the mutual support of a peer community and hence, 'to treat socially the social elements of the patients' neuroses' (Roberts, 1997b). The insubordination and subversion of military discipline this represented, however, proved intolerable to their superiors and Bion and Rickman were dismissed from their posts. Undeterred, over the next three years Siegmund Foulkes and Harold Bridger, amongst others, implemented gradually (what has been retrospectively called) 'the second Northfield experiment' in creating an avowedly democratic and therapeutic milieu – but this time with the approval of senior personnel – which again advocated the use of group analysis, regular meetings, and social activities involving the whole community (Kennard & Roberts, 1983; Whiteley, 2004).

In 1945, Northfield acquired a new hospital director, Tom Main, who sought to incorporate techniques from both psychiatry and psychoanalysis to construct a psychodynamic and interpretative exploration of his patients' objective difficulties through their subjectively experienced interpersonal frustrations and conflicts. In May 1946, Main published an article in which he argued that a neurotic, attachment disordered individual needed 'a framework of social reality which can provide him with opportunities for attaining fuller social insight and for expressing and modifying his emotional drives according to the demands of real life' (Main, 1946). He rallied his colleagues to replace the hospital as 'social refuge' with an internal community, and the role of the 'superintendent' psychiatrist with a humble 'technician', whose daily task was to study and facilitate 'the social pull and push' of the community in order to mobilise its therapeutic potential (Main, 1946). Several commentators have since timed the appearance of this 'stirring and inspirational' paper as the 'date of birth' of the democratic therapeutic community (Kennard, 1996).

It was, however, the prolific stream of publications which emanated from Maxwell Jones (inter alia 1942, 1946, 1952, 1953, 1956, 1959, 1968); his 12-year leadership from 1947 of a social rehabilitation unit for the treatment of personality and psychopathic disorders; and his international evangelising of social psychiatry, which were to secure for him the reputation of the father of the TC movement (Manning, 1976). Thus, although Main and his Northfield colleagues can claim the creation of the TC *philosophy*, it was Jones at Mill Hill who devised the *method* (Whiteley, 2004).

A 'Living-Learning' 'Culture of Enquiry'

Endorsement of Jones's distinct vision was consolidated by three years of independent research at the Henderson Hospital, conducted (at Jones's astute request) by a team of seven social anthropologists, led by Robert Rapoport. The resulting publication, *Community as Doctor* (Rapoport, 1960), identified four complementary and interdependent therapeutic community principles. These guiding tenets apply equally to staff and to residents, are intended to realise the inherent therapeutic and rehabilitative potential residing within the community, and are still widely used to define the TC 'proper' (Clark, 1965) – the ideal, power-sharing, therapeutic community whose social environment is the main therapeutic instrument.

The principle of 'democratization' exists to ensure that each member of the community can participate equally in therapeutic and administrative decision-making, with unfettered access to vertical and horizontal communication channels. This is achieved through regular whole community meetings, in which all matters relating to the running of the community – both the mundane and the substantial – are openly discussed and debated (Rapoport, 1960). Jones (1976) was acutely aware, however, that shared decision-making could encompass a wide variety of practices, ranging from the full involvement of every community member, to resigned acquiescence, managerial manipulation, or the most cursory show of hands. This principle therefore further requires residents to develop an internal commitment to, and interconnectivity with, their community, in order that they experience a high degree of ownership of the democratic process and become willing to assume responsibility for its implementation and implications, regardless of whether this coincides with their personal preference.

The most straightforward principle, *communalism*, requires that facilities and domestic arrangements are shared. Involvement in communal tasks – and the helpful realisation this frequently entails that one's seemingly unique problems are, in fact, shared by fellow residents – is intended to increase a fragile member's self-esteem and lessen his isolation and helplessness, whilst simultaneously reinforcing the community's espoused moral values of social responsibility and altruism and promoting the development of trusting, reciprocal relationships (Rapoport, 1960; Yalom, 1980). The simplicity of communalism, however, conceals the complexity of its application: people may be united in their problems but have no propensity to co-exist harmoniously, and to do so without adopting a naïve conception of community as 'phoney sharing' (Morrice, 1979) often requires a substantial and sustained effort.

Although now possessed of rather unfortunate pejorative connotations, in Rapoport's (1960) original designation *permissiveness* simply meant that residents tolerate in each other behaviours and speech that might normatively be perceived as deviant. Within the psychodynamic tradition all behaviour is meaningful, so all the individual's conscious and unconscious cognitions, emotions, motivations, and interpersonal dynamics are considered diagnostically and therapeutically informative (Yalom, 1980). This behaviour, however, will not be available for analysis if, in order to gain approval or avoid censure, one feels compelled to modify or disguise one's behaviour provisionally and instrumentally. The permissiveness principle therefore allows a TC resident to behave as he typically would – expressing and enacting habitual difficulties, secure in the knowledge of his continuing membership of an accepting environment – and this in turn facilitates the provision of plentiful 'living-learning' opportunities (Jones, 1968).

Crucially, however, this empathetic analysis is balanced by *reality confrontation* – the principle that although problematic behaviour is tolerated, it does not pass unnoticed or without criticism. Predominantly through the intimate forum of small therapy groups (typically of up to eight residents), members – as auxiliary therapists and role models – relate the effects such behaviour has upon them. This circumvents the universal tendency to deny, minimise, or rationalise one's less admirable characteristics and their objectionable consequences (Rapoport, 1960) – or, in the criminologists Sykes and Matza's (1957) memorable phrase, the deployment of 'techniques of neutralisation'. Even seemingly trivial incidents and interactions are therefore analysed within this 'culture of enquiry' (Main, 1946) in order to excavate their 'true' meaning and purpose, and to encourage members to offer support, advice, and feedback in a collaborative and pro-social manner.

This dialectical relationship between the individual and the 'miniature social universe' (Yalom, 1980) of the group additionally expedites the ability of the TC member to confront the discordance between self-image and the figurative mirror presented by one's peers, and so incrementally to acquire insight into the pervasiveness of maladaptive beliefs and behaviours. Indeed, Jones, who came to prefer the terms 'social learning' and 'facilitator' to 'treatment' and 'therapist' (1976), described social learning simply as 'two way communication of content and feeling, listening, interaction, and problem solving, leading to learning' (1980), and ultimately, personal change. (However, Jones did not explicitly accord social learning the status of an underpinning theory of TC treatment, nor does his use of the term properly correspond with social learning theory, as familiar to criminologists and psychologists.) Accordingly, the reality confrontation principle best embodies Main's (1946) exhortation that a genuine therapeutic milieu must prepare the resident for a return to 'a real role in the real world'.

Forty years after Rapoport, and as befits TCs' continually evolving and dynamic nature, Haigh (1999) updated and adapted the original principles as 'five universal qualities' of therapeutic environments, presenting them as a developmental sequence which reflects the therapeutic journey of the TC resident. The first quality, *attachment*, utilises attachment theory (Ainsworth, 1967; Bowlby, 1969, 1973, 1980) to show the importance of sensitive joining (and leaving) procedures, so that residents develop a sense of belonging to, and of valuing and being valued by, their community (Haigh, 1999). The resident then learns that the TC's culture of safety and *containment* (extending permissiveness) sets, and holds, appropriate boundaries within which they can experience their emotions; of necessity because 'it is more fundamental for a place to feel safe than for anything to be allowed' (Haigh, 1999). Only once these two elements are in place can residents confidently commit to clear, open, and honest *communication* (communalism) between and amongst staff and residents, and with the external world (Haigh, 1999). Greater *involvement* with, participation in, and responsibility for the community (reality confrontation) can then occur, so that residents become not only mindful of each other's needs and problems and how to negotiate their place within the community, but of the ultimate interdependence of all members of society (Haigh, 1999). Finally, 'a deep recognition of the power of each individual' (Haigh, 1999) (extending democracy) promotes residents' sense of *agency*, empowerment and self-efficacy.

'A Penal Institution of a Special Kind'

It will be immediately apparent that the therapeutic principles and qualities described by Rapoport and Haigh are not normally associated with the experience of mainstream imprisonment. Yet, the search for a different approach to rehabilitation had begun in 1931, nine years before the innovative work of Jones and his colleagues, when the Home Office appointed a departmental committee to inquire into existing methods of dealing with persistent offenders. Its resulting report argued that 'a certain amount of persistent crime … is due to abnormal mental factors' and thus 'certain delinquents may be amenable to psychological treatment' (Home Office, 1932). Given the paucity of scientific knowledge about crime, criminals, and effective treatment, however, both the Committee, and separately, the Medical Commissioner and Committee member, Sir Norwood East (1932), recommended that an experiment be instituted with 'willing' offenders by which the longitudinal value of psychological treatment could be assessed (Home Office, 1932).

This experiment was duly conducted between 1934 and 1938 with selected inmates at Wormwood Scrubs, under the auspices of a medical psychologist and psychotherapist, William Hubert (Faulk, 1990), and subsequently formed the basis of Drs East and Hubert's *The Psychological Treatment of Crime* (1939). Although they did not attempt to establish whether, in fact, levels of recidivism had been reduced, based upon their clinical judgements of behavioural improvement, they unequivocally concluded that 'the most satisfactory method of dealing with abnormal and unusual types of criminal would be by the creation of a penal institution of a special kind' (East & Hubert, 1939).

Although East and Hubert's recommendation was welcomed, the outbreak of World War II and prolonged bureaucratic procrastination ensured that two decades passed before building work actually commenced on the envisaged 'experimental psychiatric prison' – HMP Grendon, near Aylesbury in Buckinghamshire. When it finally opened in September 1962, during the height of penal welfarism (Garland, 1985), Grendon was tasked with caring for up to 250 men, 25 women (never, in fact, admitted), and 50 'borstal boys' who, whilst they failed to satisfy the legal criteria for insanity and were not suffering from a psychosis, were nevertheless deemed to require psychiatric treatment and management (Commissioners of Prisons,

1963). Its explicit psychiatric orientation was confirmed by the employ-ment, as recommended by East and Hubert (1939), of a forensic psychia-trist, Dr William Gray, as governor and medical superintendent, independent of the traditional Prison Service management structure; as well as psychiatrists, psychologists, and welfare officers, and the liberal prescription of psychotropic medication (Gray, 1973; Newell & Healey, 2007).

The 'patients', then, were perceived as troubled people who happened to be offenders – predominantly the less serious, though often recidivist, criminals who typically committed acquisitive rather than violent offences. In 1973, for example, 57 per cent of Grendon residents were imprisoned for property offences – compared to 17 per cent for violence, 8 per cent for robbery or its attempt, and 7 per cent for sexual offences (Cullen, 1997). Grendon's humane and civilised regime perceived rehabilitation as a holis-tic endeavour and accordingly,

> ... therapy at Grendon [was] not *primarily* directed to the prevention of crime ... the principal undertaking of therapy [was] to facilitate and promote the welfare of each individual inmate. By so doing, it may succeed in ena-bling some inmates to avoid reoffending after their release, but this [was] a secondary or consequent effect ... (Genders & Player, 1995, emphasis preserved).

By the mid 1980s, however, Grendon was forcefully and frequently criticised from within the Prison Service for being aloof, inflexible, and overly selective in its clientele, too often unresponsive to the needs of mainstream prisons struggling to manage the increasing numbers of 'heavy end' and 'control problem' prisoners (Cullen, 1998). Moreover, as political support for the ambitious rehabilitative ideal declined (Allen, 1981) – the May Committee, for example, starkly concluded that 'the rhetoric of "treatment and training" has had its day and should be replaced' (May, 1979, para 4.27) with a more limited, legalistic notion of 'positive custody'(May, 1979, para 4.46) – so the pressure on the Prison Service's 'jewel in the crown' (Genders & Player, 1995) to demonstrate its continued relevance and 'special purpose' increased.

This was the potentially hazardous context in which the Home Secretary decided to establish an Advisory Committee on the Therapeutic Regime at Grendon (ACTRAG) in order to review the prison's future orientation. The resulting report (Home Office, 1985) contained no fewer than 29 recommendations, fundamentally and irrevocably changing its referral and management practices. Grendon was henceforth to focus upon providing therapeutic community treatment for three categories of offenders: sociopaths – a term little used by British psychiatrists, but descriptively inter-changeable with the clinical constructs of psychopathy and antisocial personality disorder, and associated with a constellation of malign inter-personal and behavioural characteristics (American Psychiatric Asso-ciation, 1994); sexually-motivated offenders; and the long-term (and particularly, life-sentenced) prison population. It was, in short, to stop recruiting recidivist property offenders and replace them instead with serious violent and sexual offenders (Faulk, 1990). A 28-bed psychiatric rescue unit for those suffering acute mental breakdown or prison-induced crisis, however, was created, thus preserving some continuity with Gren-don's original objectives. Exceptionally, this unit was 'governed' by a psychiatrist, offered individual psychotherapy and (the otherwise now discontinued practice of prescribing) psychotropic medication (Selby, [1991] 1995). (Its gradual corruption, however, into a chronic long-stay unit with a high proportion of suicidal residents resulted in its 1993 closure.) Finally, and critically, ACTRAG replaced the post of medical superintendent with the conventional (non-medically qualified) 'govern-ing governor' (Cullen, 1998), thereby ushering Grendon firmly into the Prison Service fold.

Implementation of ACTRAG's recommendations, and the emergence of persuasive empirical evidence of Grendon's rehabilitative success in the early 1990s (detailed in chapter 18), proved decisive in reviving the prison's flagging fortunes. As Darwin might have predicted, by evolving, Grendon survived. In the years that followed ACTRAG, Grendon successfully re-positioned itself as a national resource and centre of excellence for the TC treatment of the most serious offenders, measurably more 'damaged, dis-turbed and dangerous' (Shine & Newton, 2000) than the 'average' inmate. Approximately three-quarters of Grendon's contemporary population are serving an indeterminate sentence, with more than 90 per cent imprisoned for murder, other violent crime, sexual offences, or robbery (Kennedy, 2008).

Diagnostically, Birtchnell and Shine (2000) found, from assessing 107 newly-arrived inmates, that 86 per cent met the criteria for at least one personality disorder, most commonly antisocial (69 per cent), paranoid (65 per cent), and borderline (60 per cent) personality disorders. Further-more, the mean number of disorders per prisoner was 4.02. The incidence of psychopathy among Grendon residents has proven more difficult to state definitively. Only around a third of current Grendon residents have been assessed for psychopathy, either prior to admission or during their time at Grendon, using the standard measurement tool, Hare's (1991, 1993) Psychopathy Checklist (Revised) (PCL-R). However, three fairly recent studies are instructive. During 1995, Hobson and Shine (1998) administered the PCL-R to 104 inmate receptions, comprising 73 per cent of receptions that year. Of this sample, 26 per cent obtained a PCL-R score (out of 40) of 30 or above, indicative of prototypical psychopathy. Shine and Newton's sample of Grendon men, resident between 1995 and 2000, scored a mean PCL-R score of 24, surpassing that (at 22) of high-security prisoners (Clark, 1998, cited in Shine & Newton, 2000). Gray *et al.* (2002) assessed 78 newly-admitted residents (59 per cent of all admissions) over a 15-month period between 2000 and 2001. Using the lower cut-off score of 25 – then recommended for British offenders as metrically equivalent to a score of 30 in North America (Cooke & Michie, 1999) – they found 47 per cent of these receptions to be psychopathic. The scores ranged from 5 to 39, with a mean of 22 (Gray *et al.*, 2002, p. 10).

Grendon and Beyond: TC Units

As a case study in successfully negotiating 'volatile and contradictory' (O'Malley, 1999) political penological policy, Grendon epitomises how, by adept re-branding of its 'unique selling point' to a new and more punitive penal marketplace, and by re-defining its optimum target population, it was able not only to thrive whilst other equally experimental penal initiatives floundered, but, moreover, to inspire the development of wholly or semi-contained TC units within mainstream prisons. The longest surviving of these units, at HMP Gartree in Leicestershire, has offered treatment for 23 men drawn from within Gartree's life-sentenced population since 1993.

Further replication of the TC regime was advanced by two important surveys of unmet psychiatric need amongst sentenced prisoners. Forensic psychiatrists from the Institute of Psychiatry in London analysed the prison files of, and conducted semi-structured interviews with, a 5 per cent cross-sectional random sample of sentenced male adult and young offenders (Gunn *et al.*, 1991), and then additionally 25 per cent of women inmates (Maden *et al.*, 1994), from 16 prisons in England and Wales. They assessed for any psychiatric disorder and determined, from five options, the most appropriate treatment modality. The authors concluded that 5 per cent of male, and 8 per cent of female, prisoners would benefit from therapeutic community treatment; 47 per cent of whom were diagnosed with a personality disorder. They suggested that this provided a rough guide to the level of need nationally and justified the development of an additional TC prison, a recommendation strengthened the same year by the Prison Service Directorate of Health Care Task Force's estimate that TC treatment would be advantageous for at least 2392 prisoners by 2001 (Genders, 2003).

Together, then, these findings provided the impetus for the 2001 inauguration of a 200-bed, entirely separate TC unit for adult males within a private sector prison, Dovegate in Staffordshire (see further chapter 3). In 2003, a 40-bed unit for adult males opened at HMP Blundeston in Suffolk. The same year, the therapeutic needs of women were belatedly addressed by the provision of a TC unit at Winchester West Hill prison. Within a year, however, this prison reverted to the male estate, requiring the TC to transfer to Surrey's HMP Send, with predictably disruptive consequences for the nascent community (Stewart & Parker, 2007). Regrettably, and notwithstanding its uniqueness within the female estate, the staff's concerted marketing efforts, and the identification by HM Chief Inspector of Prisons (2006) of 'a need for national action and responsibility to encourage and enable suitable women to be identified for the TC and take advantage of its opportunities', Send TC has yet to fulfil its maximum potential occupancy of 40 places.

There have also been some prominent TC unit 'failures'. Three separate facilities for young offenders have closed, at HMYOIs Glen Parva (1979 to 1996); Feltham (1989 to 1997); and Aylesbury (1997 to 2006). Additionally, the Max Glatt Centre at HMP Wormwood Scrubs operated from 1975 to 2002, during which time, like Grendon, it successfully transformed its target clientele to reflect its evolving remit, from adult male prisoners with addictive and compulsive behaviours to violent and personality-disordered offenders (Jones, 1997). Maintaining programme integrity and dedicated staffing levels, however, proved persistently challenging (Woodward, 1999). Ultimately, the host prison could no longer reconcile the TC's need for a stable and committed community with the exigencies of a large, overcrowded, local prison with rapid inmate 'turnover', which, at the time of its mooted closure, was beset by 'dysfunctional' management and a 'corrosive situation' following serious allegations of widespread staff brutality (HM Chief Inspector of Prisons, 2001). As Lewis (1997) rather graphically, yet presciently, warned, 'A small unit can be likened to a foreign body, or transplant, in the human body, and is subject to the same process of "rejection"'.

Most (in)famously, the Barlinnie Special Unit (BSU) in Glasgow achieved astonishing rehabilitative success with some of the most disruptive and dangerous men in the Scottish prison system (Cooke, 1989, 1991). Part of a long Scottish tradition of small units, the 10-bed BSU opened in February 1973 for the treatment of long-term and known or potentially violent inmates (Scottish Home and Health Department, 1971). Although the BSU never formally identified itself as a democratic therapeutic community, its 'social community' (Whatmore, 1990) and therapeutic regime was supported by TC principles and practices (Cooke, 1997). This semantic differentiation is perhaps explained by its specific purpose to contain and manage 'difficult' prisoners, and by residents' desire to avoid any imputation of an overtly psychiatric orientation, given that the BSU invariably represented a last resort alternative to indefinite detention in Carstairs state mental hospital or isolation in Scotland's then notorious – and evidently counterproductive – 'cages' and 'diggers' (segregation units, colloquially referred to in English and Welsh prisons as 'the block').

The BSU is now remembered by criminologists almost as much for its controversial end as for the imaginative and enlightened penological approach it pioneered. Opinions still differ as to whether its closure, in January 1995, was inevitable after becoming 'stagnant and fossilised' (Scottish Prison Service, 1994), with radical practices made routine, negative behaviour ignored, and non-involvement normalised (Cooke, 1997); or whether the – perhaps only temporary – problems it was experiencing were merely an expedient excuse to close a unit whose empathetic and tolerant treatment philosophy had become a 'political embarrassment' (Collins, 1997, cited in Sim, 2007). Certainly, it is difficult to reconcile the overwhelmingly supportive evaluation by Bottomley, Liebling and Sparks (1994) – who anticipated the correction of the problems they observed and confidently dismissed the option to close the unit (Bottomley *et al.*, 1994) – with the catastrophic 'regime slippage' highlighted by the Scottish Prison Service (1994) in its internal working party's report, partly *informed by* the findings of Bottomley *et al.* Tellingly, then, in his subsequent and exquisitely poignant memorial to the BSU, Richard Sparks (2002) writes of 'the abiding sense of unease' he still feels from 'having been implicated unwarily in someone else's arcane and somewhat ruthless stratagem'.

More positively, recently instituted procedures to audit and accredit penal TCs, and the development of a set of detailed manuals and guidelines for the delivery and management of prison TCs (discussed in chapter 2), should eradicate the re-occurrence of the sort of gradual community disengagement and regime ossification which proved so fatal to the BSU, and may help defend host-dependent units from the operational intrusions Wormwood Scrubs endured.

Furthermore, prison-based democratic therapeutic communities have provided the model for the development of ideologically and operationally similar socio-therapeutic prisons in several European countries. Most notably, Germany opened its first socio-therapeutic prison, Asperg, in 1969, seven years after Grendon (Lösel & Egg, 1997). Having consistently enjoyed political and judicial support, this type of regime is now available in approximately 30 German prisons, originally as institutions wholly independent of the rest of the prison system, or, more recently, as 'departments' within mainstream prisons (Lösel & Egg, 1997; Smartt, 2001). This independence has ensured that the inter-disciplinary staff – including (often Rogerian, client-centred) psychotherapists, (cognitive-behavioural) psychologists, and social workers – enjoy considerable latitude to shape the delivery of 'a colourful variety' of social therapy to reflect their diverse competencies and interests, within their particular institution. Accordingly, 'a uniform and systematic concept of the social-therapeutic institution does not exist' (Lösel & Egg, 1997) in Germany. This therefore directly contrasts with English prison-based TCs which, as chapter 2 elucidates, must now adhere to a Core Model and which are, in some important respects, subject to, and arguably adversely restricted by, 'top down', centralised, homogeneity-encouraging Prison Service direction. A further significant distinction is that, since 2003, social therapy is mandated by the German courts for violent and sexual offenders serving more than two years (Wößner, 2008).

Conclusion

Prison-based democratic therapeutic communities have therefore evolved, from their unlikely wartime psychiatric antecedents, into a well-established, internationally respected, alternative model of imprisonment and treatment. They have doggedly survived 'nothing works', an increased emphasis upon security and control, new public managerialism, and a now seemingly perpetual 'crisis' of penal resources and penal legitimacy (Cavadino & Dignan, 1992). Notwithstanding the estimates of need from the Institute of Psychiatry and the Prison Service Directorate of Health Care, however, TCs in England and Wales still only operate on the periphery of the prison estate, providing treatment for just 538 men and women – and this in a prison population which is projected to reach as high as 90,200 by June 2012 (Ministry of Justice 2009:2). To radical criminologists and neo-abolitionists, TCs' marginal status is a direct and deliberate reflection of the political and ideological marginalisation of penal welfarism and humanistic, holistic rehabilitation, in favour of a 'tough' law and order discourse and reductionist, deficits-focused risk management. Yet, when one ponders the fundamental incongruity of conjoining democratic therapeutic communities with coercive institutions of retributive punishment, even this numerically limited engagement with TC ideals represents an extraordinary achievement, whose 'special purpose' continues to be much admired by penologists, and much valued by those residents for whom it enables meaningful, pro-social change (Stevens, 2008). The celebration of this achievement, realistically tempered by concern for the challenges that remain, begins in the chapters that now follow.

References

Adler, A. (1924). *The Practice and Theory of Individual Psychology*. London: Kegan Paul.

Ainsworth, M. (1967). *Infancy in Uganda: Infant Care and the Growth of Love*. Baltimore: Johns Hopkins University Press.

Allen, F. (1981). *The Decline of the Rehabilitative Ideal: Penal Policy and Social Purpose*. New Haven: Yale University Press.

American Psychiatric Association (1994). *Diagnostic and Statistical Manual of Mental Disorders, 4th edition (DSM-IV)*. Washington, DC: American Psychiatric Association.

Belknap, I. (1956). *Human Problems of a State Mental Hospital*. New York: McGraw-Hill.

Birtchnell, J. & Shine, J. (2000). Personality disorders and the interpersonal octagon. *British Journal of Medical Psychology, 73* (4), 433–448.

Bottomley, K., Liebling, A. & Sparks, R. (1994). *Barlinnie Special Unit and Shotts Unit: An Assessment*. Scottish Prison Service Occasional Paper no.7. Edinburgh: Scottish Prison Service.

Bowlby, J. (1969). *Attachment and Loss, Volume I: Attachment*. London: The Hogarth Press and the Institute of Psycho-Analysis.

Bowlby, J. (1973). *Attachment and Loss, Volume II: Separation, Anxiety and Anger*. London: The Hogarth Press and the Institute of Psycho-Analysis.

Bowlby. J. (1980). *Attachment and Loss, Volume III: Loss, Sadness and Depression*. London: The Hogarth Press and the Institute of Psycho-Analysis.

Caudill, W. (1958). *The Psychiatric Hospital as a Small Society*. Cambridge, MA: Harvard University Press.

Cavadino, M. & Dignan, J. (1992). *The Penal System: An Introduction*. London: Sage.

Clark, D. (1965). The therapeutic community: concept, practice and future. *British Journal of Psychiatry, 111* (479), 947–954.

Clark, D. (1998). *Current Research*. Unpublished internal report, Planning Group, HM Prison Service, London.

Collins, H. (1997). *Autobiography of a Murderer*. London: Macmillan.

Commissioners of Prisons (1963). *Report for 1962*. London: Her Majesty's Stationery Office.

Cooke, D. (1989). Containing violent prisoners: an analysis of the Barlinnie Special Unit. *British Journal of Criminology, 29* (2), 129–143.

Cooke, D. (1991). Violence in prisons: the influence of regime factors. *The Howard Journal of Criminal Justice, 30* (2), 95–109.

Cooke, D. (1997). The Barlinnie Special Unit: the rise and fall of a therapeutic experiment. In E. Cullen, L. Jones & R. Woodward (Eds) *Therapeutic Communities for Offenders* (pp. 101–119). Chichester: John Wiley and Sons.

Cooke, D. & Michie, C. (1999). Psychopathy across cultures: North America and Scotland compared. *Journal of Abnormal Psychology, 108* (1), 58–68.

Cullen, E. (1997). Can a prison be a therapeutic community?: The Grendon Template. In E. Cullen, L. Jones & R. Woodward (Eds) *Therapeutic Communities for Offenders* (pp. 75–99). Chichester: John Wiley and Sons.

Cullen, E. (1998). *Grendon and Future Therapeutic Communities in Prison.* London: Prison Reform Trust.

East, W. N. (1932). *Report of the Commissioners of Prisons and the Directors of Convict Prisons for 1931, Cmnd 4295.* London: His Majesty's Stationery Office.

East, W. N. & Hubert, W. (1939). *The Psychological Treatment of Crime.* London: His Majesty's Stationery Office.

Faulk, M. (1990). Her Majesty's Prison Grendon, Underwood. In R. Bluglass & P. Bowden (Eds) *Principles and Practice of Forensic Psychiatry* (pp. 1347–1350). Edinburgh: Churchill Livingstone.

Freud, S. (1922). *Group Psychology and the Analysis of the Ego.* London: Hogarth.

Garland, D. (1985). *Punishment and Welfare: A History of Penal Strategies.* Aldershot: Gower.

Genders, E. (2003). Privatisation and innovation – rhetoric and reality: the development of a therapeutic community prison. *The Howard Journal of Criminal Justice, 42* (2), 137–157.

Genders, E. & Player, E. (1995). *Grendon: A Study of a Therapeutic Prison.* Oxford: Clarendon Press.

Goffman, E. (1961). *Asylums: Essays on the Social Situation of Mental Patients and Other Inmates.* Harmondsworth: Penguin.

Gray, N., Snowden, R., Brown, A. & MacCulloch, M. (2002). *Prevalence of Psychopathy and other Measures of Risk at HMP Grendon: An Investigation of Population Statistics.* Cardiff: School of Psychology, Cardiff University.

Gray, W. (1973). The therapeutic community and evaluation of results. *International Journal of Criminology and Penology, 1,* 327–334. (Reprinted in J. Shine (Ed.) (2000). *A Compilation of Grendon Research.* Leyhill Press. Available from Psychology Unit, HMP Grendon, Grendon Underwood, Aylesbury, HP18 OTL.)

Gunn, J., Maden, T. & Swinton, M. (1991). Treatment needs of prisoners with psychiatric disorders. *British Medical Journal, 303* (6798), 338–341.

Haigh, R. (1999). The quintessence of a therapeutic community: five universal qualities. In P. Campling & R. Haigh (Eds) *Therapeutic Communities: Past, Present, and Future* (pp. 246–257). London: Jessica Kingsley.

Hare, R. (1991). *Manual for the Hare Psychopathy Checklist – Revised.* Toronto: Multi-Health Systems.

Hare, R. (1993). *Without Conscience: The Disturbing World of the Psychopaths among Us.* New York: Pocket Books.

HM Chief Inspector of Prisons (2001). *Report on an Unannounced Inspection of HM Prison Wormwood Scrubs, 10–19 December 2001.* London: HM Inspectorate of Prisons.

HM Chief Inspector of Prisons (2006). *Report on an Announced Inspection of HMP Send, 13–17 February 2006*. London: HM Inspectorate of Prisons.

Hobson, J. & Shine, J. (1998). Measurement of psychopathy in a UK prison population referred for long-term psychotherapy. *British Journal of Criminology, 38* (3), 504–515.

Home Office (1932). *Report of the Departmental Committee on Persistent Offenders, Cmnd 4090*. London: His Majesty's Stationery Office.

Home Office (1985). *First Report of the Advisory Committee on the Therapeutic Regime at Grendon*. London: Her Majesty's Stationery Office.

Jones, L. (1997). Developing models for managing treatment integrity and efficacy in a prison-based therapeutic community: the Max Glatt Centre. In E. Cullen, L. Jones, & R. Woodward (Eds) *Therapeutic Communities for Offenders* (pp. 121–157). Chichester: John Wiley and Sons.

Jones, M. (1942). Group psychotherapy. *British Medical Journal, 2* (4261), 276–278.

Jones, M. (1946). Rehabilitation of Forces neurosis patients to civilian life. *British Medical Journal, 1* (4448), 533–535.

Jones, M. (1952). *Social Psychiatry: A Study of Therapeutic Communities*. London: Tavistock Publications.

Jones, M. (1953). *The Therapeutic Community: A New Treatment Method in Psychiatry*. New York: Basic Books.

Jones, M. (1956). The concept of a therapeutic community. *American Journal of Psychiatry, 112* (8), 647–650.

Jones, M. (1959). Towards a clarification of the therapeutic community concept. *British Journal of Medical Psychology, 32* (3), 200–205.

Jones, M. (1968). *Social Psychiatry in Practice: The Idea of the Therapeutic Community*. Harmondsworth: Penguin.

Jones, M. (1976). *Maturation of the Therapeutic Community: An Organic Approach to Health and Mental Health*. New York: Human Sciences Press.

Jones, M. (1980). Desirable features in therapeutic community in a prison. In H. Toch (Ed.) *Therapeutic Communities in Corrections* (pp. 34–40). Westport: Greenwood Press.

Kennard, D. (1996). Editorial: an education in sincerity and tolerance. *Therapeutic Communities: The International Journal for Therapeutic and Supportive Organizations, 17* (2), 71–73.

Kennard, D. & Roberts, J. (1983). *An Introduction to Therapeutic Communities*. London: Routledge and Kegan Paul.

Kennedy, J. (2008). *Personal communication with Jackie Kennedy*. HMP Grendon psychological assistant, April 2008.

Lewis, P. (1997). Sustaining therapeutic communities: the Grendon experience. *Prison Service Journal, 111*, 8–12.

Lösel, E. & Egg, R. (1997). Social-therapeutic institutions in Germany: description and evaluation. In E. Cullen, L. Jones & R. Woodward (Eds) *Therapeutic Communities for Offenders* (pp. 181–203). Chichester: John Wiley and Sons.

Maden, T., Swinton, M. & Gunn, J. (1994). Therapeutic community treatment: a survey of unmet need among sentenced prisoners. *Therapeutic Communities: The International Journal for Therapeutic and Supportive Organizations, 15* (4), 2229–2236.

Main, T. (1946). The hospital as a therapeutic institution. *Bulletin of the Menninger Clinic, 10,* 66–68. (Reprinted in 1996 in *Therapeutic Communities: The International Journal for Therapeutic and Supportive Organizations, 17* (2), 77–80.)

Malan, D. (1979). *Individual Psychotherapy and the Science of Psychodynamics.* Oxford: Butterworth Heinemann.

Manning, N. (1976). Innovation in social policy – the case of the therapeutic community. *Journal of Social Policy, 5* (3), 265–279.

May, J. (1979). *Committee of Inquiry into the United Kingdom Prison Services: Report, Cmnd 7673.* London: Her Majesty's Stationery Office.

Mead, G.H. (1934). *Mind, Self, and Society: From the Standpoint of a Social Behaviorist.* Chicago: Chicago University Press.

Ministry of Justice (2009). *Prison Population Projections 2009–2015, England and Wales.* London: Ministry of Justice.

Morrice, J. (1979). Basic concepts: a critical review. In R. Hinshelwood & N. Manning (Eds) *Therapeutic Communities: Reflections and Progress* (pp. 49–58). London: Routledge.

Newell, T. & Healey, B. (2007). The historical development of the UK democratic therapeutic community. In M. Parker (Ed.) *Dynamic Security: The Democratic Community in Prison* (pp. 61–68). London: Jessica Kingsley.

O'Malley, P. (1999). Volatile and contradictory punishment. *Theoretical Criminology, 3* (2), 175–196.

Parsons, T. (1951). *The Social System.* Glencoe: Free Press.

Rapoport, R. (1960). *Community as Doctor: New Perspectives on a Therapeutic Community.* London: Tavistock.

Roberts, J. (1997a). How to recognise a therapeutic community. *Prison Service Journal, 111,* 4–7.

Roberts, J. (1997b). History of the therapeutic community. In E. Cullen, L. Jones & R. Woodward (Eds) *Therapeutic Communities for Offenders* (pp. 3–22). Chichester: John Wiley and Sons.

Scottish Home and Health Department (1971). *Report of a Departmental Working Party on the Treatment of Certain Male Long-Term Prisoners and Potentially Violent Prisoners.* Edinburgh: Scottish Home and Health Department.

Scottish Prison Service (1994). *Small Units in the Scottish Prison Service: A Report of the Working Party on Barlinnie Special Unit.* Edinburgh: Scottish Prison Service.

Selby, M. (1991). Grendon – the care of acute psychiatric patients – a pragmatic solution. In J. Reynolds & U. Smartt (Eds) 1995 *Prison Policy and Practice: Selected Papers from 35 years of the Prison Service Journal* (pp. 260–265). HMP Leyhill: Prison Service Journal.

Shine, J. & Newton, M. (2000). Damaged, disturbed and dangerous: a profile of receptions to Grendon Therapeutic Prison 1995–2000. In J. Shine (Ed.) *A*

Compilation of Grendon Research (pp. 23–35). Leyhill Press. Available from Psychology Unit, HMP Grendon, Grendon Underwood, Aylesbury, HP18 OTL.

Sim, J. (2007). Barlinnie. In Y. Jewkes & J. Bennett (Eds) *Dictionary of Prisons and Punishment* (pp. 21–23). Cullompton: Willan.

Smartt, U. (2001). *Grendon Tales: Stories from a Therapeutic Community*. Winchester: Waterside Press.

Sparks, R. (2002). Out of the 'digger': the warrior's honour and the guilty observer. *Ethnography*, 3 (4), 556–581.

Stanton, A. & Schwartz, M. (1954). *The Mental Hospital*. New York: Basic Books.

Stevens, A. (2008). Therapeutic community. In Y. Jewkes & J. Bennett (Eds) *Dictionary of Prisons and Punishment* (pp. 290–292). Cullompton: Willan.

Stewart, C. & Parker, M. (2007). Send: the women's democratic therapeutic community in prison. In M. Parker (Ed.) *Dynamic Security: The Democratic Community in Prison* (pp. 69–82). London: Jessica Kingsley.

Sykes, G. & Matza, D. (1957). Techniques of neutralization: a theory of delinquency. *American Sociological Review*, 22 (6), 664–670.

Whatmore, P. (1990). The Special Unit at Barlinnie Prison, Glasgow. In R. Bluglass & P. Bowden (Eds) *Principles and Practice of Forensic Psychiatry* (pp. 1359–1362). Edinburgh: Churchill Livingstone.

Whiteley, S. (2004). The evolution of the therapeutic community. *Psychiatric Quarterly*, 75 (3), 233–248.

Woodward, R. (1999). The prison communities: therapy within a custodial setting. In P. Campling & R. Haigh (Eds) *Therapeutic Communities: Past, Present and Future* (pp. 162–173). London: Jessica Kingsley.

Wößner, G. (2008). *Sexual offenders in the social-therapeutic institutions of the Free State of Saxony, 25 June 2008*. Available at www.mpicc.de/ww/en/pub/forschung/forschungsarbeit/kriminologie/sexualstraftaeter_sozial.htm [accessed 14 August 2008].

Yalom, I. (1980). *Existential Psychotherapy*. New York: Basic Books.

Chapter 2

Dovegate Therapeutic Community: Bid, Birth, Growth and Survival

Eric Cullen and Alan Miller

Summary

In 1995 the Government commissioned the creation of a new therapeutic community (TC) of 200 beds, set within a large category B prison in the private sector. This chapter summarizes the sequence of events in the creation of this TC, which opened in 2002, as well as a first-hand account from one of the therapists, and a view of the problems that now beset it.

A Brief History

In 1939, Dr Norwood East and Dr W. H. De B. Hubert published a report entitled *The Psychological Treatment of Crime* (London: Prison Department) recommending the creation of a special kind of prison to treat those with personality disorders. Twenty-three years later, HMP Grendon Therapeutic Community Prison was opened as a direct consequence, the manifestation of a wonderful principle concerning patience. In November 2001, Dovegate Therapeutic Community Prison opened, the first and, currently, only private sector democratic TC in the United Kingdom, and only the second full-scale TC in prisons since 1939.

Grendon and the Emergence of Forensic Therapeutic Communities: Developments in Research and Practice
Edited by Richard Shuker and Elizabeth Sullivan
© 2010 John Wiley & Sons, Ltd.

The unfortunate irony of this is that therapeutic communities for prisoners generally, and Grendon specifically, are the only regime-based treatment form which has been proven by published research to work in terms of significantly reducing re-convictions, lowering institutional offending and improved psychometric measures of personality which are relevant to future pro-social behaviour. What is lamentable is that TCs can accommodate only 538 of the 83,000 plus criminals currently imprisoned, and that there are many thousands of seriously dangerous personality-disordered offenders untreated as a consequence.

This chapter is about the second democratic therapeutic community prison in the United Kingdom: HMP Dovegate in Staffordshire. The stages from the Home Office Executive Committee's Specification in 1997 to creating the consultancy team responsible for Premier Custodial Services' bid to build and run the prison, through the bidding process and preparations for opening and the first years of Dovegate, are covered. It is a story full of optimism, hard work and success but, ultimately, a genuine fear for the future and the uncertain survival of Dovegate.

Part 1: The Bid

The Prison Service opened the process by inviting expressions of interest from private sector consortia in the summer of 1997. By February 1998, Premier, along with five other consortia, presented their 'Initiative Proposals' for the design, construction, management and financing of the 600-bed category B training prison and the 200-bed therapeutic community at Marchington, Staffordshire. These extremely detailed submissions were in response to Home Office specifications. The main members of the Premier consortium were

• Premier Custodial Services;
• Kværner Construction;
• CAPITA EC Architectural Practices; and
• Lazard Brothers Banking with Joint Venture Partners: Serco and Wackenhut Corrections (USA).

The invitation to bid for private sector consortia came in the form of a document entitled *Proposals for a Second Therapeutic Community* in November 1997 (Directorate of Health Care, 1995). It is worth quoting briefly from this document:

The 'Aim' of the enterprise was 'By offering the best of therapeutic community practice and of psychological therapies to enable those individuals who have disorders of social functioning to live considerate, law-abiding lives in custody and on release'.

The 'Estimation of Need' varied, ranging between 600 and 2500 prisoners who could benefit from the new therapeutic community prison. In 2008, the unmet need was put in excess of 3000.

It is interesting to note that the Executive Committee also 'envisaged' a third therapeutic prison, which they said should 'be established to these general specifications. It is recommended that it be situated in London or South East England'. Whatever happened to that idea?

The Premier Custodial Services Therapeutic Community bid team

Dovegate was a fortunate and timely creation, coming as a product of a) the Private Finance Initiate (PFI) of the early 1990s which saw unprecedented growth of contracting and building in the private prison sector, and b) the publication of research (Cullen, 1993; Marshall, 1997; Taylor, 2000) which proved for the first time that the democratic therapeutic community approach worked in reducing re-offending. Premier Custodial Services (PCS) was one of several companies bidding for the contract with the Home Office. It was a 25-year commitment to build and run an 800-bed category B security prison on a site near Uttoxeter in Staffordshire. The first author (EC), of the Forensic Psychology Practice, was employed as the Lead Consultant for the 200-bed bid TC part of the process. The TC was to be built on the same physical site as the 600-bed main prison but was to be separated by fencing and was to have its own independent staff complement. A team of expert consultants were assembled by Premier including Dr Jeff Roberts, a psychiatrist who had worked with the management of Grendon and had published relevant treatment works including *An Introduction to Therapeutic Communities* (1983) with David Kennard; Dr Elaine Player, then a Senior Lecturer in Law at King's College, London and co-author of *Grendon: A Study of a Therapeutic Prison* (1995); Joe Chapman, formerly a senior officer at Grendon with over 10 years experience of TCs, and, crucially, Roland Woodward, who was employed by Premier as their designated Director of Therapy for the new TC. Roland was, at the time, the therapist in charge of the TC at Gartree prison, a successful regime catering exclusively for life-sentence prisoners, and he had also been a wing therapist at Grendon. He had the experience, personal skills and qualities that were essential to the successful creation and development of Dovegate

TC. The PCS team also included Michael Gander, a Director of PCS who had overall responsibility for the bid and the TC team – an exceptionally demanding task.

The primary theoretical underpinning of the PCS bid was from a professional orientation of cognitive-behavioural therapy and the group psychotherapeutic work of Yalom (1995). This was a fundamental departure from the traditional, and Grendon's, orientation of psychodynamic psychotherapy.

Premier was the successful bidder and the contract to build and run the 800-bed prison was awarded to us in 1999. The construction took just over 2 years and Dovegate TC opened in November 2001. Before it opened, the Lead Consultant Eric Cullen and the Director of Therapy Roland Woodward wrote the complete treatment and training manual for the staff teams to come.

Part II: The Preparation for Opening

Starting a therapeutic community in a secure prison from scratch was a significant challenge – the first time it had been attempted in 40 years (excluding the much smaller TC units started up in existing prisons like Max Glatt in Wormwood Scrubs, the lifers' TC in Gartree and the young offender TCs in Glen Parva, Feltham and Aylesbury).

The procedure concentrated on here concerned the preparation and training of the staff. The training programme started with a four-week course run by Cullen and Woodward for the wing therapists, managers and counsellors. These team leaders then trained their own staff teams in anticipation of opening their respective TCs. This was the longest and most ambitious staff training ever offered for prison-based TCs.

An outline of the course curriculum included:

Week One:

A history of therapeutic communities including The Retreat and the Quakers' influence: issues of class and 'moral treatment'; the military hospitals of World War II at Mill Hill (Maxwell Jones) and Northfield (Bion, Faulkes and Main) and their concepts of professional humility, collective responsibility and patient-organised groups; Rapoport's work including the four principles which characterise democratic TCs: *democratic, permissive* (in terms of tolerating behaviour sufficient to see it honestly), *communal* (in that the emphasis was on shared amenities and close relationships) and *reality confronting.* These principles continue to inform the best of TC work. The course was also experiential in that we ran it as a TC group in parallel with the didactic and informative elements, so the course members grew in their individual and collective TC insights and knowledge just as prisoner residents would. Week one continued with sessions on *The Unique Dovegate TC Staff Model*, with five primary roles: the PCO (prison officer), the *SMART* or Social Milieu And Reintegration Therapist role, which is explained below, the group facilitator role, the processor/team support role, and the recorder/data collector.

SMART was a creation of Roland Woodward's, concerned with addressing a feature uniquely strong within a TC, understanding the whole process, that TCs are far more than treatment programmes, but rather *different ways of living*. The skills required in SMART included:

1. Understanding the basic inter-group process;
2. Understanding large groups, continuity process and dynamics;
3. Understanding Rapoport's four therapeutic factors;
4. Understanding the concept of the 'healthy adult';
5. The ability to provide a model of *reasonable, rational behaviour*;
6. Understanding and performing the role of therapy arbiter;
7. Understanding, keeping and illuminating the boundaries for group and community;
8. Balancing the PCO and SMART roles;
9. Articulating the 'nicking threshold', i.e. balance insight with discipline; and
10. The ability to identify and cope with personal emotions consonant with the TC staff role.

The final sessions in week one included basic group facilitator skills, lectures on some of the philosophy and principles of TCs, and the Yalom group factors of universality and altruism.

Week Two:

Topics included interpersonal learning, attachment theory, Stack Sullivan's self-dynamism, consensual validation and the *corrective emotional experience*, which has five primary components:

1. A strong expression of emotion, involving risk in expressing, and directed towards another person;
2. A group supportive enough to permit this risk taking;
3. Reality-testing, allowing the individual to examine the incident or emotion with the group's aid;
4. Recognition of how the feelings or behaviour may be inappropriate, negative or unhealthy; and
5. Facilitation of the individual's ability to interact with the group more deeply and honestly.

Other themes covered include the group as a social microcosm, cognitive behavioural therapy and contracting, and the related and crucial process of parallel behaviour. Course members were given opportunities to practise drafting behaviour contracts, which focused on specific dysfunctional interpersonal behaviours. Entire days were given over to the SMART skills of therapy arbiters including the vital TC functions of containing residents' anxieties, facilitating residents' ability to show their genuine thoughts and feelings, and stopping the TC imploding or exploding.

Week Three:

Topics included socialising, family re-enactment, social skills and social drive theory, and experiential groups moving into unstructured, group-led dialogue; staff support procedures including:

1. Daily work/support groups – monthly individual meetings with therapy managers;
2. Full staff team meetings – annual appraisal meeting with therapy managers;
3. Access to an external consultant via the Director of Therapy;
4. Regular sensitivity meetings as determined within the unit teams and their therapy managers;
5. Daily meetings between therapy managers and the Director of Therapy. Monthly meetings for the Director of Therapy with the Prison Director;
6. The Director of Therapy meets with external mentor every two months; and
7. Support of Lead Consultant during first year of operations.

Staff boundary-breaking issues were also covered including sexual relationships with residents, making inappropriate exceptions for individual inmates, e.g. taking out letters, accepting confidences and doing extracurricular favours. The training also covered identifying signs that staff are at risk and strategies for combating these risks. The third week introduced defence mechanisms including transference/counter-transference, denial and minimisation.

Week Four:

The final week's training covered more group facilitator skills, a community meeting exercise, a culture of enquiry: its preservation or loss (a session exploring ways in which a TC can deteriorate, be threatened or close); re-integrating residents to other prisons or release upon completion of therapy or leaving early; issues of staff dissent and conflict; Addressing Offending Behaviour II; more functional analysis of behaviour; course review and evaluation.

Although it is impossible to convey it here, the month's training gave the course members many opportunities through the experiential groups to create powerful ties, bonds and even friendships that lasted. This demonstration of the power of the TC group experience is impossible in the much shorter courses run in other TCs that last no longer than a week.

Part III: The First Six Years

The place and getting in

HMP Dovegate therapeutic community is a specially designed and pur-pose-built 200-bed TC within the 800-bed category B security Dovegate prison in Staffordshire. It comprises four therapeutic communities of 40 places, each within a separate, specially designed area, a High Intensity Programme (HIP) of 20 places, and an Assessment and Resettlement Unit of 20 places.

Opening a therapeutic community: the Therapy Manager's experience

The first part of this chapter described the process of formulating, planning and constructing a new therapeutic community from a consultancy point of view. This section will reflect on the second author (AM)'s experience of the opening of the community, providing an account from the per-spective of the therapist.

The novel thing about opening a new therapeutic community is that in some respects it is a blank canvas with some basic rules set in stone: com-munalism, permissiveness, democratisation and reality confrontation (Rapoport, 1960). Despite having almost 15 years' experience of living and working in a therapeutic community for children and young people in the north-east of England, this was different, this was new, this was for those who pose the greatest risks to society. The publication *Therapeutic Communities for Offenders* (Cullen *et al.*, 1997) provided Roland Woodward and Eric Cullen with a blueprint for a purpose-built therapeutic commu-nity in a new prison. Woodward was manager and mentor and Cullen, consultant and advisor. The sages of yore were there to pass their collective wisdom to the new kid on the prison block.

Thus, Woodward and Cullen were in post to manage and open Com-munity C at HMP Dovegate Therapeutic Community Prison, Custody

Officer training had been completed, the Prison Rules learnt by rote, bodies pushed to their limit in the gym and faces rubbed in the lore of jail craft. The training team had provided each staff group with the salient elements of group facilitation and each member of staff had explored their being through the life story work of the experiential group, complete with the tears that universality of the human experience brings.

Preparation for opening also involved familiarisation with the business contract between Premier/Serco and HM Prison Service and reading core therapeutic texts such as Yalom's (1995) *The Theory and Practice of Group Psychotherapy*. Practical and technical difficulties in the commissioning of the new prison led to a delay in opening Community C. This delay resulted in clinical management responsibilities being temporarily assumed for other wings, which caused its own unique set of challenges. Clinical authority was not readily transferable and the therapeutic culture already established was not open to perceived outside interference. Boundaries were broken, for example hooch (a foul-smelling, quick-brewing alcoholic drink) was discovered within a month of opening. Lessons were quickly learned about the threats to the clinical climate whilst the culture remained embryonic and fragile and where clinical teams assume that the treatment alliance is a transferable commodity.

Pre-opening

Basic Dovegate TC therapy elements and meetings

For each community the structure is fairly simple: everyone begins the day with a business meeting chaired by staff to review happenings for that day and to listen to individual requests, complaints and comments. Each community has a full community meeting of staff and residents chaired by a resident on a Monday and Friday in which agenda items are reviewed. Agenda items can be anything from an individual's behaviour to staff responses to behaviour. Small groups facilitated by TC staff members run on the other three days. Feedback meetings for staff and residents follow each small group with process meetings for staff following that. Each individual community holds staff meetings and staff sensitivity groups, which normally follow community meetings.

Although primary responsibility was for running a 40-bed community this was also part of a much larger community, which had to be managed. To run a 200-bed therapeutic establishment efficiently and with *fewer* staff than its main competitor, HMP Grendon, was a challenge, but it was also a challenge to prove that it could be done.

How this was achieved was a magnificence of organisation and commitment to work that the authors had not witnessed before or anywhere since. That's not to say it worked perfectly all of the time because it didn't. When it worked well, it was superb and a testament to collaborative working, but at times it became as brutal as a Roman amphitheatre. The management team and the room where these meetings were held also took its name from the government of ancient Rome – the Senate.

Challenges in establishing a staff dialogue

Within the Senate was a large round table, capable of seating the team of the Director of Therapy, his PA, the six therapy managers, the four operations managers, the head of *Educom*[1], and a psychiatrist.

The structure of the meetings was broadly as follows: firstly there was the daily business meeting where overnight occurrences and daily plans were reviewed. Each week we had an operations meeting to review the practical issues of running a prison with a more comprehensive monthly meeting to supplement this. Other weekly meetings were the Educom meeting and the management's process meeting – but more of that later. Most of the other meetings were monthly, for example there was a co-lateral meeting (to review and implement the complementary cognitive behavioural programmes), therapy governance, personnel, finance, drug strategy, supervision/case study/research and risk management (a much later addition). There were additional seasonal and one-off meetings, for example, to plan *RezArt* (an annual two-week art festival held across the communities), meetings to review our research contracted out to Surrey University, and planning meetings for audits from the Prison Service and the Community of Communities.

The 'Fluffy'

The one meeting that deserves singular reflection was the management team's weekly process meeting, the *Fluffy*. Roland Woodward named the meeting after the three-headed dog in the Harry Potter stories. It was actually a very good name to describe the meeting as each head has a different way of thinking while controlling one body. Unfortunately the Fluffy had the unnerving habit of one head biting and drawing blood from the other two, with all of the heads being able to lick each other's faces on other occasions.

---

[1]Educom was a phrase devised by Roland Woodward to describe HMP Dovegate TC's activities department, meaning a mixture of academic education and commercial (vocational) training.

Collectively there was never an established definition of what the meeting represented but every attendee had their own personal definition based on their input and experience from the meeting. In the early days, the support group led by Eric Cullen also attended. Initially the team brought their individual experiences and feelings about running a therapeutic community and shared them with each other. However it wasn't too long before professional group interests and individual personalities began to use the vehicle for battle. Sometimes the Fluffy could be reasonable, rational and mature in reflection but at other times, histrionic and borderline in its personality. It often functioned in a classic T-group manner; members would accuse other members of not being honest but when people claimed to be honest in their expression of feelings, tears would flow and anger erupt. It had everything that could be witnessed in a group and had its various types of leader: the in-group, the out-group, the scapegoat, collaboration, competition, conflict, groupthink, complacency, decisiveness and compassion. It was constructive at times, destructive at others. On reflection, the Fluffy worked well for Dovegate TC and was a major contributor to its development. If the management team could not 'do' therapy it would not have been able to 'do' therapy with the residents.

Consensus management by committee, although appealing to the democratic nature of TCs, has its plusses and minuses. On the plus side, it allowed different groups and professions to have their voice heard and reach a balanced point of view. The minus to this is that the decision-making could be extremely protracted and painful in the process, and sometimes became irrelevant as time passed. As a way of managing a therapeutic community it was excellent. As a way of managing a prison therapeutic community it had its limitations, especially when it was applied to prison security and in response to governmental 'knee-jerk' reactions to media reporting on crime, punishment and victims.

However, the proof of the pudding tends to be in the eating. Ask most offenders in therapy about their experience and they will tell you quite genuinely, 'This is the hardest time you will do', and reflect that it is easy to be locked up for 23 hours per day when you can get drugs and watch television. Confronting your demons is far more scary, especially when they visit you when you are locked up at night with no one to talk to. This can be considered as the 'Prometheus effect' of the therapeutic community experience and is not always understood by the media or government. If you consider the story from Greek mythology, that Prometheus (paradoxically in ancient Greek meaning forethought) was punished by Zeus by having his liver pecked out and eaten by eagles every day, but a new liver grew overnight to be pecked out again for his crime of stealing fire and giving it to mortals, can you imagine the potential horror of being confronted by your crimes, reliving them every night only to be confronted again the next day, and the day after? This process of very public scrutiny – lasting, potentially, for years – is the reality of the TC approach to treating criminal behaviour. To those unfamiliar with therapeutic communities, the process of offenders revisiting their crimes and their past is not some form of sadistic punishment as endured by Prometheus, but works as an aid to examining the evolution of maladaptive responses for the person under scrutiny and to assist the understanding of those processes by gaining many perspectives to the behaviour under examination. There are side effects of the process of re-examination that require acknowledgement: put simply, sometimes the truth hurts.

Collateral therapies

One aspect of the bid as described by Cullen was for the therapeutic community to run other cognitive therapeutically based offending behaviour programmes alongside core therapy. The programmes agreed were Reasoning and Rehabilitation (R&R) and the Sex Offender Treatment Programme (SOTP), both of which are accredited Offending Behaviour Programmes (OBPs) of the Correctional Services Accreditation Panel (CSAP), psychodrama and art therapy. The idea was not a new one as HMP Grendon had run a number of these courses during the 1990s. The idea is a good one in that it delivers an additional 'dose' of targeted therapy to reinforce the core TC treatment. However, one issue related to courses delivered at Dovegate TC was that of cost. The bid had said it would deliver the courses in the agreed contract price; our reality was that the collateral courses had to be delivered in the agreed price without additional resource. The practicalities of this were that the courses would be administered and overseen by the therapy managers as treatment managers (mainly psychologists) and delivered by therapy staff (prison officers, psychologists in training and counsellors) engaged in all of the main therapeutic processes of the community. Many issues arose from this: training, overtime, leave and support (internal and external).

An early issue arose from psychodrama in that Dovegate TC could only afford (in the contract budget) to pay for one day (two sessions), which was not adequate for four main communities. The effect of this was that two communities had access to psychodrama and two communities did not. The communities who did not get psychodrama did get some additional support from final year trainee art therapists on placement from the University of Derby, but this was not an ideal situation. In the course of time, the resource issue became an increasing area of dispute amongst the Senate and staff who had put themselves forward as tutors. R&R was successfully delivered but quickly disappeared in a round of cuts by the Prison

Service. SOTP had a more torrid time for a number of reasons, one of which had been raised with Grendon when they delivered the programme and that was that the TC style was judged to be too confrontational. Organisational and administrative problems also beset the initial delivery of the SOTP but had improved significantly when Dovegate lost the right to run the course when SOTP was reorganised regionally. The effect of these losses on the TC was both a loss of income and a temporary lowering of morale. Resilience prevailed when the team began to develop their own collateral programmes such as the internationally reported Reintegration Programme and the ASET accredited NVQ level 2 programme 'Understanding and Managing Anger'. Despite the initial setbacks in running collateral programmes the Dovegate TC team continued with their commitment to supplementary therapies to reinforce the TC treatment modality.

C wing therapeutic community opens

'The installation and maintenance of hope is crucial in any psychotherapy' (Yalom, 1995). With the opening of C and D communities on 1 February 2002, this was the team's priority task, and as was discovered in those demanding months, the most difficult of the tasks to be faced.

The community members were embraced with their first community meeting, plotting out the base rules, expectations and hopes for the future. A feature of this meeting was to emphasise the 'culture of enquiry' (Main, 1981), that is, the ability to question and reflect upon any of the processes of therapeutic community practice and its importance to the development of the community. The culture of enquiry, however, became the club the community used upon itself to hinder the progress of its own development. The apprehension and fear of change often slowed down or stopped the change process, as the questions asked by residents could be pedantic in the extreme or the answers given were rejected through a lack of trust from the residents.

For example, after a few days most of the community complained of having problems in getting to sleep at night. The reasons were explored: the newness of the situation, prior substance dependency or feelings of anxiety as part of our fresh holistic approach to problems. The community was informed that they could spray their pillows with lavender water prior to settling down for the night, with 'three sprays' being all that was required, and they just needed to request the spray from the duty officer. The next day only two residents turned up at the business meeting, the remainder claimed they had 'slept in' as a result of the lavender water they had used.

The bottle was found to be empty, and nine residents had used 500 ml in one night, far in excess of 'three sprays' each. When the group was challenged on their collective misuse of responsibility, the staff team were told, 'Well, if you didn't want us to use it you shouldn't have made it available to us'.

Relationships with the wider organisation

The small groups appeared to be functioning effectively, and as a group, staff worked hard to process all that was observed and heard, but struggled with some of the administrative systems and the relationship with the larger sibling on the other side of the fence, HMP Dovegate main prison.

As often with siblings, there was sibling rivalry. The wider establishment were regarded as 'turnkeys', having the pick of services as they maintained control of the essential items – food, mail, property and visits. The TC was viewed as a 'care bear': there to comfort, console and collude with prisoners. These perceptions were seen across all grades, even though, when discussing this with other managers across the prison, the notion that such thoughts were held by managers was dismissed. Intense feelings of mistrust developed. For example, auxiliary grade staff were supposed to be assigned to the TC to help supervise visits but it rarely happened, so security would observe TC visits on camera and if a drugs pass was missed because of staff shortages, the TC was very publicly criticised. For the therapeutic community this was not only a breach of security, it was also undermining the therapy we were trying to deliver. This type of observation was made in many operational situations and never led to a comfortable situation between the two sides of the prison.

Despite the apparent progress in the small groups, there was an interesting, if unwelcome, development within the community. Suspicions were raised that there were drugs in the community but none had been found during searches, nor had any resident tested positive in any drug tests. There were some drug-related paraphernalia discovered in communal areas, such as the laundry, which were taken to the community meeting only to receive a response of gasps of shock, horror, denial and deflection in that the community would try to avoid the main issue of drugs by concentrating on the practicalities of communal life for example, mail delivery, food, visits and telephones.

These nuts and bolts of the therapeutic process are common to most therapeutic communities but are not without event. For example, in those new to a therapeutic community the new-found principle of a culture of enquiry allows a resident to take issues of everyday prison life to a public forum and a public protest. However, some of these public protests can be so voracious as to cause a sideshow from the main arena of therapy, but a sideshow still within Rapoport's principles of democratisation and communalism.

Threats, challenges and progress

With any new enterprise there is an early phase in which the enterprise is particularly vulnerable to threats and challenges that may restrict or prevent progress. Some threats and challenges were external, for example the enterprise was not attracting enough clients in the original volume anticipated. The host organisation (Dovegate main prison) did not either understand or want to understand the therapeutic issues and how this can lead to organisational conflict.

Internal conflicts affecting initial progress were both staff and client initiated. Staff conflicts came in the form of poor and conflicting communication both up and down the ranks and across the grades. Staff behaviour in both action and intent was not always consistent with therapeutic integrity. There was a mixture of residents genuinely wanting to change and those who were resistant to change, and there were always some residents who were continuing to engage in offence-paralleling behaviours, and in some cases blatantly continuing to commit offences of deception, theft, trafficking, extortion and assault.

Other teething problems in establishing a therapeutic culture became evident. For example, an act of assault in a therapeutic community is not only against the law (serious cases were always reported to the police) but considered to be against the 'therapeutic compact' between the individual and the community, and results in the perpetrator being removed from the community for a minimum of six months when they are free to re-apply for re-entry to the community. However, assault and violence for some people acted as a motivator for those wanting a quick exit from the therapeutic community without waiting for the ponderous workings of the prison system to move a resident from the community. More rarely the assault clause could be used by a community to expel an unpopular resident, in that a group of residents collude and accuse the unpopular resident of assault. It is reported to staff with proof being offered by the presentation of real injury to the factitious victim.

Moving prisoners out of the therapeutic community at Dovegate became unbearably slow and was the greatest threat to the community at that time (October, 2007). The delay in moving people was later discovered to be an arbitrary decision made by a bureaucrat in the Prison Service based on the rationale that as people in therapy are volunteers, the choice to leave therapy is regarded as a non-priority action. The problem with this is, as the number of residents who are out of therapy grows, the less therapeutic the community becomes. This process works like a slow-release poison for therapeutic communities in prison: 'toxic' residents infect those who are wavering and the waverers then decide to leave, increasing the number of toxic residents. With prison numbers running at over 80,000 and with fewer beds to move people into, it is easy to imagine how cumulative an effect this problem can have on a community.

Despite these negatives, an increase in the confidence of the staff and the community allowed concerns about the drug use, which had been hinted at, to be more openly talked about. Some community members had begun to make positive change and were able to disclose that, of the first 11 into the community, 9 were actively taking drugs at the opening of the community. This was the scale of the problem but progress became apparent. The culture of enquiry that was used to keep us from an exploration of the truth, whether deliberate or a sideshow, was being used in a more therapeutic way.

The increasing confidence of the staff and residents on the community allowed the acknowledgment that drug problems continued, and as a result drugs were regularly discussed in community meetings. One resident directly accused the main dealer of drug involvement, which was vehemently disputed by the dealer and his supporters. The resident raising the drugs issue was accused of 'muddying the waters' to deflect attention away from him, as the 'dealer' was going to expose his accuser as someone who was paying for sex with young prisoners with drugs. These heated exchanges were fraught with high emotions but stopped short of implied threats of violence, and when those issuing the implied violence were confronted, an apology would be issued to the potential victim, returning the situation to normal levels.

For therapeutic communities, the commitment vote is the ultimate therapeutic tool and may be used in many ways. Commitment to therapy is analogous for commitment to change, and communities putting a resident on a commitment vote should at least send a message to the individual that he needs to change, and at worst may exclude a resident from therapy and send him back into the mainstream prison to ponder his future. Giving prisoners power over the lives of other prisoners is not a concept that authorities particularly like, as wild imaginations have a tendency to jump to the worst case scenario and conjure up thoughts such as 'prisoners allowed to punish other prisoners', or 'kangaroo court'. However, giving people responsibility is a powerful rehabilitative tool, which in reality scares the individuals who have often in the past tried to evade responsibility at all costs. This was the greatest problem for the emerging community as they were reluctant to use their responsibility for keeping their community safe and rejecting the dealer and his entourage. Time and again the community was encouraged to use their authority to deal with their drugs problem. A succession of commitment votes were taken on the dealer's commitment to therapy, each time challenging him to show the community his commitment both to it and to changing himself. Each time he denied involvement in drugs but would address his presentation so that others would not be suspicious of his actions. Each time, the community vowed to help him through feedback and his small group agreed to mentor and support him through this 'difficult time' but each time it failed. The man continued his dealing.

The above scenario could represent fear of repercussion or resistance to change which prevented the dealer being rejected by the community, or represent a stage or process in the community's development. The community was behaving like an immature youth holding onto childhood, needing to be led and not yet being adult enough to accept responsibility and break the penal taboo. The prison mentality wanted the ground floor manager (staff) to take care of the problem. Although disappointing, the reality was that as the community couldn't yet act therapeutically as an independent entity, the staff felt they had to on its behalf and had those involved removed from the community.

Despite fears of how the community would react to staff intervention, their response was indicative of a further stage of its maturity if not its full independence. The community meeting held the following day was no different to any other meeting, with some residents supporting the actions of staff and some criticising them. It was well ordered, well questioned and well argued. Among many, there was the instillation of hope; among all there was a culture of enquiry. Dovegate Community C was, in essence, well on the path to becoming a therapeutic community.

Part IV: Evaluation and Audit

We were determined from the outset that the therapeutic regime at Dovegate would be evaluated, both in terms of measures regarding how well the TC met its contractual obligations to the Home Office, and in terms of how well the therapy was delivered in terms of improved behaviour and, ultimately, reconviction. Since its opening in November 2001, Dovegate TC has been the subject of two official reports by Her Majesty's Chief Inspector of Prisons (HMCIP), in 2004 and 2006, as well as three National Audit Reports (2004–5, 2005–6 and 2006–7) on behalf of the Correctional Services Accreditation Panel (CSAP). In addition to these independent scrutinies, the Dovegate management has commissioned the University of

Surrey to conduct an independent six-year 'longitudinal, multi-methodo-logical' research project led by Professor Jenny Brown.

In 1997, efforts were made to achieve formal accreditation status for therapeutic communities as a forensic intervention. They were not success-ful until 2003. Simultaneously, the Offending Behaviour Programmes Unit of HM Prison Service had commissioned the Association of Therapeutic Communities to develop a method of audit for therapeutic communities. This has been superseded by the creation of the Community of Communi-ties, composed of the ATC, the Royal College of Psychiatrists, The Prison Service and the College Centre for Quality Improvement, which has for the past three years published national audit reports on democratic therapeu-tic communities in prisons by comparing them with detailed criteria of an agreed core model. These assessments are within five themes: *Community of Communities, Institutional Support, Treatment Management/Integrity, Continuity and Resettlement,* and *Quality of Delivery.* The audit report results gave overall performance ratings for all 12 prison-based TCs – the five Wings at Grendon, the four at Dovegate and the smallest units at Gartree (lifer TCs), Blundeston and Send (females). For the first two years, the Dovegate TC ratings were between 75 per cent and 84 per cent compli-ance with standards, marks as good or better than those for all the other TCs except Gartree. In the year 2006–2007 Dovegate's overall scores dropped to between 71 per cent and 76 per cent compliance, a worrying decline matched by the Grendon TC wings. As a consequence, the authors recorded:

> It has become apparent that there is a need for senior managers, TCs and the Community of Communities to address action planning as a matter of priority in the next cycle.
>
> All HMP Dovegate communities are performing above the recommended minimum level for all sections of the standards, except for Continuity and Resettlement, where performance has decreased this year to an average of 44%. This should be addressed as a matter of priority.
>
> One issue that dominated the point-reviews was concern about staffing, nowhere was this more the case than in the multiple TC sites. The results of the process demonstrate that there is evidence for those concerns. Despite this being raised last year, *performance has plummeted ...*

Part V: The Future

Dovegate Therapeutic Community Prison faces an uncertain future with the real risk of not surviving. At the same time that tremendous progress has been made in commissioning, approving and monitoring treatment for offenders via the CSAP and the Community of Communities, the National Offender Management Service (NOMS) of the Ministry of Justice is failing year on year to adequately fund these regimes. It does this because, in spite of overwhelming evidence that TC regimes work and are significantly more humane, they insist on applying the same fiscal budget imperatives to TCs that they do to all other regimes, which automatically precludes them from being able to fund the professional staff required to do their therapeutic job. In addition to this parlous fiscal state, Dovegate and all the TCs have other significant issues to address:

a.   Prison-based therapeutic communities must change to survive. Specifically, they must focus on therapy/treatment objectives much more rigorously. One of the most serious issues concerns the lack of clarity for what constitutes successful completion of therapy. This allows residents (the overwhelming majority are now lifers and this is set to continue) to remain on the communities for years (many stay in excess of three years). Those responsible should consider reducing the time spent in therapy by obliging those responsible for the progress of therapy to concentrate on the priority of offence-relevant behaviour and thought. This in turn requires greater investment in staff sufficiently trained to differentiate the relevant from the irrelevant.

b.   Cognitive behavioural therapy (CBT) relevant to recognised dynamic risk factors should be introduced officially in the TCs with equal status to the traditional core therapy techniques. This should be done via a panel of experts commissioned to this purpose, composed of both TC practitioners and external advisers. CBT techniques including behavioural contracting could usefully be included as part of regular progress assessments. Therapy assessment must move from the subjective to the objective. Final reports for those who leave TCs should include a section that specifically addresses treatment targets set at induction and regularly reviewed and, where necessary, revised. The introduction of CBT must, however, be done whilst protecting that most essential of the core therapy activities, the psychotherapy-based small groups.

c.   Dovegate 'Therapeutic Prison': during the course of writing this chapter, the structure and direction of the therapeutic regime at Dovegate experienced huge changes. The Director of Therapy, a therapist, has been replaced by a 'Director of Therapeutic Prison', an operational manager moved from the main prison, and someone with no training or direct experience of therapy or therapeutic communities. A senior therapist will be promoted from the existing wing therapists but will take on this role in addition to current duties, and the wing therapists will become accountable to one of three 'Unit Managers', each responsible for two units within each of the Dovegate chevrons. A number of additional executive changes all add to what is a clear paradigm shift away from therapeutic to prison operational priorities. While there were definitely problems at Dovegate, and some significant improvements may accrue from these changes, especially in terms of clarity, direction and potentially enhanced credibility in the eyes of the main prison, there are also serious risks for the primacy of therapy at Dovegate.

d.　Research: at the time of writing, the University of Surrey Department of Psychology had completed a seven-year project addressing the traditional efficacy questions of the Dovegate TC. The Ministry of Justice department responsible has yet to approve release of the report, but the first author has had sight of the executive summary. The findings are consistently positive in terms of psychometric assessments, focus group appraisals, and, crucially, re-offending statistics. It must be said, however, that some of the most important findings concerning rates of re-offending relative to time at risk, raise methodological questions, so there must be some caution exercised at the time of going to press. It is to be hoped that the results can be verified, as the implications for the future of Dovegate TC are difficult to overestimate.

Conclusion

Dovegate Therapeutic Community is a qualified success, due primarily to the tremendous commitment of the staff and residents there. The best opportunity to safeguard these relatively fragile gains is full compliance with the Core Democratic Therapeutic Community model accredited by the Correctional Services Accreditation Panel, and by safeguarding the primacy of therapy over operations and the prison mentality.

Perhaps the ultimate irony for therapeutic communities in prisons concerns the basic philosophy. Conventional imprisonment is primarily for punishment, yet it is a blunt, indiscriminate form. TCs afford humane regimes where people are treated with respect yet are obliged also to look unflinchingly at their behaviour and, specifically, their crimes until they understand and accept the terrible harm they have done, and change. This process, which may last years, is a far more incisive and constructive form of punishment because it is all about accountability rather than retribution. Unless and until the Ministry of Justice accepts this basic truth and provides the funding necessary, not just for the existing TCs, but for more to be built, opportunities to save lives will be lost.

References

Cullen, E. (1993). The Grendon Reconviction Study, Part 1. *Prison Service Journal*, *90*, 35–37.

Cullen, E., Jones, L. & Woodward, R. (Eds) (1997). *Therapeutic Communities for Offenders*. Chichester: John Wiley & Sons.

Directorate of Health Care (1995). Working Party to advise on specifications for a second therapeutic prison, STP (1).

Main, T. F. (1981). The concept of the therapeutic community. First S. H. Foulkes Memorial lecture. (Reprinted in J. Johns (Ed.) (1989). *The Ailment and Other Psychoanalytic Essays*. London: Free Association Books.)

Marshall, P. (1997). *A Reconviction Study of HMP Grendon Therapeutic Community*. Home Office Research and Statistics: Research Findings Number 53.

Rapoport, R. (1960). *The Community as Doctor: A New Perspective on a Therapeutic Community*. London: Tavistock Publications.

Taylor, R. (2000). *Seven-Year Reconviction Study of HMP Grendon Therapeutic Community*. United Kingdom: Home Office, Policing and Reducing Crime Unit Research, Development and Statistics Directorate.

Yalom, I. (1995). *The Theory and Practice of Group Psychotherapy*. New York: Basic Books.

Chapter 3

The Van der Hoeven Clinic: a Flexible and Innovative Forensic Psychiatric Hospital Based on Therapeutic Community Principles

Judith de Boer-van Schaik and Frans Derks

Introduction

In this chapter we will describe the 50-plus years of experience of the Van der Hoeven Clinic in the treatment of offenders with severe mental disorders. The Van der Hoeven Clinic is a forensic psychiatric hospital in Utrecht (The Netherlands), founded in 1955 as the forensic unit of a general mental health institution, which was originally inspired by Maxwell Jones' therapeutic community model as developed in the Henderson Hospital in Sutton (Great Britain) in 1947. It has evolved into one of the most outstanding forensic treatment and rehabilitation centres in The Netherlands for offenders with severe DSM-IV axis II personality disorders (including psychopathy) and/or axis I major mental disorders. In this chapter we will highlight the factors contributing to its success. These include the continuity and consistency of the therapeutic concept from which the hospital works, but also its innovative flexibility to integrate new (scientific and other) developments and to adapt to a changing social environment (in terms of the public reaction to serious offenders).

Grendon and the Emergence of Forensic Therapeutic Communities: Developments in Research and Practice
Edited by Richard Shuker and Elizabeth Sullivan
© 2010 John Wiley & Sons, Ltd.

The History of the Therapeutic Concept

The Van der Hoeven Clinic was one of the first forensic treatment units for offenders with severe personality disorders in The Netherlands. Its founders, Pieter Baan and Anne Marie Roosenburg, were pioneering psychiatrists within the phenomenological orientated 'Utrecht School' of the physiologist/psychologist Buytendijk. In the forensic and criminological domain Baan, Pompe and Kempe are the best internationally known representatives of this school.

Baan and Roosenburg had no specific experience in the *treatment* of offenders, but were well experienced in psychiatric *assessment* on behalf of the courts. From these assessments they derived a number of specific theoretical ideas concerning the pathology of mentally disturbed offenders, including the genesis of their disorder(s), and concerning the mental and behavioural problems on which treatment should focus, but they had no fixed ideas of how treatment on the basis of their theoretical insights might be organised and brought into practice.

To gain from innovative experiences abroad, they visited several institutions in various countries, including Maxwell Jones' Henderson Hospital in Sutton. Even though the patient population here was not a forensic one, they were very much impressed by the community meetings of staff and patients and by the possibilities for patients to contribute to each other's treatment. In addition, they found the more democratic and egalitarian principles of the Henderson Hospital a good alternative to the traditionally hierarchical, medical model in general psychiatric hospitals. In their view, medicalisation, hospitalisation and a totalitarian approach should be avoided as much as possible in order to allow for an open therapeutic climate that would stimulate/motivate patients to commit themselves to the processes of change, which they deemed necessary for the prevention of re-offending.

The basic notion underlying the founders' therapeutic concept was that patients, in order to be able to reintegrate successfully after treatment, should not alienate from 'normal' society and should be given extensive opportunities and possibilities to take responsibility for their own life by maintaining already existing skills and developing new skills and a pro-social network. One of the most innovative core values in their therapeutic concept was that the patients should learn to take responsibility for their past, current and future actions and that, in order to learn this, they should have as many responsibilities as possible during treatment. A famous dictum of Anne Marie Roosenburg, the first medical director, was: 'do not unnecessarily take away responsibilities and tasks people can perform, nor give them tasks they are not able to perform'.

At the start of the new forensic unit, four basic therapeutic principles were formulated.

- Everything in the unit should be geared to prevent hospitalisation and promote the re-socialisation and rehabilitation of patients.
- The unit should, as much as possible, copy a normal life situation, where patients would be able to work, to earn (real) money, to get educational and/or vocational training, to develop a hobby and to live responsibly together in a community with their own domestic (and therapeutic) responsibilities.
- Living in a group with other patients should involve a shared responsibility to create and maintain a healthy living environment, in which they would support each other and address each other's (antisocial) behaviour in which their disorder is expressed.
- The safety in the unit should not be imposed by (mechanical and physical) external security devices such as cameras, fences, barbed wire, security gates and uniformed guards with lots of keys, but ought to be safeguarded by a shared responsibility of staff and patients, and by emphasising the possibilities inside the hospital for patients to develop their personalities and to learn the skills they will need for a better, 'normal' (i.e. pro-social, non-criminal) life outside.

To date, these four principles still underpin most of the treatment activities in the hospital and the way in which treatment is organised. The emphasis on creating 'as normal a life as possible' inside the hospital in order to avoid hospitalisation, and on the importance of 'taking responsibility' in order to promote pro-social attitudes and behaviour, are still the basic principles in the treatment philosophy.

On the other hand, more than 50 years have passed since then. Through its successes and failures, the Van der Hoeven Clinic has acquired a lot of experiential knowledge about the dos and don'ts of forensic treatment, and has gained new insights into the (non-) effectiveness of various therapeutic techniques and approaches in this population. In addition, the relatively recent developments in psychiatric pharmacotherapy and alternative treatment methods (such as cognitive behavioural therapy) have modernised the treatment model immensely. Moreover, the growth from a small 40-bed unit within a larger psychiatric hospital in 1955 to an independent forensic hospital of 165 beds in 2008 (and a prospective further increase to almost 300 beds in 2010) asked for new organisational models and structures to ensure the interdisciplinary co-operation of professionals from various backgrounds. Thus, treatment now is clearly different from treatment 50 years ago, but the basic principles as mentioned above can still be detected in the hospital's daily routines and organisational structure.

Patients and Legislative Context (TBS)

The majority of patients at the Van der Hoeven Clinic are serious offenders (homicide, sexual offences, etc.) with a penal hospital order, which in Dutch is called 'terbeschikkingstelling' (TBS). This can be translated as 'placed at the disposal of the government (in order to be treated)'. The major goals of the TBS order are the protection of society (by means of detention in a secure setting) and the reintegration of mentally ill offenders into society (by means of treatment of their mental disorder).

To impose a TBS order, the following conditions must be met:

- The offender must have been suffering from a mental disorder (major mental disorder or personality disorder) when he committed the index offence.
- The offender cannot be held fully accountable for the offence because of his mental illness (i.e. a causal relationship between the disorder and the offence must be established).
- The index offence must be a serious crime, with 'seriousness' being defined as: an offence for which a prison sentence of four years or more *may* (but not *must*) be imposed (this implies that the vast majority of TBS orders are imposed for serious violent and/or sexual offences).
- There must be an increased risk of re-offending with a further serious crime because of the disorder.

The Dutch Penal Law allows the court to impose a dual sentence on offenders with severe mental disorders. One basic notion underlying Dutch jurisdiction is that an offender can only be punished and sent to prison if (and to the extent that) he can be held accountable for his offence, and that a mental disorder may be a reason for non- or diminished accountability. Therefore, the mentally disordered offender may be sentenced to prison as a form of retribution to the extent that he can be held accountable for his actions, and at the expiry of that sentence he may be placed in a secure forensic psychiatric hospital for treatment as long as he is considered a danger to society because of a heightened risk of re-offending. Initially a TBS order is always imposed for a period of two years, but in the case of violent or sexual offences it may be prolonged indefinitely. Every order has to be periodically (i.e. every one or two years) evaluated by the same court that originally imposed it, and can only be terminated (i.e. not renewed) when the risk of re-offending with a serious crime has diminished sufficiently.

The Van der Hoeven Clinic is one of (currently) 12 forensic psychiatric institutions in The Netherlands where TBS patients can be admitted. Current total capacity of the TBS sector is about 1800 beds (in comparison, The Netherlands currently has approximately 15,000 prison cells). The Van der Hoeven Clinic can admit patients with either personality disorders and/or major mental disorders (psychosis, schizophrenia, etc.) and is one of only a few forensic hospitals that admit female offenders. To date the proportion of female patients in the hospital is about 20 per cent while the overall proportion of female TBS patients in The Netherlands is about 5 per cent.

A recent (2007) development is that the Van der Hoeven Clinic has created a ward (five beds) for crisis intervention of non-forensic patients with aggressive and/or violent behaviour from general mental health institutions.

Therapeutic Climate

In the current therapeutic climate and organisation of the Van der Hoeven Clinic, several basic principles of Maxwell Jones' therapeutic community can still be recognised. To allow for a psychologically and physically 'safe' therapeutic milieu, in which patients and staff can co-operate towards rehabilitation and can share responsibility for treatment and (internal) security, the hospital has developed and maintained a high level of transparency in its goals and in its structure of decision-making processes, including the patients' participation in these processes.

First, all staff members need to be aware that patients are not 'dangerous' all the time, but may become a risk in certain situations under certain conditions. As a consequence, staff (who 'work' therapeutically with them) and fellow patients (who literally 'live' with them) must be informed about these specific situations and conditions in every individual case. Therefore, all staff (and, to a lesser extent, all the fellow patients) have to have an extensive and shared knowledge of all the patients, their life histories and the dynamics of their criminal behaviour. Staff members, and patients also, should not be afraid of incidents, but must be alert to address inappropriate behaviour and help patients to learn from mistakes. In this respect it is imperative that all staff members share the same information at the same time and have a consistent approach towards all the patients.

Second, patients should have the feeling that staff members are working therapeutically with them and not imposing their authority upon them. Although the onus for the progress in treatment is on the patients, they should feel the support and assistance of staff members, including positive feedback on their behaviour and, if necessary, serious criticism.

Third, the decision-making processes should be transparent and not top-down: staff members working on a day-to-day basis with the patients should be the ones to discuss the decisions with them. Because of their pathology, most patients will not accept the authority of staff members who are not in the position to make decisions. Therefore staff should work together in a flat, non-hierarchical organisational structure where all staff members are collectively responsible for all decisions, and where these decisions, made in consensus, are discussed with patients on all levels in the same consistent way.

Last but not least, there has to be a number of clear rules and regulations about behaviour that is not acceptable, such as antisocial behaviour (e.g. violence) or use of drugs/alcohol or possession of pornographic material, whilst being wary of excessive bureaucracy and rigid protocols. If treatment aims at teaching the patients to take responsibility, and if the basic idea is that staff and patients are collectively responsible for a safe and healthy therapeutic environment, the culture of the organisation should be one of flexibility and dynamic 'learning'.

Treatment Model and Treatment Programme

To date, the core characteristics of treatment in the Van der Hoeven Clinic are still very much embedded in the therapeutic community principles as presented above. However, from the very start in 1955, the directors of the hospital put a strong emphasis on research, on evaluation of the effectiveness of the treatment methods and on the incorporation of new developments that might improve treatment. This focus on innovation and critical evaluation of efficiency and effectiveness has resulted in various modifications of the treatment model, treatment methods and treatment programmes in the past 50 years.

For example, it gradually became clear that the rehabilitation approach requires a multimodal theory (see figure 3.1) that addresses the interplay

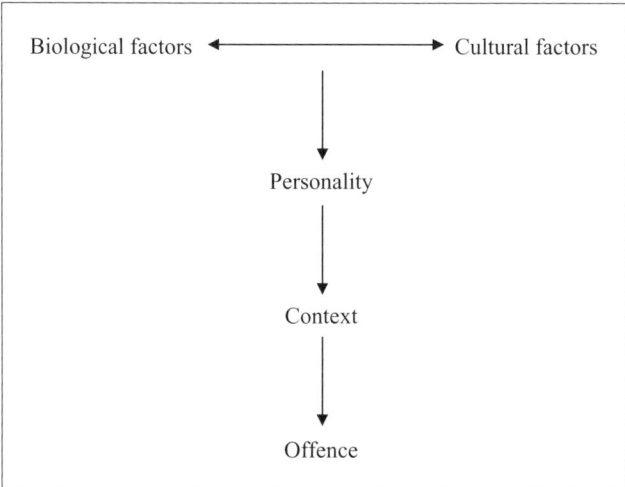

Figure 3.1   Bio-psycho-social model of offending

between biological, psychological and socio-cultural factors underlying patients' offending behaviour. Biological/physical predisposition and socio-cultural situational circumstances may contribute to high-risk behaviour.

Thus, a bio-psycho-social model was gradually adopted to explain and therapeutically address criminal behaviour. In this multimodal bio-psycho-social approach the staff members work together with the patient to analyse his life and offence history and identify the different factors and reasons for his offending behaviour. In the multimodal approach, all these factors are analysed and converge in a consistent treatment plan and risk management plan for the short and long term. This approach focuses primarily on psychological or psychiatric interventions, but also incorporates wider activities including work, leisure time, education and social networking.

The Position of Sociotherapy in the Multimodal Approach

Since the start of the Van der Hoeven Clinic, the sociotherapeutic discipline holds the central position in the psycho-education and social learning processes of the patients. They support and confront the patients in their daily life on the ward, plan the co-ordination of the different treatment activities and report to the daily staff meetings on the progress of the patient.

The sociotherapeutic team not only supports the individual patients but also orchestrates the group dynamics and the social behaviour of the patients who live together in a ward. They encourage the patients to use the group to learn to act/react/interact in a pro-social way, whilst they themselves function as role models for pro-social and responsible behaviour. By sharing information and transparency about what is going on in the group, they also encourage patients to take responsibility for their actions and collectively find solutions for daily problems. All patients have to be open about their offences and are expected to play an active role in each other's treatment processes. In short, 'living in a group' is a crucial element in the learning process of individual patients, as a preparation for responsible and pro-social behaviour in the community. It may be clear that if a patient is not able to show responsible behaviour in the relatively controlled conditions inside the hospital, he will surely not be able to do so without supervision in society.

Interdisciplinary Assessment and Treatment Plan

As part of the intake procedure, the 'head of treatment' of one of the wards of the hospital (in most cases an experienced forensic psychologist or psychiatrist) will visit a prospective patient whilst he is still in prison. At a later visit by a sociotherapist, preferably accompanied by a fellow patient, the prospective patient is informed about daily routines in the hospital, about what treatment involves and about what it means to be admitted to the hospital. These visits have a dual purpose: to inform the new patient about the hospital and the treatment programme (in addition to a comprehensive brochure that he already has received) and to check the available information about his life history, offence(s), previous assessments and actual state of mind. This information is used to write a detailed life history of the new patient, which is circulated to all staff members of the hospital.

The new patient is admitted to one of the wards ('living groups') on the basis of his or her pathology (psychosis or personality disorder) and ability to function in a group (there are wards for group treatment and for individual treatment). Type of offence or gender are not selection criteria for placement on a ward. This implies that the living groups are 'mixed' groups where male and female patients live together and that there is no special ward for female patients. At first glance this may look unusual, but it explicitly expresses the basic therapeutic notion that the internal situation in the hospital should reflect as much as possible a 'normal' situation in society, into which most patients are supposed to return sooner or later.

For many patients, male as well as female, the question of how to interact in a normal fashion with members of the opposite sex is an important treatment issue, and they can practise this in the controlled conditions of the hospital.

For most new patients the transition from the restrictive, repressive and 'macho' prison climate to the open, co-operative therapeutic climate in the hospital is a real 'culture shock'. For that reason, the first six weeks are an introduction period to the various treatment activities and facilities. At the same time a variety of staff members will undertake extensive diagnostic assessments of the patient. Staff members from the research department carry out an intensive psychological and risk assessment, using a number of internationally accepted risk assessment instruments such as the HCR-20, SVR-20 and PCL-R, and a personality assessment with questionnaires and interviews for DSM-IV personality disorders such as the SIDP–IV and MMPI. In addition, a psychiatrist will assess psychiatric disorders, staff members from the educational department and other disciplines will test the cognitive capacities, learning abilities, intelligence, creative expression and so on, to identify educational and vocational deficiencies and potentialities. The sociotherapists observe and monitor the pro- and/or anti-social behaviour of the patient on the ward and assess his social skills and behaviour. A psychotherapist will assess whether psychotherapy is indicated.

At the end of this six-week period, all staff members who have been involved with the patient until now have a meeting to exchange their impressions, observations and test results. The purpose of this meeting is to achieve consensus as to the psychiatric and psychological diagnosis, and to identify collectively the main treatment issues that need to be addressed. On the basis of the conclusions from this meeting, the 'head of treatment' of the ward where the patient is admitted will write the first draft of a treatment plan and discuss this with the patient.

The next step is the presentation of the treatment plan in a formal meeting of the treatment team with the patient, called the 'indication staff meeting', in the presence of all the therapeutic and non-therapeutic staff of the hospital. In the indication staff meeting the crucial goals and issues to be addressed are discussed with the patient, and everybody is informed about the outcome of the different assessments by all the disciplines. The aim is to reach consensus with the patient and within the staff group concerning all treatment issues.

After this meeting the treatment plan is made definitive. All the treatment activities focus on the goals formulated in the treatment plan. This applies to the daily routines of living in the group related to hygiene, eating, cooking, cleaning, social behaviour, and also to goals in the area of work, personal development in creative expression (music, mime, theatre, paint-

ing, sculpture lessons) and sport (swimming, badminton, judo, etc.), individual and group psychotherapy, educational and/or vocational training,
contact with family, establishing a pro-social network outside the hospital
and, if necessary, pharmacotherapy.

In individual psychotherapy the emphasis is on cognitive behavioural
interventions, including schema-therapy (which focuses on structural
change in the patients' personality disorders) and the 'offence script', as
part of promoting socially acceptable self-regulation. The 'offence script
procedure' focuses on internal and external management of direct dynamic
risk factors and of a pro-social life plan. In addition to individual psychotherapy there are various group therapies, such as emotion regulation
training, groups for different types of sex offenders and groups for addicted
and borderline patients. Finally psycho-education groups are delivered for
patients with major mental disorders, autism spectrum disorders, intellectual disabilities and ADHD.

Every three months treatment progress is evaluated in the group, based
on reports from the different disciplines, input from the other patients in
the group and the patient's own evaluation. Every year the treatment plan
and activities are evaluated in an interdisciplinary staff meeting and
adjusted if necessary.

The structure and organisation of the therapeutic process is represented
in figure 3.2.

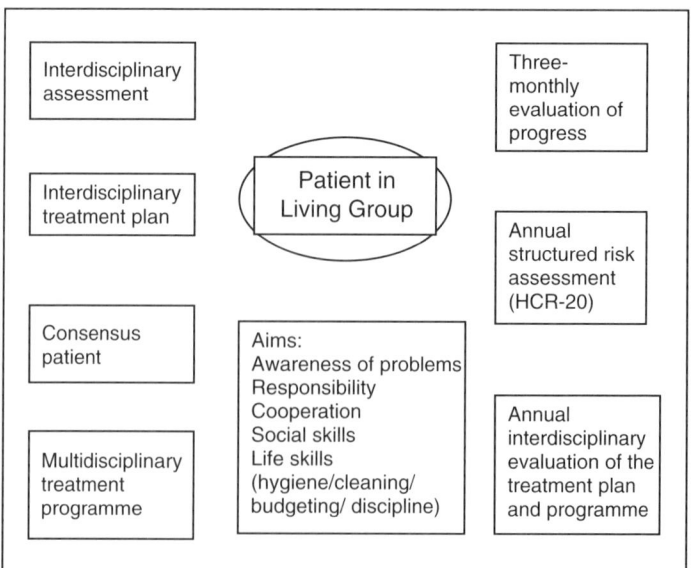

Figure 3.2   Structure and organisation of the therapeutic process

Daily Treatment Programme in the Van der Hoeven Clinic

In every treatment plan a daily programme of treatment activities is included and for every activity an 'indication' (i.e. the goal to be worked on) is formulated (see figure 3.3). The programme is evaluated every three months.

An average daily programme covers 15 hours, between 7.00 am and 10.00 pm, including a few hours of free time and a few hours which are spent on activities on behalf of the patients' community, such as group evaluations, treatment evaluations and patients' committees.

All patients have to work in one of the professional workshops, where they can earn money and gain working experience with the possibility of getting accredited vocational training and an official qualification/diploma. Patients are stimulated to comply with the programme and to take part in the activities; their participation is monitored and recorded in an electronic patient's file. Analysis of these data has shown that the average participation is about 75 per cent.

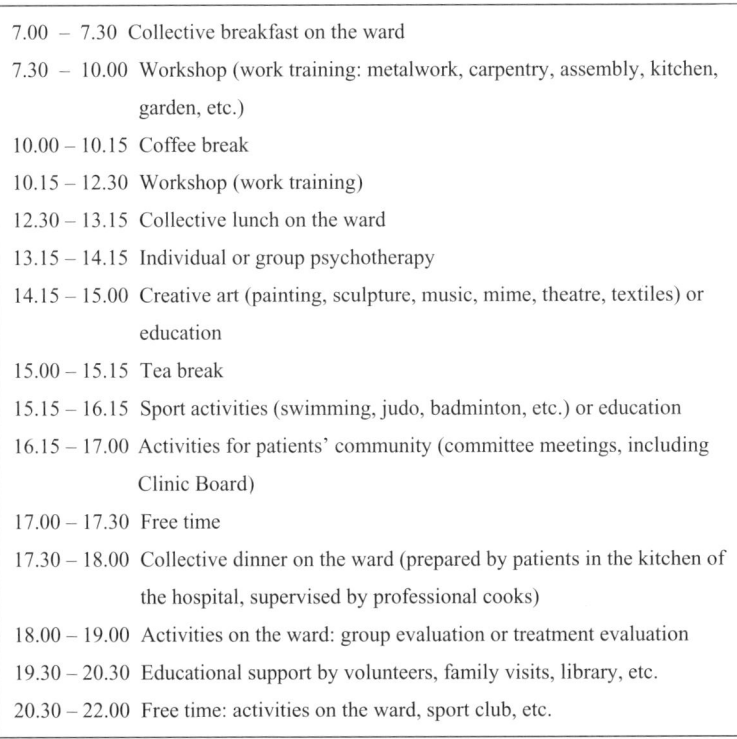

7.00 – 7.30 Collective breakfast on the ward

7.30 – 10.00 Workshop (work training: metalwork, carpentry, assembly, kitchen, garden, etc.)

10.00 – 10.15 Coffee break

10.15 – 12.30 Workshop (work training)

12.30 – 13.15 Collective lunch on the ward

13.15 – 14.15 Individual or group psychotherapy

14.15 – 15.00 Creative art (painting, sculpture, music, mime, theatre, textiles) or education

15.00 – 15.15 Tea break

15.15 – 16.15 Sport activities (swimming, judo, badminton, etc.) or education

16.15 – 17.00 Activities for patients' community (committee meetings, including Clinic Board)

17.00 – 17.30 Free time

17.30 – 18.00 Collective dinner on the ward (prepared by patients in the kitchen of the hospital, supervised by professional cooks)

18.00 – 19.00 Activities on the ward: group evaluation or treatment evaluation

19.30 – 20.30 Educational support by volunteers, family visits, library, etc.

20.30 – 22.00 Free time: activities on the ward, sport club, etc.

Figure 3.3 Hypothetical day programme of a patient in the Van der Hoeven Clinic

At 10.00 pm the patients are locked in their rooms, but one patient on each ward is on standby for fire alarm or other incidents. His room is not locked and it is his duty to alert the night shift in case of an emergency.

Patients' Involvement

The involvement of the patients in the functioning of the institution as a treatment centre is manifest in almost all areas of the hospital's policies and activities. From the very beginning the patients' involvement in the daily life of the hospital was recognised as the best way to prevent hospitalisation and to contribute to the ultimate goal of rehabilitating patients into society.

Patient involvement is formalised in what is called the 'Clinic Board', where patients and staff meet every day and discuss the issues that the patient community or individual patients want to put on the agenda of the daily staff meeting such as requests for permission for accompanied or unaccompanied leave, as well as the decisions from the previous staff meeting. The patients in the Board represent all the wards and are elected by the patients on the ward on a rota basis. In cases of incidents with an individual patient, the Board is summoned to discuss the actions to be taken. If it is decided that a patient has to be segregated, this will be carried out by staff and patients collectively. Thus, the decision to segregate a patient is a collective responsibility of staff and the total patient community, as is the responsibility to solve the problem that the incident causes.

Another form of involvement is the responsibility of the patients to look after the household work on the ward such as cleaning of the kitchen, washing, shopping and housekeeping expenses for the weekend dinners and lunches. Every ward has its own budget to buy food and drink for the weekends and one of the patients (on a rota basis) is responsible for keeping a housekeeping book. Every week there is a group meeting to discuss issues concerning group dynamics, and every three months each patient is evaluated in the group in the presence of the sociotherapists and his fellow patients.

Once a month there is an afternoon meeting for all the patients and staff members to discuss important policy issues and/or new developments. These may vary from new risk assessment instruments or antilibidinal medication to political issues such as the stigma of a TBS order or how society looks at TBS patients.

Security and Risk Management

The Van der Hoeven Clinic is the only forensic psychiatric hospital for 'high risk' patients in The Netherlands without static security devices such as fences, bars, detection ports, locked doors, etc., and without security guards. It is one of the most important characteristics and accomplishments of the hospital to have developed and maintained a full integration of treatment with internal safety on the basis of a collective attitude of staff and patients. The open and transparent atmosphere, the shared responsibility of staff and patients for safety, the in-depth knowledge all staff have of the patients and the emphasis on consistency and flexible but logical application of rules and regulations in treatment and management, provide for a safe and healthy therapeutic atmosphere for both staff and patients.

Key elements in maintaining safety within the building are:

- highly trained staff;
- full access to all information for all staff members;
- no confidentiality: all staff share the same information;
- daily staff briefings on high-risk signals of patients;
- no hierarchy in staff meetings, open communication and sharing of problems;
- no naming, shaming and blaming when something goes wrong;
- maximum collaboration with patients; and
- emphasis on responsibility of staff and patients for their own behaviour and for a safe and secure atmosphere.

A Recent Innovation: 'Transmural' Treatment

One of the most important and innovative new developments in The Netherlands in the area of forensic treatment originating from the Van der Hoeven Clinic, is the possibility to transfer patients to so-called 'transmural' facilities and services outside the hospital under close supervision, control and support of an experienced team of sociotherapists from the hospital. This implies that a patient who has been successfully treated in the hospital for a couple of years, and who has been assessed as no longer posing a high risk of re-offending under supervised conditions in society, can be transferred to a facility outside the hospital such as an apartment, flat, or a facility for sheltered housing. The patient maintains the TBS order and is still a patient of the Van der Hoeven Clinic, but he spends most of his time outside the hospital. Thus, he may have a normal job or attend a regular school, spends his free time in society, and has his own household.

The main aim of transmural treatment is to offer the patient the opportunity to put his new skills into practice, to get support from the staff who know him very well and to make mistakes under controlled conditions. Transmural treatment is a learning process in trying to live independently without relapsing into old behaviour patterns, but during his stay in a transmural facility there is always the possibility for recall when a patient is not complying with the conditions as formulated in the transmural treatment plan. There are separate transmural facilities for patients with personality disorders and for patients with psychotic disorders, as these categories have different needs and risk factors to be managed. With regard to chronic psychotic patients, the Van der Hoeven Clinic co-operates with general mental health institutions to facilitate their integration in general mental health care. This gradual reintegration, also with possibilities of recall when the patient does not comply with the conditions, has proved to be a great success.

To date, several other forms of transmural facilities are being developed, especially for chronic psychotic patients with major mental disorders who will need intensive long-term forensic care and support.

Characteristics of Staff Members Working with Patients

In the Van der Hoeven Clinic a broad range of disciplines are employed: psychiatrists, psychologists, social workers, sociotherapists, psychiatric nurses, etc., but also teachers, professional workshop supervisors, cooks, sport teachers, music teachers, drama/mime teachers, drawing/sculpture/textural art teachers and pastoral workers.

Unlike other forensic psychiatric hospitals, the Van der Hoeven Clinic does not employ occupational or creative therapists but professional workshop supervisors and professional artists/teachers, whose aim is to contribute to the personal development of a patient and thus contribute to the goals formulated in the treatment plan. An important criterion for the selection of these professionals is a high level of education, a strong ambition to excel in one's profession and, of course, a commitment to the patients. Selection criteria for the sociotherapists include a high level of educational attainment (preferably at the academic level of psychology, nursing or social work) and also the right attitudes including ability and willingness to work in a multidisciplinary team, flexibility, capacity to learn and a positive outlook on treatment of forensic patients.

Table 3.1   Escapes and absconding 2003–2007

	2003	2004	2005	2006	2007
Hospital	1	2	0	0	0
Accompanied leave	1	8	0	0	0
Unaccompanied leave	3	2	0	1	0
Transmural facility	1	5	1	0	0
Total	6	17	1	1	0

Architecture of the Building

The design of the hospital building is based on the basic therapeutic notion of normalising the constrained living conditions of patients as much as possible. The building is square-shaped and has a big inner garden, like the 'green' in an English village, where patients and staff can meet, relax, drink coffee, etc. There is a division between the living areas (wards) and the parts where patients go to work, have therapeutic sessions or creative activities. The patients themselves are responsible for getting up in time to go to the workshops and going to the planned therapeutic sessions and other activities, according to their treatment programme. In principle they are free to walk through the hospital, depending on their risk assessment and risk management plan, but they are not allowed to leave the building without permission. Due to the internal openness about everything, the transparency of the communication and the culture of 'pro-social influence' of staff and patients on each other, violent incidents and attempts to escape from the hospital are very rare. In the last two years there has not been a single escape or an absconding from a supervised leave situation (see table 3.1).

Research: Risk Assessment and Outcome Results

To evaluate treatment methods and develop 'evidence-based' treatment programmes, a number of full-time scientific researchers are employed for clinical trials and research activities. In the mid-90s the Van der Hoeven Clinic was the first forensic hospital in The Netherlands to introduce structured risk assessment tools like the HCR-20/SVR-20, and the PCL-R to assess psychopathy.

Before their implementation these instruments were translated into Dutch and validated. One of the outcomes of this research was that the

Table 3.2   Re-offending of TBS patients discharged in The Netherlands between 1999 and 2003

	Van der Hoeven (N = 76)	*All TBS hospitals (N = 356)*
General recidivism	22.8%	38.6%
Serious offences	13.9%	29.8%
Very serious offences	7.9%	12.1%

best way to implement structured risk assessment is to discuss the scores in a consensus meeting of the involved disciplines: researcher, head of treatment of the ward and sociotherapists. Another finding was that patients with a high level of psychopathy in combination with a sexual disorder/paraphilia belong to a very high-risk group.

To date the research is focused on the validation of an instrument to assess protective factors (SAPROF: Structured Assessment of Protective Factors) and an evaluation of the effectiveness of the treatment of different types of sex offenders.

On average, patients stay in the hospital for three or four years and in the transmural facility for another two or three years, which is relatively short in comparison to the average duration of treatment in the other forensic treatment centres in The Netherlands. However, the most important outcome parameter regarding the quality of treatment and risk management at the Van der Hoeven Clinic is the rate of recidivism of the patients after treatment. In 2006 a survey was carried out to record the rate of re-offending of the patients who had been discharged between 1999 and 2003. The results are excellent, compared to the rates of recidivism of ex-patients of all the forensic treatment centres in The Netherlands (see table 3.2).

Both outcome indicators (escapes/absconding and re-offending) show a good performance by the Van der Hoeven Clinic. The introduction and implementation of new (risk) assessment tools, medication for psychotic patients and for sex offenders, transmural treatment and long-term care facilities have certainly contributed to the improvement of the quality of the service. Still, the consistent and continuous way in which the Van der Hoeven Clinic has held on to the basic principles of a therapeutic community has been the main reason for its successful position in forensic psychiatry in The Netherlands. Therefore, it is the combination of consistently holding on to the basic therapeutic principles with the willingness to incorporate therapeutic innovations that predominantly accounts for 'success' in the area of forensic mental health care.

Chapter 4

A Therapeutic Distinction with a Difference: Comparing American Concept-Based Therapeutic Communities and British Democratic Therapeutic Community Treatment for Prison Inmates

Douglas S. Lipton

In the United States the use of therapeutic community (TC) programming as a means of addiction treatment for incarcerated persons has been a critical element of the programme to combat the drug problem since the middle of the 1990s, although it has been used in some American prisons for this purpose for 25 years. Consistently positive research findings from such programmes have been gathered since the mid-1980s. These findings assembled by De Leon and Melnick (1992), Wexler *et al.* (1990), Inciardi *et al.* (1997), Field (1989), Lipton (1999) and others in separate studies served as the basis for a sea change in Federal policies.

While widespread Federal support for carrying out drug abuse treatment for state prisoners was virtually unknown until late into the last decade, there had been Federal support for evaluation studies of some of the promising drug abuse treatment programmes in state prisons. When consistently positive findings for both male and female inmates began to be

Grendon and the Emergence of Forensic Therapeutic Communities: Developments in Research and Practice
Edited by Richard Shuker and Elizabeth Sullivan
© 2010 John Wiley & Sons, Ltd.

published in learned journals, a series of seven congressional hearings, chaired by Congressman (now Senator) Charles Shumer of New York, were convened in different parts of the nation to air these surprising outcomes, and allow the assembled legislators to probe the studies and the investigators that produced these findings. These hearings led to Federal appropriations and legislation supporting a nationwide programme to help state correctional administrators to create TC programmes for seriously drug-involved inmates in their institutions, as well as in Federal correctional institutions.

The evaluative research results from these studies that were presented to the Federal officials at these hearings convinced the legislators that concept-based TC treatment is an important tool capable of yielding substantial reductions in recidivism as well as in chronic drug use. From a handful of TC programmes in 1985, more than 144 programmes were created through the mid-1990s. Thus, concept-based TC programmes carried out in prison are viewed today in the United States as a significant approach to habilitate seriously addicted and persistent drug abusing persons who are typically unlikely to seek treatment for their drug abuse on their own, and who, without treatment, are highly likely to return to their drug abuse and criminality after release.

These successful programmes are termed hierarchical TCs or concept-based TCs in the United States. They differ in a number of significant ways from democratic TCs that are used to treat persons in prison custody in the United Kingdom. To understand this difference it is useful to trace the history of democratic TCs in England where they were born during the Second World War.

During World War II, TCs in the United Kingdom emerged as a process for treating military veterans during and just after World War II as these patients returned with serious neurotic conditions, e.g. called shell shock or combat fatigue then, now post-traumatic stress syndrome, that resulted from their experiences in combat. The term 'therapeutic community' was coined by Dr Tom Main in 1946, just after World War II. Dr Main pioneered a therapeutic model combining community therapy with ongoing psychoanalytic psychotherapy. This development was a modification of therapeutic work developed about the same time in England by Maxwell Jones and others with these returning veterans. By 1954 therapeutic community ideas were influencing wards in several psychiatric hospitals in the UK.

During the same era, however, the use of major tranquillisers began to emerge as the dominant 'treatment' for schizophrenia and some other mental illnesses. As patient symptoms were lessened through tranquilliser chemistry both in the US and in the UK, drastic reductions in psychiatric beds and other confinement beds occurred as facilities closed down. These closings were governed by financial and commercial priorities, as well as misunderstood research findings about the use of these tranquillisers. Nevertheless, with the rapid increase in the use of tranquillisers in the 1950s and early 1960s, the TC movement shifted from veterans and patients in mental hospitals toward other populations, notably correctional inmates. Maxwell Jones visited the US in 1959 where he became involved in the establishment of TCs with the California Department of Corrections, then the leading state in correctional treatment programme experimentation. From Jones' work, 11 TC projects were established.

His work with returning veterans also influenced Dr Harry Wilmer, who started TC treatment for returning Korean War veterans with combat neuroses at US Naval Hospitals in Japan and California. Dennie Briggs, who worked with Dr Wilmer, stimulated much of the TC development in the California prisons when Earl Warren was Governor, that continued until 1966 when Ronald Reagan became Governor and stopped virtually all treatment programming. Interestingly, it is through this US Navy connection that Dr Mitchell Rosenthal got his first TC experiences that led in part to his creation of Phoenix House, which in turn served as the original source for the development of Stay'n Out, now 29 years old and still operating successfully.

In the early 1960s some offender programmes in the United Kingdom began to be guided by Maxwell Jones' 'democratic' TC principles. This followed legislation, the 1959 Mental Health Act, which granted to psychopathy and personality disorder the status of psychological abnormality making them 'susceptible to treatment', and a new prison, HMP Grendon, was built specifically with five wings within which TCs were to operate providing treatment for psychologically disturbed offenders. TCs in prison in the UK for psychologically disturbed offenders were also established at four other institutions for psychologically disturbed offenders, and for lifers, for young offenders, and for sex offenders. None of these were designed for the treatment of drug abusers. During the mid-1990s, however, the first five prison-based TC programmes for drug abusers were established: Wayland, Swaleside, Portland, Holme House and Channings Wood.

It is important to understand that only one of all of these programmes – an 84-bed TC at Channings Wood – looks like a concept-based TC such as Stay'n Out since it is based on the American Phoenix House design; the others are all 'democratic' TCs. Although other authors in this book describe the elements and principles that characterise the classic democratic TC using the Grendon Prison model – the British exemplar of their TC – I believe it fitting to briefly add my view of them.

It must be noted that at Grendon there are no staff with prior drug or criminal histories – no recovered people. This contrasts with American concept-based TCs, which are mainly staffed by recovered drug addicts. Even in Channings Wood, which is based on the Phoenix House model, there are no recovering people (to anybody's knowledge) serving as staff, nor were there in any prison-based TC in the UK through the beginning of the twenty-first century.

At Grendon the elements of programming consist of daily, small psychotherapy therapy groups of 10 residents with two staff (serving to directly attack the emotional motivations and origins of deviant behaviour), daily community 'wing' meetings attended by all staff and prisoners, and 'feedback' sessions. At Grendon, the full treatment programme typically lasts for over two years. Since the mid-1990s, social and life skills and vocationally-based education courses have been added.

The Principles of the 'Democratic' TC

- **Democratisation** – serving to create enfranchisement and empowerment '… wherein every community member has a direct say in every aspect of how the wing is run' (including the power to vote someone out for breaching a rule), allowing healthy parts of the personality to emerge and be used, such as self-management and altruism.
- **Permissiveness** – a philosophy of tolerance allowing members to make mistakes, to assume individual and collective responsibility and to accept themselves 'with all their warts' and support each other 'regardless of their warts,' and to encourage open catharsis and self-disclosure.
- **Communalism** – fostering and encouraging individual, and especially collective, responsibility and accountability while living in a group, as well as exploring interactions and opportunities for social experimentation.
- **Reality confrontation** – encouraging continuous, direct and candid presentation of interpretation of each other's behaviour to counteract the tendency to distort, deny or withdraw from interpersonal difficulties or rule breaking.
- **Communicative open and frank discussion** – facilitating expression of distress and understanding of causes.
- **Intimate, informal** – allowing trust to develop and encouraging therapeutic playfulness.
- **Equitable, non-hierarchical** – demonstrating that all members are valued equally.

- **Peer group influence** – facilitating control and modification of inimical prison cultural values with an important role for 'community elders', members who have successfully completed the transition themselves playing a supportive role.
- **Aiming toward:**
  - relief of intra-psychic distress;
  - developing relationships with women and children;
  - developing relationships with figures of authority;
  - developing relationships with one another;
  - developing negative attitudes toward offending, especially to one's primary offence;
  - overcoming denial of past conduct and evil intent;
  - integrating morality into one's judgements;
  - heightening victim awareness, contrition, and consequences for one's victims;
  - recognising and eliminating fantasies and rehearsal in forming offending thoughts; and
  - planning strategies curtailing future offending behaviour, i.e. risk and relapse prevention.

In my visits to Grendon I met with the Governor, the Director of Therapy (what is now Director of Therapeutic Communities), and sat in during resident groups of various kinds, and during *staff* therapy groups. I interviewed staff at all levels and conducted private interviews with 25 residents. I found the staff deeply committed to their mission, as well as to a belief in the value and correctness of their approach. I believe that the professionals were convinced of the validity of the process and concerned about the interests of the residents.

During the course of my participation on the accreditation panel we examined all six outcome studies of reconviction done of clients released from HMP Grendon, and found that rates of re-offending after two years from release were not significantly different from comparison populations, in fact, in several studies the Grendon 'graduates' were less successful (worse) than the comparison populations. Nonetheless, there is a distinct time-in-programme function, i.e. the longer the term in therapy, the lower the rate of reconviction, with men over 30 years of age. This is in contrast to the six outcome studies done of US hierarchical TCs, like Stay'n Out, in which outcomes for re-arrest and return to drug use were significantly lower for those treated than for those in control populations.

The outcome research at HMP Grendon began in the late 1960s. One study (Newton, 1971) compared the reconviction rates of prisoners admitted to Grendon with similar untreated prisoners in two maximum-security prisons (Wormwood Scrubs – 1971 and Oxford Prison – 1973) and found little difference between the groups. A 1978 study (Gunn *et al.*) followed up 107 Grendon prisoners treated in 1971–2 and compared them with a matched group of prisoners not receiving psychiatric treatment. Results showed that slightly more Grendon men than controls were reconvicted during the two-year follow-up period. Questionnaires were sent out to released men at 6, 12 and 18 months. The replies suggested that the reconviction rates did not reflect the re-offending rates, and on the basis of this research, the authors argued *against* the use of reconviction rates as a measure of success (which also echoes the researchers who conducted programme evaluations with American *democratic* TCs at Chino Institution for Men in California and at New York's Clinton Prison) that utilised the Maxwell Jones model. Treatment in a therapeutic community, they said, cannot be expected to overcome all the social and environmental factors that are likely to lead to recidivism. This argument is taken up in a later paper (Gunn & Robertson, 1987) which reports a further follow-up study on the same cohorts. Again they found that more of the Grendon men had been reconvicted. The authors, as with the earlier studies, present case studies that expand on the statistical evidence, and show that the statistical results do not necessarily portray offending behaviour. Nevertheless, their research convinced them that Grendon was a paradigm for good prison management (as was concluded in the US democratic TC studies), and that much more attention should be given to aftercare in the community if the psychological changes achieved at Grendon were to be gained from.

Studies in the 1990s (Cullen, 1994; Marshall, 1997) found that men who had completed 18 months or more in therapy were less likely to re-offend than those who had stayed less time. The TIP (time in programme) effect is one that comes over strongly in much of the recent therapeutic community research. With respect to psychological changes produced by the treatment at Grendon and similar regimes, one study (Gunn *et al.*, 1978) found that therapeutic community treatment reduced psychological distress and increased interactive skills. Other studies at Grendon have demonstrated improvements in goal attainment (Sleap, 1979) and reductions in overall hostility (Newton, 1973). More recently, Newton (1998) found that treatment resulted in a variety of positive psychological changes – lower levels of psychoticism and neuroticism, higher levels of extroversion, reduced levels of hostility and increased belief in an internal locus of control. In a recent extended qualitative study, Genders and Player (1995) examined the therapeutic regime and the inmates and staff of Grendon. They found that as time in therapy went on, inmates were less likely to hold on to prison culture, and more likely to understand their own and other people's problems. As with earlier research, they found that the degree of change in inmates' views was greater for those who had been in therapy longest.

England's one democratic TC for youths (at Glen Parva Young Offenders Institute) recorded only four outstanding assaults during its 15 years of operation, despite the severity of offences and high levels of inmate disturbance prior to referral and there were no suicides, and inmates themselves provided 24-hour care for suicidal inmates from the rest of the prison (MacKenzie, 1997).

In another study (Cooke, 1989) of a special TC unit in a prison in Scotland (Barlinnie Special Unit, BSU), prisoners' violent behaviour was compared before and after admission. The unit had been established in 1973, and at the time of the study, 25 prisoners had experienced the unit, including the five currently in residence. Cooke found that the actual number of assaults and serious incident reports on the unit was far fewer than would be expected, a total of 10 compared with a predicted number of 113. After transfer from the BSU, 17 serious incidents occurred out of a predicted 26. It should be noted that both the last two noted prisons have closed their TC units.

These findings of reduced hazards for both inmates and officers are also found in the United States prison-based concept TCs. In fact, these TC units are so hazard-free that correction officers (COs) compete to get assigned to them. This contrasts with the early period of their development when COs were suspicious of programmes like Stay'n Out and sought to undermine them and, in a few cases, tried to sabotage them.

An Overview of US Concept-based TCs

For the purpose of illustration it is useful now to contrast the British model outlined earlier with a typical concept-based, community-based TC. It needs to be borne in mind that no two TCs are identical and that the material presented is a simplified model. Many of these ideas are largely due to George De Leon's influential conceptual analysis of the therapeutic community field.

A typical TC is a community-based residence with a few professional staff but primarily recovering addicts serving as staff. Residents are asked to spend about 9 to 18 months in residence, but the drop out rate is quite high – usually 60 to 80 per cent are gone within the first three months. A core characteristic of most TCs is the use of work as an organising therapeutic activity. This means residents are involved in all aspects of the community's operations including administration, maintenance and food preparation. Drug abuse is seen as a disorder of the whole person, so the treatment problem to be addressed is the person, not the drug, i.e. drug abuse is seen as a symptom not the essence of the disorder, and the pattern of drug use is less important than the psychological and behavioural disorders. Drug abuse is seen as a symptom of immaturity, thus the abuser is seen as unable to postpone gratification, unable to tolerate frustration, and has difficulty maintaining stable healthy relationships. Beside immaturity, most abusers have conduct or behaviour problems and low self-esteem. These characteristics are targets for the behaviour-change techniques used by the TC staff and senior residents. Recovery is considered to involve the development of a personal identity and global change in lifestyle including the conduct, attitudes and values consonant with 'Right Living', and is a lifelong continuing process. Right Living develops from committing oneself to the values of the TC community including both positive *social* values such as the work ethic, social productivity, and communal responsibility, and positive personal values such as honesty, self-reliance, and responsibility to oneself and significant others. The goals of treatment are congruent with these values; abstinence from drug use, termination of illicit behaviours, gainful employment, school matriculation and maintenance of positive stable social relationships.

TCs are hierarchically organised or stratified. Staff and resident roles are aligned in a clear chain of command. New residents are assigned to work teams with the lowest status, but can move up strata as they demonstrate increased competency and emotional growth. They thus have an incentive to earn better work positions, associated privileges and living accommodation.

For success in the TC, one must accept the notion of 'acting as if' that requires new residents to suspend judgment and *make believe* that they accept the basic TC values and rules of conduct. The TC resident then continues to 'act as if' until the community values and attitudes become internalised. Maturity develops as roles and responsibility are taken on and increase. The stratified nature of the TC facilitates the working through of authority problems and helps residents to accept appropriate authority as they move out to assume responsible positions within the society. The distinguishing feature of the TC in contrast with other treatment approaches is the 'purposive use of the community as a primary method for facilitating social and psychological change in individuals' (De Leon, 1995a) as it blends confrontation and support to help residents undergo the difficult changes that are necessary. This perception of *community* is constantly emphasised.

The concept-based TC uses groups and meetings to provide 'positive persuasion' to change behaviour, and confrontation by peer groups whenever values or rules are breached. On the other hand, peers also provide supportive feedback such as reinforcement, affirmation, instruction and suggestions for changing behaviour and attitudes, and assist residents during group meetings as they recall painful memories from childhood and adolescence. In addition, TCs often provide additional services such as family treatment, and educational, vocational, medical and mental health services, and staffing is often augmented by increasing proportions of professional from the mental health, medical and educational fields.

Distinctions Between US Community and Prison-based Concept TCs

Now, I will present 10 distinctions between the concept-based, *community*-based therapeutic communities (CBTCs) and concept-based, *prison*-based therapeutic communities (PBTCs):

- First, in prisons, a TC is much more constrained by rules and policies, particularly those relating to security.
- Second, as a corollary, the range of programming autonomy, clinical creativity and independence of action normally seen in a CBTC is much narrower in a PBTC.
- Third, PBTCs usually have fewer recovering persons as staff compared with CBTCs. Thus, usually there are fewer role models consisting of recovering ex-addict offenders with whom the inmates may identify, and from whom they may draw encouragement.
- Fourth, in PBTCs, mixed gender resident groups are rarely found unlike in CBTCs. This difference obviously denies each gender the opportunity to learn how to develop positive working and social relationships with the other.
- Fifth, in CBTCs, work plays a major organising role in the development of responsibility. In PBTCs a number of work functions are performed by work crews in prison industry, e.g. cooking, landscaping, painting and maintenance, not by residents. This places limits on growth in personal development, opportunities for hierarchical movement, learning about leadership, and learning the responsibilities of being an employee. Thus, surrogate tasks need to be created, some of which may not be real enough to facilitate the desired changes.
- Sixth, when there is rule violation in a CBTC, such as theft of another resident's personal property, this is viewed as a constructive

opportunity to teach the offender the consequences of his or her act. In a PBTC a breach of this kind may have to be reported to the security staff for adjudication and possible criminal action. Thus, in the CBTC there is a greater opportunity for growth, but in a prison similar circumstances are likely to bring punishment.

• Seventh, as a corollary, staff are compelled to report the offence and failure to do so would negatively affect the programme's reputation in the facility and could bring the force of the institutional administration down on the programme. In the CBTC, the offence would be brought to the resident group. Together with staff, residents would participate in an encounter or a group meeting where the incident would be discussed and appropriate consequences assigned such as loss of job status.

• Eighth, there is a restricted range of rewards and incentives that a PBTC can use compared with a CBTC. The absence of a variety of housing, work and clothing options in prison inhibits the number and variety of positive sanctions than can be used as incentives for positive growth during treatment.

• Ninth, PBTCs have much lower drop out rates, averaging around 40–50 per cent within a year, as compared with 70–90 per cent in CBTCs.

• Tenth, within PBTCs residents are exposed daily to inmates of the general prison population. Thus, they have an opportunity to see their changed selves and behaviour in contrast with persons like themselves who have not experienced the PBTC. They thus see more clearly the changes in themselves since they began treatment. This tends to accelerate the rate of personal change. CBTC residents don't have this opportunity until they are furloughed.

Now that we've examined both the democratic and the hierarchical TC models, let us examine what key factors could account for the dramatic differences in outcomes for the British 'democratic' model as at Grendon and the US 'hierarchical' concept-based model as we see in Stay'n Out.

First, the prison-based TC for substance abusers in the US has a rather different origin and history than Grendon and its English cousins. In the US, current TCs for addicted persons (both alcoholic and drug addicted) derive from Synanon, founded in 1958 by Charles Dederich in California. Synanon's immediate roots lie in the Oxford movement and Alcoholics Anonymous, with earlier prototypes existing in religious, temperance and communal healing communities in North America and abroad. Stay'n Out is a prison-based hierarchical (or concept-based) TC, like Phoenix House and Project Return that generally subscribe to a self-help, social learning model approach and a holistic human change perspective. In contrast, the

British model grew out of a psychoanalytic psychotherapy within a 'community' treatment structure designed for a pro-social group – returning veterans suffering from combat fatigue, shell shock, etc. which was transformed into a correctional treatment approach when the growing use of tranquillisers made in-hospital treatment less possible.

Second, hierarchical TC programming as it is used in US prisons focuses on drug abusers and drug addicts whose crimes in most instances flow from, are connected with, or are accelerated by their drug misuse, whereas democratic TC members at Grendon and the like are prisoners with a history of psychological disorder. Many of these men are also drug and alcohol abusers but this abuse is not the primary focus of the therapeutic process.

Third, the staff of the democratic, prison-based TCs in the UK are mainly therapeutically-trained correction officers led by psychodynamically-orientated therapists and psychologists working with a cognitive, criminogenic framework whereas the staff of hierarchical, concept-based, prison-based TCs like Stay'n Out have some graduate professionals but are comprised mainly of recovering addict-offenders who have graduated themselves from TC programmes, and have been trained to serve in staff roles.

Fourth, in the British prison-based TC, the treatment is aimed not at individuals, but at, and by, the whole community. There is a principle of permissiveness allowing psychopathic persons with severe personality difficulties to be tolerated in the belief that, while they may be more likely than others to leave at an early stage due to difficulties in settling in, therapeutic communities can be modified to accommodate such residents more readily and staff can be trained to work more effectively with these difficult residents. Highly psychopathic residents exhibiting hostile or potentially harmful conduct in a hierarchical TC like Stay'n Out, however, would after one or two warnings be discharged in the belief that his or her behaviour would be so destructive to the community that the treatment process for other residents, or the residents themselves, would be disadvantaged, or worse, damaged.

Fifth, several views guide the hierarchical TC approach to the treatment of substance abuse and related problems: a) the view that substance abuse and criminality are symptoms of a disorder of the whole person, b) the view that both social and psychological characteristics must be changed in the person, c) the view that 'right living,' pro-social values and moral requirements are essential to sustaining recovery, d) the view that recovery from addiction is a developmental learning process, and e) the view that abstinence is a prerequisite to recovery. In the democratic TC the process of change is guided by a multimodal psychotherapeutic model with an in-depth understanding of the origins of one's conduct being important conditions for change; abstinence is not a prerequisite to change, and psychotherapy occupies a position which is of equal importance to community principles such as adherence to truth, honesty, self-responsibility, work ethic, community responsibility and responsible concern for peers.

Sixth, in the democratic TC such as Grendon equality among all members is a key principle. Work is not an organising principle, thus, assuming job responsibilities although important has perhaps a lesser role as a means of learning responsibilities and behaviours toward authority figures than it has in a hierarchical TC. The entire process is also less structured than in a Stay'n Out-type programme. Interaction between staff and residents is much more familiar and the day is less tightly scheduled than in Stay'n Out and similar US prison-based TCs.

Seventh, aftercare or continuing treatment after release from incarceration is not provided in any systematic way for persons released from Grendon or other prisons with TCs in the UK. Research conducted with US prison-based TCs, in contrast, clearly demonstrates the importance of aftercare programmes for at least six months after release to maintain the positive gains made in the prison TC.

There are many other differences that are less critical than those noted above, but there are also many surface similarities given the 'community' orientation.

Conclusion

1. The evidence suggests that both kinds of prison-based TCs can be helpful in reducing distressing psychological symptoms and improving behaviour, but they differ in their ability to reduce re-offending with the American concept-based TCs consistently producing 17–22 per cent less recidivism.

2. While the evidence from the concept-based TCs in the US for substance abusers looks particularly impressive, in all fairness the British believe these figures cannot be directly compared to the evidence from democratic TCs for two main reasons. First, hierarchical TCs are organised essentially to deal with a narrower group of individuals – those who are serious drug abusers. Since the crimes committed by drug abusers are held to be directly associated with their drug use for the most part, the TCs tackle drug abuse issues (e.g. immaturity, susceptibility to peer group pressure, inability to postpone gratification, etc.) rather than the personality disorders, underlying or otherwise,

connected with offending behaviour. Second, Grendon Prison inmates comprise a more difficult to treat population (50 per cent psychopaths, 30 per cent sex offenders, 40 per cent violent predatory felons, 80–90 per cent personality disordered (Birtchnell & Shine, 2000)) than most concept-based TCs ever see. In fact, persons such as the Grendon population would probably not be accepted in most American TCs. American research might counter this point by arguing that concept-based TCs frequently encounter persons like Grendon's population and their successful graduates were often as violent and as disturbed prior to treatment.

3. The emphasis of evaluative research on concept-based TCs has provided a great deal of evidence of their effectiveness, based on large numbers of clients. In turn, this has assisted their becoming accepted as a mainstream drug abuse treatment approach in prisons in the United States. Democratic TCs in the United Kingdom, on the other hand, have provided only limited evidence of their effectiveness in reducing reconviction rates of personality-disordered offenders. This probably underlies the differences in proliferation of TCs. TCs in Her Majesty's prisons in particular seem to have been established very sparingly, and often last only a few years.

4. Concept-based TCs in the US for substance abusers provide programme graduates with aftercare programming that continues to positively reinforce the therapy long after treatment has ended. No such system for continuing treatment after release exists for British TC graduates. Concept-based TCs also seem particularly efficient at re-integrating inmates back into the community. Some American in-prison TCs operate community-based TCs which function almost as pre-release facilities or halfway houses for ex-prisoners, and which continue the familiar therapeutic regime. Again, however, reintegration for ex-addicts often involves a break with past environments and adoption of a new, positive way of life and groups of friends. Aftercare for inmates from British democratic TCs (if it is carried out at all) is carried out after discharge from prison under the auspices of the Probation Service, and ex-prisoners often find themselves back in their old neighbourhoods among their old crime buddies without the 'cushion' of a TC environment to help them readjust.

5. There is general agreement that inmates behave better in both kinds of TCs than in mainstream prisons, even though the particular inmates who elect to join TCs often have lengthy records of prison disruption and violence. Studies of psychiatric disturbance show that disturbance tends to decrease during both kinds of TC treatment and that test scores on positive traits tend to rise. Evidence from the Amity

programme's research at Donovan Prison in California shows that the rate of inter-inmate assaults and attacks on officers substantially declined almost to zero in the 800-man quad where the TC was located but did not change in the other three equal-sized quads where no TC was located (Wexler *et al.*, 1999). An examination of much of the evaluative literature demonstrates the effectiveness of both kinds of TC treatment for personality disorders both inside and outside prisons. This is an important finding for the management of inmates of correctional institutions in dealing with inter-inmate prison assaults and inmate–officer assaults and other violations such as trafficking and actual clandestine substance use.

6. There is less knowledge about the efficacy of either kind of TC treatment for the more severely personality-disordered inmate, particularly those who are judged to have the type of psychopathic or antisocial personality disorder that may lead, or has led, to their committing violent crime. However, the data from Stay'n Out outcome studies indicates that 70 per cent of *successful* residents followed up for three years also evidenced pre-treatment histories of violent offences.

7. There is a positive relationship between time spent in therapy and outcome. This may be through some kind of self-selection procedure, in that only those most committed to change are prepared to stay the full course, or it may be an effect of the experience. Self-selection through early drop out seems to be a particular feature of community-based, concept-based TCs, which have especially high drop out rates in the early weeks of the programme, but both kinds of prison-based TCs have roughly the same proportion of drop outs because of the requirement that members should be willing to continue, and the community should be willing to let them continue.

8. There are very few TCs for women in prisons, and very few studies have been conducted evaluating TC treatment for such women. Stay'n Out is one of the few programmes where evaluative results – favourable ones I might add – have been collected. In the UK, only one democratic TC exists for women and this remains as yet unevaluated.

I wish to add some comments about the programme I have been citing in this piece – Stay'n Out. I'm using the label '*Stay'n Out*' to mean all the New York Therapeutic Communities, Inc. programmes – Bayview, its women's facility, Serendipity I and II (its aftercare facilities), as well as the original programme, Stay'n Out, now 29 years old. We do know that treatment in a prison-based therapeutic community such as Stay'n Out creates a social and psychological environment conducive to bringing men and women to recovery – of this the research evidence is profoundly clear. Not only has Stay'n Out consistently demonstrated success for both men and women, it is also the longest continuously functioning prison-based TC in history. This commends its achievements and is a powerful testament to its leadership, its staff and its commitment.

An intensive analysis of Stay'n Out shows that it changes negative patterns of behaviour, thinking and feeling so as to foster a responsible drug-free lifestyle. Its residents achieve stable recovery by successfully integrating conduct, emotions, skills, attitudes and values. Stay'n Out focuses on lifestyle, rather than drug abuse, criminality or any one problem alone. Stay'n Out fosters the process of human change, allowing each resident's passage through stages of incremental learning in which changes at each stage facilitate change in the next stage, each in turn reflecting movement toward recovery.

Recovery, however, depends on positive and negative pressures to change, and the programme uses these pressures well. Remaining in treatment requires continued motivation to change. Successful concept-based therapeutic communities, like Stay'n Out, provide elements in the daily regime that are designed to sustain motivation and detect premature termination signals at the resident level, and to sustain programme integrity at the programme level. To paraphrase George De Leon, 'Treatment is not provided by Stay'n Out, but made available to the individual in the programme's environment, in its staff and peers, the daily regime of work, groups, meetings, seminars, and recreation. However, the effectiveness of these elements is dependent upon the Stay'n Out resident who must fully engage in the treatment regime. Self-help recovery means that the Stay'n Out resident makes the main contribution to the change process … each Stay'n Out resident in the process contributes to change in other residents. With all elements mediated by peers through confrontation and sharing in groups, by example as role models, and as supportive, encouraging friends in daily interactions' (De Leon, 1995b, cited in Lipton, 1999). Democratic TCs (DTCs) also encompass many of these values and principles and have survived the various political and ideological moods. Adopting such principles, Grendon has predated and outlived many of its rivals and many of the outcome measures referred to above have also been consistently demonstrated in the English DTCs (Lees *et al.*, 1999, Newton 1998).

To achieve recovery for a Stay'n Out resident means, and this mirrors processes within DTCs, participating as a community member in a variety of socially responsible roles, and learning how to deal constructively with anger, jealousy and other triggering emotions as they arise. As in the prison DTCs, changes in lifestyle and identity are gradually learned through participating in various roles, supported by other residents similarly engaged, and a trained, experienced and highly supportive staff of recovered ex-offender-addicts (in the case of Stay'n Out) and professionals. It is clear from experience and from research that the process only begins in prison, and to be genuinely and lastingly effective, *it must continue in the community*. The struggle to achieve successful recovery is snagged with obstacles inherent in general society – such as racism, lack of employment opportunities and absence of inexpensive housing – that are doubly difficult for ex-offenders to overcome. Stay'n Out must continue to be creative and forceful to help residents achieve solid jobs and adequate housing in the face of prejudice and social and economic obstacles. Stay'n Out has met this challenge well with Serendipity I and II, and by maintaining warm and helpful relationships with its former clients as they move on in general society.

References

Birtchnell, J. & Shine, J. (2000). Personality disorders and the interpersonal octagon. *British Journal of Medical Psychology*, *73*, 433–448.

Cooke, D.J. (1989). Containing violent prisoners: an analysis of the Barlinnie Special Unit. *British Journal of Criminology*, *29*, 129–143.

Cullen, J.E. (1994). Grendon: the therapeutic community that works. *Therapeutic Communities for Offenders*, *15*, 301–311.

De Leon, G. (1995a). Therapeutic communities – is there an essential model? In G. De Leon (Ed.) *As Community as Method. Therapeutic Communities for Special Populations and Special Settings*. Westport, CT: Greenwood Publishing Group.

De Leon, G. (1995b). Therapeutic communities for addictions: A theoretical framework. *International Journal of Addictions*, *30*, 1603–1645.

De Leon, G. & Melnick, G. (1992). *Therapeutic Community Scale of Essential Elements Questionnaire*. Center for Therapeutic Community Research. NDRI. New York: Community Studies Institute.

Field, G. (1989). A study of the effects of intensive treatment on reducing the criminal recidivism of addicted offenders. *Federal Probation*, *53*, 51–56.

Genders, E. & Player, E. (1995). *Grendon: A Study of a Therapeutic Prison*. Oxford: Oxford University Press.

Gunn, J. & Robertson, G. (1987). A ten-year follow-up of men discharged from Grendon prison. *British Journal of Psychiatry*, *151*, 674–678.

Gunn, J., Robertson, G., Dell, S. & Way, C. (1978). *Psychiatric Aspects of Imprisonment*. London: Academic Press.

Inciardi, J.A., Martin, S.S., Butzin, C.F., Hooper, R.M. & Harrison, L.D. (1997). An effective model of prison-based treatment for drug-involved offenders. *Journal of Drug Issues*, *27*, 261–278.

Lees, J., Manning, N. & Rawlings, B. (1999). *Therapeutic Community Effectiveness: A Systematic International Review of Therapeutic Community Treatment for People with Personality Disorders and Mentally Disordered Offenders.* CRD Report 17, University of York.

Lipton, D.S. (1999). Therapeutic community treatment programming in corrections. In C.R. Hollin (Ed.) *Handbook of Offender Assessment and Treatment.* Chichester: Wiley.

MacKenzie, J. (1997). Glen Parva therapeutic community – an obituary. *Prison Service Journal, 111,* 26.

Marshall, P. (1997). A reconviction study of HMP Grendon Therapeutic Community. Home Office Research Findings no 53. In J. Shine (Ed.) *A Compilation of Grendon Research.* Leyhill Press. Available from Psychology Unit, HMP Grendon, Grendon Underwood, Aylesbury, HP18 OTL.

Newton, M. (1971). Reconviction after Grendon. (Reprinted in J. Shine (Ed.) (2000) *A Compilation of Grendon Research.* Leyhill Press. Available from Psychology Unit, HMP Grendon, Grendon Underwood, Aylesbury, HP18 OTL.)

Newton, M. (1973). *Progress of Follow Up-up Studies and Comparison with Non Patients Carried out at HMP Oxford.* Grendon Psychology Unit Report, Series A, no.15.

Newton, M. (1998). Changes in measures of personality, hostility and locus of control during residence in a prison therapeutic community. *Legal and Criminological Psychology, 3,* 209–223.

Sleap, H. (1979). Goal attainment scaling: the technique and some initial findings. In J. Shine (Ed.) *A Compilation of Grendon Research.* Leyhill Press. Available from Psychology Unit, HMP Grendon, Grendon Underwood, Aylesbury, HP18 OTL.

Wexler, H.K., De Leon, G., Thomas, G., Kressel, D., & Peters, J. (1999). The Amity prison evaluation: Reincarceration outcomes. *British Journal of Criminology, 26,* 147–167.

Wexler, H.K., Falkin, G.P. & Lipton, D.S. (1990). Outcome evaluation of a prison therapeutic community for substance abuse treatment. *Criminal Justice and Behavior, 17,* 71–92.

Chapter 5

Towards a Social Analytical Therapy

John Shine

Introduction

Democratic therapeutic communities (TCs) have a long history in forensic settings and have shown some success in managing and treating offenders with personality disorders. However, previous research (Hobson *et al.*, 2000; Ogloff *et al.*, 1990; Shine, 2001a), has indicated that offenders scoring highly on measures of severe personality disorder or psychopathy are likely to pose particular difficulties when admitted to this treatment approach, such as high levels of therapy-interfering behaviours and institutional misconduct leading to elevated attrition rates. Nevertheless, as this chapter outlines, there are good therapeutic reasons to support the TC approach as an overarching model for working with severely personality-disordered offenders. The challenge for those who work in TCs and are involved in developing treatment models, is how to incorporate innovations and modifications of this approach in order to meet the clinical needs of this group, rather than adopting referral systems based on exclusion, diversion or therapeutic nihilism.

This chapter describes the development of the Millfields Unit: an innovative pilot scheme in East London for patients with severe personality disorder detained under the Mental Health Act in a medium secure setting. The model utilises a TC approach but with important adaptations specifically to deal with the needs of patients with severe personality disorder.

Grendon and the Emergence of Forensic Therapeutic Communities: Developments in Research and Practice
Edited by Richard Shuker and Elizabeth Sullivan
© 2010 John Wiley & Sons, Ltd.

The changes include modifications of some of the key TC principles, provision of a wide range of individual and group-based support therapies available to patients and a step-down supportive housing facility close to the unit intended to provide a continuum of care and therapy to assist reintegration to the community.

The theoretical basis for the model owes much to the work of Livesley's (2001) framework for an integrated treatment approach for personality disorder, which will be outlined. However, in this chapter I argue that Livesley's approach, though extremely helpful, pays insufficient attention to the holistic nature of treatment and the importance of day-to-day or 'here and now' social interactions as a basis for therapeutic intervention. The importance of assessing and working with present day behaviour in the social context of the therapeutic environment offered within the TC model is highlighted. It is argued that greater emphasis on '*social analysis*' – that is, the significance of present day, clinically relevant behaviour – (Kohlenberg & Tsai, 2007) as a focus of therapeutic intervention could make a major contribution to the embryonic literature on 'What Works' for severely personality-disordered offenders.

Background to Dangerous and Severe Personality Disorder (DSPD) Programme

The DSPD programme was instigated following a number of high-profile cases attracting considerable media attention in the 1990s when former patients discharged from secure psychiatric care were convicted of serious violent offences. A notable example was the case of Michael Stone who was convicted of attacking Lin Russell and her two daughters Megan and Josie in 1996. Lin and Megan died and Josie survived but with serious head injuries. Michael Stone had been discharged from a medium secure unit as 'untreatable' and was being managed in the community under the Care Plan Approach.

Michael Stone was assessed by psychiatrists as suffering from Personality Disorder and drug-induced psychosis (Dyer, 2006). His background contained many characteristic features that would be familiar to those who work in secure forensic services such as HMP Grendon (Shine & Newton, 2001), and are recognised risk factors for violence in later life (Wong & Gordon, 2000). These included both witnessing and suffering domestic violence as a child, early and sustained exposure to male antisocial role models, admission to children's homes, early acquisition of criminal attitudes and beliefs leading to convictions from the age of 12, substance misuse from an early age and previous convictions for violence and weapon use.

Following this case, psychiatrists were condemned by Jack Straw, the Home Secretary at the time, for washing their hands of 'dangerous psychopaths' (www.guardian.co.uk/society/2002/apr/17/mentalhealth.crime). A Government consultation document (Home Office, 1999) acknowledged that successive administrations had recognised the threat to public safety from a '... minority of people who, because of their disorder pose a risk of serious offending' and estimated that there were just over 2000 people, mainly in prisons or secure hospitals, who would fall into this group.

In terms of treatment and management systems, the consultation paper acknowledged that, with a few small-scale exceptions, existing arrangements were not satisfactory and that: '... the kind of therapeutic treatment needed to ensure that they are not released back into society whilst they still present a significant risk is not generally available' (Home Office, 1999, p. 4).

Draft mental health legislation and proposals to manage this group were proposed, including a new classification system of Dangerous and Severe Personality Disorder (DSPD) and the setting up of a number of pilot sites to develop expertise in the assessment and management of personality-disordered offenders. The new services were intended to form the basis of a new infrastructure, provide a focus for research, offer specialist training and consultation to other services, develop methods for staff selection, training and support for this work.

The draft proposals initially attracted considerable criticism from a range of professions concerned that they posed a potential threat to civil liberties because of the risk of indeterminate detention based on a dubious clinical/legal category without empirical support. In the light of these concerns, the DSPD programme was changed to a pilot project designed to undertake extensive research and provide clinical services to a group who had previously been neglected. The programme is now broadly welcomed as offering the possibility of developing innovative models of service delivery to a challenging and previously marginalised group (British Psychological Society, 2006, p. 46).

Since these modifications the DSPD programme has attracted less controversy and criticism from professionals, although, by their very nature, DSPD units are high-risk services and vulnerable to adverse media coverage, especially in terms of decision making to discharge patients or prisoners to the community (see below for further details).

Planning and delivery guides for the new services were produced in 2005 for high and medium secure services (Ministry of Justice and Department of Health, 2005). Provision was set out for 300 high secure beds and approximately 95 beds in medium secure sites.

The criteria for severe personality disorder is defined by the most recent DSPD planning and delivery guide (http://www.dspdprogramme.gov.uk/media/pdfs/High_Secure_Services_for_Men.pdf) as:

> … a PCL-(R) score of 30 or above (or the PCL-SV equivalent); or
>
> A PCL-(R) score of 25–29 (or the PCL-SV equivalent) plus at least one DSM-IV personality disorder diagnosis other than antisocial personality disorder; or
>
> Two or more DSM-IV personality disorder diagnoses. (DSPD Planning and Delivery Guide, 2008, pp. 14–15)

The delivery guide stresses that the most important criterion is the strength of the relationship between personality disorder and a person's offending behaviour. The concept of a 'functional link' between personality disorder and offending is therefore a key criterion that differentiates DSPD units from secure units in prisons that admit cases on the basis of disruptive behaviour alone.

The Millfields Unit

The Millfields Unit, located in East London, is one of four DSPD pilot sites in medium secure settings. The unit opened in 2006 and is comprised of two 10-bedded wards and two multidisciplinary teams. A supported housing hostel, run in partnership with a housing agency and supported by a community multidisciplinary team, is located nearby as a step-down provision for patients completing treatment at the inpatient service. The aims of the service were outlined in a Philosophy of Care document published in 2005 (East London and City Mental Health Trust, 2005):

a)   Assess and treat patients suffering from severe personality disorder who pose a serious risk to others, according to the most rigorous available evidence.

b)   Evaluate the risk posed by these individuals and contribute to its management, whilst recognising that not all adverse events can be predicted or prevented.

c)   Promote where possible, and in close alliance with other agencies, the safe reintegration of our patients into the community, whilst recognising their human need for consistency and continuity in the longer term.

d)   Promote a model of close collaboration with our patients as integral to their care.

e) Add to the evidence base for effective treatment.

f) Provide a service that is accessible to those previously excluded, including individuals from ethnic minorities.

g) Develop our understanding of how best to support clinical teams in this work. (East London Mental Health Trust, 2005)

In terms of the treatment model, the unit has drawn heavily from the work of Livesley (2001) who has argued for an eclectic and integrative approach to the treatment of personality disorder. Livesley argues that, although differential effectiveness has been established for some types of psychological disorders (such as cognitive therapy for panic disorder and behaviour therapy for child conduct disorder), for personality disorder there is evidence that many interventions have demonstrated effectiveness. However, differential superiority has yet to be shown for a particular approach through randomised control trials (although see a recent paper by Giesen-Bloo *et al.* 2006). Therefore an integrative approach is best suited to the current stage of evidence for this group of patients.

Following Lambert (1992), Livesley (2001) argued that there are two sets of factors that effective therapies have in common. Firstly, generic change factors common to all therapies arising from the therapeutic alliance and secondly, structured components linked to the acquisition, testing and practising of new skills.

Livesley outlines a set of principles designed to inform a framework for an integrated approach to treatment. In the next section these are described together with the approach used at Millfields to meet each of the principles. Before outlining these principles it is important to stress that personality disorder is a heterogeneous category and most of the research with personality disorders has been conducted on non-forensic populations. In the DSPD programme, however, it is clear that the main function of the new units is to work with clients who pose a risk of serious violent or sexual offences to the public. In the new services therefore, the forensic principles of criminogenic assessment and management of risk factors that predispose individuals to offending are paramount.

Forensic Context of the Millfields Personality Disorder Unit

In common with all DSPD Units, all patients admitted to Millfields complete a set of structured risk assessment tools designed to measure whether the assessment criteria are met, to identify treatment needs and assist in the assessment of change in attaining treatment targets (www. dspdprogramme.gov.uk/media/pdfs/High_Secure_Services_for_Men. pdf). The assessment tools include measurement of violence, sexual offending, personality disorder and other mental disorders (as defined in DSM 4 Axis 1, American Psychiatric Association, 2000). This is known as the 'common dataset' as it is used across all the DSPD sites for evaluation and monitoring purposes. The common dataset is supplemented with additional measures specific to each DSPD pilot site; those used at Millfields are given in appendix 1.

The structured risk assessment tools form an important part of the assessment of an individual's suitability for treatment and contribute both to clinical formulation and identification of long-term treatment goals.

In addition to the structured tools, forensic issues are addressed by:

- Close attention to offence-paralleling behaviours (Daffern *et al.*, 2007);
- Daily observation and behavioural monitoring of ward behaviour and behaviour in core and specific therapies;
- Provision of staff training on the Correctional Services Accredited model for democratic therapeutic communities in prisons (HM Prison Service, 2007);
- Awareness of treatment responsivity issues in the treatment of psychopaths such as the creation of illusory therapeutic alliances and duping delight (Meloy, 1994; see below for explanation of these processes);
- Provision of criminogenic interventions such as substance misuse, anger control and sexual offending;
- Daily handover meetings to manage risk, clinical and security issues, regular multidisciplinary team (MDT) meetings; and
- Formulation meetings in which structured risk assessments are scored and discussed with the MDT to help in the development of a shared clinical formulation of the patients' difficulties and identification of long-term treatment goals.

In the next section the principles for an integrated approach to treatment as set out by Livesley (2001) and their specific application to Millfields is outlined.

Principle one – personality disorder involves
multiple domains of psychopathology

As mentioned above, personality disorder is a heterogeneous category and covers a wide range of symptomatology; typical problems include:

... anxiety, dysphoria, self-harming acts and transient psychotic features, situational problems, difficulty in regulating affect and impulses, maladaptive expression of basic traits such as dependency and social avoidance; dysfunctional interpersonal relationships, problems forming integrated representations of self and others and failure to develop a cohesive self and the capacity for intimacy and mature attachment. (Livesley, 2001, p. 572)

In addition to the above list, DSPD populations are characterised by high levels of psychopathy (Hare, 2003), which is known to present particular difficulties in treatment settings. These include problems such as the creation of 'illusory alliances' in which the patient manipulates or conditions the therapist into believing he has changed through the use of flattery, superficial charm and using the language of therapy without the corresponding gains in insight and sustained affective, cognitive and behavioural change. Clinical experience from professionals who work with this group suggests that psychopaths may also engage in a process of 'duping delight' in which the process of conning therapists is intrinsically rewarding for the patient leading to an increased sense of triumph and grandiosity (see Meloy, 1994, for a discussion of these processes). The case of Lee Porritt (http://www.thesun.co.uk/sol/homepage/news/article1347748.ece) who was discharged from a high secure hospital after completing treatment only to go to a national newspaper to try and sell his story of how he conned the therapy staff and lived in conditions of luxury whilst doing so, may serve as an illustration of these processes.

The wide range of psychopathology typically exhibited by personality-disordered patients indicates that comprehensive approaches are needed to target a range of pathology. This requires an eclectic range of therapies, based on the principle of 'what works for each individual'. In terms of the Millfields model this is addressed by the provision of a range of therapies designed to address specific areas of need, including:

- Therapeutic community groups including community meetings, small groups, feedbacks, group activities concerned with developing communalism such as participating in social events, open days and organising visits from external members of staff;
- A wide range of occupational therapy groups including gardening, cooking, hobbies and other life skills;
- Orientation to therapy groups;
- Cognitive-behavioural therapy (CBT) groups such as substance misuse, anger control and sex offending;
- Creative therapies such as art therapy, group and individual and communal activities such as creation of murals for the unit;

- Educational and vocational training;
- Individual psychotherapy and psychology work; and
- Nursing-led mood diary work for patients in the initial stages of therapy.

Principle two – personality disorder involves general features common to all cases and specific features observed in some cases and not others

Livesley (2001) argues that comprehensive treatment of personality disorder should involve

> '... general strategies to manage and treat general psychopathology and specific interventions tailored to the specific features of individual cases.' (p. 572.)

The 'core features' of personality disorder are identified by Livesley (2001) as chronic interpersonal problems and self-pathology. Within the therapeutic community model these core features are highlighted in terms of the difficulties encountered by patients in pro-social behaviour and co-operative living. One of the defining features of the therapeutic community approach is the community meeting where all members of the unit meet on a regular basis to discuss how they are getting on with each other. Indeed the very definition of a therapeutic community is offered by Kennard (1998) as: 'an opportunity to learn about oneself in relation to other people' fits well with this concept as through the process of community living difficulties in pro-social behaviour and co-operative behaviour are highlighted.

The dynamics that are explored in these meetings are taken to regular small group meetings facilitated by a small pool of consistent staff to allow therapeutic work to take place at the deeper level of self-pathology, offending behaviour, attachment processes and interpersonal relationships.

Principle two, therefore, is addressed through the provision of the core therapies that every patient regularly attends and the availability of specific therapies based on treatment need identified for each individual case (see above).

Principle three – personality disorder is a bio-psychological condition with a complex biological and psychosocial etiology

It is well established that personality traits are highly heritable (British Psychological Society, 2006). In DSPD populations, high scores on the Psychopathy Checklist (Hare, 2003) are one of the criteria for admission.

Recent research has shown a high heritable component for the factor one (interpersonal and affective) components of psychopathy, as much as 70 per cent (Viding *et al.*, 2005). The antisocial and lifestyle components are more influenced by environmental, rather than heritable, factors. Despite this, most treatment approaches are based on psychological or psychosocial interventions with scant regard to the role of biological factors in the origin and maintenance of these complex disorders.

The implications of the biological contribution to personality disorder are identified by Livesley (2001) in three areas: highlighting the contribution of biological interventions, awareness of the limitations that some personality disorders are amenable to change and conceptualising change in personality disorder, not as a cure, but an improvement in flexibility and adaptation of core personality systems.

Within the Millfields model, principle three is addressed by limited use of pharmacological interventions to treat significant degrees of over-arousal, emotional deregulation, depression, anxiety, PTSD and psychotic-like symptoms (East London and City Mental Health Trust, 2005). A paper by Cartwright and Gordon (2007) argues for the use of medication in promoting readiness for psychological treatment for men suffering from severe personality disorder in the treatment of co-morbid mental illness, personality traits such as emotional dysregulation and offending behaviour. However they add important caveats concerned with clear boundaries and MDT involvement to avoid the pitfalls that have been associated with these approaches in the past, such as splits in the therapy team or perceiving medical staff as the most powerful team members.

In addition there is provision of individualised specific psychological interventions that can help build competence and resilience.

Principle four – psychosocial adversity influences the contents, processes and organisation of the personality system

Experiences of trauma are common in personality-disordered populations. As Livesley (2001) describes, these experiences can affect behaviour in several ways; firstly, through the well documented experiences of psychological sequelae to trauma such as flashbacks and de-realisation; secondly, through the development of schemas in manner of experiencing and relating to others, for example in the view that others are 'untrustworthy, unreliable, unhelpful and unpredictable'; thirdly, experiences of adversity can affect personality development resulting in ' ... poorly defined self and interpersonal boundaries, poorly integrated self-states and a self system that lacks integration and cohesion'.

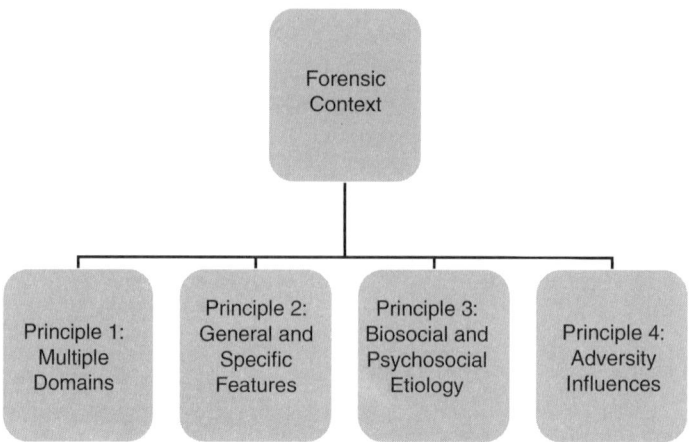

Figure 5.1   Principles for an integrated approach to PD treatment (Adapted from Livesley, 2001)

Within the Millfields model, this principle is addressed by:

- Close attention to the processes of attachment and consistent and supportive therapeutic alliances;
- Provision of individual psychotherapy based on need and readiness; and
- Regular attendance at small psychotherapy groups to help work with the memories of traumatic events particularly in the context of day-to-day relationships with others.

In summary, the Millfields model is an eclectic approach to working with severe personality disorder based on the four principles identified by Livesley for an integrative and pragmatic framework for treatment; these principles are applied within a forensic context of criminogenic risk assessment and management as shown in figure 5.1.

An Adapted Forensic Therapeutic Community

The principles set out by Livesley (2001) provide the basis for the adapted therapeutic community model at Millfields; however, it is noticeable that within the *Handbook of Personality Disorders* (Livesley, 2001) the therapeutic community (TC) approach is not included in the range of therapies described in the book as offering effective treatment for this group. This is an unfortunate omission as there are good theoretical and empirical reasons to support the TC approach as an overarching model with working for personality disorder. Some of the main reasons are described below:

- Therapeutic communities have well-established processes to contain and manage the characteristic difficulties presented by this group. For example, the use of emergency therapeutic meetings to contain the crisis states that personality-disordered patients often present during treatment. Staff support groups are also well established in most therapeutic communities to help staff deal with the emotional pressures of working with personality-disordered patients. The culture of 'taking issues to groups' rather than to individuals in the team helps militate against splitting dynamics. All these, and other processes, have evolved out of a long clinical tradition of working with patients with severe personality and mental health problems.
- Therapeutic communities work within a holistic model in which interactions across a range of different settings (small groups, community meetings, specific therapies, and communal activities) can be a focus for therapy. The richness of therapeutic material generated by this approach is, in the author's view, far greater than that found in therapies that just work in one therapeutic modality.
- There is a strong emphasis on the therapy relationship as a focus for change, which is supported by the empirical literature on effectiveness in psychotherapy generally.
- Prison therapeutic communities are accredited by the Correctional Services Accreditation Panel and have standards for training, monitoring, evaluation and focusing on criminogenic risk factors. In addition, most therapeutic communities (forensic and non-forensic) are audited through a peer review body, the Community of Communities, aligned to the Royal College of Psychiatrists.
- Although there have been few randomised control trials, which has attracted criticism, for example Rutter and Tyrer (2003), both forensic and non-forensic therapeutic communities have conducted a considerable amount of research demonstrating their efficacy in managing disturbed populations and leading to changes in functioning and improved mental health following treatment, although the evidence from reconviction studies is mixed (Manning, 2005; Shine, 2001b).

However, although there are many positive features of the democratic TC model there are difficulties in adopting this in its pure form to DSPD populations; some of the main difficulties are presented below:

- Traditional therapeutic communities for forensic populations have relatively high attrition rates, for example at HMP Grendon around half of all admissions fail to complete 18 months or more of therapy, the period when clinically significant change usually occurs. High attrition is marked for men with severe substance misuse and personality characteristics that are associated with DSPD populations, such as outwardly directed hostility and psychoticism (Shine, 2001a).
- Many TCs have a strict line prohibiting the use of psychotropic medication based on the view that this will contribute to the patient or prisoner seeking symptomatic relief rather than engaging with psychological therapies (Cartwright & Gordon, 2007).
- Standard TC therapy groups may not meet the specific needs of personality-disordered offenders, many of whom have a wide range of co-morbid Axis 1 disorders and specific criminogenic needs such as substance misuse and deviant sexual fantasy.
- Several studies have shown that psychopathic offenders present particular difficulties in therapeutic communities resulting in problems in terms of therapeutic management. One study by Harris *et al.* (1991) found that psychopaths treated in a high secure therapeutic community in Canada had higher reconviction rates than would have been expected, although there are many differences between this model and that offered within contemporary forensic TCs (see, for example, Shuker, chapter 7 of this edition).
- Traditional democratic therapeutic communities have also been criticised for failing to offer choice and flexibility to residents and for not differentiating clearly enough the types of clients that benefit from this approach (Rutter & Tyrer, 2003). This is not in keeping with contemporary approaches to the treatment of mental disorders based on specific evidence-based therapies for recognised clinical conditions.

These reasons suggest that the traditional democratic model is probably not sufficient to work with DSPD populations, which are characterised by multiple problems and high risk of recidivism. The experimental nature of these units also offers an opportunity to develop innovative approaches to treatment not bound by the constraints of existing models of practice. The adapted therapeutic community approach at Millfields offers an integrated approach to therapy, including pharmacological treatment and includes a range of psychological therapies according to need. The model retains key aspects of the therapeutic community approach such as community meetings and small groups but modifies these in some respects, for example the role of democracy in patient decision-making is constrained by the nature of detention under the Mental Health Act. These procedures allow for

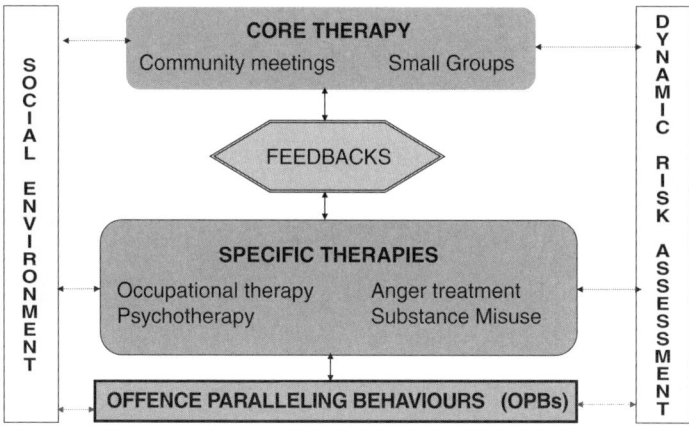

Figure 5.2 Model of the Millfields Adapted Forensic Therapeutic Community

greater provision to work with acting out behaviour of the type that often leads to early termination of treatment in other forensic therapeutic communities.

A diagram of the model in practice is shown in figure 5.2. The core therapies, small groups and community meetings are defined by all members of the community attending on a regular basis. Specific therapies as described above are available according to need. All these therapies are fed back through regular feedback sessions. The social environment, or therapeutic milieu, is all the interactions that take place outside of therapy groups. The therapeutic community environment is designed to maximise opportunities for social interaction; in this environment the patterns of behaviour and relating that underpinned a patient's offending behaviour can be evoked and provide a focus for therapy and dynamic risk assessment through observation and assessment of offence-parallelling behaviour (Morris, 2004; Shine & Morris, 2000).

Synthesis – a Neglected Concept in the Treatment of Personality Disorder

The above model shows the elements of the adapted therapeutic community model at Millfields Personality Disorder Unit. The issue of how the therapeutic elements connect to each other is, arguably, more important in this context than the elements themselves. The reasons, in the author's view, are primarily to do with the assessment of clinically valid and reliable change in patients for whom this is notoriously difficult. The adapted therapeutic community model offers an opportunity for the enduring problems of personality-disordered patients to be understood at different levels.

For example, consider the case of a patient with anger control problems. As figure 5.2 shows, each of the elements is connected through bi-directional arrows illustrating how problem behaviour can be addressed in each element. In the case of anger control problems, these will be shown within the social environment in terms of interactions between patients and between patients and staff. These in turn can be brought to the community meetings and discussed openly in a safe environment based on group rules that are identified, and regulated if the model is working properly, by the patients themselves. In turn, the issues identified can be worked on at a deeper level of understanding of the underlying beliefs that underpin anger and aggression. Specific anger control and skills-based groups can help equip the patient with skills such as assertiveness, challenging automatic thoughts and internalised rules that govern aggressive behaviours, for example, 'I must never be mugged off' (humiliated or shamed by another person). These can then be practised and reinforced within the social environment and in the other therapeutic activities of the unit.

The model therefore works on the principle of skills generalisation. As Kohlenberg and Tsai (2007) point out: 'Therapy is ineffective if the client improves in the therapy environment, but the gains do not transfer to daily life.' This principle is, in the author's view, critical to measuring change in forensic clients, many of who are skilled in detection evasion (Daffern *et al.*, 2007) and engage in processes associated with psychopathy such as duping delight or the creation of illusory therapeutic alliances. Therapeutic communities, such as Millfields, offer the opportunity to test whether skills learnt in therapy are being generalised on a consistent basis, rather than just in the environment of the therapy room. Interestingly, the need to adopt a holistic model of working with severe personality disorder, rather than focusing primarily on a clients therapy group behaviour, was one of the main learning points identified in the review of a DSPD Forensic Personality Disorder Unit in the first two years (Clark & Ndegwa, 2006).

The important point about the TC approach is that the deliberate creation of a social environment to maximise social interaction generates opportunities for these interactions to occur naturally and thus provide a focus for therapeutic intervention. As Genders and Player (1995) highlighted in their seminal review of Grendon prison, the emphasis of the therapy is *social analysis*. For this to be effective, however, it is important that staff have a shared approach to the assessment and formulation of patients' clinical needs and treatment aims. This requires a detailed functional analysis of offending behaviour and staff training to highlight the awareness of each patient's personality disorder, offending and treatment needs. Of particular importance is how patterns of attachment and offending behaviour may be paralleled in the therapeutic environment (Morris, 2004; Shine & Morris, 2000). The model would be seriously undermined if, for example, evidence of offence-paralleling behaviour or other types of antisocial activity was neglected in favour of assessments of progress based on therapy sessions alone. For effective change to occur it is important that patients show evidence of generalisation of skills across different situations, and across time periods related to the severity of the persistence and gravity of the risk behaviour being treated (Wong & Gordon, 2000). In this way, clinical staff may have more confidence that patients or prisoners are 'walking the talk' rather than just 'talking the talk' of therapy.

Appendix 1 – Structured Assessments Used in the Common Dataset

1.   **Violence**
1.1   **The Violence Risk Scale (VRS).** Wong, S. & Gordon, A. (1999, 2000). *Violence Risk Scale (VRS)*. Saskatoon, Saskatchewan: Regional Psychiatric Centre.
1.2   **The Historical and Clinical Risk Scale (HCR-20).** Webster, C., Douglas, K., Eaves, D. & Hart, S. (1995). *HCR-20 Assessing Risk for Violence (Version 2)*. Vancouver: Simon Fraser University.
2.   **Sexual Offending**
2.1   **Static 99.** Hanson, R. K. & Thornton, D. M. (1999). *Static 99: Improving Actuarial Risk Assessments for Sex Offenders*. Ottawa, Canada: Public Works and Government Services Canada.
2.2   **Risk Matrix 2000.** Thornton, D., Mann, R., Webster, S., Blud, L., Travers, R., Friendship, C. *et al.* (2003). Distinguishing and combining risks for sexual and violent recidivism. In R.A. Prentky, E.S. Janus & M.C. Seto (Eds.) Sexually Coercive Behaviour: Understanding and Management. *Annals of the New York Academy of Sciences, 989*, 225–235.
2.3   **Violence Risk Scale – Sex Offender Version.** Wong, S. C. P., Olver, M. E., Nicholaichuk, T. P. & Gordon, A. E. (2003). *The Violence Risk Scale-Sexual Offender version (VRS-SO)*. Saskatoon, Saskatchewan: Regional Psychiatric Centre and University of Saskatchewan.

3.   **Personality Disorder**

3.1   **The Psychopathy Checklist – Revised (PCL-R).** Hare, R. D. (2003). *The Psychopathy Checklist – Revised, 2nd edition (PCL-R).* Toronto: Multi-Health Systems.

3.2   **International Personality Disorder Examination (IPDE).** Loranger, A. W. (1999). *International Personality Disorder Examination (IPDE): DSM-IV and ICD-10 Interviews.* Odessa, Florida: Psychological Assessment Resources, Inc.

4.   **Mental Disorder**

4.1   **Structured Clinical Interview for DSM-IV Axis I Disorders (SCID-I).** First, M., Spitzer, R., Gibson, M. & Williams, J. (1997). *Structured Clinical Interview for DSM-IV Axis I Disorders (SCID-I).* Washington, DC: American Psychiatric Press, Inc.

5.   **Cognitive Functioning**

5.1   **Wechsler Adult Intelligence Scale.** Wechsler, D. (1997). *Wechsler Adult Intelligence Scale, 3rd edition (WAIS-III).* San Antonio, TX: The Psychological Corporation.

6.   **Millfields Specific Assessments**

6.1   **State-Trait Anger Expression Inventory-2 (STAXI-2).** Spielberger, C. (1999). *State-Trait Anger Expression Inventory-2 (STAXI-2).* Florida: Psychological Assessment Resources, Inc.

6.2   **Personality Assessment Inventory (PAI).** Morey, L. (1991). *Personality Assessment Inventory (PAI).* Florida: Psychological Assessment Resources, Inc.

6.3   **Symptom Checklist-90-R (SCL-90-R).** Derogatis, L. (1994). *Symptom Checklist-90-R (SCL-90-R).* Minneapolis: NCS Pearson, Inc.

6.4   **Paulhaus Deception Scales (PDS).** Paulhaus, D. (1998). *Paulhaus Deception Scales (PDS).* Toronto, Ontario: Multi-Health Systems Inc.

6.5   **The Psychological Inventory of Criminal Thinking Styles (PICTS).** Walters, G. (2006). *The Psychological Inventory of Criminal Thinking Styles (PICTS).* Allentown: Centre for Lifestyle Studies.

6.6   **The Multiphasic Sex Inventory (MSI).** Nichols, H. (2007). *The Multiphasic Sex Inventory (MSI).* Tacoma, WA: Nichols & Molinder Assessments, Inc.

6.7   **The Basic Empathy Scale (BES).** Jolliffe, D. & Farrington, D. (2006). Development and validation of the Basic Empathy Scale. *Journal of Adolescence, 29,* 589–611.

6.8   **Treatment Motivation Questionnaire (TMQ).** Ryan, R.M., Plant, R.W. & O'Malley, S. (1995). Initial motivations for alcohol treatment: relations with patient characteristics, treatment involvement and dropout. *Addictive Behaviours, 20,* 279–297.

References

American Psychiatric Association (2000). *Diagnostic and Statistical Manual of Mental Disorders, 4th edition, revised.* Washington, DC: American Psychiatric Association.

British Psychological Society (2006). *Understanding Personality Disorder. A Professional Practice Report.* The British Psychological Society, St Andrews House, 48 Princess Road East, Leicester, LE1 7DR. www.bps.org.uk

Cartwright J. & Gordon, H. (2007). Beyond the 'Quick Fix': The role of medication in readiness for psychological treatment of severe personality disorder. In E. Sullivan and R. Shuker (Eds) *Issues in Forensic Psychology*, No. 7, pp. 55–61.

Clark, A. & Ndegwa, D. (2006). Forensic personality disorder in an MSU: lessons learnt after two years. *British Journal of Forensic Practice*, 8 (4), 29–33.

Daffern, M., Jones, L., Howells, K., Shine, J., Mikton, C. & Tunbridge, V. (2007). Editorial – Refining the definition of offence paralleling behaviour. *Criminal Behaviour and Mental Health*, 17, 265–273.

Dyer, C. (2006). Better care for Michael Stone might still not have prevented the killings. *British Medical Journal*, 333, 670.

East London and City Mental Health Trust (2005). *Philosophy of Care: A Forensic Therapeutic Community.* Unpublished paper. Available from: The Millfields Unit, Centre for Forensic Mental Health, 12 Kenworthy Road, Hackney, London, E9 5TD.

Genders, E. & Player, E. (1995). *Grendon: A Study of a Therapeutic Prison.* Oxford: Clarendon Press.

Giesen-Bloo, J., Van Dyck, R., Spinhoven, P., Van Tilberg, W., Dirkson, C., Van Asselet, T. *et al.* (2006). Outpatient psychotherapy for borderline personality disorder. *Archives of General Psychiatry*, 203, 649–658.

Hare, R. (2003). *The Hare Psychopathy Checklist – Revised* (2nd edn). Toronto, Ontario: Multi-Health Systems.

Harris, G., Rice, M.E. & Cormier, C.A. (1991). Psychopathy and violent recidivism. *Law and Human Behaviour*, 15, 625–637.

Hobson, J., Shine, J., & Roberts, R. (2000). How do psychopaths behave in a therapeutic community? *Psychology, Crime and Law*, 6, 139–154.

HM Prison Service (2007). *Training Manual for Democratic Therapeutic Communities.* London: Home Office Publications.

Home Office (1999). *Managing Dangerous People with Severe Personality Disorder: Proposals for Policy Development, July 1999.* www.dspdprogramme.gov.uk/media/pdfs/Proposals_for_Policy_Development.pdf

Kennard, D. (1998). Review of 'Therapeutic Communities for Offenders'. *Therapeutic Communities*, 19 (4), 331–332.

Kohlenberg, R.J. & Tsai, M. (2007). *Functional Analytical Therapy.* New York: Plenum.

Lambert, M.J. (1992). Psychotherapy outcome research: Implications for integrative and eclectic therapists. In J.C. Norcroft & M.R. Goldfried (Eds), *Handbook of Psychotherapy and Behaviour Change* (4th edition, 143–189). New York: Wiley.

Livesley, W.J. (2001). A framework for an integrated approach to treatment. In W.J. Livesley (Ed.) *Handbook of Personality Disorders: Theory, Research and Treatment*. New York: Guilford Press.

Manning, N.P. (2005). Does the therapeutic community work? The politics of knowledge. *Therapeutic Communities, 26* (4), 385–396.

Meloy, R. (1994). *The Psychopathic Mind*. Northvale, NJ: Aronson.

Ministry of Justice and Department of Health (2005). *Dangerous and Severe Personality Disorder (DSPD) Planning and Delivery Guide for High Secure Services for Men*. www.dspdprogramme.gov.uk

Morris, M. (2004). *Dangerous and Severe: Process, Programme, and Person: Grandson's Work*. London: Jessica Kingsley.

Ogloff, J.P.R., Wong, S. & Greenwood, A. (1990). Treating criminal psychopaths in a therapeutic community programme. *Behaviour, Science and the Law, 8,* 81–90.

Rutter, D. & Tyrer, P. (2003). The value of therapeutic communities in the treatment of personality disorder: a suitable place for treatment? *Journal of Practical Psychiatry and Behaviour, 9* (4), 291–302.

Shine, J. (2001a). Characteristics of inmates admitted to Grendon Therapeutic Prison and their relationships to length of stay. *International Journal of Offender Therapy and Comparative Criminology, 45* (2), 252–265.

Shine, J. (2001b). *A Compilation of Grendon Research*. Leyhill Press. Available from Psychology Unit, HMP Grendon, Grendon Underwood, Aylesbury, Bucks, HP18 0TL.

Shine, J. & Morris, M. (2000). Addressing criminogenic needs in a prison therapeutic community. *Therapeutic Communities, 21* (3), 197–218.

Shine J. & Newton, M. (2001). Damaged, disturbed and dangerous, a description of the Grendon Prison population. In J. Shine (Ed.) *A Compilation of Grendon Research*. Leyhill Press.

Viding, E., Blair, J., Moffitt, T. & Plomin, R. (2005). Evidence for a substantial genetic risk for psychopathy in 7-year olds. *Journal of Child Psychology and Psychiatry, 46* (6), 592–597.

Wong, S. & Gordon, A. (2000). *The Violence Risk Scale*. Research Unit, Regional Psychiatric Centre, P.O. Box 9243, Saskatoon, Saskatchewan, Canada, S7K 3X5.

Part II
Practice

Chapter 6

Putting Principles into Practice: The Therapeutic Community Regime at HMP Grendon and its Relationship with the 'Good Lives' Model

Michael Brookes

Introduction

Stevens (2009), in chapter 1, has provided an overview of therapeutic communities and outlined the history and development of HMP Grendon. Shuker (2009), in chapter 7, sets out the guiding principles of democratic therapeutic communities, describes how a therapeutic culture is established and explains the theoretical underpinnings of therapeutic communities.

This chapter seeks to complement those of Stevens and of Shuker and will describe how the regime at HMP Grendon operates and the process by which treatment needs are addressed. It will also provide an account of how the Good Lives Model (Ward, 2002) goals are met.

Factors Informing the Therapeutic Community Regime

In his classic work, based on his research at the Henderson Hospital, Rapoport (1960) established the characteristic features of a therapeutic community (see Stevens, this volume). Kennard (1998) determined that some

Grendon and the Emergence of Forensic Therapeutic Communities: Developments in Research and Practice
Edited by Richard Shuker and Elizabeth Sullivan
© 2010 John Wiley & Sons, Ltd.

of the defining characteristics of therapeutic communities are that a group of people who live together or meet together regularly:

- participate together in a range of purposeful tasks, therapeutic, domestic, organisational, educational;
- strive for non-hierarchical relationships where there is frequent sharing of information between all members of the group;
- with a shared commitment to the goal of learning from the experience of living and/or working together (a living learning situation);
- alongside a joint commitment to open examination and resolution of problems, tensions and conflicts within the group (culture of enquiry);
- that is theoretically informed by bringing a psychodynamic awareness of individual and group process to bear on this examination;
- all of which requires a clear set of boundaries concerning time, place and roles within which the above can take place.

These attributes position therapeutic communities as providing a distinctive environment, especially within custodial establishments, in which therapeutic interventions can take place. Essential factors in all therapeutic communities are the development of a communal atmosphere, the importance of group meetings and the sharing between staff and residents of the responsibility for the maintenance and running of the community. Indeed, it is establishing a residential community with a therapeutic exploratory ethos that leads to the effectiveness of the treatment being increased. This is because it 'becomes a culture that is lived, rather than a group that is attended' (Morris, 2004).

Maxwell Jones, who founded and operated the most famous therapeutic community at Belmont Hospital, which then became the Henderson Hospital, considered that what is required for change to occur are (a) people who are motivated to change or grow; (b) the presence of a facilitator with skilled neutral leadership; (c) the creation of a group setting or milieu where those people can communicate openly and freely together leading to an appropriate level of feeling with one another; (d) face-to-face confrontation occurring around an individual or more general problem area; and (e) timing of interventions (cited by Briggs, 2005).

It is within therapeutic communities that these personal change conditions are most clearly met. The selection criteria for residents focuses on their motivation to engage in therapy, while for staff it is an ability to suspend immediate judgement and to encourage residents to share previously undeclared aspects of their lives. This takes place in a group or community meeting setting with the immediacy of recent events providing an effective means of exploring deeper rooted concerns or patterns of behaviour.

The therapeutic potency is enhanced because each member of the community shares in decision making about community affairs. It means they can express their views and opinions and that members tolerate distressed or antagonistic behaviour by other residents when this is expressed within a therapeutic context. Community members working together and supporting each other in all aspects of community life increases the strength of their relationship with one another. Through being challenged when their actions and behaviour impact on others and why this is so, community members gain a greater insight and understanding of their own behaviour. The processes of interpersonal feedback and personal accountability make residents more aware of the consequences of their actions.

Accordingly, in a therapeutic community environment, it is fellow residents who often provide the strongest challenges to other residents. This is because they may have often lived similar lives. Consequently, their challenges carry greater strength and validity. It is in therapeutic communities that the therapeutic capabilities of the client group are best utilised, where the environment is structured in such a way as to establish a sense of shared aim and to facilitate the participation of the clients. Residents then do much of the therapeutic work, with the staff role being to facilitate that process.

Morris (2004) considers there is an argument that:

> ... this sort of therapeutic set-up is the most effective way of delivering psychodynamic treatment to a severely personality disordered population. It is more effective because it increases the intensity and dose of the treatment. With the deeply ingrained maladaptive patterns that comprise this group's personality disorder, high intensity, high dose treatment is required. (p. 36)

The Regime at HMP Grendon and the Therapeutic Process

At HMP Grendon, every weekday morning residents attend either a community meeting or a small therapy group. Community meetings are held on Mondays and Fridays and last, on the majority of the communities, for an hour and a half. They are attended by residents, all available staff on duty (operational and non-operational) and the chaplain with specific responsibility for that community. Also, during the month, the art therapist, that community's education liaison officer and other senior managers will attend the community meeting. Given the number of therapeutic communities at Grendon it is not possible for a senior manager to be present at every meeting.

In the community meetings, all aspects of community life are subject to discussion and community voting. This includes paid work (cleaning, education, cooking) or rep jobs (healthcare, catering, gym). Rep jobs are when representatives from each of HMP Grendon's six communities meet with staff that work in or are responsible for a particular area to discuss issues and concerns, or to clarify operating procedures. The reps are as responsible as the members of staff for determining the agenda of each meeting.

At HMP Grendon there is also a twice-monthly 'interwing', when 'interwing' reps have the opportunity to ask senior operational and non-operational (specialist) managers, residential and security principal officers, specific questions from the community. These should be related to matters which cannot be addressed by other meetings (e.g. the 'privileges committee' for items that can be purchased from the 'prison shop') but which are of concern to residents. This is particularly important when a prison-wide decision has had to be made centrally. The 'interwing' provides a forum where senior managers can be asked about that decision and an explanation provided.

In the thrice-weekly small groups, every facet of a resident's life is considered and discussed: offences, family backgrounds, early life (childhood and adolescence) experiences including those of abuse (physical, emotional, psychological and sexual). School histories and, if residents have been in work or married, are also considered. Discussed as well are incidents residents have been involved in, or outbursts of behaviours displayed, which caused them, other residents or staff discomfort. The more recent these events are, then the greater the opportunity for thoroughly exploring what actually occurred, cognitions and feelings at the time. This then provides the opportunity for considering how the next time a similar situation occurs, it could be handled better. Offence paralleling behaviour is anticipated and examined when it occurs.

Also considered within the small groups is the impact of offences on victims and those associated with the victim (for example, their family). One of the most distressing times for residents is when they begin to fully realise and acknowledge the hurt and harm they have actually caused to others.

The discussions that take place in the small groups are then fed back to both resident and staff groups. This is with a view to everyone within the community having knowledge of areas and issues that are being discussed and the progress that is being made in therapy.

Therapeutic work at Grendon is based on the totality of what happens within the prison. What occurs in the workplace, in education and the gym, and on the landings is open to analysis and discussion. These discussions take place in the small therapy groups and in community meetings with the other prisoners and staff who live and work together on that wing, not in a place away from the wing and with others who are not part of that community. So, therapy at Grendon does not occur in isolation from what is happening in the rest of the prison, rather every aspect of prison life is an integral component within the therapeutic community environment that is HMP Grendon.

Staff and the Therapeutic Community Regime

Being a series of therapeutic communities and with its unique regime based on therapy, the therapeutic process at HMP Grendon is embedded in the way that the establishment functions. This impacts on and influences the actions of all staff, of whatever grade or profession. It holds not only for those who form part of the community staff teams: therapists, psychologists and uniformed prison officers, but also those who form part of the security or works departments, those who are chaplains, teachers, physical education instructors or caterers, those who work in the healthcare centre and those who are administrators.

Amongst the whole staff team there is the recognition that they need to adapt the way they worked previously to the demands of an establishment whose *raison d'être* is therapy. Staff have to be sensitive to the fact that they cannot resolve issues in the way that they used to, and that they have to take account of what it means to work in a therapeutic community environment. Members of staff therefore have to be prepared to engage with the community in a way in which staff in other prison establishments would not seek to engage with prisoners. It means that consultation and involving the community is of primary importance. This is as true for the prison governor as it is for everybody else. They too have to 'learn ways and means of overcoming traditional rivalries by developing procedures characterised by consultation and working together' (Bennett, 2007, p. 211).

Similarly, Leggett and Hirons (2007), Prison Service operational managers who were at one point responsible for security at Grendon, have written:

> The basic principles of the democratic TC allow the residents, through their agreed meeting and decision-making structure, to influence and change the way they interact within set boundaries. In a prison environment, the areas over which the Community can have legitimate influence are significantly reduced because of security constraints, some of which are mandatory.

Unless sensitively managed, this can lead to conflict between those responsible for managing the TC and those responsible for maintaining security. (p. 233)

The operational staff on each community consists of two senior officers and twelve main grade prison officers. The non-operational staff comprises a wing therapist, a psychologist and a group facilitator. Together they provide at least one member of staff to each of the five small groups, which are held on Tuesday, Wednesday and Thursday mornings, with the average number of residents per group being eight.

The role of prison officers is key to the therapeutic effectiveness of HMP Grendon. Their particular and unique role has been described by Coltman (2004) as one where:

We staff, a collection of the experienced and inexperienced, with frequent staffing shortages, ask these men to attend a difficult alien experience, namely to attend groups, lower walls built up by years of abuse and self-abuse and to speak their truth – or partial truth – and understanding about their most humiliating and degrading experiences. In short, not only to lose the masks that we all wear, but also to lose the deeply ingrained mask of the long-term criminal, so that collectively each can help the other to address problems and obtain relief … we are asking them to learn to trust prison officers – authority figures, bearing in mind that their experiences with authority figures from the past (parents, abusers, children's home workers), not forgetting physical fights with prison officers (almost all have had numerous prison sentences), have often been disastrous. (p. 145)

Kennard (1998) has set out the various important roles staff have within therapeutic communities. These include:

- participating oneself as a member of the community;
- preserving the boundaries necessary for the community to be therapeutic;
- modelling desired behaviour, provision of learning experiences;
- using therapeutic interventions in groups;
- encouraging explanation of the meaning of behaviour;
- attending to the dynamics of the community, in particular, where processes destructive of the community as a learning environment may arise;
- attending to one's own emotional involvement; and
- being able to describe and explain the community.

With staff being cognisant of the need to include the community, as far as is possible, in discussions that affect residents, a process has been created in which residents can feel part of the wider discussions that take place in the establishment. Indeed, on occasions, residents have submitted, on paper and through attendance, proposals to the monthly Therapy Policy meeting. These have concerned setting up a group for determinate sentence prisoners, similar to that which existed for indeterminate sentence prisoners, or for the Incentive and Earned Privilege scheme not to apply to 'in therapy' men on a particular wing.

The Good Lives Model

McAdams (1994) is of the view that personality should be understood as involving three levels or domains: traits, personal strivings and self-narratives. Traits may be difficult to change, with the other two being more susceptible and amenable to psychological intervention. Personal strivings express the sense of who we are and what we would like to become (Emmons, 1986). Narrative identity, the construction and reconstruction of this narrative, integrating one's perceived past, present and anticipated future, is itself the process of identity development in adulthood. These self-narratives then act to shape and guide future behaviour, as persons act in ways that agree with the stories or myths they have created about themselves (Bruner, 1986; McAdams, 1985, 2006). There is growing evidence from research in criminology and criminological psychology that development at this level of personality is a facilitative condition for desisting from offending (Ward & Maruna, 2007). In his research with offenders, Maruna (2001) found that individuals needed to establish an alternative, coherent and pro-social self-identity in order to justify and maintain their desistance from crime.

Michalak and Grosse Holtforth (2006) have considered that what gives purpose, structure and meaning to life are personal goals. When goals meet an individual's explicit and implicit needs, where these are achievable and where there is commitment to goal attainment, it is likely that well-being will be experienced.

However, over the past two decades, the reducing re-offending emphasis has tended to focus on the risk-needs-responsivity (RNR) model (Andrews & Bonta, 2003; Andrews *et al.*, 2006). The risk principle asserts that criminal behaviour can be reliably predicted and that treatment should focus on the higher risk offenders; the need principle highlights the importance of criminogenic needs in the design and delivery of treatment; while the responsivity principle describes how the treatment should be provided.

This model has been criticised because of the focus on the offenders' deficits (Lynch, 2006; Ward *et al.*, 2007). Consequently, more recent approaches have emphasised a strengths-based approach (Maruna & LeBel, 2003; Ward & Gannon, 2006) for it has been found that motivating correctional clients and creating a sound therapeutic alliance are pivotal components of effective treatment (McMurran, 2002). Similarly, working collaboratively with clients in developing treatment goals results in a stronger therapeutic alliance (Mann & Shingler, 2006). Additionally, therapist features such as displays of empathy, warmth and encouragement facilitate the change process (Marshall *et al.*, 2003).

When interviewing 129 convicted adult male prisoners, McMurran *et al.* (2008) found that a range of positive, anti-criminal goals were expressed, including stopping offending, improving self-control, finding and keeping jobs, having stable accommodation, quitting drink and drugs, changing support networks and finding new leisure pursuits. Furthermore, prisoners expressed life-enhancing goals such as improving their lifestyle, gaining work experience, having good family relationships, gaining skills, and getting fit and healthy.

The Good Lives Model (Ward & Brown, 2004; Ward & Marshall, 2004; Ward & Stewart, 2003) was formulated as an alternative to correctional treatment based on the RNR approach. The model was devised by Ward and colleagues to integrate aspects of treatment not dealt with well by the RNR perspective, such as the formulation of a therapeutic alliance and motivating individuals to engage in the difficult process of changing their lives.

Underpinning the Good Lives Model is the assumption that offenders are essentially human beings with similar needs and aspirations to non-offending members of the community. It is based around two core therapeutic goals: to promote human goods (aspects of life that bring satisfaction and meaning) and to reduce risk. The Good Lives Model is an approach based on the pursuit of a better life, ways of living that are constructed around core values and concrete means of realising goals. There is a focus on the promotion of specific goods or goals that are likely to automatically eliminate (or reduce) commonly targeted dynamic risk factors (or criminogenic needs). By proceeding in this manner, individuals do not need to abandon those things that are important to them, only to learn to acquire them differently. In the Good Lives Model, crime and psychological problems are hypothesized to be a direct consequence of maladaptive attempts to meet human needs (Ward & Steward, op. cit.).

The Good Lives Model of offender rehabilitation then, is a strength-based approach that seeks to ensure primary human goods (goals) are attained in socially acceptable and personally meaningful ways. It is concerned with the enhancement of offenders' capabilities in order to improve the quality of their life and, in so doing, reduce their chances of committing further crimes when they are released. The issue of treatment responsibility is an important component within the Good Lives Model, as is the offender's motivation to change.

Provided by the Good Lives Model is a framework for intervening therapeutically with individuals of all types. This applies to sex offenders (Ward *et al.*, 2007a) and non-sexual offenders (Whitehead *et al.*, 2007). Being a positive model, based on the assumption that offenders want to embrace positive change and personal development, treatment objectives are based on creating new skills and capabilities within the context of individuals' life plans. They aim to encourage fulfilment through the achievement of human goods.

Ward and Maruna (2007) considered that psychological, social, biological and anthropological research evidence supports the existence of at least 10 groups of primary human goods:

(i)   Life (including healthy living and physical functioning);
(ii)   Knowledge;
(ii)   Excellence in play and work (including mastery experiences);
(iv)   Agency (includes autonomy and self directedness);
(v)   Inner peace (freedom from emotional turmoil and stress);
(vi)   Friendship (including intimate, romantic and family relationships);
(vii)   Community;
(viii) Spirituality (in the broad sense of finding meaning and purpose in life);
(ix)   Happiness; and
(x)   Creativity.

Prison-based therapeutic communities provide an ideal environment in which these good lives goals can be achieved. Some of these goals can be provided within other prison establishments, but it is the holistic treatment environment of therapeutic communities that provides a setting in which all these goals can be achieved and integrated at the same time.

For as 'Martin' is recorded as saying in the *Guardian* newspaper (7 May 2008): 'Things changed for me after spending time in Grendon … if you want to break the cycle you have to show the kindness, that's what has helped me'. Risk-needs-responsivity issues can also be addressed within the richness of the therapeutic community environment. At HMP Grendon this occurs during the six-monthly therapy assessments and annual reviews, when sentence-planning targets are considered and integrated into the treatment targets. Addressing these targets provides the platform for many of the discussions that take place within the small therapy groups. How this process works and its effectiveness has been described by Jones (1997), Shine and Morris (2000), Jones and Shuker (2004) and Shuker and Jones (2007).

Attainment of the Good Lives Goals Within HMP Grendon

Within all prisons there are opportunities for prisoners to be physically cared for in respect of diet, accommodation, access to healthcare, exercise, education, religious 'services' and meetings, and gym. This assists in the meeting of the life, knowledge, excellence and spirituality good lives goals. However, at HMP Grendon prisoners also have the prospect of achieving the other good lives goals in a way that is not possible in other prison environments: Grendon provides opportunities for dialogue, discussion and debate. This involvement fosters a sense of responsibility, and enables Grendon men to have greater ownership over their lives. It is a process that importantly allows creativity to develop.

For those prisoners who chose to apply for a place at Grendon, it is what happens throughout their stay at Grendon that impacts on and changes their lives, and that process starts as soon as men arrive:

> *I got off the bus and was greeted by my first name. Staff brought my stuff over. I was put in the office and introduced. It seemed weird – I was given a key! I was nervous but excited, felt I was made welcome. ... invited to sit next to an officer in the office.*

and:

> *It was different – mind blowing! It was 'My name's so and so, What's yours!' ... Then they shook hands and gave me tea.* (Sullivan, 2007, p. 28)

The approach of staff at HMP Grendon helps facilitate the good lives goals of friendship, community and happiness. It assists with the development of inner peace, which is one of the words used by men in exit interviews to describe the impact that Grendon has had upon them. Other words used were 'trust', 'respect', 'insight' (into self and others), 'pride in achievement', 'relationships', 'balance', 'strength' (mental health), 'self-worth', 'sense of belonging', 'sense of achievement', 'a voice' and 'attachments – to staff'. For, as one resident said of staff: 'How they interact with inmates, their honesty, care, not taking sides, respect they show. They're the crucial components of success' (Sullivan, 2007).

In her interviews with prisoners at HMP Grendon, Rivlin (2007) found a similar assessment of staff. As one prisoner said to her: 'The staff are very different here because they actually care about the inmates – they don't just want to bang you up, they want to see why you've got your problems or how to overcome your problems and support you.' (p. 37.)

With regard to prisoner–prisoner relationships, Rivlin (2007) considered that while 'inmates very rarely admitted to having friends in prison and although in Grendon 'friendship' was a closely guarded term, inmates did confess to having formed 'positive relationships' with the other men on the wing' (see also chapter 16, this volume).

The development of relationships with family members is another key feature of prison therapeutic communities. As a prisoner told Sullivan (2007): 'We have family days when we put on a meal, family can see your cell, we play bingo. It's a very positive part' and 'Family day is excellent, it blows my family away' (p. 29).

Prisoners also indicated to Rivlin (2007) that they had greater contact with their social support group than would otherwise be possible in the wider prison estate through the family and children's days and social evenings that were held at Grendon. Rivlin also found that Grendon men experienced companionship, a safe environment, had lower levels of boredom and had a positive vision of the future. They also had hope, and felt empowered with more control over their life path.

As one prisoner said to Sullivan (2007): 'It has allowed me to grow up emotionally. I have a better understanding of who I am and of the consequences of my actions and the victims I create. I am responsible for the decisions I make.' (p. 31.)

The attainment of good lives goals is interwoven with the way that HMP Grendon functions. Through the processes that operate and the opportunity men have to make decisions that affect what happens within the community, they gain the goal of agency through being held to account and made responsible for their actions. They are expected to take the lead in bringing issues to their small groups. They also feed back during community meetings what took place during group specials and in art therapy and psychodrama sessions. Key also to this is the fact that it is a resident who chairs the community meetings, which both staff and residents attend.

Conclusion

HMP Grendon, as a prison with five therapeutic communities and an assessment and induction unit, provides a regime that is based on the development of safe, secure and open relationships. It also cultivates a culture of belonging, participation, empowerment, democratisation and reality confrontation. For it is by staff and residents sharing the responsibility for the maintenance, running and therapeutic functioning of the community that the impact and effectiveness of the treatment is increased. This process is further enhanced because what occurs in the work place, in education and the gym, and on the landings can be brought into the therapeutic space, open to analysis and discussion. It means that recent events can be addressed promptly and all the implications and ramifications explored – particularly if it parallels individual residents' offending behaviour.

Treatment targets within HMP Grendon can focus both on risk factors and on gaining life goals including work, education and improved social functioning. The integration of therapy assessments and the sentence planning process means that both criminogenic needs and resettlement objectives can be identified and then addressed through the therapeutic process. It is within the therapeutic communities that risk-needs-responsivity factors can be identified and met alongside good lives goals.

As men apply for a place at HMP Grendon they are motivated to begin the process of addressing deficit areas in their lives. They want, at some level, to improve their sense of self-worth, to achieve personal goals, to desist from offending and to gain new skills to ensure that their life on release is more successful than the last occasion they were in society. The way in which therapeutic communities operate means that there is an emphasis on improving each resident's self-identity and providing purpose, structure and meaning to life. This is assisted by the development of a strong therapeutic alliance between staff and residents and through both staff and residents displaying empathy, warmth, and encouragement.

HMP Grendon, as a series of therapeutic communities, is also a place where prisoners can obtain primary human goods (goals) in socially acceptable and personally meaningful ways. It is concerned with the enhancement of offenders' capabilities in order to improve the quality of their life and, in so doing, reduce their chances of committing further crimes when they are released.

The attainment of good lives goals is interwoven with the way that HMP Grendon operates. As in most prisons, life, knowledge, excellence and spirituality good lives goals are met through the meeting of dietary, accommodation, health, fitness, learning and religious needs. But at HMP Grendon prisoners also have the opportunity to achieve the other good lives goals in a way that is not possible in the majority of other prison environments; there are greater openings for prisoners to be creative, to experience friendship, community, happiness, agency and inner peace.

References

Andrews, D.A. & Bonta, J. (2003). *The Psychology of Criminal Conduct*. Cincinnati, OH: Anderson.

Andrews, D.A., Bonta, J. & Wormith, S.J. (2006). The recent past and near future of risk and/or need assessment. *Crime and Delinquency*, *52*, 7–27.

Bennett, P. (2007). Governing Grendon Prison's Therapeutic Communities: the big spin. In M. Parker (Ed.) *Dynamic Security: The Democratic Therapeutic Community in Prison*. London: Jessica Kingsley Publications.

Briggs, D. (2005). *Learning To Live: Social Learning in Practice*. Occasional Paper, 11, PETT Archive.

Bruner, J. (1986) *Actual Minds, Possible Worlds*. Cambridge, MA: Harvard University Press.

Coltman, J. (2004). Working at the coalface. In D. Jones (Ed.) *Working with Dangerous People: The Psychotherapy of Violence*. Oxford: Radcliffe Medical Press.

Emmons, R. (1986). Personal strivings: An approach to personality and subjective well-being. *Journal of Personality and Social Psychology*, *51*, 1058–1068.

Jones, D. & Shuker, R. (2004). Concluding comments: a humane approach to working with dangerous people. In D. Jones (Ed.) *Working With Dangerous People: The Psychotherapy of Violence*. Oxford: Radcliffe.

Jones, L. (1997). Developing models for managing treatment integrity and efficacy in a prison-based TC: the Max Glatt Centre. In E. Cullen, L. Jones & R. Woodward (Eds) *Therapeutic Communities for Offenders*. Chichester: Wiley.

Kennard, D. (1998). *An Introduction to Therapeutic Communities*. London: Jessica Kingsley Publications.

Leggett, K. & Hirons, B. (2007). Security and dynamic security in a therapeutic community prison. In M. Parker (Ed.) *Dynamic Security: The Democratic Therapeutic Community in Prison*. London: Jessica Kingsley Publications.

Lynch, J.P. (2006). Prisoner re-entry: beyond program evaluation. *Criminology and Public Policy*, *5*, 401–412.

Mann, R.E. & Shingler, J. (2006). Collaboration in clinical work with sexual offenders: Treatment and risk assessment. In W.L. Marshall, Y.M. Fernandez, L.E. Marshall & G.A. Serran (Eds) *Sexual Offender Treatment: Controversial Issues*. Chichester: John Wiley.

Marshall, W.L., Serran, G.A., Fernandez, Y.M., Mulloy, R., Mann, R.E. & Thornton, D. (2003). Therapist characteristics in the treatment of sexual offenders: Tentative data on their relationship with indices of behaviour change. *Journal of Sexual Aggression*, *9* (1), 25–30.

Maruna, S. (2001). *Making Good: How Ex-convicts Reform and Rebuild Their Lives*. Washington, DC: American Psychological Association.

Maruna, S. & LeBel T.P. (2003). Welcome home? Examining the 're-entry court' concept from a strengths-based perspective. *Western Criminology Review*, *4*, 91–107.

McAdams, D.P. (1985). *Power, Intimacy, and the Life Story: Personological Inquiries into Identity*. New York: Guilford Press.

McAdams, D.P. (1994). Can personality change? Levels of stability and growth in personality across the life span. In T.F. Heatherton & J.L. Weinberger (Eds) *Can Personality Change?* Washington, DC: American Psychological Association.

McAdams, D.P. (2006). *The Redemptive Self: Stories Americans Live By*. New York: Oxford University Press.

McMurran, M. (2002). *Motivating Offenders to Change: Guide to Enhancing Engagement in Therapy*. Chichester: John Wiley.

McMurran, M., Theodosi, E., Sweeney, A. & Sellen, J. (2008). What do prisoners want? Current concerns of adult male prisoners. *Psychology, Crime and Law, 14* (3), 267–274.

Michalak, J. & Grosse Holtforth, M. (2006). Where do we go from here? – The goal perspective in psychotherapy. *Clinical Psychology: Science and Practice, 13*, 346–365.

Morris, M. (2004). *Dangerous and Severe – Process, Programme and Person: Grendon's Work*. London: Jessica Kingsley Publications.

Rapoport, R.N. (1960). *Community as Doctor*. London: Tavistock.

Rivlin, A. (2007). Self harm and suicide at Grendon Therapeutic Community Prison. *Prison Service Journal, 173*, 34–38.

Shine, J. & Morris, M. (2000). Addressing criminogenic needs in a prison therapeutic community. *Therapeutic Communities, 21* (3), 197–220.

Shuker, R. & Jones, D. (2007). Assessing risk and need in a prison therapeutic community: an integrative model. In M. Parker (Ed.) *Dynamic Security: The Democratic Therapeutic Community in Prison*. London: Jessica Kingsley Publications.

Sullivan, E.L. (2007). 'Seeing beyond the uniform': Positive views of a prison through prisoners' eyes. *Prison Service Journal, 173*, 27–33.

Ward, T. (2002). Good lives and the rehabilitation of offenders: Promises and problems. *Aggression and Violent Behaviour, 7* (5), 513–528.

Ward, T. & Brown, M. (2004). The Good Lives Model and conceptual issues in offender rehabilitation. *Psychology, Crime and Law, 10* (3), 243–257.

Ward, T. & Gannon, T.A. (2006). Rehabilitation, etiology, and self-regulation: The comprehensive Good Lives Model of treatment for sexual offenders. *Aggression and Violent Behavior: A Review Journal, 11*, 77–94.

Ward, T., Mann, R.E. & Gannon, T.A (2007a). The comprehensive Good Lives Model of treatment for sexual offenders: Clinical implications. *Aggression and Violent Behavior, 12*, 87–107.

Ward, T. & Marshall W.L. (2004). Good lives, aetiology and the rehabilitation of sex offenders: A bridging theory. *Journal of Sexual Aggression, 10* (2), 153–169.

Ward, T. & Maruna, S. (2007). *Rehabilitation: Beyond the Risk Assessment Paradigm*. London: Routledge.

Ward, T., Melser, J. & Yates, P.M. (2007b). Reconstructing the risk need responsivity model: a theoretical elaboration and evaluation. *Aggression and Violent Behavior, 12*, 208–228.

Ward, T. & Stewart, C.A. (2003). The treatment of sex offenders: Risk management and good lives. *Professional Psychology: Research and Practice, 34,* 353–360.

Whitehead, P., Ward, T. & Collie, R. (2007). Time for a change: applying the Good Lives Model of rehabilitation to a high-risk violent offender. *International Journal of Offender Therapy and Comparative Criminology, 51,* 578–598.

Chapter 7

Personality Disorder: Using Therapeutic Communities as an Integrative Approach to Address Risk

Richard Shuker

The direction of the debate about the treatability of high-risk psychopathic personality disordered offenders was influenced to a large degree by a study at Oak Ridge in North America in the early 1990s. The authors, Rice *et al.* (1992), maintained that intervention was not only ineffective but, they argued, was associated with increased risk of recidivism. Reflecting to some extent approaches associated with the era, the study described involved controversial, unconventional and experimental practices, those such as 'encounter groups', sensory deprivation and the clinical use of LSD, in an environment of rather unfettered patient autonomy. Whilst this highly cited study influenced clinical practice and informed theoretical positions on the issue of treatability, it also came to be misleading. The intervention described was labelled a 'therapeutic community' despite these procedures having no resemblance to the treatment processes within therapeutic communities in most health or penal establishments. These practices became associated with therapeutic communities, perhaps because of the element of patient involvement rather crudely embedded within its approach. Whilst prisoner involvement is a defining feature of democratic therapeutic communities (TCs) in the UK, the carefully defined treatment procedures and clear recognition of the limits to prisoner involvement make any

Grendon and the Emergence of Forensic Therapeutic Communities: Developments in Research and Practice
Edited by Richard Shuker and Elizabeth Sullivan
© 2010 John Wiley & Sons, Ltd.

comparison redundant. However, the words 'therapeutic communities' and Oak Ridge continue to be used interchangeably, which may go some way to explaining why certain myths still exist regarding practice within TCs, and why their contribution to the debate about the treatment of personality disordered offenders remains unrecognised. This chapter seeks to describe how the principles and practices within TC intervention provide a highly relevant and informative contribution to interventions with personality disordered offenders.

Recent Developments in Interventions for Personality Disordered Offenders

Implications from research evidence

Despite the apparent robustness of the literature focusing on 'criminogenic needs' in the understanding and treatment of criminal behaviour within general offender populations (Andrews & Bonta, 2003; McGuire, 2002), interventions attempting to incorporate the same methods in the treatment of offenders with personality disorders have not been developed and implemented with the same level of empirical support (Hodge & Renwick, 2002). Whilst there is an intuitive rationale for assuming that there will be overlap between the needs of disordered and non-disordered offenders, the evidence supporting the assumption that similar treatment methods can be successfully applied to both groups lacks empirical support. Duggan *et al.* (2007), reviewing the evidence base for the treatment of antisocial personality disorder, considers that although positive outcomes have been achieved (for example in relation to substance misuse), where treating the core construct of the disorder is the goal of intervention, there is little evidence demonstrating the efficacy of treatment. However, Duggan (2008) goes on to suggest that, although there may be 'limited evidence to support intervening with antisocial personality disorder' (p. 2604), consistent evidence does support the more general effectiveness of correctional programmes in leading to reductions in offender recidivism. This, he argues, gives grounds for optimism that interventions aimed at reducing some of the symptoms associated with personality disorder could be successful.

The strategy paper *Personality Disorder: No Longer a Diagnosis of Exclusion* (www.dh.gov.uk/en/Publicationsandstatistics/Publications/Publication sPolicyAndGuidance/DH_4009546), produced by the Department of Health in 2003, advocated the development of clinical services for those with personality disorders, arguing that the shortage of interventions for this client group was no longer ethically or empirically defensible. The thrust of this paper highlighted that, although interventions could lead to successful outcomes with this group, no single treatment approach has a monopoly on success. Although this position remains somewhat at odds with the 'what works' literature, which advocated an almost exclusive cognitive behavioural framework for mainstream forensic interventions, it has some support. Studies reviewing interventions for personality disordered populations (Bateman & Fonagy, 1999; Duggan *et al.*, 2006; Piper & Joyce, 2001; Warren *et al.*, 2003) reiterated the view that although evidence for treatment efficacy was only tentative, and certain interventions could be seen as 'promising', no single treatment method has been shown to be superior to any other. Duggan *et al.* (2007) concur with this view, concluding that although good quality evidence from well-conducted studies is sparse, certain psychological approaches across different modalities (including schema focused, dialectical behaviour therapy, cognitive behavioural approaches and psychodynamic psychotherapy) have produced encouraging results.

Issues in treatment in forensic settings

Although reconviction studies lent support to the view that interventions may well be worthwhile, the evidence base suggesting that interventions with personality disorder may lead to positive outcomes is drawn largely from non-forensic populations. McGuire (2007), however, has argued that, given the multi domains of psychopathology associated with forensic populations, interventions for offenders need to draw from a range of methods, a view echoed by Livesley (2003). He argues that because of the complex range of needs presented by this population, interventions that incorporate a one-dimensional clinical approach are unlikely to be successful (Livesley, 2003).

The Good Lives approach (Ward, 2002) has also challenged the significance given to 'criminogenic' factors arguing that quality of life factors such as autonomy, spirituality, relationships, health and creativity are important treatment goals and that interventions simply directed at rectifying skill deficits form too narrow a focus (see Brookes, this edition). Livesley (2007) further argues that, rather than being geared around one focal problem, personality disorder can be construed as involving multiple problems from which a complex pattern of symptoms ensues. Severe personality disorder presents a 'diffuse array of psychopathology' for which he argues that comprehensive interventions are required in the form of an integrated and multi-modal approach, supporting the assertion of Bateman and Tyrer (2002) that a combination of treatments needs to be employed to address the complex range of treatment and responsivity needs.

Engaging people with personality disorder in interventions presents its own set of issues in forensic settings. Traits such as mistrust or hostility can become exacerbated (Benjamin, 1993) especially where those working clinically are also involved in risk assessment and progress evaluation. Behavioural deficits such as impulsivity, aggression and self-harm are also likely to impact on treatment engagement (Jones, 2007), and interpersonal traits which can undermine the treatment programme present obstacles to those delivering treatment (Shine & Hobson, 2000). This becomes a challenge for practitioners where, in order to achieve effective outcomes, they need to be able to engage personality disordered offenders in interventions that they may feel they neither want nor need, and where the offender may, on a number of different levels, not be adequately prepared or psychologically 'ready' for treatment. Ward *et al.* (2004) developed the Multifactor Offender Readiness Model (MORM) model of treatment readiness which suggests that to engage effectively in and benefit from intervention, offenders must possess necessary cognitive, interpersonal, affective and behavioural attributes. Personality disordered offenders often have considerable deficits in these areas which impact adversely upon readiness, and McMurran and Theodosi (2007) highlight the difficulties of engaging personality disordered offenders in treatment citing the high drop out rate and subsequent negative impact on recidivism.

The difficulties observed in engaging those with personality disorders in treatment within the criminal justice system may not be altogether unexpected where interventions are frequently unadapted to meet their needs. A further issue clinicians need to confront is to respond to the psychological and mental health needs of individual patients or prisoners, whilst at the same time demonstrating that as a primary treatment target, reductions in risk have been demonstrated. This issue has led to confusion about treatment priorities and sequencing treatment and an unhelpful demarcation between criminogenic and non-criminogenic targets, which have been polarised as conceptually distinct rather than clinically complementary focuses of intervention.

Developing a treatment model

The growing recognition by clinicians and policy makers that personality disorder is worth researching and is potentially treatable, has shifted the balance and seen important clinical developments (see Shine, chapter 5 this volume). Programmes have seen developments from a narrow focus on cognitive behavioural methods to a recognition that the treatment regime and environment are important treatment components (Wong & Hare, 2005).

When adapting mainstream interventions to meet the needs of personality-disordered offenders, certain factors need to be taken into consideration. Implications from research suggest that interventions need to be theoretically inclusive, address a broad range of treatment targets, and target overtly criminogenic needs, in addition to psychological and mental health needs. Outcomes from meta-analytic studies support the value of incorporating multi-modal methods. McGuire (2002) suggests that when developing an effective service, delivering it as a single integrated and cohesive programme provides the most promising approach. Another central requirement is that forensic interventions targeted at personality disordered populations must be 'fine tuned' or adapted to take into account the core personality characteristics of the individual (Andrews & Bonta, 2006). This particularly applies to CBT approaches. Duggan (2008), referring to antisocial personality disorder states that:

> One could argue that ... this modest effect of current correctional programmes might be enhanced if the specific psychological vulnerabilities of the subset of ASPD were addressed in programme development. (p. 2609)

Where interventions have the capacity to be flexible, to adapt to specific learning styles, to respond effectively to individual mental health needs, and most importantly, to be able to meaningfully engage and involve participants, they are more likely to be of relevance to those with personality disorder. Within his conceptualisation of an integrated approach to the treatment of personality disorder, Livesley (2007) argues that treatment should be 'integrative', that is it should be based on an eclectic approach that is underpinned by a framework that emphasises the contribution of diverse therapeutic approaches. Integrative interventions (see figure 7.1) should have the capacity to:

- integrate core therapeutic factors to engage participants in a supportive and collaborative therapeutic alliance and provide opportunities to learn and test out new skills in a consistently delivered clinical process;
- incorporate treatment methods that can engage and motivate participants and, delivered within an environment which can provide a 'corrective' experience, target *general* psychological deficits whilst addressing *individual* learning styles and treatment needs; and
- form the basis on which specific therapeutic interventions can be delivered through an integration of different theoretical perspectives (see Shine – chapter 5 – who discusses Livesley's theory in more detail).

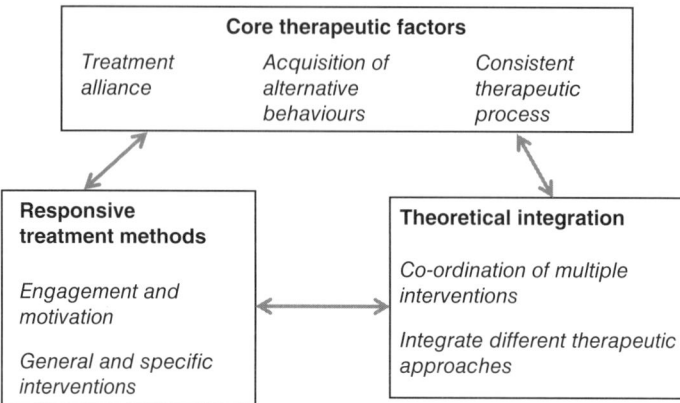

Figure 7.1   Integrative treatment approach (adapted from Livesley 2007)

Making reference to Livesley's framework, this chapter will explore the contribution that the therapeutic community model can have towards promoting an integrative approach to treatment, arguing that the TC model presents a framework for integrated practice in the treatment of personality disorder in forensic settings.

TC Principles and the Development of a Treatment Model for Working with Personality-disordered (PD) Offenders

Within Livesley's (2007) eclectic framework he argues that 'empirical and conceptual considerations point to the merits of an integrated and eclectic approach that combines interventions from different theoretical perspectives' (p. 31), and he suggests that treatment is at its most effective where diverse approaches from different frameworks can be incorporated. The difficulties presented by people with complex interpersonal needs in engaging in and responding to treatment, require specific therapeutic approaches (Birtchnell, 1996), which should be incorporated in treatment design and orientation.

TCs and eclectic practice

An important point in the development of the TC treatment model is that its practice has emerged without rigidly adhering to particular clinical or

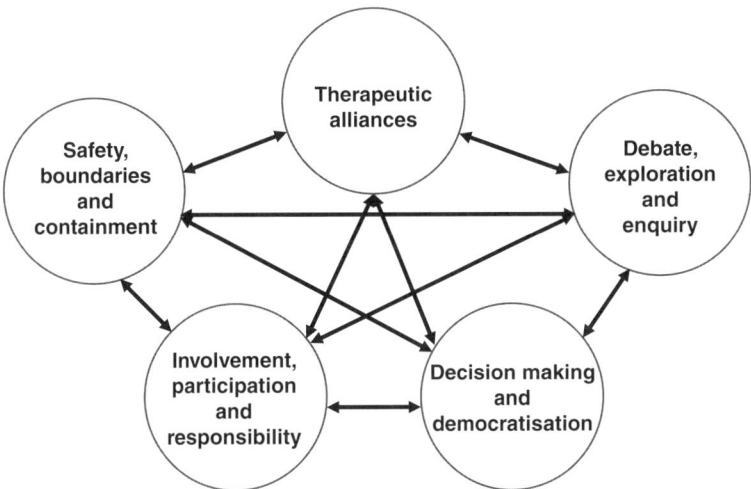

Figure 7.2   Guiding principles of democratic TCs

theoretical doctrines. Rather, it has evolved in part as a reaction to ortho-dox psychiatric and medical approaches and has, as a consequence, reflected a diversity of treatment methods (Haigh, 2002; Kennard, 1998). The TC model arose through more of a pragmatic belief that a supportive, positive and safe clinical environment, which could empower and involve patients, promote healthy relationships and enhance self-esteem and psychological well-being, was essential to therapeutic change. Based on these ideas, a set of therapeutic techniques developed which can be as much construed as social learning (Genders & Player, 1995; Shine & Morris, 2000) as they can cognitive-behavioural and psychodynamic (Shuker & Jones, 2006). TC principles and the inter-relationship between these (see figure 7.2) forms the basis for this multi-modal and integrative approach.

Therapeutic alliance: establishing collaborative and supportive alli-ances, where prisoners feel secure when exploring paranoid beliefs or deviant fantasies, is a core requisite when working with personality disor-dered offenders.

Safety, boundaries and containment: therapeutic communities have clear boundaries detailed in a written constitution. Part of this constitution also recognises that prisoners will demonstrate behaviour which mirrors offending patterns and this behaviour will, within limits, be tolerated if explored within treatment.

Involvement, participation and responsibility: a central part of the learning process involves prisoners learning skills from taking an active role within the wing and wider regime. This is seen in the emphasis given on prisoners taking positions of responsibility within the community.

Decision making and democratisation: the process of giving prisoners opportunities for decision making is fundamental to TCs. Whilst the possibility for a staff veto always remains, voting on key issues, such as other prisoners' suitability for treatment, forms a central part of community living.

Debate, exploration and enquiry: structures that allow and encourage channels of community, discussion and conflict resolution represent a defining feature of TC practice.

The structures and practices that TCs adopt to create a clinical climate underpinned by the above principles will be explored later on in this chapter.

TCs as a Framework for Integrated Practice

Core therapeutic factors

Treatment alliance

The importance of the therapeutic alliance in clinical outcome is widely recognised across a range of psychotherapies. Studies have consistently demonstrated that a therapeutic alliance characterised by a collaborative and supportive relationship is a significant predictor of therapeutic outcome and an essential component of any therapeutic intervention (Hatcher & Barends, 1996; Horvarth & Greenberger, 1994; Ryle, 1997). Within forensic settings, forming a therapeutic alliance with personality disordered individuals presents its own set of challenges, with problems concerning mistrust, overdependence, the intensity of the transference relationship and fluctuations between idealisation and hostile projections, presenting potential obstacles to treatment engagement.

One potent clinical feature of therapeutic communities is the relationship that becomes established between residents and, more significantly, that which develops between residents and the staff group. Collaborative, mutually supportive and trusting alliances have been shown to be a feature of relationships between residents and staff (Genders & Player, 1995; McKenzie, 2000; Sheffer, this edition) and improvements in attitudes towards authority figures reported as a treatment outcome (Gunn & Robertson, 1982). Given that the therapeutic alliance remains one of the core underlying principles of TC treatment, it is important that the structures, processes and conditions that establish and maintain this alliance are identified, and this is explored in more detail later in this chapter.

Acquisition of alternative behaviours

Livesley (2001) argues that a defining feature of integrated practice is the opportunity to acquire behaviours which provide alternatives to offending. He suggests that this involves a number of stages: generating alternatives; maintaining motivation; encouraging new behaviours; inhibiting old patterns and teaching new skills. Once learnt, these new behaviours need to become 'habitual patterns of action that are generalisable to everyday situations' (p. 580; Shine, chapter 5 this edition).

Kennard (1998) describes a therapeutic community as a 'living learning' experience where the principles of community living promote therapeutic change. This feature of treatment is central to TCs where opportunities for skill development and generalisation form the core of TC life, and where opportunities for communication, problem solving and dialogue are vital to its structures. The emphasis on the resolution of domestic and interpersonal problems, the ownership of community decision making, domestic responsibilities, social affairs, finances and business matters provide a potent means to identify interpersonal, emotional and criminogenic needs. Treatment objectives designed to promote skill development, address unhelpful belief systems and promote personal responsibility can be formally set during clinical reviews. The co-ordinated inter-linking of the regime's varied functions promotes a clinical climate, which provides the opportunities for learning.

The clinical emphasis on dealing with problems in the 'here and now' presents diverse treatment opportunities where, for example, conflict resolution skills are practiced, or hostile assumptions and appraisals explored. The immediacy with which antisocial activities are responded to gives potency to the behavioural component of TC practice (Jones, 1997). Offence-paralleling behaviours can be identified and explored (Shine & Morris, 2000) and importantly, therapeutic targets, such as taking greater community responsibility or completing a task that may test the prisoner's ability to cope with perceived stress, can be set. Such a process becomes the inevitable product of a 'culture of enquiry' where the exploration of behaviour is an ingrained response to community rule breaking.

The principle of prisoner involvement presents a powerful therapeutic tool when prisoners can assume positions of responsibility which present meaningful opportunities for participation. The community becomes able to create its own carefully defined roles with clear responsibilities when the community and wider regime recognises their value and their legitimacy. Positions such as 'cleaners' foreman' (where a prisoner is given the responsibility of supervising the cleaning of the community) only become possible where they offer a genuine opportunity for involvement and where the extent and limitations of these roles are clearly understood. Where they are, the therapeutic benefits of such a role are immense; interpersonal and organisation skills can be learnt, developing conflict resolution skills become essential, and liaison with previously untrusted authority figures in the staff team is a routine part of the role.

Consistent therapeutic process

The presence of a consistent therapeutic process is especially important in the treatment of personality disorder given difficulties with trust, regulation of affect and impulse control, and other aspects of personality that impair a stable therapeutic process (Livesley, 2001). TCs offer a highly boundaried, clinical environment where the emphasis on consistency of therapeutic process, adhering to the requirements of a defined therapeutic constitution, and accountability for breaking community regulations, form governing principles for practice. Shared goals by residents and staff further promote consistency, as does the process of collaborative target setting, procedures for self and peer review of the integrity of the clinical processes, and the continued reflection on the quality of treatment alliances and relationships.

Responsive Treatment Methods

Establishing a therapeutic culture

Engaging the regime

This culture of the TC regime, which regards work, leisure, education, life skills and, critically, the security and discipline strands as inextricably linked to the clinical process, promotes integration and collaboration. The therapeutic community explicitly seeks to involve the different components of the prison regime to provide a treatment environment that offers a range of opportunities for learning. By giving recognition and legitimacy to multidisciplinary contributions, fragmentation and marginalisation are avoided. Activities such as work and education are key parts of the treatment process and any behaviours which emerge in these contexts are important in informing the assessment of risk reduction and treatment progress. The assumptions and expectations shared by staff and prisoners are that these will be 'fed back' into the clinical pot for exploration, challenge and, where appropriate, community sanction.

However, the ability of the regime to incorporate its various strands into a clinical programme can only exist where collaborative systems are present, allowing for close organisational communication and liaison. Without

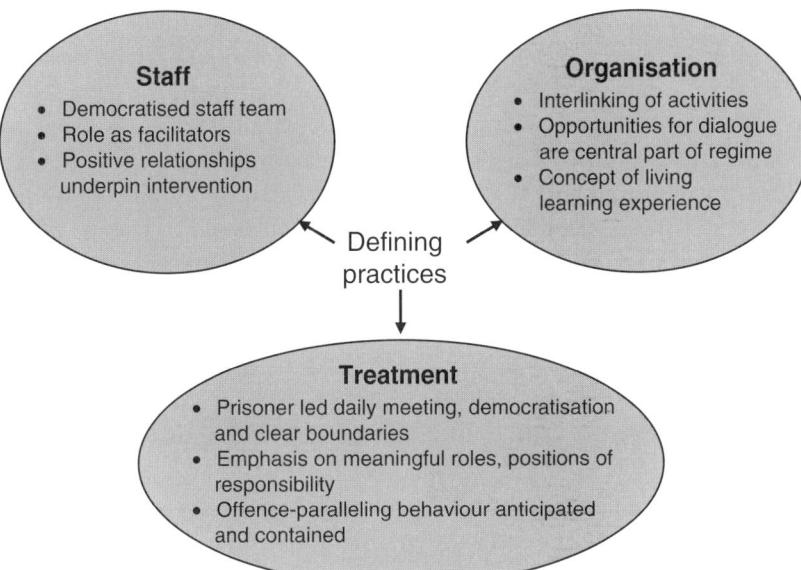

Figure 7.3 Showing the practices that support the integration of the wider organisation

these systems, multidisciplinary contributions cannot be utilised. In a multi-modal intervention, where one specific clinical dogma is not allowed to dominate practice, it becomes possible to incorporate different disciplines and recognise and reinforce their significance and value within the regime. This is represented in figure 7.3, which illustrates the practices that support the integration of the wider organisation, utilising its multidisciplinary components, to engage the staff team, prisoners and regime.

Engaging the staff

Attempting to engage personality disordered offenders in a complex, long-term intervention may be relatively futile unless the staff team delivering that treatment are themselves fully engaged, involved and committed to its delivery. Within a TC, where only a small handful of clinical staff work with over 40 prisoners, the prison officer grade represents by far the largest and potentially most potent professional group. For both pragmatic and clinically relevant reasons, treatment procedures aimed at engaging the staff team have developed at the heart of the clinical practice.

Underpinning the treatment model is the principle that collaborative alliances with front-line staff are central to the clinical process. This alliance is established foremost by mechanisms that are able to involve and engage the staff group in the clinical work. There is an overt recognition that front-line prison staff have a role of equal significance to clinical specialists in promoting change. Prison officers are more likely to embrace a less rigid and more consent driven nature to their authority where their role in treatment, and position as clinicians within the TC, is explicitly defined and acknowledged. They provide a key role in the co-facilitation of treatment groups and meetings, and structures such as full community meetings foster collaborative interest and involvement. The decision-making structures seek to capture democratised working practices, where the staff team actively share decisions such as deselection, community sanctions and treatment planning, and promote an ownership of the treatment process. Practices such as the use of first name terms also help to promote a treatment environment of trust and respect. More complex cultural aspects of the regime that question the implicit assumption that the staff group necessarily hold the answers or the intellectual authority also promote alliance between staff and prisoners. The therapeutic community principles of openness, debate and inquiry allow residents to explore paranoid assumptions about staff without fear of rejection or punishment, and to explore their feelings of hostility, suspicion and insecurity.

Engaging the prisoners

The clinical activities that engage staff become those that engage and involve prisoners. Following submitting an application, prisoners are communicated with regularly before they are formally invited for assessment. This provides the opportunity for a relationship to be established prior to their participation in treatment. This sense of collaboration prior to entering the therapeutic community is an important treatment component. The relationships, which are fostered by the use of first name terms, the collaborative nature to authority and the emphasis on communication and dialogue, create mutual respect and understanding, which becomes the foundation for engagement in the therapeutic process.

Figure 7.3 shows the key practices which function to engage and involve prisoners in treatment. Full wing meetings, attended by all staff and prisoners, are a central component of the TC treatment process and provide a forum for discussion and debate, conflict resolution between members, and planning events and activities. These mandatory meetings are chaired by elected fellow prisoners, and all community issues, ranging from how to spend the wing budget to who should be deselected from treatment, are explored and voted upon.

Elected roles, where prisoners are assigned key responsibilities within the community (see Brookes, chapter 6 this edition), play a crucial role in creating a culture of involvement and ownership. Therapy groups and community meetings allow the opportunity for prisoners to suggest ways of managing or responding to acts of rule breaking, and staff and prisoners share the understanding that all behaviour will be the focus of community discussion and exploration. These activities take place within established boundaries, which provide clear parameters for conduct within the community. Additionally, the emphasis on prisoners being given legitimate opportunities for involvement and decision making, which may present a degree of risk taking by the regime, provides the mechanism to engage interest and involve its participants.

General and specific interventions

Whilst the therapeutic role of the treatment environment provides an anchor to the TC process, group work is also a fundamental aspect of treatment. In addition to the larger community-based meetings, which form the arena for decision making, conflict resolution and debate, it is important to understand the role of the treatment groups. Small therapy groups are a central component of TC treatment and what needs to be considered is how a model of group-based intervention without a clearly defined structure can be of relevance to reducing offender recidivism. Andrews (1995) argues that unstructured group therapy is an ineffective treatment method for offenders, claiming that interventions 'designed according to the principles of clinical sociology, principles of deterrence and labelling, innovative and immediate punishments and unstructured psychodynamic therapy, all constituted an ineffective approach where recidivism was the aim' (p. 56). Unstructured treatment groups may well lack clarity of focus with offending populations unless they are clearly anchored in the therapeutic principles and structures described in the above section. It is argued that where they are, they offer a method which gives a clear focus on cognitive, affective and behavioural deficits with direct relevance to the prisoner's offending, and which are able to identify and focus upon individual need. The exploration of offence paralleling behaviours becomes a principal role of small group work where a range of behaviours, observed from different activities, are explored. In doing so, individual needs can be identified and addressed using specific therapeutic approaches.

Theoretical Integration

Co-ordination of multiple interventions

Livesley (2007) suggests that an integrative approach should be able to incorporate effective components from different schools of therapy and implement them in a co-ordinated way. Figure 7.4 highlights the therapeutic community processes which enable pathology to be addressed from a

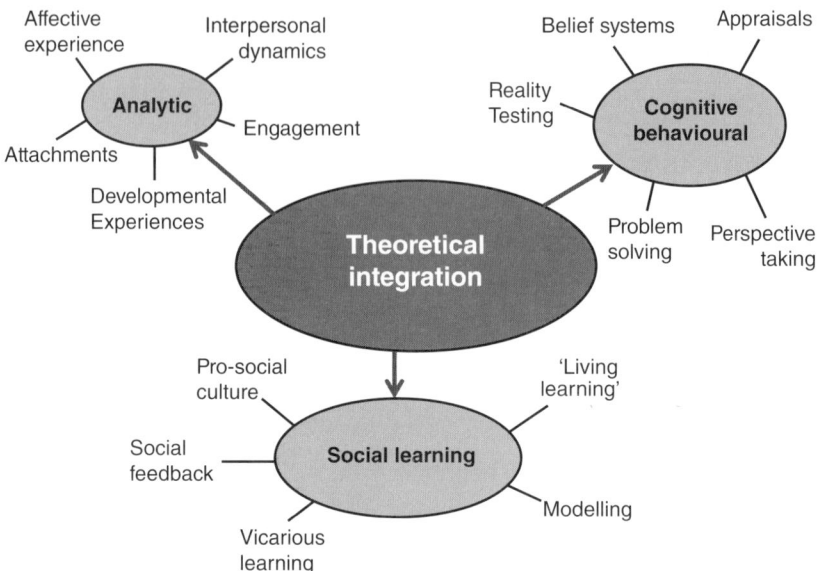

Figure 7.4   Theoretical integration

number of different theoretical perspectives, and where TCs provide the arena which allows a specific, individualised approach in addition to core therapeutic factors being present.

Core to the treatment process is the involvement of prisoners in exploring and challenging other prisoners' beliefs and behaviour (Shine & Morris, 2000). Cognitive behavioural mechanisms operate where fellow prisoners will challenge irrational thinking, identify inconsistencies between expressed attitude and behaviour, and make links between behaviour observed within the community and those with a functional link to their offending. Linked to this is a process of 'reality testing' where prisoners are able to test out the assumptions and beliefs they may hold about other community members and have these explored and supportively challenged by fellow prisoners. Evidence supporting the hypothesis that TCs have a strong cognitive behavioural component comes from research that suggests that changes in offence supportive beliefs and attitudes occur following treatment (Gunn & Robertson, 1982; Newton, 1998; Shuker & Newton, 2008). Therapeutic community practice has also been observed as incorporating social learning approaches (Genders & Player, 1995) where the living learning culture enables the modelling, observation and learning of alternative behavioural repertoires. Early definitions of the TC model emphasised the role of psychodynamic principles with the exploration of early attachments, developmental factors, emotional experiences and group and unconscious processes demonstrating the application of psychodynamic approaches to TC treatment.

Integration of different therapeutic approaches

This integration of approaches allows pathology to be understood and addressed from contrasting theoretical perspectives, and within the therapeutic groups, clinical needs can be recognised and explored from different angles. For example, the development of maladaptive belief systems can be addressed from different clinical formulations of their development and function. Complementary therapeutic methods, from cognitive behavioural to psychodynamic approaches, are adopted to work towards change. The clear value here is that different conceptualisations of mistrustful beliefs can be explored from different perspectives and by using different approaches. For example, interventions are able to incorporate cognitive behavioural conceptualisations or more psychodynamic object relations approaches, emphasising the role of the early infant–caregiver relationship in perpetuating maladaptive relationships. Given the range of factors involved in both the aetiology and maintenance of specific disorders, the group process enabling interventions to be responsive to individual need provides a relevant and potent clinical method.

Case example: Carl was assessed as having a number of borderline, avoidant and antisocial traits. He had a deep-rooted lack of trust and believed himself to be inadequate and worthless. Work within his group was able to explore developmental experiences relating to the onset of such traits within his family where his attachments were tentative and insecure. His relationship with other group members became a focus of exploration and this was observed to fluctuate between being clingy and needy to being distant and withdrawn. On occasions he would flair up aggressively within the treatment setting. Issues including attachment patterns and transference reactions were explored by the facilitator and by other group members who had previously addressed similar issues. Group work was then able to focus on his interpersonal suspicion, exploring what lay behind the mistrustful beliefs he held about other group members and exploring how valid and rational his beliefs were. This work took place whilst simultaneously exploring his index offence (arson), which had occurred after he was rejected by his partner, and his rumination over beliefs that he had been taken advantage of and exploited. His group, together with the wider community, set him objectives to become more socially involved on the wing. By assigning him positions of responsibility (organising wing-based events) they aimed to expose him to potentially testing social interactions where he could be supported in working through and resolving his difficulties.

Therapeutic Communities and Risk Reduction: an Interpersonal Model

As Jones (1997) points out, when working with personality disorder it is critical to have a model that can understand community behaviour and the mechanisms by which the clinical processes impact upon and modify behaviour. It is argued here that the TC methods that impact directly on criminogenic factors can be understood in interpersonal terms. A brief summary of interpersonal theory and a conceptualisation of the processes underpinning offending is provided.

Personality disorder has been conceptualised by a number of theorists as a disorder of relating which can be best understood in interpersonal terms (Benjamin, 2003; Carson, 1979; Kiesler, 1996). Interpersonal approaches developed by Leary (1957) regarded personality disorder, as in object relations theory, as primarily a problem in interpersonal relationships. The interpersonal circle, a theoretical development of interpersonal theory, regards personality disorder as representing extremes of relating on two fundamental axes – dominance versus submissive, and friendly versus hostile. It considers that disorder arises due to the inflexibility and extremes of the preferred modes of relating. Blackburn (1998) suggests that the notion of an 'inflexible' interpersonal style provides a means of understanding criminal behaviour, arguing that the construct of psychopathy and other personality disorders reflect extremes of hostile and dominant interpersonal styles. Birtchnell and Shine (2000) found that particular interpersonal deficits are present within specific personality disorders, providing further support for personality disorders being considered as disorders of relating.

An inflexible interpersonal style can also be understood as reflecting deficits in social cognition (Wiggins, 1991). This may be indicative of motivational concerns such as power and status, with antisocial and violent behaviour motivated by maladaptive appraisals and interpersonal beliefs. Blackburn (1998) goes on to suggest that the interpersonal model is useful in providing a theoretical understanding of the functional link between personality disorder and antisocial behaviour. He argues that constructs such as psychopathy can be construed in interpersonal terms where appraisal biases and belief systems promote callous, aggressive and irresponsible behaviour, providing a mediating link between the personality disorder and offending.

Jones (1997) suggests that the treatment methods within a therapeutic community and the process by which the community is able to impact upon criminogenic deficits can be conceptualised in such interpersonal

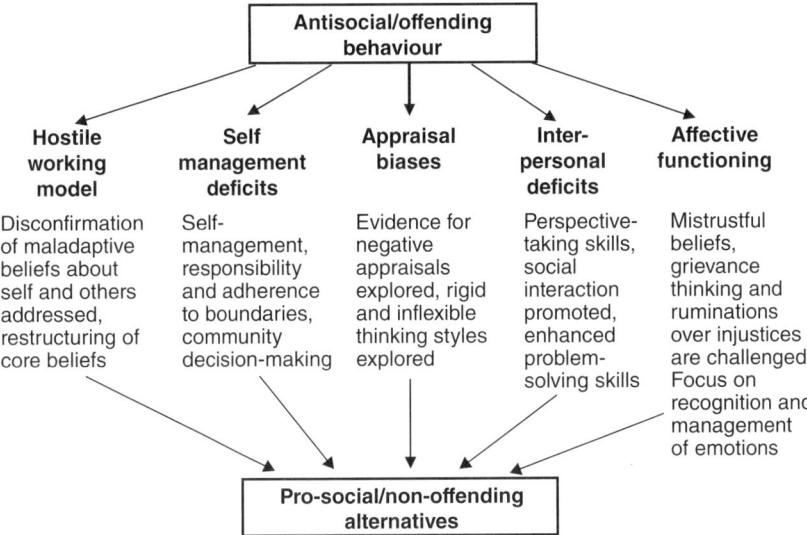

Figure 7.5 TC treatment model (Shuker, 2003)

terms. Drawing from relating theory and providing support to this position, Birtchnell *et al.* (2009) found that deficits in interpersonal relating improved during treatment in forensic therapeutic communities. This suggests that the interpersonal processes which operate within a TC function to address a number of key interpersonal and criminogenic needs.

Figure 7.5 shows the psychological processes that impact upon treatment needs (Shuker, 2003). It illustrates the role of the cognitive and interpersonal processes that provide the link between personality disorder and offending, and suggests a model for how these are addressed in a therapeutic community. For example, an offender with callous and unemotional traits may be observed taking advantage of and exploiting other members of the community. Within the group and community meetings, this pattern of behaviour is explored. From a schema-based perspective (Young, 1990), it could be hypothesised that core beliefs, which provide a hostile working model of the world, for example, and 'dog eat dog' attitudes, are being explored, and the legitimacy of these beliefs challenged.

A central aspect of this process is the potential for disconfirmatory responses (Blackburn, 1990) where prisoners experience events discrepant with their belief systems, providing the dissonance where their beliefs and values become challenged. For example, a belief system that non-aggressive behaviour will make somebody vulnerable is challenged through experiences, for example where non-aggression is able to effectively resolve conflict, with these experiences providing evidence which is able to counter former negative beliefs. From a schema-focused approach, this process could be understood in terms of the learning of more adaptive core beliefs allowing for non-hostile interpretations of interpersonal experience.

The emphasis on self-management and personal responsibility provides prisoners with a clear framework for pro-social behaviour. For example, domineering and intimidating interpersonal styles become confronted and explored, guided by a clear set of boundaries. The rigid and inflexible thinking styles that underpin hostile and antisocial behaviour become a central focus for intervention where the exploration of interpersonal conflicts becomes a focus of attention in groups and community meetings. Negative appraisals, which trigger aggressive incidents, are explored where, for example, a benign interaction on the wing that had been interpreted as signifying hostile intent can be examined, and hostile appraisals that have previously triggered aggressive reactions can be identified. Interpersonal deficits form a continued focus for therapeutic community treatment, and the focus on communication and interpersonal feedback promotes more adaptive and realistic perspective-taking skills. Developing skills with which to appropriately manage and regulate emotions is a central feature of the prisoner's commitment to the community, with any expression of affect taking place within the parameters necessary to ensure that safety is maintained. Social learning processes operate within this context, with more senior members of the community modelling pro-social means of demonstrating and regulating emotion. In this context social feedback can be effectively used to reinforce the appropriate expression of affect and used to suggest alternative management strategies where deficits have become evident.

Conclusion

TCs provide a clinical environment in which to engage personality-disordered offenders in treatment. The strength of TCs is their capacity to engage prisoners, staff and the organisation in its clinical processes and present a framework for integrating contrasting theoretical approaches. Whilst TCs provide a forum for a multi-modal approach, the community-based processes within TCs can be understood in interpersonal terms. Although further empirical support is necessary, it is argued in this chapter that TC treatment provides an interpersonal approach to conceptualising and addressing social, cognitive and behavioural deficits.

TCs need to respond to a number of challenges presented by developments in research and practice. Defining the limitations to their treatment model, and addressing questions concerning what level of risk and need they are equipped to meet, continues to be necessary. The question of how far their current practice is robust enough to work adequately with psychopathic offenders, remains one which needs further consideration by all prison-based TCs. Effective methods for assessing and monitoring progress, particularly in relation to addressing psychopathic behaviour and its impact upon the staff team, need to be a routine part of practice. Furthermore, clinical safeguards designed to prevent the erosion of treatment integrity must be built into the clinical audit procedures. Incorporating more rigorous research methods to evaluate their efficacy is essential (Rutter & Tyrer, 2003) and remains a priority if TCs are to become more centrally positioned within both criminal justice and health settings.

TCs have considerable potential to provide a framework for effective intervention with personality-disordered offenders, and offer a treatment model of clear relevance to personality disorder and psychological disturbance. Despite the need for more research, and for TCs to enhance their work by incorporating additional clinical interventions, they present an important opportunity to inform wider forensic practice.

References

Andrews, D.A. (1995). The psychology of criminal conduct and effective treatment. In J. McGuire (Ed.) *What Works: Reducing Offending: Guidelines from Research and Practice*. Chichester: Wiley.

Andrews, D.A. & Bonta, J. (2003). *The Psychology of Criminal Conduct* (3rd edn). Cincinnati, OH: Anderson.

Andrews, D.A. & Bonta, J. (2006). *The Psychology of Criminal Conduct* (4th edn). Newark, NJ: LexizNexis.

Bateman, A.W. & Fonagy, P. (1999). Effectiveness of partial hospitalization in the treatment of borderline personality disorder: A randomized controlled trial. *American Journal of Psychiatry, 156*(10), 1563–1569.

Bateman, A.W. & Tyrer, P. (2002). *Effective Management of Personality Disorder*. NIMHE, www.wmrdc.org.uk/silo/files/effective-management-of-personality-disorder.pdf

Benjamin, L.S. (1993). *Interpersonal Diagnosis and Treatment of Personality Disorders*. New York: Guilford Press.

Benjamin, L.S. (2003). *Interpersonal Diagnosis and Treatment of Personality Disorders* (2nd edn). London: Guilford Press.

Birtchnell, J. (1996). *How Humans Relate: A New Interpersonal Theory*. Hove: Psychology Press.

Birtchnell, J. & Shine, J. (2000). Personality disorders and the interpersonal octagon. *British Journal of Medical Psychology, 73*, 433–448.

Birtchnell, J., Shuker, R., Newberry, M. & Duggan, C. (2009). The assessment of change in negative relating in two male, forensic therapy samples using the Person's Relating to Others Questionnaire. *Journal of Forensic Psychiatry and Psychology, 20*, 387–407.

Blackburn, R. (1990). Treatment of the psychopathic offender. In K. Howells & D. Hollin (Eds) *Clinical Approaches to Working with Mentally Disordered and Sexual Offenders. Issues in Criminological and Legal Psychology, 16*, 54–66. London, British Psychological Society.

Blackburn, R. (1998). Psychopathy and personality disorder: Implications of interpersonal theory. In D. J. Cooke, S. J. Hart & A. E. Forth (Eds) *Psychopathy: Theory, Research and Implications for Society.* Amsterdam: Kluwer.

Carson, R. C. (1979). Personality and exchange in developing relationships. In R. L. Burgess & T. L. Huston (Eds), *Social Exchange in Developing Relationships.* New York: Academic Press.

Duggan, C. (2008). Why are programmes for offenders with personality disorder not informed by the relevant scientific findings? *Philosophical Transactions of the Royal Society of Biological Sciences, 363*, 2599–2604.

Duggan, C., Adams, C., McCarthy, L., Fenton, M., Lee, T., Binks, C. & Stocker, O. (2006). A systematic review of the effectiveness of pharmacological and psychological treatments for those with personality disorder. *Personality and Mental Health, 1*, 95–125.

Duggan, C., Huband, N., Smailagic, N., Ferriter, M. & Adams, C. (2007). The use of psychological treatments for people with personality disorder: A systematic review of randomised controlled trials. See www.nfmhp.org.uk/MRD%20 12%2033%20FinalReport.pdf.

Genders, E. & Player, E. (1995). *Grendon: A Study of a Therapeutic Prison.* Oxford: Outpatient Psychotherapy for Borderline Personality Disorder, Clarendon Press.

Gunn, J. & Robertson, G. (1982). An evaluation of Grendon prison. In J. Gunn & D. Farrington (Eds) *Abnormal Offenders, Delinquency and the Criminal Justice System.* Chichester: Wiley.

Haigh, R. (2002). The quintessence of a therapeutic community. In P. Campling & R. Haigh (Eds) *Therapeutic Communities: Past, Present and Future.* London: Jessica Kingsley Publications.

Hatcher, R.L. & Barends, A.W. (1996). Patient's view of the alliance in psychotherapy: Explanatory factor analysis of three alliance measures. *Journal of Consulting and Clinical Psychology, 64*, 1326–1336.

Hodge, J.E. & Renwick, S.J. (2002). Motivating mentally disordered offenders. In M. McMurran (Ed.) *Motivating Offenders to Change: A Guide to Enhancing Engagement in Therapy.* Chichester: Wiley.

Horvarth, A. & Greenberger, L.S. (1994). Introduction. In J. Horvath & L.S. Greenberger (Eds) *The Working Alliance.* New York: Wiley.

Jones, L. (1997). Developing models for managing treatment integrity and efficacy in a prison-based TC: the Max Glatt Centre. In E. Cullen, L. Jones & R. Woodward (Eds) *Therapeutic Communities for Offenders.* London: Wiley.

Jones, L. (2007). Using case formulation for assessing and interviewing with engagement difficulties. *Issues in Forensic Psychology, Readiness for Treatment, 7,* 42–47.

Kennard, D. (1998). *An Introduction to Therapeutic Communities.* London: Jessica Kingsley Publishers.

Kiesler, D.J. (1996). The 1982 interpersonal circle: An analysis of DSM-III personality disorders. In T. Millon & G.L. Klerman (Eds) *Contemporary Directions in Psychopathology: Toward the DSM-IV.* New York: Guilford Press.

Leary, T. (1957). *Interpersonal Diagnosis.* New York: Ronald Press.

Livesley, J. (2007). The relevance of an integrated approach to the treatment of personality disordered offenders. In C. Hollin, P. Koppen, S. Penrod & K. Howells (Eds) *Psychology, Crime and Law. Special Issue: Personality Disorder and Offending, 13*(1), 27–46.

Livesley, W.J. (2001). A framework for an integrated approach to treatment. In W.J. Livesley (Ed.) *Handbook of Personality Disorders: Theory, Research, and Treatment.* New York: Guilford Press.

Livesley, W.J. (2003). Diagnostic dilemmas in the classification of personality disorder. In K. Philips, M. First & H.A. Pincus (Eds) *Advancing DSM: Dilemmas in Psychiatric Diagnosis.* Washington, DC: American Psychiatric Association Press.

McGuire, J. (2002). *Offender Rehabilitation and Treatment.* Chichester: Wiley.

McGuire, J. (2007). A review of effective interventions for reducing aggression and violence. *Philosophical Transactions of the Royal Society of Biological Sciences, 363,* 2577–2597.

McKenzie, J. (2000). An analysis of therapeutic factors on 'A' wing HM Prison Grendon. In J. Shine (Ed.) *A Compilation of Grendon Research.* Leyhill Press. Available from Psychology Unit, HMP Grendon, Grendon Underwood, Aylesbury, HP18 OTL.

McMurran, M. & Theodosi, E. (2007). Is treatment non-completion associated with increased reconviction over no treatment? *Psychology, Crime and Law, 13*(4), 333–343.

National Institute for Mental Health for England (2003). *Personality Disorder: No Longer a Diagnosis of Exclusion. Best Practice Guide.*

Newton, M. (1998). Changes in measures of personality, hostility and locus of control during residence in a prison therapeutic community. *Legal and Criminological Psychology, 3,* 209–223.

Piper, W.E. & Joyce A.S. (2001). Psychosocial treatment outcome. In W.J. Livesley (Ed.) *Handbook of Personality Disorders: Theory, Research, and Treatment.* New York: Guilford Press.

Rice, M.E., Harris, G.T. & Cormier, C.A. (1992). An evaluation of a maximum security therapeutic community for psychopaths and other mentally disordered offenders. *Law and Human Behaviour, 16*(4), 399–412.

Roberts, J. (1997). The history of the therapeutic community. In E. Cullen, L. Jones & R. Woodward (Eds) *Therapeutic Communities for Offenders.* London: Wiley.

Rutter, D. & Tyrer, P. (2003). The value of therapeutic communities in the treatment of personality disorder: A suitable place for treatment? *Journal of Psychiatric Practice, 9*(4), 291–302.

Ryle, A. (1997). *Cognitive-Analytic Therapy and Borderline Personality Disorder.* Chichester: Wiley.

Shine, J. & Hobson, J. (2000). Institutional behaviour and time in treatment among psychopaths admitted to a prison-based therapeutic community. *Medicine, Science and Law, 40*(4), 327–335.

Shine, J. & Morris, M. (2000). Addressing criminogenic needs in a prison therapeutic community. *Therapeutic Communities, 21*(3), 197–291.

Shuker, R. (2003). *Therapeutic communities as an approach to address risk.* Presentation at: British and Irish Group for the Study of Personality Disorder, Dublin, February 2003.

Shuker, R. & Jones, D. (2006). Assessing risk and need in a prison therapeutic community: An integrative model. In M. Parker (Ed.) *Dynamic Security: The Democratic Therapeutic Community in Prison.* London: Jessica Kingsley.

Shuker, R. & Newton, M. (2008). Treatment outcome following intervention in a prison-based therapeutic community: a study of the relationship between reduction in risk and improved psychological wellbeing. *British Journal of Forensic Practice, 10*, 33–44.

Ward, T. (2002). Good lives and the rehabilitation of offenders: Promise and problems. *Aggression and Violent Behaviour, 7*, 513–528.

Ward, T., Day, A., Howells, K. & Birgden, A. (2004). The multifactor offender readiness model. *Aggression and Violent Behaviour, 9*, 645–673.

Warren, F., McGauley, G., Norton, K., Dolan, B., Preedy-Fayers, K., Pickering, A. et al. (2003). Review of treatments for severe personality disorder. *Home Office Online Report*, 30/03.

Wiggins, J.S. (1991). Agency and communion as conceptual co-ordinates for the understanding and measurement of interpersonal behaviour. In W.M. Grove and D. Cicchetti (Eds) *Thinking Clearly about Psychology: Essays in Honour of Paul E. Meehl, 2*, 89–113. Minneapolis: University of Minnesota Press.

Wong, S.C.P. & Hare, T.D. (2005). *Guidelines for a Psychopathy Treatment Programme.* Toronto: Multi-Health Systems.

Young, J. E. (1990). *Cognitive Therapy for Personality Disorders: A Schema-Focused Approach.* Sarasota: Professional Resource Exchange.

Chapter 8

Psychodrama as Part of Core Therapy at HMP Grendon

Jinnie Jefferies

Psychodrama has been a treatment method at HMP Grendon for the past 27 years. It was first established as a complementary therapy and recently, alongside art therapy, it has been recognised as part of the core therapy. It operates on all wings on a weekly basis. It is my intention in this chapter to give a brief overview of psychodrama and role theory, discuss how psychodrama works as a treatment method within the forensic setting, giving clinical examples, and describe how it links with other theoretical concepts when describing or reflecting on the offender patient.

Baim *et al.* (1999) describes psychodrama as an action method that is structured and focused on the needs of the individual and the group, based on role playing and dramatic action. In a psychodrama session, group members have an opportunity to create a three-dimensional, active environment, which is at one and the same time both imaginary and yet deeply relevant to every aspect of real life (Moreno, 1940). It offers the space for focused dramatic exploration of life situations with developmental feedback from the psychodramatist and the group members. During a psychodrama session, clients are assisted with the help of other group members to use dramatic action to re-enact scenes from their lives. A number of scenes may be portrayed, representing memories of specific events in the past, current unresolved conflicts, inner thought processes, fantasies, dreams or anticipated future events. The scenes either approximate real-life

Grendon and the Emergence of Forensic Therapeutic Communities: Developments in Research and Practice
Edited by Richard Shuker and Elizabeth Sullivan
© 2010 John Wiley & Sons, Ltd.

situations or are externalisations of mental processes. Throughout a psychodrama, the individual at the centre of the enactment, known as the protagonist, is encouraged to gain insight into his common patterns of thinking, feeling and relating to others, to take responsibility for his behaviour and to gain sufficient spontaneity to effectively deal with recurrent and entrenched difficulties. Where appropriate, the protagonist may also be assisted in coming to terms with traumatic or debilitating life events, to correct any resultant maladaptive learning or behaviour, and to express unresolved or repressed feelings about these events. The client is also encouraged to identify and alter common patterns whereby his negative feelings are projected and transferred inappropriately from his inner world onto other people and events. This complex and deeply entrenched process of projection and transference is often at the core of violent and sexually abusive behaviour. Psychodrama also uses the well-known method of role play to assist clients in practising effective and appropriate interpersonal skills. In this way, the destructive patterns of relating, both on a behavioural and emotional level, can be corrected, with clients taking new roles and expanding their role repertoire. As the protagonist takes the roles of significant others in the scenes (role reversal), he is faced with the impact of his behaviour on them, and is encouraged to take responsibility for his actions and to develop empathy for the feelings of others.

As psychodrama is primarily a group method, the members of the group as a whole are encouraged to be active participants. Group members often take on the roles of significant others, known as auxiliary roles, in the protagonist's drama. Auxiliary work is not just intended to benefit the protagonists, taking such a role itself benefits group members as they often gain useful insight into their own problems by participating in the enactment of others' life stories. Furthermore, playing a positive auxiliary role can also provide beneficial behaviour practice for group members. In addition, with its specific focus on role theory and role analysis, psychodrama identifies dysfunctional behaviour and distorted belief systems (cognitions) about self and other, and the associated emotions that motivate offending behaviour. By use of psychodramatic techniques we are able to intervene in these dysfunctional behaviours and beliefs by challenging and correcting mental representations of early childhood experiences. Through role reciprocity the forensic patient is encouraged to take an active part in dealing with his relationships by taking responsibility for his part of any interaction. The techniques of role reversal and doubling encourage the sense of other and other's perspective of self.

Psychodrama developed by J.L. Moreno integrates emotion, intellect and imagination through the development of spontaneity and creativity. Blatner and Blatner (1998) say of Moreno:

In addition to his other contributions Moreno was also one of the founders of social psychology and along with George Herbert Mead and a few others, one of the prime developers of role theory. The idea of using the concept of role as bridge between social and individual psychodynamics was obvious to Moreno. Moreno's intention was that the concept of role could function as a tool in therapy, group work and everyday life. Although role theory as an approach in sociology is essentially descriptive in nature and has thus become an academic theoretical system, Moreno's viewpoint of role is orientated to clinical application and more involved with methodology and is essentially different from the traditional sociological usage (pp. 101–102).

Moreno defined role as:

> The functioning form the individual assumes in the specific moment he reacts to a specific situation in which other persons and objects are involved. The form is created by past experiences and the cultural patterns of the society in which the individual lives … every role is a fusion of private and collective elements. (Moreno cited in Fox 1987, p. 62)

Developing this further, Jefferies (2005) goes on to say:

> As a treatment process, with role theory at its foundation, psychodrama concerns itself with the way an individual responds to a particular situation (context of role), the individual's behavioural responses, his belief system about himself, the other and the world that he inhabits, his feelings and the consequences of such a response. (p. 372)

Williams (1989) describes how an examination of context of action reveals how the interactions of individuals to the reactions of other individuals are organised in time. Investigating the context of role implies an initial enquiry about what the other significant members do and say when the protagonist is in a given scene. Such enquiry often reveals the coalition positions of other members.

By focusing on the individual's behavioural responses, the therapist focuses on what people do and say in relation to the problem they face rather than settling for generalities. Detailed information about behaviour can reveal important distortions or contradictions that are key to understanding the systemic function of behaviour.

The ability to select out, and respond to, information about difference depends largely on the individual's beliefs, presumptions or personal constructs, which exist largely out of consciousness and provide restraints on spontaneity and new action. In a psychodrama the therapist is curious as to who are the major actors who have steered or influenced the protagonist's life in a certain direction. The personal constructs or beliefs pertaining to a role are the elements least likely to emerge from the enactment. It is of little use to ask what a person believes until they are warmed up to a role, whereas the context and behaviour can be established from the outset. Changing old code books and the establishment of new ideas is a prime goal of any therapy. The belief aspect of role is one of the most complex factors involved in role assessment.

Williams suggests that change in the individual cannot occur until the person feels adequately and accurately defined. Only then can their perception of a problem and the consequent perceptions of solutions begin to be helpful. In order for this to occur, people's emotions need to be part of this definition since emotions are primary sources of information about one's own experience of the world. Emotion is the direct experience of the self. It is a crucial regulator of action and furnishes the basis of awareness of what is important to the person. Because it is so dominant, emotional experience can be a powerful tool for changing perceptions and meanings.

Often the meaning or function of a role only becomes clear when one observes what the outcome of the role is. It is only for the sake of analysis that role is broken up into five components: context, behaviour, belief, affect and effect. In reality these all merge into each other. Williams (1989) argued that 'roles are not "things" nor are the components of role "things", they are a construction on experience, a way of making sense of complicated data, a form of distinction that turns behaviour into information for the therapist' (p. 66).

The Process

The process of psychodrama:

- begins by establishing a contract with the client involving a therapeutic formulation and what needs to be addressed in the session;
- moves on to examine the present problem as it relates to the client in the here and now, examining the client's responses to the specific situation in which other persons and objects are involved. It is at this stage that a role analysis is made;
- finds similarities in the recent past in order to check the role analysis and confirms the internal working models operating;
- explores a link between current problems and early developmental experiences;
- helps the client understand his or her own process in life;
- achieves a catharsis if necessary with regard to repressed emotions;
- concretises the issues: the choices and actions that keep the client in the dysfunctional state;

- helps the client see the choices and options in life;
- aids integration of the cognitive and the affective states; and
- achieves closure so that the client can apply what he has learnt from the therapeutic situation.

Psychodrama relies on Vaihinger's 'as if' concept by creating in action the moment when a particular response took place (Vaihinger, 1911). In psychodrama the client is encouraged to *show* the problem rather than tell the group and the therapist about it. There is no script, the drama is spontaneous, created in the moment by the protagonist, group members and the therapist, and as such the *there and then* of the moment is created in the *here and now* of the psychodrama space. John will play Fred's perception of his abusive father, Pete his abandoning mother, whilst other group members may join in to double the emotions that Fred may be feeling but not stating. Psychodrama techniques, such as role reversal, doubling and mirroring are all used in the therapeutic process.

Each psychodrama session starts with a warm-up, using creative techniques to increase a sense of trust and encourage interactions between group members. It stimulates the creativity and spontaneity and helps focus on personal issues. The warm-up phase leads to the selection of the offender whose work will be the focus of the enactment. In this way the protagonist works for himself and the group.

The enactment stage explores the issues heightened by the warm-up process. During this phase, the offender will place characters that form part of his internal world on the psychodrama stage. Because psychodrama is intrinsically an action method, the protagonist is encouraged to move quickly into action, creating the space in which events took place. The physical setting of scenes and their portrayal evokes memories and emotions associated with the space, and counters the distortions and evasive manoeuvres that may be introduced by verbal disclosure. Pete relentlessly stuck to his account of how his victim accidentally drowned in the bath, despite being constantly challenged by his small group, that is, until in a psychodrama as he played out the scene in which the event took place, his distorted version of events could no longer be sustained.

At the end of the enactment stage the group comes together to share what they have resonated with. Jim shared with George, who had been working on his sister's murder, that his own sister had died some 20 years ago and that it wasn't until George's work that he realised he had never mourned her death. Marvin wept the tears he failed to weep as a child as he remembered his mother's death. On another occasion Paul shared with Simon his own brutal beating at the hand of his father.

Attachment Theory and Psychodrama

The work of John Bowlby (1969, 1973, 1980), Mary Ainsworth *et al.* (1978) and Mary Main (1998) support and provide a framework for my experience as a psychodramatist at Grendon. Bowlby's attachment theory states that the kinds of experience a person has in childhood and the kinds of attachments created are crucial to the development of the personality and the attachment styles they develop (Bowlby, 1979). Research supporting Bowlby's ideas indicates that many people suffering from anxiety, insecurity or showing signs of dependency, immaturity and low concept have been exposed to pathogenic parenting resulting in much partially unconscious resentment persisting into later life, and usually expressed away from parents towards someone weaker (Henderson, 1974).

The concept of 'internal working models' derived from Bowlby's attachment theory is also significant in understanding criminal behaviour. Internal working models are mental maps an individual has about himself and his environment, in particular about self and relationship to other. They act as a filter by which the individual makes sense of himself, of other and of his world. The quality of the model will be based on two judgements: whether or not the individual sees himself as worthy of support or care and whether or not important others are seen as people who will give support or care. Attachment theorists argue that it is not the experience alone but what the individual does with their early experiences that is significant for the attachment styles they develop. Internal working models are dynamic and as such can be changed through psychodrama and other psychotherapies. For Bowlby, treatment entails reversing those experiences in the most honest way possible (Bowlby, 1979). In the context of therapeutic work with individuals Bowlby (1998) defined five tasks:

1.   Create a safe place, or secure base, for clients to explore thoughts, feelings and experience regarding self and attachment figures.
2.   Explore current relationships with attachment figures.
3.   Explore relationships with psychotherapist as an attachment figure.
4.   Explore the early relationship between early childhood attachment experiences and current relationships.
5.   Find new ways of regulating attachment anxiety (i.e. emotional regulation).

Jeremy Holmes (2001) suggests attachment-based psychotherapy is a process of story making and story breaking. One needs to break the rigid unemotional and unrelated story of the avoidant individual and create a story with greater emotional content, a better balance of positive and negative experiences and more descriptive and realistic narrative descriptions of relationships. With the preoccupied individual, one must break the emotional dysphoria by creating a story that is infused by logic and perspective and balance of affect and reflective understanding.

Psychodrama offers a forum for the offender to consider in detail how their modes of procuring and dealing with others may be influenced by the experiences they have had in earlier childhood. As a therapeutic method, psychodrama employs action methods to encourage the expression of suppressed and repressed emotions and to introduce the possibility of change by correcting the maladaptive learning that has taken place. It helps the offender understand how he has projected negative feelings and transferred his inner disruptive world onto other persons and situations.

Within the context of the group, the prisoner is encouraged to find new ways of perceiving and reacting to past and present life experiences.

This means taking the offender back to his early attachment relationships, the 'there and then' becomes the 'here and now' created by the auxiliaries holding the roles of early attachment figures. As previously stated, this enables expression of repressed negative feelings towards these early attachment figures, often displaced on members of the public who have been caught up in the transference, but it also makes it possible for the offender to understand what he has done with the experience, how he has let his interpretation of the experience affect his life, his view of himself, his relationship with others and his view of the world in general. It also provides the offender with the ability to self-soothe when confronted by attachment anxieties.

Roy presented two scenes in the early part of his psychodrama, in the visiting room where his girlfriend boasted of her sexual exploits with men she was seeing (as a lifer, they had come to an arrangement that she should be free to live her life without restraints as long as she was honest with him) and the scene of his offence where the prostitute he had murdered had laughed at his inability to have an erection and terrified him by having an epileptic seizure (he was unaware at the time of the offence that this was what happened). Both scenes held memory traces of his early experiences of a humiliating, rejecting, terrorising mother and his belief or working model, 'that women are bitches, they are out to hurt me and therefore cannot be trusted'. With this internal working model, his response was one of anger and violence. Roy was helped to see how the present situation and his offence held memory traces of past experiences, how his actions were influenced by distorted belief systems and negative feelings associated with early childhood. It was important for him to have an opportunity to trace his anger back to its source, to confront his persecutory mother, to speak his anger as well as to cry his tears. Simply venting his anger and despair was not enough however. Brennan *et al.* (1998) suggest that by learning to self-soothe attachment anxieties, and to find other mechanisms besides avoidance to deal with fear and vulnerability that can be activated within close relationships, clients can begin to develop more secure relationship experiences. It was necessary for Roy to develop such an ability when faced with attachment anxieties in the present. The ability to self-soothe can be achieved by making use of the concept of surplus reality.

Surplus reality refers to that part of our experience that remains within us when the external world has taken its share of attention; the psychic reality is 'made wider' and the intangible, invisible dimensions of the protagonist's life are given expression (Moreno & Moreno, 1969, p. 124 cited by Kellerman, 1992, p114). In its use of surplus reality, psychodrama offers the emotionally hungry prisoner the experience, perhaps for the first time, of finding out what it would have been like to be held, to be told he was loved, to receive tenderness rather than the cruelty. Roy needed the experience of a holding and attuned mother, experienced in the surplus reality of the session and then internalised. In John's psychodrama, as his mother lies dying in hospital, John hears what he thinks and hopes she might have said before she died. The auxiliary holding his mother's role takes his hand. Nigel, at the end of his psychodrama when asked what he wanted but never had says, 'To sit on my father's lap and have him read me a story.' In the 'as if-ness' and the surplus reality of the moment, Nigel sits on the lap of the prisoner who holds his father's role and hears the story he never heard. Such experiences in psychodrama have the potential of reducing the persecutory internalised figure that often drives the inmate's sadistic behaviour. In this case it also provided the auxiliary, who had captured the moment with his storytelling, to reflect on his own fathering role. 'I have never read to my kids. When I am released this is the first thing I am going to do.' The experience in the auxiliary role had not only provided Nigel with an important moment but also allowed the auxiliary to increase his own role repertoire.

In John and Roy's psychodramas, both were given the mother they needed, thus developing a self-soothing aspect within themselves, enabling them to meet their emotional needs in the present. Roy also needed to differentiate between anger at his mother and present anger towards himself for maintaining patterns developed in the past and transferred onto his victim. Finally in the psychodrama, Roy was given an opportunity to address his victim, to share his realisation that he had unwittingly transferred onto her his unresolved feelings towards his mother and encouraged to explore new ways of dealing with the situation with his girlfriend, free from the internal persecutory figure of his mother.

Transference and Psychodrama

Many of the men who come to Grendon have been abused against, as well as being abusers. Some of them experienced extreme cruelty in their child-hood. There are tales of children beaten, degraded and abandoned by one or both parents or by care workers. There are stories of violent incest, of children who were fed their own faeces, whose hands were placed on elec-tric fires or who were required to give sexual pleasure to fathers and mothers. Many helplessly witnessed scenes of violence between parents or became the chosen object of redirected anger. Traumatised by these early experiences they have grown up with little trust in relationships and are resentful and angry at what has happened to them. In some cases they have internalised and identified with the aggressor and have come to despise that part of themselves that they perceive as weak and helpless. There is often a frightening similarity between their sadistic behaviour and these early experiences.

Zane, having been regularly sexually abused by his social worker, often talks in his psychodrama group about despising weakness in others. When others shed their tears he physically withdraws, his face hardens and he has great difficulty in staying in the room. He hates himself for, as he sees it, allowing the abuse, for not doing anything about it. He has hidden his vulnerability behind a facade of extreme cruelty and is serving a sentence for attacking an old woman: 'I hated her for being so weak and helpless.' Through his work in psychodrama, Zane has come to acknowledge that he had projected his despised weaker self onto his victim and attacked that part of himself that he saw in her. He truthfully says he has no empathy and wishes that he had but he will never do so until he can find empathy for his own vulnerability and helplessness. At present he chooses to dis-tance himself from the little boy who used to sit on the doorstep hungry to be loved and noticed. He blames his emotional neediness for his abuse.

Other inmates, when they re-experience rejection and abandonment, displace their primitive rage onto their victims. John, in the middle of his psychodrama in which he was attempting to understand his rape of a woman, broke down in tears saying:

> *Every time I start thinking about what I did to you I just want to pick up a glass and smash it into my arm … It sounds crazy but I want to rip myself to bits. I hate myself for what I have done to you. The only person I wanted to hurt was my Mum. God knows what was going through my head that night because I don't … I did worse to you than my mother ever did to me.* (Jefferies, 1991, p. 195)

Kernberg (1984) emphasises the dangerous violence inherent in paranoid attitudes of some offender patients. He states that it is therefore difficult to work with ordinary psychotherapeutic approaches because such approaches rely on the therapeutic relationship to represent symbolically the client's internal world, a world full of destructive feelings that places the therapist at considerable risk. Psychodrama is also concerned with the symbolic representation of the offender's external and internal reality but the representation takes a different route. The 'as if-ness' developed between client and therapist through the transference is achieved through the enactment itself, relying on auxiliaries and scene setting to represent time, place and other. The therapist's interpretations are expressed through the psychodramatic interventions themselves, thus relieving the therapist of the task of becoming everything to the protagonist and thus enabling her to stand alongside the expression of aggression rather than becoming the recipient of these primitive emotions. John, for example, was helped within the psychodrama session to understand how his early experiences with his mother and his angry feelings about her treatment of him had been displaced onto someone he perceived as weaker than himself. Within the session he was taken back to the scene of his mother's ill treatment and dealt with his anger directly. He had an opportunity to speak to her about how she would abuse him and his brothers and his sisters.

> All I wanted to do when you were drunk and in a bad mood was go up and hold you, but I was so scared … all I wanted was for you to love me. All I wanted was a wife and three kids, that was all I wanted … but I always questioned when people said, 'I love you'; I always pushed them away. I couldn't take it. I thought they were going to do things you did, be all lovey-dovey and then kick me in the teeth.
>
> By role reversing with his mother in an attempt to understand her actions he was able to reduce the internal rage. The psychodrama session ended with him placing a flower on her grave stating, 'I love and forgive you'. John's mother died whilst he was serving a previous prison sentence. He had failed to make peace with her and therefore with himself. The psychodrama allowed him such an opportunity. (Jefferies, 1991, p. 195)

Expression of aggression for many offenders has been their only form of survival and meaning. It has also been said that the persecutor of violence is as traumatised by their violent behaviour as is their victim(s). In order to survive this trauma they cut off from the feeling part of themselves with devastating consequences for themselves and for others, as is seen in the offender's behaviour. This phenomenon has also recently been witnessed in the brutalised and brutalising behaviour of the soldiers in Iraq and depicted in the film *The Valley of Eliah*. Morris (2004, p. 48) states 'they (the psychopath) simply disavow the trauma. … The psychopathic defence adaptively builds up to such, that the effects of intensely traumatising experiences are not felt. Likewise, the infliction of intense cruelty to others is not felt.' It is essential then, that the offender who has cut off from the early trauma finds a way to re-connect, to return to the emotion, to the memory and so collapse the psychopathic defence in order for empathetic resonance to return. Psychodrama re-enactment, be it in mirror, facilitates this process.

Development of Empathy through Role Reversal, Doubling and Mirroring

What is clear with some offenders is their difficulty of keeping the other in mind, to understand the other's subjective experience or 'mentallisation'. Fonagy states that 'when mentallization fails, violence results' (Fonagy, 2003).

The capacity to empathise with others, to perceive and share an emotional response, is related to caring, co-operative, pro-social behaviour. It is contingent upon cognitive ability to discriminate affective cues in others; the cognitive skill in assuming the perspective and role of another person; and upon emotional responsiveness – the ability to experience the other person's emotions (Feshbach, 1989).

Role reversal was developed by Moreno as a tool to encourage the protagonist to understand the point of view of the counterpart role and to find a peaceful co-existence, captured in Moreno's poem on encounter.

> A meeting of two: eye to eye, face to face,
> And when you are near I will tear your eyes out
> and place them instead of mine
> and you will tear my eyes out
> and place them instead of yours
> then I will look at you with your eyes
> and you will look at me with mine.
>
> (Moreno, 1914)

Role reversal as a technique is considered by many practitioners as the single most effective psychodrama instrument. According to Brind and Brind (1967), role reversal 'naturally compels the protagonist to deepen and widen his empathic identification with the opponent, just as this same process compels him to see his own self enactment through the eyes of his adversary or the adversary substitute (auxiliary) who portrays him'. With regard to the offender, it is a technique that encourages the offender to understand the subjective experience of his victim. William, who is serving a life sentence for killing his common-law wife, failed to understand her position and minimised his actions because of hurtful comments made by her prior to the incident. It was not until he was placed in her role in a psychodrama session conducted from her position that he became aware of her distress and anger at him for constantly having affairs, fathering children by other women and her sense of betrayal. Events came to a head on the night of his offence when he returned home having used cocaine with one of his other partners and she struck out verbally to take her revenge. In the psychodrama, in her role, he broke down, as he was able to understand her 'subjective experience' of the relationship and his behaviour. He moved from justifying and defending his position to one of remorse for the pain and cruelty he had inflicted and understood the context of her verbal attack for which she had lost her life. In William's psychodrama, the techniques of doubling and mirroring were also used to increase empathy. The doubling technique is used to express verbally the hidden contents of the protagonist's communication (Kellerman, 1992). William listened to clarifying voices (doubling) from other group members, both in his own role as he reflected on his actions and in the role of his victim. This not only provided further insight for him but also enabled other group members to develop their own empathy skills by placing themselves alongside, trying to understand the thoughts and feelings of both parties. At times, William was also asked to look at the situation involving himself and his partner from the outside, the technique of mirroring.

To take the offender beyond their manifest aggression to the latent despair about what they have done to others, and what has been done to them, is a journey to be taken with caution. Guy, a life-serving prisoner at Grendon unable to live with what he had done and what had been done to him, made a decision to end his life. His last message, written before his death, reminded us that no one was to blame, or was at fault but himself, and as such he was obsessed by a death wish which he finally turned upon himself, becoming the last victim in a line of victims. 'My thank you is for your help and for your concerns.' Sadly our concern for him did not prevent him from taking his own life. His final message caused me to reflect on Zulueta's statement when commenting on Bowlby: 'Human infants are pre-programmed to develop in a socially co-operative way: whether they do so or not relies to a high degree on how they are treated' (Bowlby, 1988: 9). In other words: 'The forensic patient does to his objects what was once done to him (Zulueta in Cordess & Cox, 1996, p. 186).' Guy not only destroyed the life of others as his own life had been destroyed, but by taking his life he completed the full circle by re-enacting the ultimate abuse.

Practical Implications

Naturally there are difficulties in running a psychodrama group in such an environment. To start with, the group is made up of offenders who have committed different offences: there is no one so intolerant of offenders than fellow offenders. The psychodrama and the protagonist depend on the support of the group to provide a secure base in which the work can be achieved. This means that introducing psychodrama and building group unity cannot be hurried. If they are, one pays the price later as the work intensifies and the therapist looks for support from the group. Comments from other offenders such as, 'I have no time for sex offenders' or, 'You are an animal' fail to provide a setting that encourages the offender to share their feelings about themselves or their offences. During the early sessions, the therapist needs to make sure that everyone, whatever their offence and however well they can articulate their feelings, has space to explore issues that need to be explored, however disturbing these issues are to others. Using psychodrama warm-ups helps group members to begin to share of themselves and to realise that in order to help each other, this group (in contrast to other groups they experience) needs to be supportive, facilitating and encouraging, rather than confronting. If the action is stopped by another offender passing judgement on what is happening in the psychodrama space, all can be lost. Many weeks of building up to the stage where a father who had killed his child dared risk looking at his actions, or holding the murdered child in his arms, can be lost by a hostile comment. Such a comment can force the protagonist back into his world of isolation, defensive manoeuvres or self-recrimination, once again unable to speak about the unspeakable.

As well as these initial difficulties there is the fact that offenders often fear the emotional side of psychodrama. 'If I lose control, what then?' is a familiar question expressing real fear. Their inability to control their violence brought them into prison, and acts of violence against each other can lead to them being transferred out of Grendon. Experiencing emotions that have not been dealt with before raises anxiety as to whether the group, protagonist, and therapist can survive the emotions that need to be expressed.

Tony came to the session and warned the group of the intensity of his anger towards his uncle who had forced him to eat his own faeces before sexually abusing him. The group noticeably withdrew, not knowing whether they or the therapist could contain his anger. No one wanted to volunteer to hold the role of the abusing uncle, fearful of his own safety in the face of negative transference. At such times, the protagonist and the group are in different places. However warmed up and ready for work the protagonist might be, it is inadvisable to go ahead if the group is not warmed up to the protagonist and to the issue itself. It is essential to acknowledge the group's need for some form of containment and its lack of readiness to deal with certain issues. It was several weeks before the group felt able to address Tony's work. Together we found creative and psychodramatic ways of making it safe for everyone, including Tony, to express the anger he was fearful of expressing at the age of 12.

More often or not, angry outbursts are followed by tears of regret and remorse for what they have done and for not receiving what was rightfully theirs as a child. For many of us, tears are a natural expression of emotion, but for the offender, who has been brought up in an environment where to be a man is to adopt an unfeeling macho image or where one has been beaten for crying, the psychodrama session might be the first acceptable place to share these emotions.

In a psychodrama session it is important to ask oneself, 'What more do I need to achieve in this session?' One can ruin the impact of a session by attempting too much. It is vital to keep to the contract. To take the prisoner, without further negotiation, beyond what he has been asked for or wants to do is to put it all at risk.

In conclusion, psychodrama treatment continues to be an effective way of working with the offender patient at HMP Grendon, supported by the small and large group in the context of a living and learning environment. Because they have been incarcerated for their behaviour it is important that we, and they, learn to manage behaviour but we also need to interpret it and change it. Offenders have primitive communications. If the offender does not have the capacity to put feelings into words then he resorts to action. Acts have symbolic meaning and so we need to ask, why now? why this person and not another? Often the offender, and to some degree ourselves, are reluctant to do this thinking; too much focus is put on incarceration.

References

Ainsworth, M.D.S., Blehar, M.C., Waters, E. & Wall, S. (1978). *Patterns of Attachment: A Psychological Study of the Strange Situation*. Hillside, NJ: Erlbaum.

Baim, C., Allam, J., Eames, T., Dunford, S. & Hunt, S. (1999). The use of psychodrama to enhance victim empathy in sex offenders: an evaluation. *The Journal of Sexual Aggression*, 4(1), 4–14.

Blatner, A. & Blatner, A. (1998). *Foundations of Psychodrama*. New York: Springer.

Bowlby, J. (1969). *Attachment and Loss Vol 1: Attachment* (2nd edn). London: Hogarth Press.

Bowlby, J. (1973). *Attachment and Loss Vol 2: Separation.* New York: Basic Books.

Bowlby, J. (1979). *Making and Breaking of Affectional Bonds.* London: Tavistock.

Bowlby, J. (1980). *Attachment and Loss Vol 3: Loss, Sadness and Depression.* New York: Basic Books.

Bowlby, J. (1988). *A Secure Base: Clinical Applications of Attachment Theory.* London: Tavistock.

Bowlby, J. (1998, reprint). *A Secure Base: Clinical Applications of Attachment Theory.* London: Routledge.

Brennan, K.A., Clark, C.L. & Shaver, P.R. (1998). Self report measurement of adult attachment: An integrative overview. In J.A. Simpson & W.S. Rhodes (Eds) *Attachment Theory and Close Relationships* (pp. 46–76). New York: Guilford Press.

Brind, A.B. & Brind, N. (1967) Role reversal. *American Journal of Psychodrama & Group Psychotherapy, 20,* 88–9.

Feshbach, N.D. (1989). Empathy training and pro-social behaviour. In J. Grobel & R.A. Hinde (Eds) *Aggression and War: Their Biological and Social Basis.* Cambridge: Cambridge University Press.

Fonagy, P. (2003). Towards a development understanding of violence. *British Journal of Psychiatry, 183,* 190–192.

Fox, J. (1987). *The Essential Moreno.* New York: Springer Press.

Henderson, A. (1974). Care-eliciting behaviour in man. *Journal of Nervous and Mental Diseases, 159,* 172–181.

Holmes, J. (2001). *In Search of a Secure Base.* London: Routledge.

Jefferies, J. (1991). What we are doing here is defusing bombs. In P. Holmes (Ed.) *Psychodrama Inspiration and Technique.* London: Routledge.

Jefferies, J. (2005) Psychodrama: Working through action: 'My thank you is for your concern'. *Group Analysis, 38,* 371–379.

Kellerman, P.F. (1992). *Focus on Psychodrama.* London: Jessica Kingsley.

Kernberg, O. (1984). *Severe Personality Disorder: Psychotherapeutic Strategies.* New Haven: Yale University Press.

Main, M. (1998). *Adult Classification System.* Unpublished manuscript, University of California.

Moreno, J.L. (1914). *Einladung zu einer Begegnung (Invitation to an Encounter).* Vienna: Anzengruber Verlag.

Moreno, J. (1940). Psychodrama treatment of marriage problems. *American Journal of Sociometry, 3,* 1–23.

Morris, M. (2004). Psychopathy: the dominant paradigm. In D. Jones (Ed.) *Working with Dangerous People* (pp. 48–49). Oxford: Radcliffe Medical Press.

Vaihinger, H. (1911). *Philosophie des Als Ob* [The philosophy of As If]. Berlin: Reutner & Reinhard.

Williams A. (1989). *The Passionate Technique.* London: Tavistock/Routledge.

Zulueta, F. (1996) Theories of sexual aggression and violence. In C. Cordess & M. Cox (Eds) *Forensic Psychotherapy.* London: Jessica Kingsley.

Chapter 9

Self and Social Function: Art Therapy and Readiness for Treatment in a Therapeutic Community Prison

Bill Wylie

Introduction

Thinking, feeling, acting are requisites for self-expression. If not in harmony, then there will be inhibition in one or other, if not in all of them. Such inhibition may be described as a blockage in the natural flow of harmonious being. The result is a dysfunction of communication either externally with society or internally with the whole self. The population of HMP Grendon is characterised by high levels of personality disorder, psychiatric symptomatology, significant loss or separation from parental figures and incidence of physical and/or sexual abuse (Shine & Newton, 2000). Research evidence indicates that certain factors showed a high correlation with the risk of future recidivism and these criminogenic factors are affected by multi-factorial therapy supported by a multidisciplinary team: 'The significance of this milieu is in understanding the functioning of the multidisciplinary team and contributions made from the different therapeutic paradigms.' (Shine & Morris, 2000, p. 202.) Art therapy provides a significant contribution to this holistic process and by formally describing, analysing and evaluating art therapy on the Assessment Unit at HMP Grendon, it is the aim of this research to clarify the value of its use as a contribution to the assessment of readiness or lack of readiness for therapeutic community engagement.

Grendon and the Emergence of Forensic Therapeutic Communities: Developments in Research and Practice
Edited by Richard Shuker and Elizabeth Sullivan
© 2010 John Wiley & Sons, Ltd.

Art Therapy

Waller and Dalley (1992) suggest that 'art therapy' describes a collection of diverse practices held together fundamentally by their practitioners' 'belief in the healing value of image-making'. The focus of art therapy is the image and the process involves a transaction between the maker, the artefact and the therapist. As in all therapy, bringing unconscious feelings to consciousness and thereafter exploring them holds true of art therapy, but here the richness of artistic symbol and metaphor illuminates the process.

According to the British Association of Art Therapists (BAAT), art therapy is a form of therapy in which the making of visual images – paintings, drawings etc. in the presence of a qualified art therapist – contributes towards externalisation of thoughts and feelings that may otherwise remain unexpressed. The images may have a diagnostic as well as a therapeutic function, in that they provide the individual and the therapist with a visible record of the session and give indicators for further treatment. Art therapists may work with transference – that is, feelings from the past, which are projected onto the therapist. Such feelings are usually contained by the artwork, and this enables resolution to take place indirectly if necessary (BAAT, 1989).

HMP Grendon's purpose as a therapeutic community is to increase individual confidence and self-esteem, to reduce offending tendencies and to develop more positive relationships with others. Art therapy contributes by encouraging pro-social behaviour in the context of a complementary group process; therein is the possibility for creatively addressing and promoting such qualities as empathy and communication skills, listening to others, appropriate expression of emotions and awareness of own behaviour. According to Schaverien (1987):

> Once an image exists 'out there', in the world, it interacts with and affects the artist. It also interacts with and affects other people, the consequences of which have repercussions for the artist. For the client in therapy, who is unable to relate easily to other people, who is also perhaps unable to relate to herself, the image-making process may play a fundamental part in enabling her to begin to do so. To make something that can be seen can authenticate her experience and even her existence. (pp. 84–85)

Creativity is a process of perception, the interaction of unconscious and conscious modes of thinking. The art therapist is involved with creative expression and the making of visual equivalents for inner feelings. This is a psychodynamic process that facilitates self-awareness through reflection on the imagery produced, thus influencing behaviour and social functioning. By this process the self is externalised; communicated through creativity, emotion is viewed in imagery, interpreted and acknowledged. Art therapy is an exploratory process that enables the individual to reflect upon the past and its influence on the present and on the future. The artwork encourages the maker to engage with their true thoughts and feelings. For instance, personality disorders are ingrained and enduring behaviour patterns; reflecting on past history through image making develops awareness of the person's responses to life experience while the images facilitate acknowledgement of the individual's emotional reaction to events, promoting the potential for change. In execution and content, the picture reveals evidence of the true person rather than how they choose to present or see themselves. As such, art therapy is a unique psychotherapeutic service providing support for improvement with coping skills and in the long term contributes to personal and social integration.

Setting

In the Assessment Unit at Grendon, sessions begin with a description of the art therapy process and the group is offered a theme, which does not vary from week to week, but it does contain an element of choice. The men are asked to consider their reasons for coming to Grendon, their past lives and their hopes for the future. Additionally, they may use the session as an opportunity to express what they are feeling at this particular moment. So, the participants are asked to think about their lives and express that engagement in visual equivalents. No suggestion or specific directive is given about the placement of elements within the compositional structure. Referring to the initial stage of working with the art therapy process, Case (1998) concluded that in an assessment there are twin tasks: discovering if the person is able to make use of a therapeutic space, and assessing their state of mind in terms of their inner world and the effect of the outer environment upon them.

Rationale

The purpose of the research described here was to define aspects of image making that might be used to assess readiness to engage in the therapeutic community model of treatment, which is highly demanding emotionally, intellectually and socially, requiring motivation and readiness to engage. A qualitative research method was employed in which extensive analytical notes were written about each image, in addition to the conventional case notes, in order to facilitate the emergence and interpretation of meaningful graphic elements. This process was informed by psychoanalytic theory and the literature on interpretation of images in art therapy. This research lays the foundation for further quantitative research to demonstrate the extent to which predictions of readiness for treatment based on these elements are accurate.

Method

As stated above, participants were asked to consider their reasons for coming to Grendon, their past lives and their hopes for the future. Data was collected between March 2004 and May 2005 and the images reproduced here were extracted from the study of more than 200 images. Session notes and detailed research notes were kept on the conscious and unconscious symbolism of the images produced, noting participants' behaviour and demeanour. The resulting analysis was compared with summaries of assessment contributed by the other members of the multidisciplinary team and the subsequent progress of the men was noted in terms of whether they were allocated to a therapy wing and whether they remained on wing or left without completing therapy. Eight examples are presented here that exemplify common characteristics, found in images made by this population, which are used as indicators of readiness for treatment.

Time, Space and Colour

Analysis shows that many participants chose to engage with the task in terms of three aspects of life experience – past, present and future. Graphically, this temporal symbolism was often constructed such that the picture could be read from left to right, from past to future with the present centrally placed. Buck and Warren (1995) observed that 'the proportion, perspective, and details in a drawing are general characteristics that can provide information about the functioning of an individual in the context of their expected level of functioning' (p. 25). Thus the image provides an indication of the psychological propensity of the maker. In addition, according to Edwards (1999): 'Image-making, story-telling, therapy and research are each, in their way, concerned with joining together actions, intentions, emotions, perceptions and events into meaningful narratives, though these narratives may take different forms.' The picture produced in art therapy is a story of being in time, a history of experience, a narration of the maker's passage through life.

Figure 9.1 is a drawing made by a man who had difficulty with emotional expression but who persisted in his endeavour to visually describe aspects of his life. He sat for some time before starting to draw. He could not think of a satisfactory image to describe his past or future so he concentrated on the present, which he described as 'going through a tunnel with a light at the other end'. This referred to his coming to Grendon and the hope that therapy would help him to change. The centrally placed image of a railway track going through a dark tunnel inspired him to talk about his past; remembering childhood holidays by the seaside, he began to draw sandcastles to the left of the central, 'present' metaphor. In the area below the sandcastles there was a weapon and as he drew, he related the reason for his imprisonment. Becoming more relaxed, the participant was able to imagine a future that he hoped would be tranquil and peaceful. To the right of the tunnel he drew mountains and a lake that encapsulated his hopes for the future. The participant had been anxious and uncommunicative at the beginning of the session, reticent to reveal himself. However by the end of the session he had become more relaxed and communicative. This man had been in the army and then in prison, environments where control over the self is of primary importance, where emotional expression is unacceptable. Yet within a single session of two hours' duration he had revealed much about his life experience and had expressed feelings regarding these experiences. Art therapy may be described as a process

Figure 9.1

Figure 9.2

of revelation – a revealing of oneself to oneself and to others. The image produced provides evidence of the maker's being at the time of coming to Grendon and in conjunction with his affect during the session, contributed to the assessment of that individual's readiness to engage in further group work.

Figure 9.2 is that of a man who appeared not to be ready for group therapy at the time of attending the art therapy session. He too found difficulty with emotional expression, seemed anxious with the situation and was reticent to communicate. However, the outcome of the session was quite different to the previous example. After sitting motionless for some time the man decided to fold his paper in half, an indication that he was unwilling to address the 'enormity' of the task placed before him, i.e. he was unable to openly express his feelings by using the whole of the paper. Again this area of paper was too great for he drew a tiny gravestone to the right of centre, an image insignificant in proportion to the potential area available for the construction of a picture. Nothing more was added. Yet this small revelation had been too great, for he put down his pencil, rose and left the room. He remained in Grendon for just four months.

The Form of Intention

In figure 9.1 the participant addressed the three periods of his life – the past, the present and the future – thereby exhibiting a capacity to engage with all three aspects and was able to discuss them in a social context. The structure of the imagery is such that the journey of his life could be read from left to right – the past was drawn on the left, the present was centrally placed and the future was on the right. It is suggested that this narrative movement, the telling of a story and consequent reading of it from left to right is indicative of someone who has a capacity to participate in therapeutic process. That he has a willingness to attend to all three aspects of his life with the intention to change is evident from the placement of the three chronological periods, starting with the past, moving to the right across the paper and concluding with a symbol for the future. In this example the movement towards the future is emphasised by the railway track, which curves to the right through a dark tunnel to the light of future peace and tranquillity. Further, the accompanying change of affect from inhibited unease to open self-expression communicated readiness to become involved with therapy.

In comparison figure 9.2, the drawing of a gravestone, indicates someone who was not ready for therapy at that time. The man folded his paper in half, thereby indicating restraint, an unwillingness to openly express himself. Reticence to communicate emotion was symbolised by the difficulty he experienced with starting to draw, then by the minimal size of the object placed on the paper to the right of centre. This placement was also unusual in that the subject matter relating to a past event was positioned to the right in the area normally reserved for illustrating the future. The gravestone was surrounded by empty space, it was without context, again showing difficulty in addressing the subject. Finally the need to leave the room was an indication that the man was not ready for therapy.

In a study designed to assess the impact of drawing topic on children's colour use when drawing affectively salient topics, it was concluded that children tend to associate a negative emotion with dark colours, e.g. black or brown, while yellow and orange are often associated with positive, happy feelings (Burkitt & Newell, 2005). Additionally, children depict the emotional significance of a drawn topic through size, whereby appealing figures are exaggerated in size and potentially threatening figures are reduced in size (Thomas *et al.*, 1989). It is suggested that these conclusions regarding colour and size are also pertinent in the consideration of artwork made by adults who do not have the experience of art education. Men on the Assessment Unit often choose black paper to symbolise their unhappy past or use bright colour, especially yellow, to represent a positive hope for the future. A negative approach is described in figure 9.2, where the participant produced a small drawing relating to an unhappy event. The two images described were monochrome drawings, the positive image was a pencil drawing and the negative one made using a black felt tip pen, both on white paper. The first illustration was a positive example of someone who was willing to enter a therapeutic alliance through visual expression. He did this by imaginatively conveying a desire to address the totality of his life; the past, present and future were graphically communicated in chronological sequence across the paper from left to right, from past to future. However, the lack of colour may indicate a degree of emotional reserve.

In his book on art and psychoanalysis, Fuller (1980) described aesthetics as 'the specific structuring of feeling' (p. 187). In considering image-making as a depiction of the outside world and expression of the internal world of the maker, Fuller identified an underlying biological influence on aesthetics that can be defined in terms of object relations theory, or the concept of fusion and separation related to child development. Fuller cites Milner's book, *On Not Being Able to Paint* (1950), in which the analyst described her attempt to find visual equivalence to her psychological/emotional experiences. She noted when painting, there occurred, 'a fusion into a never-before-known wholeness; not only were the object and oneself no longer felt to be separate but neither were thought and sensation and feeling and action' (p. 142). This led her to suggest that a sense of union is achieved in attempts to create a work of art: 'this transcendence of separateness, might it not have its parallel in the union with other people that working together for a common purpose achieves?' (p. 143). For Milner there was a fear to be encountered in the abandonment to colour, and fear of what might happen if one let go of one's mental hold on the drawn outline which kept everything in its place – the outline represented the world of facts. This suggests that, in addition to representing external reality, drawing facilitates a definition of reality and this expression is more clearly enhanced by the use of colour. Naumberg (1958) observed that 'the process of art therapy is based on the recognition that man's most fundamental thoughts and feelings, derived from the unconscious, reach expression in images rather than in words'. The following examples show positive engagement, emphasised by the additional use of colour, indicating either an increased capacity for emotional expression, or that what is being communicated is of particular importance to the artist.

In figure 9.3 the surface area of the white paper has been divided into four sections: the two left sections address childhood and happier times prior to criminal activities, the two right sections deal with imprisonment and consideration of the future. Words dominate each quadrant of the composition, illustrating reserve regarding artistic ability (many participants add words to their pictures believing themselves unable to adequately express themselves in visual terms). Initially this man used pencil to describe his childhood experiences and, in the top left quadrant, drew his family home. The word 'love' dominates this section, along with other positive feelings such as 'confidence' and 'security'. There are heart shapes on which he has written family members. The section below also engages

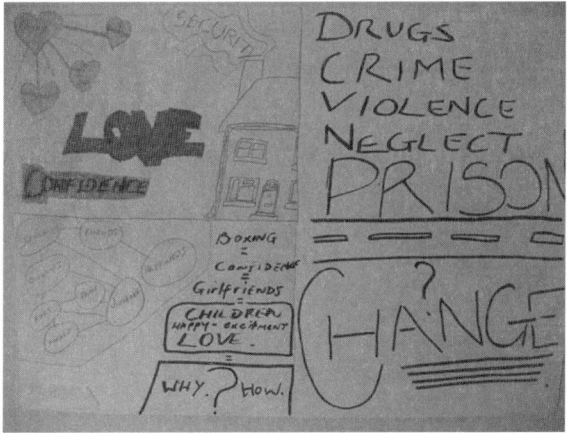

Figure 9.3

with the past, but is divided between early childhood bullying (placed to the left), and later positive developmental experiences that compel him to ask why it went wrong. In the top right section, in large letters, is a list of words – 'drugs, crime, violence, neglect, prison'. Finally, in the bottom quadrant the word 'change' is underlined many times. It is separated from the negative, top right area by a road, which represents his journey through Grendon. It is significant that the participant began his image using a pencil but later used felt tip pens. The use of pencil on white paper to illustrate his childhood is emotionally symbolic of returning to the past, to a time as a child when he would have used such materials to make a drawing, and that choosing to exchange the pencil for felt tip pens was a means of differentiating childhood and later experience. It is also significant that this section, which addressed early emotional experience, is the only area in which the participant used colour. It would seem that the man's childhood was a positive experience as he has attempted to embody that period of his life by drawing the family home rather than simply writing the words. He repeated this process when he drew a road to symbolise the importance of his journey through Grendon.

Figure 9.4 further exemplifies the use of colour to emphasise meaning. The paper is divided into two sections, past and future, separated by the present symbolised by a road (life's journey). Past (left section) and future (right section) are emotionally contrasted by the use of colour – black to represent the negative past and yellow to express a happy future. Yellow is used to emphasise a positive aspect of the artist's life, similar to the use of yellow to represent the positive feeling aroused by thoughts of the family environment expressed in figure 9.3. Again, words describe feelings but

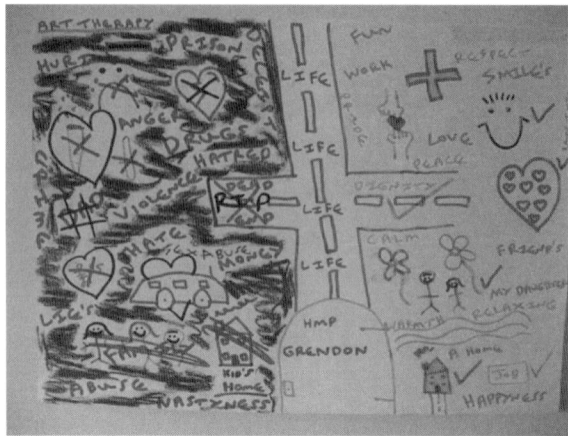

Figure 9.4

colour is used to emphasise the contrast – red for negative emotions such as hate and violence in the 'past' section, whereas orange and green are positively used in the future, 'love' is written in orange and 'peace' is green. A road representing life's journey is often shown as a crossroad by the residents in Grendon and represents the choice between returning to a criminal lifestyle or moving on to a socially acceptable way of being. When this road is placed horizontally, a return to the past way of life will be directed to the left while a change in life will show movement to the right area of the picture. In addition to the present being situated centrally, that which is of immediate concern will be positioned towards the bottom edge of the paper, the area nearest to the artist. In this instance, the entrance to Grendon is drawn in a central position from the bottom of the paper, illustrating the importance that the participant has placed on coming to Grendon (see Buck & Warren, 1995, on placement).

In figures 9.5, 9.6 and 9.7, willingness to fully participate in the thera-peutic experience is indicated by attending to each time sequence (past, present and future) on individual sheets of paper. This decision shows a degree of openness and an intention to thoroughly explore each period. This does not imply attention to details, more a desire for explicit engage-ment. Each period is symbolically portrayed on white paper, using felt tip pens but with the additional use of crayons to convey the future. The first image (figure 9.5) conveys the participant's journey from one children's home to another, terminating in prison. The man portrays himself on a road, going from one institution to another, from the left area to the right, culminating in an entrance to a prison. Above there are black clouds and broken hearts representing the unhappiness that he has experienced in the

Figure 9.5

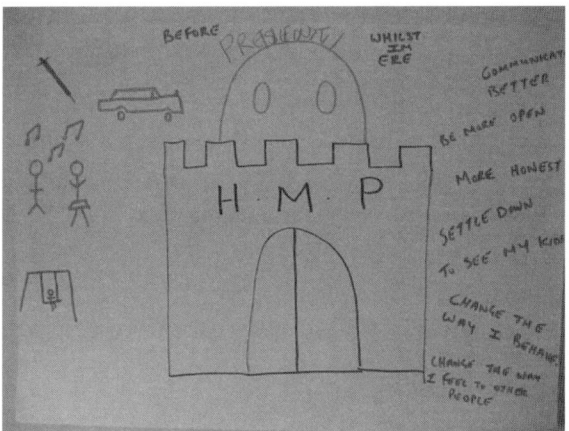

Figure 9.6

past. On the second sheet of paper (figure 9.6) the prison is centrally placed and dominant, expressing the importance of the man's present situation – being in Grendon, which he feels is positive, as he has added a large sun rising above the edifice. To the left are the participant and his partner, drawn with the same orange colour as the rising sun – on reflection the past had not been all bad. The two people are to reappear in the final picture (figure 9.7) accompanied by children. Also in the second picture, to the right of the prison, there are several statements regarding the participant's positive desire for change through engagement with therapy in Grendon, e.g. 'be more open', 'more honest', 'change the way I feel to other people'. The final drawing shows the hope for a better future symbolised

Figure 9.7

by a house with a garden, the participant and family. Overhead there is a colourful rainbow and smiling sun emphasising a positive approach to a future by participating in therapy. The above examples are illustrations of positive approaches to therapeutic engagement, and they are indicative of the symbolism, use of materials and pictorial composition used by the many new arrivals.

Imagery Produced by Men Unsuitable for Group Work

In the following examples, artwork and affect suggested that these partici-pants were unsuitable for therapy at that time. Later, these conclusions were justified, and the men were returned to their sending prisons.

The image in figure 9.8 was made by someone who had difficulty express-ing himself. At the start of the session, without hesitation the man picked up a sheet of deep pink paper and a black felt tip pen. This seemed decisive, but after moving to a corner of the room away from the other members of the group, he struggled to begin his image. For the first half of the session (the image-making period), he sat in a corner with his back to the group. After some time he drew two vertical lines thereby separating the surface area of the paper into three sections – past, present and future. More time elapsed as he attempted to find an appropriate symbol to express his life experiences. Eventually he drew a house within a circle in the left section of the paper (he later described this as the family setting from which he had to escape); however, he could go no further with the image-making

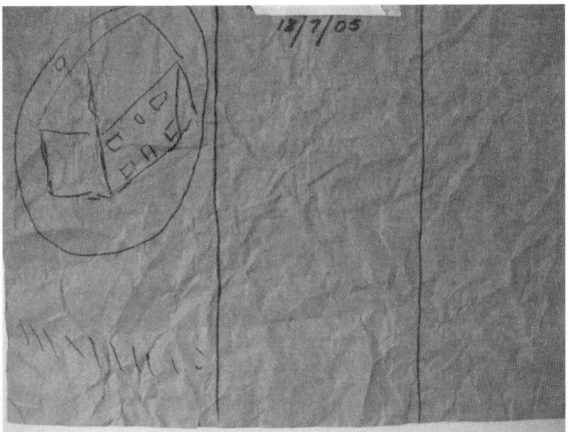

Figure 9.8

Figure 9.9

process or was unwilling to do so, crumpled the paper and placed it in a bin. Afterwards, he retrieved the paper from the bin at my request, but confessed to having difficulty talking about himself. He felt unable to engage with the process and could not envisage the future.

In figure 9.9, the man declined to participate in art therapy to begin with, admitting that he had no artistic ability and had never drawn, not even as a child. However, after some persuasion he came to the session. He used brown crayon on ochre-coloured paper to draw three buildings relating to his past. These were simple rectangular shapes that represented sequentially his family house, a children's home and a prison, with the house to the left, the prison to the right and the children's home in the middle. The structures were naïvely executed with windows at the corners and only the house had a door. This man has spent most of his life in institutions where he suffered abuse; he scribbled black crayon across each structure to indicate that all were places associated with negative experiences, including the family house where he was anxious and mistrustful of authority, his mother had mental health problems and he feared being sent to a psychiatric hospital. Turning the paper over he drew two more rectangles to represent the present and the future; the first rectangle in the bottom left corner of the paper represented Grendon and next to it, another rectangle symbolised a house of his own in which he would live when he leaves prison. The composition was simplistic in conception – three rectangles representing buildings, with windows supported at the corners; the position of the windows echoed the placement of two buildings at the lower corners of the paper. The positioning of the buildings, their simple design and the overall naïve composition indicated diminished intellectual capacity suggesting that he was unsuited to the challenges of the therapy at Grendon. Later, psychometric testing concluded that his very limited intellectual capabilities would reduce his chances of success in such a setting (Bond & Newton, 2005). Buck and Warren (1995) suggest that use of the side of the paper as a sidewall line for the house suggests general insecurity, as does use of the bottom edge of the paper as a ground for the structure. This need for support is echoed in the placement of windows at the corners of the buildings. In addition there are no representations of people (as with figure 9.8) excepting the lone stick figure symbolising the artist, indicating a problem with interaction.

Although figure 9.10 addressed all three aspects of his life (past, present and future), with each period being colourfully visualized on individual sheets of paper, the formal presentation resembles a comic strip. This creates a feeling of fantasy and of unwillingness to engage with reality. The final picture in the series, 'The Future', will suffice to illustrate this dissociated state. To symbolise a future, the participant used felt tip pens on white paper – the theme, space flight. In the top left quadrant there is a bright yellow star while in the bottom right quadrant a partial view of Earth can be seen. The participant has written 'future' in the top right corner which he coloured yellow similar to the star and below this he added a rocket leaving Earth in the direction of the star. This picture symbolised freedom for the artist, he was leaving behind his problems. However, it suggests that he was escaping from, or avoiding, the reality of his existence. Primarily this is indicated by the choice of subject matter and the use of fantasy rather than direct consideration of the practical

Figure 9.10

consequences of actions. Further, avoidance of reality is emphasised in the pictorial composition; although the past is presented on the left and the future is on the right, and the symbol for the man's journey into the future (the spaceship) is placed in the appropriate section of the paper, the direction of flight is to the left indicating a return to the past, or regression to a previous state of being.

The emotive use of colour is worthy of consideration in this picture. Yellow is a positive colour associated with happiness. In this instance, yellow is used to emphasise both the word 'future' and the future destination of the rocket indicating that the artist wishes for a happy future (albeit an unrealistic one). The rocket is the means by which the artist will reach his destination; it is the container and may be identified as a symbol for the individual himself. The body of the rocket is red – the colour of strong emotion, yet the wings are blue – the colour of the sea and a symbol for the unconscious. Also, wings facilitate movement – to take flight. There may be a strong desire to escape to an earlier place of refuge, to return to a more pleasant state of being rather than address the consequential realities of his life experience. Eliade (1969) says:

> Images, symbols and myths are not irresponsible creations of the psyche; they respond to a need and fulfil a function, that of bringing to light the most hidden modalities of being. Consequently the study of them enables us to reach a better understanding of man – of man 'as he is' before he has come to terms with the conditions of History. (p. 12)

All three men left Grendon within three months of their arrival.

Conclusion

By formally describing, analysing and evaluating examples of art on the Assessment Wing at Grendon Therapeutic Community Prison, the value of art therapy as an assessment tool indicating readiness (or lack of it) for TC engagement has been explored. Specific aspects of the artworks have been described, such as temporal placement and use of colour, and their analysis, informed by the art therapy literature, shown to have relevance to assessment of readiness. The examples described here are taken from a set of 200 that were similarly analysed, showing that the interpretations described can be usefully applied to other work. The outcomes, in terms of those 200 participants staying or leaving Grendon, will not be fully known until sufficient time has elapsed, however early indications are that art therapy assessments do have utility.

References

Bond, N. & Newton, M. (2005). *Report on the Psychometric Tests Carried Out on Reception at HMP Grendon*. Unpublished Prison Service report.

British Association of Art Therapists (1989). Artists and arts therapists: a brief discussion of their roles within hospitals, clinics, special schools and in the community. In D. Waller & A. Gilroy (Eds) *Art Therapy: A Handbook*. Buckingham: Oxford University Press.

Buck, J.N. & Warren, W.L. (1995). *House-Tree-Person. Projective Drawing Technique. Manual and Interpretive Guide*. Los Angeles: Western Psychological Services.

Burkitt, E. & Newell, T. (2005). Effects of human figure on children's use of colour to depict sadness and happiness. *International Journal of Art Therapy*, *10*(1), 15–22.

Case, C. (1998). Brief encounters: thinking about images in assessment. *Inscape, The Journal of the British Association of Art Therapists*, *3*(1), 26–33.

Edwards, D. (1999). The role of the case study in art therapy research. *Inscape, The Journal of the British Association of Art Therapists*, *4*(1), 2–9.

Eliade, M. (1969). *Images and Symbols. Studies in Religious Symbolism*. USA: Search Books.

Fuller, P. (1980). *Art and Psychoanalysis*. England: Writers & Readers Publishing Co-operative.

Milner, M. (1950). *On Not Being Able to Paint*. London: Heinemann.

Naumberg, M. (1958). Art therapy: its scope and function. In E. F. Hammer (Ed.) *Clinical Applications of Projective Drawings*. Illinois: Thomas.

Schaverien, J. (1987). The scapegoat and the talisman: transference in art therapy. In T. Dalley *et al.* (Eds) *Images of Art Therapy*. London: Tavistock.

Shine, J. & Morris, M. (2000). Addressing criminogenic needs in a prison therapeutic community. *Therapeutic Communities*, *21*(3), 197–219.

Shine, J. & Newton, M. (2000). Damaged, disturbed and dangerous: a profile of receptions to Grendon therapeutic prison 1995–2000. In J. Shine (Ed.) *A Compilation of Grendon Research*. Leyhill Press. Available from Psychology Unit, HMP Grendon, Grendon Underwood, Aylesbury, HP18 OTL.

Thomas, G.V., Chaigne, E. & Fox, T.J. (1989). Children's drawings of topics differing in significance: Effects on size of drawing. *British Journal of Developmental Psychology*, *7*, 321–331.

Waller, D. & Dalley, T. (1992). Theoretical, political and institutional issues. In D. Waller & A. Gilroy (Eds) *Art Therapy. A Handbook*. Buckingham: Open University Press.

Chapter 10

Undertaking Therapy at HMP Grendon with Men Who Have Committed Sexual Offences

Geraldine Akerman

Introduction

This chapter examines the work of staff on A Wing, HMP Grendon, whose residents have committed offences of a sexual nature or with sexual motivation. The development and ethos of therapeutic communities (TCs) has been described extensively elsewhere in this book, and by Genders and Player (1995), and Shine and Morris (1999), so this will not be repeated in detail here. However, it is useful to remind the reader that the TC works on the principle that society can be the agent of change. Examples of residents' fantasies, thoughts, feelings and behaviour in the thrice-weekly small therapy groups, the twice-weekly community meetings, and all other places where residents spend their time, are integrated into their therapy. The principles of democratisation (learning from mistakes, decision making, and living with consequences of these); tolerance (i.e. allowing pre-offending behaviour to emerge so it can be examined and challenged); and communalism, (acknowledging that basic emotions and instincts are common and learning how others manage these) and reality confrontation (observed behaviour is challenged and pro-social behaviour practised) underpin the work described in this chapter.

Grendon and the Emergence of Forensic Therapeutic Communities: Developments in Research and Practice
Edited by Richard Shuker and Elizabeth Sullivan
© 2010 John Wiley & Sons, Ltd.

The staff team is comprised of a wing therapist, a senior forensic psychologist, a group facilitator, two senior prison officers, and ten officers. The staff team endeavour to maintain a flattened hierarchy in which each person has a voice, and opinions on running the TC are taken into consideration. The resident and staff/resident relationships are discussed, along with the dynamics of group work in this context. This chapter describes the development of a programme to help manage offence-related attitudes and arousal.

Setting the Scene

Residents in therapy at Grendon regularly describe it as the most difficult time of their sentence, yearning to be back in a prison where they can act out their feelings by 'smashing up', and then going to segregation units for respite from others. Instead they live in a TC where they are under the constant scrutiny of others, and subject to challenge, which results in an emotionally volatile environment. There are 40 residents on A wing, all of whom have committed offences that involve some sexual motivation. When new residents join the wing, it is expected that they will go through a series of phases akin to maturation. Genders and Player (1995) described the stages of this process as:

- entry;
- attachment;
- developing a sense of belonging, or 'community mindedness', that is, considering problems from a group and community perspective, rather than an egocentric one (described further in Akerman, 2002);
- individuation; and
- detachment as they prepare to leave.

As a result, the residents should then develop a sense of belonging and attachment to a community, as opposed to the isolation and detachment felt previously. This process can take between one and three years, and can provide the stability that has been lacking for the resident in the past. Before they leave, residents need to spend time working through the feelings evoked by leaving what has become a safe place for them, taking with them the templates they have internalised for future relationships.

The TC seeks to aid the development of pro-social attitudes and ways of relating to others in line with the Good Lives Model (Ward & Stewart, 2003). The Good Lives Model indicates that all people strive for goals, called 'goods' by Ward and Stewart (see Brookes, chapter 6 this edition). The model suggests that offenders may have sought these 'goods' through inappropriate, ineffective or unlawful means such as offending. Ward and Stewart suggest that individuals have an innate drive that determines our psychological well-being: each individual will flourish when these needs are met; and being able to achieve these needs is reliant on internal strengths and opportunities to work towards achievable goals. Ward suggests that individuals should seek approach-focused goals, developing their skills rather than removing a problem (or risk factor), leaving a 'pinhole'. The model suggests that it is important that there is a balance between all of the goods, rather than excelling in one area whilst neglecting another. The individual treatment plan at Grendon takes account of individual strengths to help men develop the necessary resources to achieve these 'goods'. Therefore goals are set in the TC to enable this process to take place, building on strengths in line with positive psychology to: 'amplify client's strengths rather than repair weaknesses' (Seligman, 2002, p. 5). For example, if a resident is able to converse well on a one-to-one basis he would be encouraged to develop his relationship to members of his group and then to the wing generally. Residents are also encouraged to keep a feelings diary, describing how they are managing emotions and new behaviours, and this is discussed in the group.

   The TC model encourages men to overcome past difficulties in relating to others by facilitating attachment to the community. Attachment theory (Klein, 1993) indicates that each individual is born with the innate potential to relate to others, but difficulties in early relationships can leave people feeling 'fragmented, liable to fall apart' (p. 7), and as a result they may develop the inflexible and rigid relating styles that are often evident in those with personality disorders. Rich (2006) notes that poor attachment in childhood has been linked to sexually aggressive behaviour. The TC seeks to provide a reparative relationship so that the resident can experience the feeling of being held in a safe environment, and given time to develop a secure attachment with a view to developing appropriate adult relationships by the time they are released. Ward and Gannon (2006) highlight the need to understand the human condition and the importance of social relationships within therapy, emphasising the importance of social success in effective treatment. They describe sexual offending as arising from a 'complex weave' of influences resulting from early development, individual biology, the social environment, circumstances, and psychological processes. The TC environment provides an effective setting to examine and address such complex and interacting influences within a microcosm of society. Through discussion in the therapy group primarily, but also in other interactions in the community, residents make links between past and present behaviours. Through recognising how they relate to a wide range of people in the community they can access thoughts, feelings and behaviour from the past and recognise patterns.

The Therapeutic Relationship

In all therapy, the relationship between therapist and client is of paramount importance in determining how effective the treatment will be. Recent research focuses on different aspects of this dynamic, for instance Marshall and Serran's (2004) work on therapists' style and Frost's (2004) research on engagement in treatment, both emphasise the importance of the relationship, indicating that therapy at Grendon needs to attend to such issues. Ackerman and Hilsenroth (2003) discuss a range of studies looking at therapist styles. They found that the therapist should demonstrate that they are working *together with* the client, and that the therapeutic alliance was developed and enhanced through referring to common ground, for instance, being able to disclose similar incidents from your own life experience. This may present problems when working with men who have committed sexual offences as the therapist may find it difficult to refer to common ground when it comes to understanding deviant sexual fantasy and arousal.

In order to work effectively with men who have committed sexual offences, therapists need to be able to tolerate hearing details of violent and sexual offences against others. Lewis (1997, p. 211) spoke of the 'corrective emotional experience', as distinct from the 'defective emotional experience' that existed in the early years of rejection and inconsistency of care. Consistency, continuity and a caring environment provide the context for 'the personal journey to personality reformation'. Pearlman and Saakvitne (1995) describe how clients in therapy unconsciously invoke re-enactments of previous relationships, making the relationship between the therapist and client potentially healing or threatening, which presents a considerably complex environment in which the therapists' skills are constantly tested.

It is vital that there is a supportive therapeutic relationship. Nitsun (2006) suggests that 'group psychotherapy has marginalized sexuality and desire in the evolution of theory' (p. 13), and yet this is the focus of work on A wing. Nitsun draws on his experience of many years working with clients in psychotherapy and finds that they feel unable to discuss sexuality. Given that the residents of A wing have committed serious transgressions of sexual boundaries, it would seem likely that they would find it even more difficult to discuss their sexuality and sexual behaviour. Davies (1998) describes how therapists use themselves in an affirming therapeutic relationship to help the client form a template for future relationships. The therapeutic culture within Grendon provides the reparative role so that the resident can develop more appropriate relationships.

The facilitators tread a fine line between being authority figures, holding parental roles and establishing a therapeutic alliance where residents feel safe to disclose deviant attitudes. As stated above, discussing sexual issues is not easy to do; discussing sexual offending can prove even more difficult. Much of the power of a sexual fantasy stems from its secrecy and so to expose it to public scrutiny can make the resident feel very vulnerable. This relationship with staff can be particularly difficult for men who have spent long periods of time in higher security prisons, often preceded by other institutions such as children's homes. These experiences can result in residents testing boundaries as a means of finding out where those boundaries are in order to feel safe, because staff in similar positions of power have abused them in the past. It is worth noting that the prison officers at Grendon do a highly specialised job and whilst most will have received some training in TC concepts and treatment methods, few will have undertaken any professional training. Whilst most clinical staff are experienced practitioners who have completed specialist training, most prison officers gain their training by facilitating groups alongside a more experienced facilitator until they feel sufficiently confident to do so alone. Adjusting to, and dealing with, the tensions inherent in this role becomes part of the clinical discussion within the TC, and structures such as staff post-group 'feedbacks' and weekly staff support, or 'sensitivity' meetings, form essential components of the treatment process. In these meetings, staff are able to discuss the impact that the toxic content of therapy has on them, so that they do not project any feelings evoked onto residents (or other members of staff) when working with them throughout the day. Members of staff must also ensure that splits do not develop amongst the different disciplines. In addition the staff should act as role models to residents, and if they can not work through issues between them, they would not be demonstrating conflict resolution.

The Content of the Work on A Wing

The nature of the offences committed by the residents on A wing leads to a need to discuss intimate issues such as sexual fantasy and masturbation, which Nitsun (2006, p. 39) describes as 'the part of an individual that is most difficult to share with others in a group'. However, on A wing, in addition to discussing their offences, a culture has been developed and sustained that enables residents to safely question each other about the content of their sexual fantasies, and their masturbatory habits, as a means of assessing the ongoing risk each poses. Issues such as the use of pornography, what television programmes an individual is watching, how they relate to other residents and staff, and the use of sexual banter are regularly commented on by other residents in order to draw attention to offence-paralleling behaviour, inappropriate sexual attitudes and behaviour. Offence paralleling describes the way a person interacts with others in a similar pattern to that which has already led them towards committing an offence, and is 'functionally similar to behavioural sequences involved in previous criminal acts' (Daffern *et al.*, 2007). The men regularly question the use of pornography which, given its link to sexual preoccupation, and its role as a disinhibitor prior to offending (Frost *et al.*, 2006), is an issue that is better challenged by other residents than by staff, whose views can be construed as moralistic. Morris (p. 13 in Shine, 2000) describes how 'the work of the group is amplified by the therapeutic community environment with forty therapists (or fellow inmates) who carry on the psychotherapy in between formal sessions ... they ferret out evasions with tenacity and vigour that far surpasses what a therapist can muster' ... adding a well-used phrase, 'you can't con a con'. The staff team continually need to evaluate both present and potential future risk to themselves and others, and so it is essential that the residents feel able to disclose their most intimate thoughts and behaviour.

Discussing current sexual interests and past sexual offences can evoke powerful feelings. Mollon (2003) suggests that seeking psychotherapy itself can be shame-provoking because it requires the disclosure of private material, thus having to disclose sexual offending magnifies the strength of feeling evoked during the disclosure of such shameful material in psychotherapy. Following each small group session the whole community meets to hear a summary of the group's work. This frequently causes further discomfort, as the intimate details of their sexual acts are now shared not only with eight others, but also with the entire community. These feedback sessions are frequently ended with the words 'please be aware of those who have used the groups' because, unlike traditional therapy where the group members will disperse until the next session, these men will continue to work and live together with their innermost secrets exposed to all. This can result in a powder keg of emotions, and consequently requires a high level of commitment from the residents to remain in therapy within the TC.

Dynamics Within the Group Setting

Nitsun (2006) states that the therapy group can 'hold in creative balance the emergence of sexual desire and the recognition that this must be contained without enactment' (p. 175). Facilitators must show to the group that they are able to tolerate discussion of an intensely intimate nature. At the same time the facilitator must be able to monitor how other group members are responding to disclosure and if they can tolerate what is being described. For instance, could they be overwhelmed by the material because of their own previous experiences? Or will they respond in an inappropriate manner? Many of the residents have had childhoods characterised by dysfunctional attachments to significant caregivers. This may impact on how they engage in group treatment and relate to others generally in the community. Group members can show disrupted patterns of attachment and detachment, depending on their relationships with others in the group and larger community. In addition, the presence of a number of people inevitably produces rivalry for the attention of the facilitator, and former sibling rivalries and infant–mother/infant–father relationships are played out on a daily basis and need to be attended to in an atmosphere highly charged with emotion.

The structure of the groups is open, in that more experienced members (the culture carriers) are joined at intervals by new members who then learn from the senior members. Inevitably, maintaining stable and therapeutically cohesive treatment groups becomes an ongoing focus. One benefit of residing in a TC is the provision of a reparative relationship to the resident in order to help him form mature erotic attachments. The disrupted childhood experienced by many residents has resulted in significant emotional neglect, leaving the resident with an intense longing for intimacy with another, and the drive to meet this need has often been met through sex. The therapy group can provide a transitional object through which to replace erotic infantile relationships with mature ones (Nitsun, 2006). The facilitator needs to be able to recognise family dynamics being re-enacted within each group and be aware of their own erotic response in the therapy session. This response provides material for the ongoing supervision of all facilitators. Within a TC treatment group this leads to complex and intense therapeutic dynamics, including feelings between group members and the facilitator (for instance envy, anger, irritation, love) as well as group members to each other, many resonating with those from their families of origin. This does not even account for actual present day sexual feelings between one community member and another, or for a member of staff.

The Development of an Additional Fantasy Modification Programme

A central focus of the work on A wing involves the exploration of the role of sexual fantasy and sexual offending. Research (Marshall, 2006) has consistently indicated that interventions aimed at sex offenders need to incorporate multi-modal treatment methods and behavioural and skill-based approaches when addressing deviant sexual arousal. To reflect these findings and to ensure clinical approaches were sufficiently diverse and responsive to the treatment needs of residents, a Fantasy Modification Programme (FMP) was devised as a means of teaching the skills with which to manage inappropriate violent or sexual fantasies, while keeping in mind the prosocial goals developed in therapy. In line with TC principles, each session is fed back to the whole community so that participants will be supported during the ongoing work.

The FMP (see Akerman, 2008) draws a great deal from techniques used on other programmes, such as Sex Offender Treatment Programmes (SOTPs), and particularly the Healthy Sexual Functioning Programme (HSFP), an intervention developed by the Interventions Group within HM Prison Service to manage sexual arousal and develop intimate relationship skills. The FMP is able to be specific in teaching the strategies because a great deal of the work of the HSFP is covered in groups generally, for instance in developing intimacy, challenging offence-supportive attitudes, and getting support to try new strategies. The programme also focuses on giving residents the chance to practice new behaviour through the use of role-play. During (and between) sessions, group members can think about their future lives by focusing on the Good Lives Model Comprehensive (GLM-C, Ward & Gannon, 2006) and the steps they need to take to achieve their aims; for instance managing emotions and considering what the motivations were in the development and maintenance of their fantasies and how these needs can be met in another manner. The application of the GLM to fantasy modification has been described previously by Akerman (2005). In addition, the programme addresses potential problematic scenarios such as disclosing offences to an employer or future partner, and enables participants to practice how this may be managed.

The FMP was piloted with four men and has since been run again with four more participants. The programme begins by developing cohesion between the men, and teaches fantasy modification techniques, such as:

- directed masturbation, described by Marshall *et al.* (2006) as pairing masturbation with arousal associated with appropriate images, thus reinforcing the excitement of those images;

- covert sensitisation (Marshall & Serran, 2006), a technique that pairs personally aversive consequences (such as being in prison, creating more victims, or being publicly humiliated) with each step of an offence-related fantasy;
- satiation, associating offence-related fantasies with boredom;
- the principal of 'urge surfing' or 'distress tolerance' (that is remaining in a state of arousal without reinforcing it through masturbation, with the knowledge that the urge will pass in a few minutes); and
- the use of thought stoppers as a means of managing arousal are discussed and practised.

The programme helped participants to learn to manage high levels of sexual preoccupation and develop their intimacy skills through setting goals for what they wanted in future relationships. The TC provides an environment in which new skills can be practised among those who understand and support the changes in behaviour. One man who undertook the programme identified offence-related fantasies, and then developed strategies to manage his sexual preoccupation by finding ways to spend his time more productively whilst developing more relationships and being less reliant on his fantasy world. He was trying to stop using pornography and so informed the community about this and asked them to challenge him should he seek such material. In addition, he took opportunities to form relationships with others, for instance through learning to play the guitar, thus spending his time in a more pro-social and relationship-focused manner. During the programme he undertook a role-play in which he placed himself in the position of a potential victim, recognising the intense distress he could cause if he were to carry out his fantasy, as well as the potential consequences to himself. Later, he found himself in the position about which he had fantasised, and was able to manage his arousal in an appropriate manner.

Another participant practised what he would do if he found himself in a position similar to the one in which he offended. He was able to take the role of those who would be affected should he continue with his fantasy, and think about future consequences for all concerned. He had been sceptical about his ability to think himself into the role (as role-play requires the participant to place himself in the position as if he were there) but rather than him being unable to put himself in role, once he was there he found it difficult to leave what was a risky situation. With the guidance of other group members he challenged his offence-supportive thoughts and developed appropriate self-talk to get himself out of the area of risk.

One participant focused his work on violent thoughts he had following an incident that had occurred on the exercise yard, role-playing how to challenge the violent fantasies he had experienced and using calming self-talk to manage his violent thoughts. Throughout the programme the participants practiced fantasy modification techniques and discussed their effectiveness with their therapy groups. As stated previously, the wing houses men with a diverse range of needs, some with experience in managing sexual arousal, and so when it is disclosed that participants are undertaking this work, others will talk with them explaining which strategies have helped them in the past. Participants can maintain a diary and discuss this with their therapy groups between sessions to help them to integrate their personal work into their ongoing group work. Residents are able to recognise signs of discrepancy in behaviour on the group and on the wing generally, and challenge that which is inappropriate or not consistent with the stated goals. The participants developed relapse prevention plans so that they had a range of options available to them, depending on how close they were getting to acting on their fantasy, and developing a support network so that they did not feel isolated. Residents who have been released from prison in the past and failed to access help when they needed it can advise what resources may be required. The programme continues to be evaluated and updated in line with current theory.

Conclusion

This chapter discussed the complexities of relationships between residents and staff working in a highly charged atmosphere, where all must be able to tolerate hearing about sexually violent acts perpetrated by or against residents. They must be able to see past the acts and support the development of appropriate relationships for the future. The chapter discussed the development of a FMP, which was well received within the community with further participants being identified, and the remaining graduates of the first course providing support and guidance for later group members. The culture on the wing needs to be constantly assessed to ensure that relationships remain healthy and appropriate, and to ensure the community is safe to support the work so the therapeutic alliance can be most effective. Future research possibilities include developing measures of the environment so that it remains safe for such intense therapy, and developing measures of sexual arousal so that change can be assessed.

References

Ackerman, S.J. & Hilsenroth, M.J. (2003). A review of therapist characteristics and techniques positively impacting on the therapeutic alliance. *Clinical Psychology Review, 23*, 1–33.

Akerman, G. (2002). Development of a checklist to measure community minded behaviour in a prison-based therapeutic community. *Forensic Update, 69*, 17–29.

Akerman, G. (2005). Applying fantasy modification techniques in line with the Good Lives model with learning disability as a confounding factor: A case study. *Nota News, 49*, 12–14.

Akerman, G. (2008). The development of a fantasy modification programme in a prison based therapeutic community. *International Journal of Therapeutic Communities, 29*, 2.

Daffern, M., Jones, L., Howells, K. *et al.* (2007). Refining the definition of offence paralleling behaviour. *Criminal Behaviour and Mental Health 17*, 265–273 (published online in Wiley InterScience).

Davies, J.M. (1998). Between the disclosure and foreclosure of erotic transference–countertransference. *Psychoanalytic Dialogues, 8* (6), 747–766.

Frost, A. (2004). Therapeutic engagement styles in child sex offenders in a group treatment programme: A grounded theory study. *Sexual Abuse: A Journal of Research and Treatment, 16*, 191–208.

Frost, A., Daniels, K. & Hudson, S.M. (2006). Disclosure strategies among sex offenders: A model for understanding the engagement process in group work. *Sexual Abuse: A Journal of Research and Treatment, 12* (3), 227–244.

Genders, F. & Player, E. (1995). *Grendon: A Study of a Therapeutic Prison.* Oxford: Oxford University Press.

Klein, J. (1993). *Our Need for Others and its Roots in Infancy.* London: Routledge.

Lewis, P. (1997). Context for change (whilst consigned and confined): A challenge for systematic thinking. In E. Cullen, L. Jones, & R. Woodward (Eds) *Therapeutic Communities for Offenders.* Chichester: Wiley.

Marshall, W.L., Marshall, L.E., Serran, G.A. & Fernandez, Y.M. (2006). *Treating Sexual Offenders: An Integrated Approach.* Routledge: UK.

Marshall, W.L & Serran, G.A. (2004). The role of the therapist in offender treatment. *Psychology, Crime and Law, 10*, 309–320.

Mollon, P. (2003). *Shame and Jealousy.* London: Karnac.

Nitsun, M. (2006). *The Group as an Object of Desire. Exploring Sexuality in Group Therapy.* London: Routledge.

Pearlman, L.A. & Saakvitne, K.W. (1995). *Trauma and the Therapist: Countertransference and Vicarious Traumatization in Psychotherapy with Incest Survivors.* London: Norton.

Rich, P. (2006). *Attachment and Sexual Offending: Understanding and Applying Attachment Theory to the Treatment of Juvenile Sexual Offenders.* Chichester: Wiley.

Seligman, M.E.P. (2002). Positive psychology, positive prevention and positive therapy. In C.R. Snyder & S.L. Lopez (Eds) *Handbook of Positive Psychology* (pp. 3–9). New York: Oxford University Press.

Shine, J. (Ed.) (2000). *HMP Grendon: A Compilation of Grendon Research*. Leyhill Press. Available from Psychology Unit, HMP Grendon, Grendon Underwood, Aylesbury, HP18 0TL.

Shine, J. & Morris, M. (1999). *Regulating Anarchy: The Grendon Programme*. England: Springhill Press.

Ward, T. & Gannon, T. (2006), Rehabilitation, etiology, and self-regulation. The good lives model of rehabilitation for sexual offenders. *Aggression and Violent Behaviour, 11,* 77–94.

Ward, T. & Stewart, C.A. (2003). Criminogenic needs and human needs: A theoretical model. *Psychology Crime and Law, 9,* 125–143.

Part III
Research and Outcomes

Chapter 11

Reflections on Grendon: Interviews with Men Who Are About to Leave

Elizabeth Sullivan

Introduction

This chapter describes HMP Grendon Therapeutic Community Prison, and the experience of living and working in a therapeutic community through the reflections of men as they are about to leave. Candid views were gathered from 48 prisoners during exit interviews as they were about to leave Grendon for a variety of reasons. The purpose of the interviews was to discover, from their perspective, why some men leave Grendon before their therapy is completed. While necessarily focusing on the negative aspects of men's experiences at Grendon in order to explore drop-out rates, in all but one or two of the 48 interviews undertaken, a huge amount of positive material was also collected. This related particularly to the relationships of trust and equality that men enjoyed with staff, and to the immense personal benefits men felt themselves to have gained from being at Grendon. This chapter draws together the dominant themes, positive and negative, that emerged from the interviews and offers some commentary on them. An account of the original research, which used exit interviews at Grendon as part of a larger research study to find out why men leave before finishing their therapy, can be found elsewhere (Sullivan, 2006).

Grendon and the Emergence of Forensic Therapeutic Communities: Developments in Research and Practice
Edited by Richard Shuker and Elizabeth Sullivan
© 2010 John Wiley & Sons, Ltd.

HMP Grendon is unlike most prisons (Genders & Player, 1995) in that the men who live and work there have chosen to be there, and sometimes they also choose to leave. Thus, within the constraints of their sentence, spending time at Grendon is voluntary. Men who want to change their offending behaviour and reduce their risk of further offending may consider Grendon to be a potential step towards a prison-free future. They discover from Grendon's literature, and by word of mouth, that Grendon offers a relatively unique therapeutic community (TC) regime in which men live together and regulate each other's behaviour, alongside regular intensive group therapy and additional therapies such as psychodrama and art therapy (see chapters 8 and 9 in this volume respectively). They must respond to Grendon's 'admissions' criteria and demonstrate a wish to change, and they must be drug-free and be free of active mental illness, although around four-fifths of the population have personality disorders. It is expected that they will stay at Grendon for the duration of their therapy, which will usually last between 18 months and 2 years. When they leave, it is usually to return to the 'normal' prison system to finish their sentence.

Why Use Exit Interviews?

Since Grendon is in essence voluntary, men can choose to leave before they are assessed as having finished therapy. In addition, they can be asked to leave by their community or staff if it is believed that they are no longer engaging in the therapeutic process, or are not sincere in their wish to address their offending behaviour, or break the rules. Living in a therapeutic community has benefits and advantages, but it is hard and often painful work. Like other prisons HMP Grendon must be economically viable. It must strive to fill cells and help as many men to complete their therapy as possible. However, in one regard, HMP Grendon is like an employing company because its roll is subject to fluctuations when men choose to leave or are made to leave. Like any employer, Grendon could benefit from understanding not just how many men leave unexpectedly but why they leave, in order to plan strategically and provide an effective therapeutic environment. Exit interviews provided a way of capturing this information from the prisoner's otherwise unsought point of view (Bailey, 1996; Skyrme, 2001). Unexpectedly, however, the interviews also yielded as much positive and enthusiastic comment from the leavers as it did criticism. A sense of belonging, identification with and loyalty to the individual's wing and to the prison as a whole, characterised many comments, even where men also had severe criticisms to make.

The Causes of Premature Leaving

The research found no single cause for men leaving Grendon early. Rather, there were a combination of factors that contributed to premature leaving. There were reasons relating to individual prisoners such as ill health or inability to engage in therapy. There were wider contextual reasons relating to the Prison Service such as the economic imperative to maintain prisoner numbers at a high level, which has a potential impact on Grendon's ability to afford due importance to assessments of motivation, readiness and ability to benefit from therapy. In addition, competition for suitable candidates from interventions such as programmes for Dangerous and Severe Personality Disorder (DSPD) and other prison TCs may have depleted the pool of eligible men that Grendon has traditionally drawn from, thus increasing the likelihood that potentially unsuitable men will be offered a place only to drop out after a short time. Although this chapter will give a flavour of the original research report 'Reasons for Leaving Grendon: A study of drop-out rates' (Sullivan, 2005), its main purpose is to give a balanced account of what men actually think about Grendon – to give an 'insider's' view.

Methods

Exit interview development

A semi-structured exit interview schedule was produced following discussions with inmates and staff. Examination of the 'End of Therapy Reports' of recently left men was also helpful in the development of the exit interview schedule. Three versions of the interview were designed and piloted, with minor differences to accommodate three types of leaver: Interview 1 for men returned to their sending prison from the Assessment Unit (Group 1); Interview 2 for men dropping out of therapy or being moved on (Group 2); Interview 3 for 'progressive moves' at the end of therapy where men were leaving at an agreed time[1] (Group 3). The interview lasted approximately an hour and was a confidential process (within agreed limits) in order that men felt able to be honest. Detailed notes of each interview, identified only by a serial number, were made contemporaneously using

[1]Progressive moves are where a man has come to the end of his therapy and is moving on in a planned manner. However, it does not necessarily imply that his therapy is complete or considered 'successful'.

as many of the participants' original descriptive words and phrases as possible.

Participants and conduct of the research

Short presentations were made to each wing community about the purpose and nature of the research to engage interest and participation. It was intended to interview all men leaving Grendon during a six-month period. Men making progressive moves were included as a comparison group. During the period of the study, while 68 men left Grendon, interviews were administered to only 48. Among these, 22 were planned or progressive leavers, 17 unplanned leavers or drop-outs and 9 were returned to their sending prison from the Assessment Unit, while 3 refused to be interviewed and 17 men were missed for a variety of practical reasons. An information and consent form was produced and a system for obtaining the names of men, meeting them to make appointments, and keeping a record of progress was devised. Each of the three types of interview was recorded separately, and each individual interview was given a unique number so that it could be tracked during the analysis without using the participant's name in order to maintain anonymity. Probes were used to invite participants to enlarge on their answers and the words written by the interviewer were checked back with the participant to ensure accuracy. Following interview, handwritten notes were transcribed onto a database according to categories suggested by the questions. Subsequent iterations of the categorisation process enabled the identification of underlying themes.

Results

The results are presented and discussed in the following way:

Assessment Unit: in order to explore the question of why the Assessment Unit has a higher rate of drop-outs than other wings, the Assessment Unit data was analysed separately. The men's criticisms and dissatisfactions are reported and commented upon and contrasted with the positive things that they had to say about Grendon.

Therapy Wings: the question of why men drop out from therapy wings or are moved on against their will was explored and their accounts were compared with the accounts of men who stayed until their therapy was concluded. Again, the positive things that both groups had to say are reported.

The Assessment Unit

The Assessment Unit uses a number of formal and informal measures and observations to assess a man's suitability for life on a democratic therapeutic community. Factors such as intelligence, psychological mindedness (openness to therapy), potential and readiness for change, emotional robustness and ability to fit into a community and ability to obey the rules are assessed. This process takes between 8 and 12 weeks although can be extended where the prisoner needs more in-depth assessment or more preparation time prior to beginning treatment. Nine men being returned to their sending prison from the Assessment Unit were interviewed. In this sample, 5 were assessed as unsuitable for therapy, 3 made their own decision to leave and in one case both reasons were given. The men's own accounts and the account given in their official Transfer Summary are very similar as the examples below demonstrate.

'Unsuitable for therapy'

In the present sample, five men received an assessment of 'unsuitable for therapy', which was made on grounds of:

a) **Transfer summary: 'emotional fragility'**

I was told I'm not strong enough emotionally to take the challenges.

b) **Transfer summary: 'inadequate intellectual capacity'**

I got low scores in the tests … I get the feeling its because I'm a bit slow.

c) **Transfer summary: 'lack of capacity for insight and reflection and not being ready to address his problems'**

One of my great problems is talking about (…) my offences (…) I'm not certain if I do need therapy.

Other men in this category who were not interviewed were described in their transfer summaries as finding group participation difficult and having difficulty in accepting responsibility.

The similarity between official and interviewee accounts of the reasons for being returned to their sending prison suggests that there is a transparent decision-making process shared with the man himself. However, this did not stop men from feeling that the decision was wrong or unfair and that they weren't being given a chance to change the minds of the assessors. In one or two cases they would rather not have come in the first place:

(F Wing[2]) felt they had come as far as they could as far as therapy is concerned. It wouldn't be fair on me sending me to a wing to fail. (…) I'd rather they didn't accept me in the first place.

Two of the men in this category were subsequently allowed to remain for further assessment and were eventually allocated to a wing, demonstrating a degree of flexibility in the decision-making process. However for those who had been assessed as too fragile emotionally to be able to survive on the therapy wing, the assessment process and its outcome was experienced as negative and damaging:

I'd like to stay. At the moment I'm a bit on the low side. I came off anti-depressants to come here but maybe I'll need to go back on them[3]. (…) my short sentence is not very conducive to returning (to Grendon in the future). I feel I've failed.

Some of the men in the 'unsuitable for therapy' category were unsuitable because they were unable to adapt to the social and democratic life on the wing:

They said I can't do menial tasks e.g. dining room cleaning and I have a problem with fairness and equal-ness. That pissed me off, it wasn't fair. Also I was too sensitive toward issues and being challenged, but I would have worked on it. I agree to an extent – but I always felt I had a valid point (about the cleaning) but I got shot down.

Arrival phase – avoiding sub-groups

The accounts of at least three men across the whole sample brought up an issue associated with men arriving together in groups, particularly from the same sending prison, or forming a friendship on arrival together. Three issues arise related to:

a)   The difficulty of engaging in intimate therapeutic disclosure in front of someone with whom you share a history:

I came with a fellow I knew at Swaleside, so was attached to him, which is a big mistake because you can't be yourself with someone you know. I never had my chance to say my piece and do my thing because he was there.

---

[2]F Wing is the Assessment Wing.
[3]Men must be medication-free before they arrive at Grendon. Anti-depressants are thought to interfere with the therapeutic process.

b)   The potential for men carrying 'prison subculture' to exert minority influence and have a negative effect on, or undermine, the majority:

Me and two others of similar age hang out together and people have got it in for us, saying we're intimidating. The staff say it too. … Staff take the side of the community against us.

c)   The potential for importing a group of men supporting each other, reinforcing unhelpful attitudes and behaviours, and resisting the therapeutic community ethos:

They're disruptive, and it's worse when two or three who are friends on F wing are sent together. We have this on a regular basis. Most get thrown out after six to twelve months.

Research by Robin McPherson, Senior Psychologist at Grendon in the 1980s found that men were more likely to leave prematurely if more than one man arrived on the same day. These situations may stem from men arriving at Grendon, a new and anxiety-provoking situation, seeking comfort in attachments to other new arrivals. This would suggest that men should arrive one at a time, although if this was logistically difficult other measures might prevent these 'cliques' from forming. A mentor or buddy system, whereby each new man spends a large part of his time with a 'senior' member of the Assessment Unit and is discouraged from spending too much time with other newcomers, could prevent the problem from arising. In addition, it suggests that groups of friends should not be sent to the same therapy wing, or at least not at the same time.

Men who chose to leave the assessment unit

The three men who made their own decision to RTU[4] did so for a variety of reasons and dissatisfactions, sometimes in agreement with wing staff, and sometimes despite persuasion to re-consider:

Length of time on F Wing made me decide to leave as it is a seriously boring place … also wages are low and I have no private cash and there is no work.
*   *I thought it would be more one-to-one. Groups are weird, everyone's arse-licking but out of group they talk shit (…) they're all liars. I would have stayed if people were genuine. Grendon is right for me but things in it are wrong – things shouldn't be taken from you, you should be given things on a plate.*

---

[4]RTU means return to unit. When men arrive, it is on the understanding that they can be returned to the prison they came from if they leave, for whatever reason, within six months.

They're taking things away from me. They're making my mind up for me (…)
I'd stay if they introduced TV[5]. I'd address my problems. It's my decision to go.
… had a better offer to do a course, more likely to be more eligible for D cat
at the end of the year. If I stay here I may have to commit to two or three years.
I wanted to stay for the good visits and family days but decided it's wrong to
take up a place someone else could use for therapy.

The men in this category appear to have had a very different idea of what they could expect at Grendon, and may have misunderstood what the purpose of the Assessment Unit is. Access to better introductory information about Grendon might avoid such misunderstandings.

Feelings about leaving

Understandably, most men on the Assessment Unit would have preferred to stay. Even those who chose to leave felt that they could have stayed if only their grievance, however unrealistic, had been acted upon.

It'll do my head in when I leave, I need to be here (but) can't get past it [not having a TV].

The effect of gaining a place and then losing it again so soon is experienced in the words of the interviewees as '*victimisation*', '*failure*', a '*kick in the face*', '*being let down*' and '*not being given a chance*'. A degree of distressed bewilderment comes across in the quotations because, despite the explanations that they have been given, they are either unable to grasp what the explanations mean, or are unable to accept them.

I've got just as many problems as the others, I need the therapy (…) I have the
same rights. I poured my heart out and got nothing in return.

There are also practical consequences of being sent back relating to sentence planning (see Padfield, 2002), and several men felt disadvantaged in real terms by the decision to reject them.

I feel let down by the staff – victimised. It's wrong to kick someone out who is
asking for help because they can't understand big words. My parole is due at
the end of the year but was willing to waive that to come here. But when I go
for it they'll say 'you've not done any courses'. (Subsequently allocated to a wing.)

---

[5]TVs are not allowed on the Assessment Unit during the 6 to 12 weeks of assessment, but they are allowed in the rest of the prison.

Clearly an intervention has an ethical duty to minimise any potential harm or distress caused to participants. However it is also difficult to avoid some short-term distress for unsuccessful men who would have a high likelihood of future failure if allocated to a therapeutic community, and problems associated with early termination from treatment for those not ready or suitable have been recognised (Dowden & Serin, 2001; Jones, 1997). Those men who show low aptitude for community living conditions, or for addressing their offending behaviours, or for engaging in therapy with their peers could not only experience more distress themselves, but could have a negative effect on the therapeutic community overall.

Positive comments

Without exception, the Assessment Unit interviewees also had many positive things to say. They reflected on aspects of the quality of life that they felt HMP Grendon got right:

> *I feel safe here.*
> *You can be yourself* [sex offenders] *not tolerated in the system.*[6]

They spoke in positive terms about staff and how they were treated by them.

> *Officers treat you better here, they try to help you the best they can.*
> *Staff have more time for you, even the psychologists make time for you.*

Given that each of these prisoners was experiencing either rejection or self-de-selection, their ability to reflect positively on the brief relationships they had enjoyed with staff is evidence of the TC ethos at work, but losing this positive experience so soon contributed to their negative feelings.

Therapy Wings: Drop-outs and Expulsions

Drop-out and expulsion rates from therapy wings have remained relatively stable since 2000 despite a small upturn in 2004. Reasons for leaving fall into two main categories: involuntary (voted out) and voluntary (own request). Men were asked what their primary reason for leaving Grendon at this point was. A range of reasons were offered, with roughly twice as many men choosing to leave as being voted out.

---

[6] 'The System' means other prisons or the prison system at large.

Voted out: of 6 men interviewed only 2 agreed with the decision made about them. Two were voted out for violence or aggression, one for drugs, one for dishonesty, one for sex and one was assessed by his community as unsuitable for therapy:

> *Been kicked out. Pressured by the group to talk about what I didn't want to talk about (…) so I said what they wanted to hear. A percentage of the wing voted me out. (…) I do understand but I don't. I was put in a position by my group. (3+ yrs)*

Own request: of 11 men who chose to leave, none said that staff agreed with his decision. Criticisms of Grendon were given as the primary reason by 7 men who chose to leave:

> *I don't think the place works. Majority are here to get cat C and parole. There's a tremendous amount of drugs on the wing. Staff don't care. When I first came it wasn't up to my expectations but therapy was done, but last year many devious people came, not prepared to change. (2 yrs 1 month)*
> *Prison is not good at doing reports on time (…) had enough. Feel I've done what was asked (…) not really convinced it's the right timing (…) overwhelming and repetitive, bores the life out of me now. (2.5 yrs)*
> *My decision to go. (…) Environment and policy mean it's not working. No order of importance. Not happy with people being able to manipulate on groups and wings, but staff seem to encourage it. (2.5 yrs)*

One gave health reasons and one assessed himself as unsuitable for therapy:

> *I can't cope with what's going on in my head. Getting stressed out, no tolerance for people. You can't shut yourself away here like you can in the system. (5 months)*

Others gave reasons related to their sentence plans:

> *Got to do SOTP. I want to get back on track and get a job. (22 months)*
> *I feel I've got to the stage where I've got what I need from the wing. (…) I need to do SOTP, I need a new challenge. (3 yrs 11 months)*

It is likely that there will always be problems with unacceptable behaviour, although there is general acknowledgement that the unique Grendon regime is responsible for keeping this at a remarkably low level. Men who fall into the unacceptable behaviour and unsuitability for therapy categories of leavers are probably unlikely to be affected by any mitigating strategy Grendon might adopt. However, dissatisfied men might, in some cases, be reflecting areas of Grendon that are amenable to change. In other words, if things had been different they might have stayed. It is perhaps significant that many of the criticisms made by disgruntled men were echoed by those otherwise satisfied men interviewed who stayed to finish therapy and make a progressive move. Thus, some criticisms are less readily dismissed as arising from individual resentment or personal dysfunction. The themes of dissatisfaction that arose are summarised in table 11.1.

While some criticisms may need more exploration before they can be fully made sense of or can be explained in terms of 'clinical defences' or low readiness for treatment, others may indicate opportunities for organisational change that could contribute to the reduction of general drop-out rates by improving the least desirable aspects of Grendon's infrastructure, amenities and environment.

Planned leaving from therapy wings

The third type of interview was with men who had finished their therapy (although not necessarily successfully in all aspects of it) and who were moving on in their sentence in a planned and agreed way. For some this is to a C or D cat prison to finish their sentence, and for others it is discharge. For many, completion of therapy had lengthened their sentence considerably or postponed their re-categorisation. It is interesting to note that their criticisms of Grendon were largely the same as those of men who dropped out, despite which they managed to finish their therapy.

> *Conditions we live in: sanitation facilities, lack of amenities or up-keep. This is the 21st century, they need to get their act together. Other prisons stay on top of all infrastructure faults and are aware of the impact this can have – here they aren't, so complaints get in the way of therapy.*
>
> *Infrastructure: paperwork. The shortcomings of the prison have an adverse effect on the wing. It's becoming more of a system prison.*
>
> *Therapy is two to three hours per day but should be the whole environment (…) due to lack of involvement of staff (who are) doing off-wing duties, e.g. security. Since the escape, the culture is more rule-bound (…) impinges on quality of therapeutic life. This diminishes the individual's voice – we are seen as cons rather than men.*

It is likely that many of the men who stayed to complete their therapy have a more robust way of dealing with the frustrations, ambiguities and disappointments than those who dropped out. Ongoing exit interviews

Table 11.1   Themes of dissatisfaction

Dissatisfaction theme	Examples
Perceived lack of transparency and proper democratic process, particularly in managerial decision-making	*'It's becoming more of a system prison, it creates the illusion that you have a real voice but when you ask to air that voice it seems that the decision has already been made'* *'Instead of integrating changes slowly they are imposed suddenly with no communication or reason'*
Timely completion of paperwork to deadlines, such as reports required for parole or re-categorisation applications. This was perceived as particularly problematic for lifers	*'Paperwork can't be done and groups are left unstaffed, general admin gets left, which is very important for lifers when boards are delayed'*
Stresses and strains on staff that affect prisoners	*'Staff have left because of stress. Staff don't know what the messages from upstairs mean, leading to stress'* *'Therapy is 2–3 hrs per day but should be the whole environment. It is due to lack of involvement of staff doing off-wing duties, e.g. security'* *'Staff regularly get pulled out to work elsewhere in the prison, this occasionally disrupts groups. Staff are constantly under pressure from the top. These things can be a distraction in therapy, e.g. chasing paperwork, Governors who are supposed to visit but don't'*
Perceived disagreements between therapy and security resulting in actions experienced as incomprehensible, unexpected or petty	*'I've lost faith in what people say and what they actually offer'* *'I had 2 (requests) backed by the wing but refused by the Governor, which was unfair. The (request) was based on therapeutic need, but refused. Therapists don't have the power anymore. The refusals broke my heart because my hard work wasn't being recognised'*
Therapy staff perceived as fending off criticisms by 'blaming' the individual's inability to change or understand, or attributing complaints to resistance	*'Lack of honesty, favouritism; collusion, inconsistent rules, everything in life can't be related to offending behaviour'*

Table 11.1   *Continued*

Dissatisfaction theme	Examples
Security perceived as having a heavy handed, inflexible, black-and-white approach, often cutting across therapeutic decisions and with no explanation	*'It's like 'them and us' now – becoming more like a system prison. Less trust from security we have to be escorted everywhere now. Governors are not pro-therapy, just administrators'* *'There is a constant battle between therapists and management to keep therapy safe'*
Poor amenities such as gym access and sport, lack of workshop and work opportunities. Poor maintenance of the environment, e.g. inadequate or broken heating and hot water systems	*'There is definitely not enough to do here. Only therapy and no real relief from it. We could do with more job training, workshops, life skills, job interview skills, experiential learning – make the workshops work'* *'Gym provision is inadequate and inflexible'*

plus psychometric data might be used to examine why successful men are successful and how they managed these difficulties.

Summary of leaving from therapy wings

Some prisoners reported a mismatch between the feeling that they have been 'given a voice' by Grendon, and the real opportunity to exercise that voice. These men were as likely to feel disempowered by therapeutic decisions as they were by security decisions, leaving some feeling unable to continue to live and work at Grendon. The operation of the 'democratic' aspect of the prison TC, which is the locus of empowerment and pro-social behaviour, is sometimes felt to be weak.

You don't know where you stand anymore here, you do in other prisons even if it is negatively.

Decisions made by the community can appear to be over-ridden by the therapy staff, and expectations of fairness and 'rights' may be over-ridden by the security agenda. To some extent this may be practically unavoidable, and such perceptions may sometimes relate to the lessons men are learning about the responsible use of democracy and living within social boundaries. However, an inability to cope long-term with perceived inconsistencies and disappointments arising from the therapy and security agendas, which are sometimes inevitably incompatible, contributes to the sense of grievance some men develop against their community and the establishment. Thus, men who are making progress on their criminogenic risk factors may still become disillusioned and wish to leave. Continued efforts to promote as far as possible a culture of transparency, unity and consistency between therapy, management and security (staff and function), as well as tailoring men's expectations and understanding of TC democratisation as it operates within a prison-based TC, may help to prevent some men becoming disillusioned and subsequently dropping out.

Steps to address some of the more basic complaints (e.g. environment and leisure time occupation) that seem most prevalent among prisoners whether they have completed therapy or not, and on which dimensions men compare Grendon unfavourably with other prisons, could contribute to a more stable population less prone to drop-outs. The fact that four times as many men choose to leave as get voted out highlights the significance of this group of men. Criticisms of amenities and environment in particular may relate to stretched budgets and equally stretched maintenance staff. However, in the modern world of competition from attractive modern establishments, Grendon may find itself slipping behind in the league where once it was the only player.

Positive Comments

Alongside criticisms the participants, with only one exception, made positive comments, some solicited by questions on the interview schedule and many unsolicited, in response to a range of other questions. These comments fall broadly into two categories, firstly relating to what each felt he had gained on a personal level at Grendon; and secondly how each had experienced staff relationships and behaviours.

Personal gains

Most men made some comment about what they felt they had gained from Grendon. Common themes related to gains in confidence, self-esteem and feeling listened to:

It has changed my life, I have self-esteem and confidence – I would never have had this before. (pl)[7]
   First time ever (in my life) I have had a voice. (pl)
   '*For me to survive here for three years is massive, I feel proud of myself. I know I've done well.*' (vo)

These comments, and others like them, were offered enthusiastically and with genuine warmth toward Grendon, even when they were expressed alongside quite severe criticisms about the regime or the physical environment, imparting considerable veracity to them.

The relationship that individuals were able to make with staff members was described as being unlike that in any other prison. Themes of trust, honesty and equity arose:

The SO who gave me the chance, he's been honest and I see him as a person not a screw. (pl)
   Staff use first names. (pl)
   There is more respect and common courtesy here than in other prisons. (pl)
   Staff are brilliant, spot on, fully supportive, recognise people who work, strong. (vo)

A number of staff qualities were highlighted as unique to Grendon in the experience of the participant, such as being welcomed on their first day by an officer using their first name and inviting the prisoner to address them by their first name. This was mentioned so often that its power to impress cannot be underestimated. Some men confessed that they were suspicious of this approach for some time before they realised it was a genuine attempt to make them welcome, while others appreciated it immediately. The lasting and positive effect of this welcome appears to serve as an introduction to the unusual environment of mutual respect that is encouraged between prisoners and staff in several ways: by the use of first names; by the sharing of day-to-day decisions about life on the community; by the supportive but challenging work that both are engaged in and by the openness, approachability and reliability of the staff. The environment was felt to be '*supportive and open despite your background*' and people felt treated as individuals. The therapeutic 'work' that men had come to Grendon to do was often mentioned:

---

[7](pl) indicates a planned leaver, while (vo) indicates someone who was voted out, expelled or who chose to leave.

I'm here to struggle not settle in, I'm trying not to have rigid thinking. (pl)
… therapeutic ethos, challenges set for you. (pl)
You feel you can talk in here, in the system you can't so you respond in other ways (…) self harm, drugs etc. (pl)
You get out what you put in. (pl)

These quotations demonstrate the centrality afforded to the therapeutic process by men, even when they are opting to leave, although some (see above) found it repetitive and boring. Men at Grendon share something unique, talking about having a 'therapy head' on. They learn to talk about difficult areas of their lives and they learn to help others do the same. They become skilled at challenging each other in order to 'move people on' so that work on childhood trauma, on criminogenic factors and on antisocial and crime-related behaviours moves forward in fits and starts.

Conclusion

Exit interviews have the potential to reveal important information about the impact an organisation has on the people in it. As a way of evaluating various aspects of prison life, the exit interview has the advantage of exposing the details of individual experience, invested with all the meaning that individuals attach to those experiences, unlike traditional survey-style instruments. In addition, asking departing prisoners to talk about their experiences and feelings provided them with an often-welcome opportunity to reflect on their time at Grendon. However, the interviews were time-consuming, lasting about an hour, as was the writing up and analysis. The impartiality of the interviewers may have aided the interview process but for many establishments, on-site researchers would be unlikely and external researchers expensive. On the other hand, once the first round of interviews is done, the results can be used to inform the development of a more wieldy exit interview or questionnaire that could contribute to the prison's ongoing collection of knowledge about itself leading to improvement in services and outcomes.

Acknowledgement

With thanks to the men at Grendon who participated in these interviews, and to the therapeutic communities at Grendon for their co-operation.

References

Bailey, C.A. (1996). *A Guide to Field Research*. Thousand Oaks, CA: Pine Forge Press.

Dowden, C. & Serin, R. (2001). *Anger Management Programming for Offenders: The impact of program performance measures*. Research Branch, Correctional Service of Canada. Accessed 23 Feb 2009 from www.csc-scc.gc.ca/text/rsrch/reports/r106/r106_e.pdf

Genders, E. & Player, E. (1995). *Grendon: A Study of a Therapeutic Prison*. Oxford: Clarendon Press.

Jones, L. (1997). Developing models for managing treatment integrity and efficacy in a prison-based TC: the Max Glatt Centre. In E. Cullen, L. Jones & R. Woodward (Eds) *Therapeutic Communities for Offenders*. London: Wiley.

Padfield, N. (2002). *Beyond the Tariff: Human Rights and the Release of Life Sentence Prisoners*. Oregon: Willan Publishing.

Skyrme, D.J. (2001). *Disappearing Knowledge: Are Exit Interviews the Wits End?* 1[3] Update / Entovation International News no 55. Accessed 23 Feb 2009 from http://209.85.229.132/search?q=cache:http://skyrme.com/updates/u55.htm

Sullivan, E.L. (2005). *Reasons for Leaving: A Study of Drop-out Rates*. Unpublished report of research for HMP Grendon.

Sullivan, E.L. (2006). Moving on: Exit interviews in a therapeutic community prison. *Therapeutic Communities*, *27*(3) Autumn.

Chapter 12

'This can't be real': Continuity at HMP Grendon

Lorna A. Rhodes

Introduction

If you had the opportunity to visit a community 30 or 40 years ago, in many respects it would be the same as a community today. There would be the same clamour for time to be heard ... the same politics and community problems that are at the same time impossible to live with for another moment, and yet utterly compelling and absorbing ... Bob Healey (2000, p. 65)

HMP Grendon has maintained an unbroken practice of community therapy for over 40 years. As Healey documents in his history of the prison, much has happened in that time – both in internal governance and in relation to the larger Prison Service – with many changes reflecting Grendon's position as a small and experimental regime within a larger system. Yet a robust thread of continuous practice is apparent in Grendon's daily life. Staff members remark that it is almost as though an expectation of community permeates the very walls. Prisoners – who have been describing the place to outsiders ever since its inception – confirm Healey's description of a recurring movement from 'distrust ... to uncomfortable and ambivalent belonging' (2000, p. 65). Somehow, Grendon's communities do the work of reproducing themselves through time, recreating for each

Grendon and the Emergence of Forensic Therapeutic Communities: Developments in Research and Practice
Edited by Richard Shuker and Elizabeth Sullivan
© 2010 John Wiley & Sons, Ltd.

prisoner the sense that he has entered a stable – almost inevitable – yet new and surprising world.

In this chapter I take up the question of social reproduction at Grendon by considering the relationship between, on the one hand, the therapeutic community as a regime of *practice*, and on the other, the larger institutional logic in which it is embedded. As Genders and Player (1995) have pointed out, what is remarkable about Grendon is that it is *both* prison and therapeutic community; the one is embedded in and inextricable from the other, yet their goals are in some ways radically different. I argue that the continuity of Grendon's regime crucially depends on its strategic creation of an interface at which 'prison' becomes both 'same' and 'other'. It is this interface that creates the initial conditions – the social world, matrix, or 'assemblage' – within which prisoners can articulate new versions of themselves. Looking at Grendon in this way opens up the question of how an institution might work to contain and transform the damaging effects of institutional practice itself.

During a month of ethnographic research at Grendon in 2008, I formally interviewed 17 prisoners with stays of up to five years, as well as 7 staff members; I also attended community and staff meetings, spoke informally with prisoners and staff, and attended Grendon events. My brief study does not pretend to be a complete description; rather, my previous research on supermax prisons in the US led me to focus on the contrast between the isolation imposed by such regimes and Grendon's emphasis on sociality (Rhodes, 2004). Because I shared with Grendon residents an initial experience of disbelief at the prison's egalitarian and informal atmosphere, my interviews – and thus my choice of topic here – were undoubtedly influenced by their desire to make sure I understood the contrast between Grendon and the prisons from which they had come.

I have organised this essay around three questions centred on Grendon's strategic relationship to the institutional logic that surrounds and permeates it. The first is the question of what makes a total institution 'total'? What do such institutions actually do to their inhabitants to 'institutionalise' them? The second question is: how does Grendon strategically 'reverse' or 'play with' the elements of this institutionalising process? That is, what signals to Grendon residents that they are no longer, as one man put it, in 'prison as they knew it'? I will take up three features of this process that stood out in my interviews: mortification, seniority, and 'delinquency'. The third question, standing in contrast to reversal, is what other aspect of the total institution is actually intensified at Grendon, and how is this intensification accomplished – again, through a strategic re-visioning of 'prison'? Finally, I conclude with a brief consideration of the implications of this institutional strategy for the broader issue of mass incarceration.

Grendon as a Total Institution

One way to think of institutions is as assemblages of practices – including ways of talking and feeling – within which people come into alignment with certain possibilities for making sense of themselves. From this perspective, what happens in an institution is neither that anonymous forces act upon passive subjects, nor that people 'discover' who or what they are as a result of managed 'intervention'. Rather, the assembled practices into which individuals are inserted – forms of speech, definitions of conditions, rules for behaviour, routines of daily life – enable some actions (and thus also thoughts) while making others difficult or impossible (cf. Downie, 2004). What Nikolas Rose (1998) calls 'being-assembled-together' – in any human situation – produces the corresponding 'inner' assemblage of thoughts, emotions, and desires that make up what we experience as our sense of self. This process occurs in relationship to all sorts of 'authorities' – not only parents, teachers and doctors but also techniques, images, and affects – as a result of multiple more or less coherent practices (pp. 171–198).

Total institutions can be understood as unusually bounded and constrained assemblages organised to produce habits of docility through specific practices of authority. Erving Goffman, the American sociologist who coined the phrase 'total institution', published *Asylums: Essays on the Social Situation of Mental Patients and Other Inmates* the year before Grendon opened in 1962. Based on ethnographic fieldwork at St. Elizabeth's Hospital in Washington, DC, *Asylums* centres on how institutional practices within such no-exit enclosures as convents, psychiatric hospitals, and prisons serve to encompass individuals so that all of their behaviour is (in theory) open to being observed and managed (Castel *et al.*, 1982, p. 31). Specific rituals accompany entrance to such places, and once inside inmates discover themselves in a world where – in the absence of both privacy and relationships with the larger world – social life collapses in upon itself. Sooner or later this experience destabilises the inmate's previous identity and induces variable combinations of passivity, porosity to authority, and resistance (Goffman, 1961, p. 14).

Goffman's description of the total institution is rooted in the same historical moment that produced Grendon. He was an important voice in the critique of psychiatry as social control that initiated deinstitutionalisation and eventually – in concert with psychotropic medication – transformed public psychiatry in the United States (Castel *et al.*, 1982, p. 85; Cohen & Scull, 1983). As with deinstitutionalisation, the parallel historical thread that led to the establishment of Grendon relied on notions of community and a hope for less authoritarian, more democratic modes of interaction (Harrison, 2000). But unlike the problematic experiment of dismantling total institutions altogether – as it turned out, with little 'community' support – Grendon is founded on the retention of the 'total' apparatus. In addition to its locked wings, intensive rules for entrance and exit, and round-the-clock control, Grendon features long stays, elaborate disciplinary expectations, and a regime of non-confidentiality that make it even more encompassing than most.

But Grendon is also a *response* to the total institution, one that highlights and strategically uses the fact that its residents have already been institutionalised elsewhere. While the therapeutic community is meant eventually to address the resident's original 'home world', its starting point is the 'home world' of other prisons from which the men come. Features of this larger system include rituals of degradation, strict inmate and staff hierarchy, and emphasis on 'respect'. Practices that address these features aim to convey the expectations and potential of a different, yet familiar environment. But this is not a simple matter of substitution for, as Goffman notes, 'total institutions do not really look for cultural victory [over the 'home world']. They [instead] use this persistent tension as strategic leverage in the management of men' (1961, p. 13). What Grendon reproduces over time is precisely this 'strategic leverage': the use of differences between 'home' (in the form of other prisons) and Grendon's regime. But while in one sense 'management' is a consequence of this strategy, the therapeutic community aims eventually to disarticulate management as such from the individual's capacity to reassemble himself.

We can imagine, then, a triangular relationship among assemblages. On one leg is the larger prison system, which – regardless of the specific ways in which it is encountered by any given individual – is defined by Grendon as embodying certain 'criminal values' (such as the rule against snitching or 'grassing' on another prisoner) and as requiring specific counterpractices in order to be left behind. On the second leg is the therapeutic community itself, but also Grendon's practices as a prison (such as the admission ritual I discuss below, through which Grendon presents itself as a commentary on and challenge to the values of the larger system). Finally, the prisoner finds himself for a while 'between two worlds' as he is inserted into practices – including ways of talking about himself – that are the conditions of possibility for a revised 'interior' landscape.

The Logic of Reversal

Mortification

One of the prisoners Tony Parker met at Grendon in 1970 described the period following his admission. 'Frankly,' he said, 'I was shattered when I first came here.' (Parker, 1970.) This sense of being 'shattered' is echoed in these comments by men I interviewed:

> When I first came here, it was a complete culture shock to me. This place was like something that I've never known in my time in prison. When I got off the bus ... [a member of staff], he's going, 'Hello, my name's [giving his first name]. Welcome to Grendon.' And I thought, 'What? Hang on. Have I just arrived in some parallel universe?'

> I had a high-ranking staff [member] shake my hand and tell me his first name. I couldn't believe [it] ... [I was] very stunned. Eventually I was left in [a] room on me own, the door wasn't even locked. Even though the reception is secure and it's all double fenced, you still felt that door should be closed. It just weren't prison as I knew it.

> And then to come here ... thinking is there an agenda, what's that all about, this can't be real, this isn't real prison, this isn't the safety I feel. I [felt I'd] rather be in a prison ... where you know where you belong, you're used to it, and that's how it is.

The admitting officers introduce entering inmates to a 'parallel universe' by reversing familiar elements: the hierarchy that precludes shaking hands or using first names, the mistrust conveyed by multiple locks, the pervasive indifference in contrast to which the offer of a cup of tea is an unheard of act of kindness (cf. Sullivan, 2006, p. 9). What is addressed by these rituals of reversal is the process of 'mortification' – encompassing both shame and death – that is normally brought to bear on new arrivals, who are stripped of their possessions, given special clothing or uniforms, submitted to tests of their submission to authority, and humiliatingly inducted into the lack of privacy they can expect from confinement (Goffman, 1961). Mortification breaks down resistance, removes many protective elements of social life (such as the ability to control how one is addressed), and emphasizes the 'bare' or biological aspects of human existence (Agamben, 1998). Describing the admissions process at other prisons, one Grendon prisoner pointed out that 'there's no one got any time for anyone really because the flow of people is quite busy'. And not only does the institution's need for efficiency come first, but 'you [experience] ... degradation, strip searching and showers and all that'.

In contrast, the induction process at Grendon presents a series of unexpected gestures that offer a preliminary map of the therapeutic community. Before their arrival, 'safety' and 'realness' for these men has been constituted in part by a numbing of response; the prisoner who uses the term 'degradation' goes on to say 'you know that occurs, but you don't let it ... you don't have any feelings about it.' Another remarked that in contrast he found Grendon:

> ... *unlike any other prison that I've ever been in and that in itself takes some getting used to, and it's kind of a shock tactic ... There's a shock thing there at the beginning because you think it's unreal. What we experienced just coming off the bus is different, very different ... and kind of hard to trust at the beginning and very unnerving and unsettling, even to the point where ... I didn't think I'd be staying because I didn't feel safe enough.*

One message in this tactic is that the defensiveness and numbing of feeling induced or exacerbated by mortification are about to be challenged.

A second message conveyed by the 'shock' of entry concerns the notion of 'respect' as it pervades prison culture. Richard Sennett (2003) points out that 'in places where resources are scarce and approval from the outside world is lacking social honor is fragile; it needs to be asserted each day' (p. 34). 'Honor' in this sense 'signals a kind of erasure of social boundaries and distance' a world in which the impingement of others is not only a matter for immediate vigilance, but also one in which one's 'image' is 'indistinguishable from that presented to him by other people' (p. 55, quoting Bourdieu, 1966, p. 211). In prison settings this sense of honour comes closest to what inmates mean by 'respect'; it includes a system of hierarchy among crimes, a need to quickly redress even minor insults, and a code of allegiance to fellow prisoners. Many prisoners thus describe a defensive 'front' or mask through which they hope to control their interactions with others (Rhodes, 2004).

> *In the standard prisons ... everyone's just really out for themselves. They've all got masks. You're all bigging yourself up all the time.*

> [The new arrival] *wants to know what everyone thinks about him, and he wants to know where he stands with everyone, and that's what it's like in most jails. You are showing utter respect to everyone. You don't want to upset no one. Little idiots can stick a knife in you.*

The suspicion with which new arrivals respond to Grendon's entry rituals suggests how easily a respectful gesture can seem mocking, ambiguous and potentially shameful. Arrival at Grendon begins to destabilise the expected situation, in which 'respect' is a scarce resource to be hoarded and displayed. As they look back later, residents describe their understanding that they were being offered a kind of proposition – the provocative suggestion that respect could acquire a different horizon.

And it took me about, I don't know, it took me about three, four weeks to come to terms with what they were actually trying to do. And what they were actually trying to do was to treat me like a human being and to show me a bit of respect, you know something which I hadn't been shown for a long, long time, and something which I hadn't shown to anyone else for a long, long time. So I look at that little interaction back then and how important that actually was. That was a very, very important step for me because they weren't just treating me as a murderer.

Seniority

Speaking about the 'new prison at Grendon Underwood' shortly after it opened, Dr H.K. Snell remarked that '[prisoners] often assimilate from their fellows in this kind of group setting home truths and good advice which they would not otherwise accept – certainly not from an authoritarian figure' (Snell, 1962, p. 178). This reliance on peer teaching is described by a prisoner I interviewed who was leaving after several years.

[In group] I have to accept what I've done in order for me to explore that, to let my barriers down and reduce my defences so that we can take a look at that. So there's the process of building trust and making newer guys feel comfortable … It feels really hard, and you know I feel shame, and I feel guilt, and I don't want to do this. But the hope is, and generally it works, that people end up divulging what it is that they experienced, and then we encourage [them] – those of us that have lived through that – to try new things … So that's the thing: we give each other things to think about. Sometimes we take that on board, and sometimes we don't. Sometimes we'll say, 'Why should I? Who are you?' But the group provides the setting where we should feel safe to explore the nature of our lives.

'Giving each other things to think about' – a centrepiece of Grendon's process ever since Dr Snell's day – is puzzling and potentially threatening to a more recently arrived prisoner.

When people express themselves honestly [about] what they would like to do to you – that's the bit you don't normally hear, and I struggle with that. My motto is don't create an enemy. If I tell someone that they just brought up certain feelings, then I expect that person to go away thinking about doing me harm. So, therefore … I'm going to attack him. But that doesn't happen. I don't know how it doesn't happen. These people lived the same lives I've lived, so why, why are they not doing it? I don't know. I honestly don't know. It's the desire to change obviously.

The change represented by these contrasting responses is mediated by seniority as 'older' residents serve as models and teachers for those who are newer to the community.

The senior members show you. The senior members are very honest. They talk about their feelings. They talk about their violent thoughts, their anger. It's like leading the way, there is a hierarchy. There is a peer system because you've got your new members who've just come in and then you've got your lads who've been here for 18 months, and then you've got your senior members who are at the back end of their therapy.

It becomes apparent to newer residents that the more experienced have learned a complex set of skills – being able to 'take on board' unpleasant truths about the effects of one's actions on others, being emotionally expressive beyond anger, dealing effectively with aggression – that they too might be able to master. As with the entry ritual, these new relationships draw on, yet simultaneously shift, pervasive notions of respect.

He's a guy I respect … And to become him, with his characteristics and with his personality and how he was, he kind of showed me that this place was quite serious. If he can do it, no one's going to laugh at me.

As Sennett suggests, 'the acts of recognition and regard which orchestrate the experience of respect' are acutely responsive to hierarchy and inequality (2003, p. 149). The substitute hierarchy created at Grendon, on the other hand, asks residents to live with 'nonces' (sex offenders) while offering respect not for murder but for specific interpersonal skills. Describing how he felt shortly after admission, one man said that the more experienced prisoners seemed to have 'no one to impress … and they end up not inmates, but more of an inspiration.' Such a figure of emulation is not an 'inmate' – absorbed by the prison hierarchy – but rather a person of whom he thought, 'Oh, I'd love to be like that.'

'Delinquency'

Inmates of total institutions are treated as 'not yet adult' by staff and like children often maintain a secret zone of tacitly permitted transgression. This combination of infantilisation and 'removal activities' means that 'every total institution can be seen as a kind of dead sea in which little islands of vivid, encapturing activity appear' (Goffman, 1961, p. 69). At Grendon, these 'little islands' – what some prisoners describe as 'delinquency' – are a third way in which the normal mode of prison life is reversed and played upon by the therapeutic community. As one staff member put it, 'You have to have a culture which allows for and perhaps even encourages breakdowns in good behaviour without it being too punitive, so that the shared understanding is that this is a kind of emotional workbench that you're all sitting around.'

The sense in which the workbench is 'emotional' can be heard in this resident's answer to my discovery that Grendon staff neither punished nor moralised about milder forms of bad behaviour.

> LAR: [So] *there's the therapeutic community. And then inside of that there's a little gang or ...*
> Resident: *Aye. You've the therapeutic side, the therapeutic gang, and then you've got the criminal element, the criminal gang ... I've had loads of battles with it ... but it's been healthy for me because I've been on both sides. I had to own me behaviour. I had to work on it. I had to talk about why I had come here, started off so good, and then went back to the criminal element in the wing and start taking drugs again. So I had to explore them powerful feelings and what they meant for me.*

Here the 'therapeutic gang' refers to residents, not 'therapists'. The contrasting 'criminal gang' is valued for its potential to represent the resident's 'home world' – first the 'home' of the prison system itself and later on, as he becomes more able to tolerate distress, the home from which he came. The ebb and flow of 'delinquency' opens up and problematises the very territory most compelling to many inmates.

> *At one time* [on my wing] *the therapeutic element was really strong, and we were proper governing things in the community but* [now] *there's been more new people, so it's been a lot harder. But that's only right because that's part of the struggle, because standing up to your criminal feelings is a hard, difficult thing to do, to face your anger, your violence, why you rob people, why you steal ... It's a huge emotional thing.*

Thus in the parallel universe of Grendon, the previously taken-for-granted world is still available but has fallen under question; as one resident put it, '[My] normal wasn't normal at all.'

> *There might be someone that's brought drugs in and the community's damaged* [and] *I'm thinking, 'Oh, look what you've done.' Then I say, 'Hold on a minute,*

that's what you *were doing.' Now you can see. These are the people whose shops you burgled or whose son you harmed or I took someone's life, and that raises itself up and speaks to you, and they're very profound moments when you allow yourself to humble yourself and acknowledge that and say this is what it's about, this is the choice you made.*

The energy that emanates from 'encapturing islands' of delinquency thus mirrors what happens in prisons generally, but in a context in which each element starts to come into view – what the taboo against grassing suggests about affiliation, what drug use suggests about the desire to escape responsibility. In other words, before these can be brought into the 'container' of the therapeutic community they are held in the 'container' of Grendon as a prison linked to other prisons. It is from there – in fits and starts – that the possibility for 'thinking' then emerges (Downie, 2004).

When I come here I was up on the landing, and I could smell loads of dope being smoked around us, and one of the staff downstairs said, 'Could you smell any dope being smoked up on the landing?' I'd never ever been asked anything like that before, and for the first time I says, 'Yes. I could.' Well, that brung up a huge amount of feelings. I felt disgusted. I felt like I had done something really wrong … I started rejecting them feelings, so I got involved again in cannabis, just to make meself feel more accepted in the criminal fraternity. [When, again, the use of drugs came out and was brought up in a wing meeting] it shocked me … to face the consequences of me actions. So then I started to face my feelings. And that was the beginning of the journey.

It's good that every 8 or 12 months somebody brings drugs into the prison and spreads it about and there's a big huge drug issue. You know I wouldn't recommend it to happen all the bloody time, but I think that's good because that highlights so many things that are going on for people, and they can't deny it. They've got to start facing it. They've got to start making choices. And that's really good. That's the therapeutic community thing.

Looping

What I have described so far is a triangular relationship in which the prisoner finds in Grendon a kind of encapsulated tinkering with the familiar prison world. But in one respect entry into Grendon greatly intensifies one of the most problematic aspects of any total institution: unlike people living under ordinary circumstances, inmates are unable to keep their behaviour compartmentalised. Through what Goffman (1961) calls 'looping', 'spheres of life are desegregated, so that … conduct in one scene of activity is thrown up to [the inmate] by staff as a comment and check upon his conduct in another context.' An angry outburst in the dining hall, for example, might be brought up when the inmate requests permission to receive a visitor or goes up for parole, so that 'his reaction to his own situation is collapsed back into this situation itself …' (p. 37). Prisoners are of course well aware of this danger, for as one Grendon resident explained, 'I was brought up never, never to tell the police or the authorities anything about me self. I was always very guarded … because I always thought [that] the more you open your mouth to the police, to the government, the more trouble you get yourself in.' For someone already well schooled in this perspective, prison is a powerful reinforcer. As a different man said, 'In the system you don't talk to screws. And if you do start talking to them, it can get you into trouble because you can be misjudged … and they'll go away, and they'll write down … stuff.'

This aspect was uppermost when prisoners spoke of the difficulty of being at Grendon, with its daily meetings, rule of non-confidentiality and emphasis on the retrieval of trauma. 'It was very frightening [at first] because revealing stuff about myself was one of the hardest things I've ever done. It felt really uncomfortable.' Prisoners stressed that this aspect of Grendon is not optional. As one man put it, 'When I come here I had to reveal a lot of things, and it was expected, and that put us under a lot of pressure.' Keeping a secret is one of the few powers available to prisoners; to give it up is to surrender a compelling vision of how the world works that has been confirmed by prior experience. Seen more broadly, the technologies of surveillance and record keeping that enforce transparency also serve to produce the inmate as an institutional subject who is, even from prisoners' own perspective, 'institutionalised' (Foucault, 1979; Rose, 1998).

But this intensification of looping at Grendon stands in a complex relationship to the way knowledge of prisoners is used in prisons more generally. The most intense situations I observed during my research centred on whose knowledge would count when institutional pressures – such as recategorisation – bore down on inmates' lives. Prisoners spoke about how 'honesty' – the willingness to align with the ethic of transparency by owning up to violent thoughts and feelings – could serve them poorly in the larger system.

> I've struggled sitting on our group because [the group is] me jailer as well, and it's really uncomfortable … how honest am I going to be with people to the point where I'm going to keep meself in prison?

At the same time, transparency also represents a shift in the nature of attention, away from the parsimonious prison economy in which positive attention is a scarce resource while negative attention is dangerous. As the resident's thoughts and actions come into visibility at Grendon, the glare of attention is on *his* response to them. Transparency is used to break old habits – and may ultimately affect the prisoner's fate in the larger system – but the context is the group. There he is asked to revisit the social context in which secrecy became necessary, and while at first the emphasis is on its meaning in prison, eventually secret-keeping itself can be brought into question. Speaking of a traumatic event in his childhood, one man said:

> *That's the one thing what gets me. Why should it be a secret? I've held all my things – obviously it's painful, right – thinking that I should carry shame for it. Why should I? Why should it be a secret? It shouldn't be. I've done nothing wrong. My offence I've done wrong, and I'll own that all day … But what's happened to me and what's happened to other people, why should they hold it as a big secret?*

By insisting that each man tell the story of himself, for himself, therapy at Grendon thus uses the no-exit strategy of the total institution, but enlists it to effect change that is inherently person-centred and unpredictable. In this sense it shifts not only the content but the nature of institutional discipline. As Andrew Jefferson (2003) puts it, the management of change in the therapeutic community 'is not a disciplining of subjects as much as it is a creation of space for the working of discipline itself … the constitution of necessary and sufficient conditions such that self-discipline can function in the modes non-specifically prescribed by the local, particular community' (p. 67).

Conclusion

By emphasising the institutional practices that emerge from Grendon's relationship to the larger prison system, I do not address the question most often asked of Grendon, which is whether its residents 'really' change. Instead I have asked: under what conditions – within which specific social arrangements, in relation to what assemblages – do prisoners at Grendon come to think that they *can* change? What I've outlined here is a specific relationship to the prison system as a whole that both reverses and intensifies its logic. This relationship positions the prisoner – especially early in his experience of the new and 'unreal' environment – so that tensions around institutional practice become a proxy for his relationship with himself. Aligning with the experience of those senior to him, he moves through the 'process of distrust turning to uncomfortable and ambivalent belonging and moving on to … realisation of what Grendon had provided' (Healey, 2000, p. 65). Of course this transition is not a given, and I have only been able to touch on the different kinds of work that make it possible. But one of its conditions of possibility seems to be the balance of powers among institutional traditions that undergirds Grendon's longevity.

The contemporary dominance of mass incarceration would have been unimaginable at the time of Grendon's founding. As prisons expand and become increasingly punitive, as sentences lengthen and the use of isolation becomes routine, the experience of confinement leaves ever-deeper marks on prisoners' lives. Through a long, organic process of mostly unrecorded trial and error, staff and prisoners at Grendon have evolved a way of using institutional practice itself to address the harm done by institutional practice. Although the specifics of this knowledge are tied to Grendon's history and position, the larger lesson is that this harm is not without its remedies.

Acknowledgements

I am deeply grateful for the support and kindness of the prisoners, staff, and administration of HMP Grendon. I also thank the University of Washington's Royalty Research Fund for the small grant that made this research possible, the Simpson Center for the Humanities at the University of Washington, and Andrew Jefferson, David Jones, Michelle Newberry and Elizabeth Sullivan for helpful comments. Quotations are from semi-structured, recorded interviews conducted in private and have been edited for length and clarity.

References

Agamben, G. (1998). *Homo Sacer: Sovereign Power and Bare Life* (trans D. Heller-Roazen). Stanford: Stanford University Press.

Bourdieu, P. (1966). The sentiment of honour in Kabyle society (trans P. Sherrard). In J.G. Péristiany (Ed.) *Honour and Shame: The Values of Mediterranean Society*. Chicago: University of Chicago Press.

Castel, R., Castel, F. & Lovell, A. (1982). *The Psychiatric Society* (trans. A. Goldhammer). New York: Columbia University Press.

Cohen, S. & Scull, A.T. (1983). *Social Control and the State*. New York: St Martin's Press.

Downie, A. (2004). Thinking under fire: the prison therapeutic community as container. In D. Jones (Ed.) *Working with Dangerous People: The Psychotherapy of Violence* (pp. 71–80). Oxford: Radcliffe Medical Press.

Foucault, M. (1979). *Discipline and Punish: The Birth of the Prison.* New York: Vintage Books.

Genders, E. & Player, E. (1995). *Grendon: A Study of a Therapeutic Prison.* Oxford: Oxford University Press.

Goffman, E. (1961). *Asylums: Essays on the Social Situation of Mental Patients and Other Inmates.* New York: Doubleday.

Harrison, T. (2000). *Bion, Rickman, Foulkes and the Northfield Experiments: Advancing on a Different Front.* London: Jessica Kingsley Publishers.

Healey, B. (2000). *Grendon Prison: The History of a Therapeutic Experiment 1939–2000.* Grendon Underwood: HM Prison Grendon.

Jefferson, A. (2003). Therapeutic discipline? Reflections on the penetration of sites of control by therapeutic discourse. *Outlines, 1,* 55–73.

Parker, T. (1970). *The Frying-pan: A Prison and its Prisoners.* London: Hutchinson.

Rhodes, L.A. (2004). *Total Confinement: Madness and Reason in the Maximum Security Prison.* Berkeley, CA: University of California Press.

Rose, N. (1998). *Inventing Ourselves: Psychology, Power, and Personhood.* Cambridge: Cambridge University Press.

Sennett, R. (2003). *Respect in a World of Inequality.* London: Norton.

Snell, H.K. (1962). The new prison at Grendon Underwood. *Medico-Legal Journal, 31,* 175–188.

Sullivan, E.L. (2006). Moving on: exit interviews in a therapeutic community prison. *Therapeutic Communities, 27*(3), 1–9.

Chapter 13

The Experience of Officers in a Therapeutic Prison: an Interpretative Phenomenological Analysis

James McManus

Introduction

It has been increasingly recognised in the last 10 years that therapists may experience negative effects as a result of exposure to the material discussed in therapy. Indeed, the diagnostic criteria for post-traumatic stress disorder in the DSM-IV-TR (American Psychiatric Association, 2000) state that the disorder can arise by being confronted with traumatic events that affected others. It has been suggested that exposure to clients' narratives of traumatic events can result in disruptive psychological and physical symptoms analogous to post-trauma symptoms in the therapist (McLean *et al.*, 2003).

Vicarious traumatisation (VT) has been defined as 'a process through which the therapist's inner experience is negatively transformed through empathic engagement with clients' trauma material' (Pearlman & Saakvitne, 1995, p. 31). The terms secondary traumatic stress (STS) and compassion fatigue (CF) have also been used to refer to symptoms 'nearly identical' to post-traumatic stress disorder (PTSD) applied to those emotionally and cognitively affected by the trauma of another (Figley, 1995).

Studies of psychological distress in therapists have found inconsistent results. For example, Schauben and Frazier (1995) found significant correlations between the percentage of sexual violence survivors in

Grendon and the Emergence of Forensic Therapeutic Communities: Developments in Research and Practice
Edited by Richard Shuker and Elizabeth Sullivan
© 2010 John Wiley & Sons, Ltd.

counsellors' caseloads and symptoms of PTSD, self-reported VT and disruption in beliefs. In contrast, Steed and Bicknell (2001) found no relationship between percentage of caseload made up of trauma work and therapist reports of STS. Some researchers have attempted to design specific measures to assess vicarious or secondary trauma. These include the Traumatic Stress Institute (TSI) Belief Scale (Pearlman *et al.*, 1992), which has been used to measure disruption in beliefs thought to be relevant to VT, and the Compassion Fatigue Self-Test for Practitioners (CFST; Figley, 1995), developed to measure compassion fatigue and burnout. However, research evidence based on these measures has been described as inconsistent and reliant on small and variable correlations between symptomatic distress and traumatic exposure (Sabin-Farrell & Turpin, 2003).

Steed and Downing (1998) interviewed 12 psychologists and counsellors working with survivors of sexual abuse or sexual assault about their responses to hearing traumatic material. All of the therapists interviewed reported a range of negative effects that occurred inside and outside the therapy sessions. These included affective responses (such as anger towards the perpetrator or society in general), physiological effects (such as fatigue and disturbed sleep), intrusive images and thoughts and increased vigilance regarding their own safety and that of others. In addition to the responses viewed as negative, several participants also reported positive changes in beliefs about themselves and others, including positive changes in their sense of identity and a greater sense of compassion for their clients. As a result, Steed and Downing (1998) argued for a broader conceptualisation of VT than a focus on negative changes.

A small number of studies have investigated the impact on staff of undertaking therapeutic work with offenders. For example, Crawley (2004) interviewed therapists involved in a sex offender treatment programme. Respondents described a sense of inner conflict between their desire to help to reform sex offenders and their feelings of revulsion towards such offenders and their crimes. The author described a 'fear of moral contamination' (Crawley, 2004, p. 217) in that participants were concerned that prolonged contact with sex offenders, including listening to graphic details of their crimes, could change their own perceptions, attitudes and behaviour.

Way *et al.* (2004) described some of the unique factors involved when working therapeutically with offenders. These included the necessity for therapists in this field to 'manage strong emotional reactions to hearing clients' traumatic material (e.g. stories of perpetration, deviant fantasies) and cognitive distortions while striving to remain helpful, appropriately empathic and professional. As a result, clinicians who treat offenders may experience different effects when compared to those who treat survivors and non-offenders' (p. 51).

Overall, more research is required to understand the impact on therapists of their work and how staff and organisations can prepare for and
protect against any negative consequences. The concepts of VT and STS
require refinement in terms of their validity and of contributory therapist
and client factors. The following study was an attempt to explore in detail
the experience of prison officers undertaking therapeutic work with offenders. With little research conducted in this area, no comprehensive measures
and lack of agreement about what factors may be relevant, a qualitative
approach was considered most appropriate.

Method

There were 8 participants: 5 men and 3 women. The mean age was 39.5
years (standard deviation = 6.02). All participants were white and British
and all were employed as prison officer facilitators. The mean length of
time spent in this role was 28.1 months (SD = 22.5). A cross-sectional
qualitative methodology was selected, using semi-structured interviews.
The information from these interviews was analysed using Interpretative
Phenomenological Analysis (IPA; Smith, 1996).

IPA is a qualitative method that aims to explore individuals' perceptions
of objects or events. It has been increasingly used in psychological research
particularly in the areas of health, social and clinical psychology (Reid
et al., 2005). The aim of IPA is 'to explore the participant's view of the
world and to adopt, as far as is possible, an insider's perspective of the
phenomenon under study' (Smith, 1996, p. 264). At the same time, it is
explicitly recognised that access to this perspective is dependent on the
interpretative activity of the researcher whose own conceptions are
employed to understand the information provided.

An interview schedule was developed which consisted of four broad
questions:

1   How would you describe your job/role?
2   What is it like to do this work?
3   Tell me about any personal impact of undertaking this work; and
4   What helps you to do the work?

Information from the interviews was transcribed and themes were identified in each transcript, in terms of how the text related to psychological
theory and what the nature and meaning of the experiences reported were.
Possible relationships between the themes were then considered. For

example, whether themes were similar or clustered together in hierarchical relationships, with 'super-ordinate' or master themes providing an over-arching title to explain related, subordinate themes. Once all transcripts had been considered at an individual case-study level, the themes for all participants were considered collectively. Attention was given to themes that reflected shared aspects of experience for all participants (consistency) and any areas of difference (divergence).

Results

The researcher developed 3 super-ordinate and 13 subordinate themes based on the interpretative phenomenological analysis (figure 13.1).

Theme 1: role conflict

This super-ordinate theme encompasses some of the tensions and conflicts described by participants in association with their role as prison officer facilitators. These included security-oriented and therapy-oriented aspects of their job. Additionally, participants reported some difficulties associated with helping or empathising with offenders. All participants reported observations of change in offenders, or faith in the potential for a positive outcome of therapy, as a way of maintaining motivation and justifying the work.

Theme 1.1 Balancing therapy and security

Participants stated that there was some degree of conflict between these two roles of therapy and security, both on a personal level and within the system in which they worked.

> For me it's if I'm sat in a group listening to somebody er talk about their abuse, talk about very sensitive things, which 9 out of 10 times you do, and then I have to issue them with a warning in the afternoon. That, it's very hard to do that because you know how much stress they've been through, and then you've got to tell them off for something else. (Participant 8: 237–248)
>
> You know I can be sitting on a group, them telling me all about their sexual abuse they covered or about some quite horrific stuff the way they were treated by their parents, and at 1 o' clock I can be strip searching them as they're coming out. Now that's a difficult thing to balance because I've got to be aware of the sensitivity and their needs and saying right yeah, you know, I know this is not pleasant … but you know I'm not going to abuse you, I want you to build

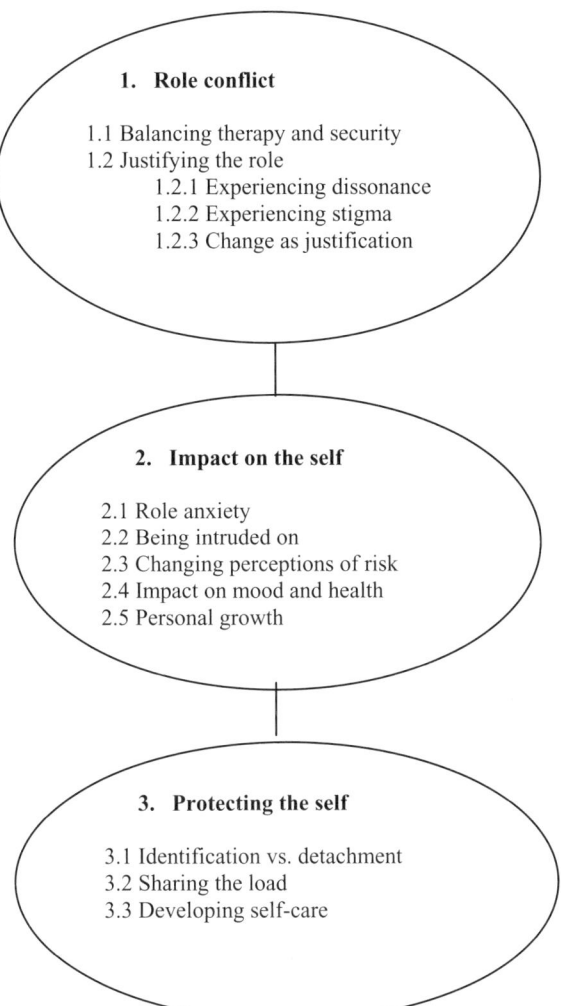

Figure 13.1   Super-ordinate and subordinate themes

confidence and trust me, so I tend to use it as that way but it's still a fine line.
(Participant 5: 633–648)

Based on retrospective accounts, Crawley (2004) suggested there was a qualitative difference between staff–prisoner interactions before the 1980s, when prison was seen as 'a place of and for punishment' (p. 105) and close relationships between the two groups was regarded as inappropriate, and more recent policies that have emphasised rehabilitation and understanding of prisoners and their crimes. The following quote highlights the dual purpose at the heart of the conflict in the functioning of a prison – both to punish and to rehabilitate offenders.

> *People will rail up against you and they'll say what you're doing now is anti-therapeutic if you're having to do searches or cuff them for visits and such like, but [...] you say this is how it is I want to be protected from you people [...] they're not cured, you're not cooked yet and things like that ..., and in due time, you will earn that right, but within any prison sentence there has to be the sort of justice element, and one hopes that here we do the sort of rehabilitative side of it as well.* (Participant 7: 819–838)

Theme 1.2 Justifying the role

All participants described some conflict inherent to working in a therapeutic way with people who had committed violent or sexual offences against others. This theme encompasses the need expressed by many of the participants to justify the role to themselves (perhaps as a way of reducing cognitive dissonance; Festinger, 1957) and to people outside the prison.

Theme 1.2.1 Experiencing dissonance

All participants commented that they had developed good relationships with some prisoners and been able to get to know them rather than regarding them simply as 'offenders'.

> *Just an understanding and sort of you know, yeah there's some really nasty people here. But ... take their offence away from them, they're no different from me or you. You know, their upbringing, you know I've seen deprivation I've seen how people have been treated.* (Participant 5: 1894–1901)

Having developed relationships with the prisoners, most of the participants felt that at times it was difficult to reconcile an awareness of the prisoners' offences with the people they had got to know.

> *It can make you that sort of, how can someone do that, I mean some of the things you hear are quite, how can human beings do that to each other, it's ... horrible, and then you can be angry about that, sad with that erm ... and you can get sort of melancholy and depressed about it.* (Participant 4: 1277–1282)
>   *For me it's the extreme violence that some people can go to, but then you talk to someone who has been capable of that and they're a normal person, you don't see any evidence of that, you see some character traits but you don't see the extreme violence that brought them to jail. And sometimes you will sit across a room like this and look at somebody and you think how are you capable of that?* (Participant 7: 656–667)

Theme 1.2.2 Experiencing stigma

Several participants reported a concern regarding a potential stigma attached to working with offenders, particularly violent and sex offenders.

> *The two don't always mix cos socially members of the public don't understand what Grendon is about, they don't understand how you can work with sex offenders, they don't understand how you can actually be pleasant to these people.* (Participant 3: 781–782)

Some participants gave examples of potential stigma in relation to being around children. Participant 4 was aware that colleagues had been concerned about their actions around children in the context of increased awareness of child abuse in society.

> *But I don't feel … I don't think oh I can't go near them cos I work with a paedophile. It hasn't had that sort of … I know some people have felt funny about bathing their children and stuff because … you know the sexual abuse they hear but I've been quite fortunate that I haven't felt that way about it so … I'm quite lucky.* (Participant 4: 1488–1501)

This replicates a previous finding that some prison officers reported a feeling of being 'contaminated' by contact with people who had committed violent and sexual crimes (Crawley, 2004). That study suggested that officers were concerned that prolonged contact with sex offenders, including listening to details of their crimes, could change their own attitudes and behaviour, or that others would perceive this to be the case. One way of conceptualising this would be in terms of counter-transference. This refers to the responses in the therapist in relation to the client. In particular, hostile counter-transference behaviours relate to a fear of being 'infected' by the client's disturbing thoughts or behaviour (Watkins, 1989).

Theme 1.2.3 Change as justification

The majority of participants discussed the sense of reward that came from observing change in the prisoners. Participants attributed such change to the therapeutic process, and this may be one of the ways in which participants overcame the conflicts discussed above.

> *When you get a prisoner that's been here a couple of years and you see the change from start to finish, that's actually quite rewarding […] and that actually gives you a feeling that you're doing a half decent job.* (Participant 3: 338–346)

Positive changes observed by the participants included changes in attitudes, social interactions and a reduced reconviction rate following release from prison. Participant 3 suggested that it was better to try and help people to change (and therefore not re-offend, or re-offend at a less serious level) than to use prisons for punishment and confinement alone.

> *We can either keep people behind doors, and release angry people, or we can actually try and work with them and make them a better member of society.* (Participant 3: 669–676)

Theme 2: Impact on the self

This theme encompasses the descriptions participants gave about the different ways that their work affected them personally.

Theme 2.1 Role anxiety

This theme relates to participants' concerns about their ability to do the job well, and the consequences of getting it wrong. Most of the participants reported feeling able to complete the security-oriented duties well but felt additional training was required for the therapeutic role.

> *You have absolutely no idea what therapy is about and you learn as you go and you make your own mind up, but you're getting various opinions from various departments cos it's quite … multi discipline; but it would have certainly helped coming in, yeah, the introduction, to get a feel for that.* (Participant 2: 227–235)
> *Then you also have the anxiety of, because I wasn't that experienced in the group process itself, was the anxiety of putting your foot in it, saying the wrong thing sometimes or getting the trust of the people you're working with was quite difficult, took a bit of time.* (Participant 8: 165–171)

Theme 2.2 Being intruded on

This theme represents the way that stories that were described or events witnessed could 'stay with' the participants. Most of the participants reported that listening to graphic descriptions in therapy groups of events in the prisoners' lives was distressing. For some participants, they continued to remember these stories vividly and to experience distress subsequently.

> *I think they always stay with you. I think everything, every story you hear stays with you. I don't know, I just get on with it. Well, yeah, it's all part of the job*

isn't it? To … yeah, just accept it … but each person leaves something with you. I think that's quite a pressure in some ways. Cos you're giving part of you to them. (Participant 1: 1541–1558)

Participant 4 also described this, although some benefits were apparent. It was suggested that imagining what had happened enabled a sense of empathy for the prisoners to develop and this was regarded as helpful to the therapeutic process.

Some of the descriptions are very graphic and you can't help but imagining it, you can see, you can have a 35-year-old man talking about when he was six years old […] and you see a six-year-old boy […] you can't help but imaging that and that's quite … can be disturbing. Erm (pause) but it also … it can give you some sort of insight as to what it might have been like and have some sympathy for that, you know then you can, if you're onto how it is how it makes you feel you can use that again to help. (Participant 4: 1297–1313)

Theme 2.3 Changing perceptions of risk

This theme was described by three of the participants, who described a change in their perceptions of risk in situations outside of work. Theories of VT would predict that listening to potentially traumatic material, for example descriptions of abuse and violent or sexual offences, could lead to disruptions in therapists' beliefs about the world (Sabin-Farrell & Turpin, 2003). This study suggested that this was the case for specific beliefs about personal safety and the trustworthiness of others.

With working with such potentially violent prisoners you're walking round making risk assessments all day long and the way you talk to people, it's just a natural thing after a while. But sometimes I'll pull into a garage and I'll think he looks like a sex offender, he looks like he's selling drugs, he looks a bit shady. (Participant 4: 1472–1488)

Some of the participants regarded this as a negative effect, but Participant 3 acknowledged that a similar process contributed to them feeling protective of their family and this was regarded as a positive effect to some extent.

It makes you very over-protective, but it's also the case that I'd like to think I could sort of spot signs they were up to no good, and at least I'm aware that other people are the way they are and that's been quite a positive thing, I think in this day and age. (Participant 3: 456–462)

Theme 2.4 Impact on mood and health

This theme relates to an awareness expressed by several participants that the stress associated with work could have negative consequences on their mood and health. Participants tended to discuss the impact of stress in terms of observations they had made of colleagues rather then their own experiences. Additionally, all participants found it difficult to provide a clear description of the impact of stress.

> *I think you can see something in people, a colleague was sitting on a group and I could see something in him that just couldn't cope with it, and again it's hard to put your finger on it cos people never sort of break down and say I can't deal with this, it's just something that isn't quite there. (Participant 3: 579–585)*
>
> *I don't know what the signs are for burnout, but I've seen it enough times on people that have been in the job long enough and then you say well where's this person gone, where's this officer gone, because you do become quite close and you don't see them passing in the corridor, and then people will talk in hushed tones of well you know he's having a few problems at the moment, I've seen that too many times. (Participant 7: 495–507)*

Theme 2.5 Personal growth

In addition to the outcomes described above, all of the participants described changes in their personal relationships and emotional well-being that they regarded as positive. In particular, all participants stated that they had experienced a therapeutic process themselves through facilitating group therapy in their work with the prisoners. This is perhaps an inevitable consequence of the work. 'It is not possible to ask a patient to focus upon interpersonal relatedness without examining one's own modes of relating' (Yalom, 2002, p. 256).

> *I think I've changed quite dramatically. I used to … be very aggressive, very erm (pause) bolshy I think is the word, and I came here and I start, I was like it here for a little while. And then you kind of get it knocked out of you a bit, not forcibly or anything but you just begin to change. (Participant 1: 958–975)*
>
> *If I'm honest I've been looking for something like this, in a purely selfish way … because I had a relatively difficult childhood, I wanted some answers for me. If I'm honest that was probably the most, the biggest drive, I've always wanted to care for people … and that's probably linked to the fact that I wanted to be cared for as a child and (pause) being able to come here and do that and yet behind the scenes work out what that is for me has been incredibly useful. (Participant 4: 1135–1148)*

Theme 3: Protecting the self

This theme encompasses ways that participants attempted to manage the negative impact of the work. Participants emphasised a need to maintain boundaries between themselves and the prisoners. However, all participants also identified emotions and experiences shared with the prisoners. Additionally, all participants emphasised the importance of sharing thoughts and feelings related to the work with colleagues.

Theme 3.1 Identification vs. detachment

This theme describes the participants' view of themselves as both similar to and separate from the prisoners. For example, several participants mentioned the surprise and distress aroused when they recognised shared thoughts, emotions and experiences between themselves and the prisoners.

> *Some of the, the hardest stuff I went through was ... there's a guy on the wing was sexually abused and murdered a boy and he was talking about some of his difficult emotions and I ... I've experienced similar emotions. And of course then the fear straight away is, my God could I do this? And that's really hard to think about ... actually that that person sitting there has done this most heinous crime and actually I've felt and thought like he has at times.* (Participant 4: 901–918)
>
> *Sometimes just even the simplest of things like relationships that people have had over their lifetime and how it went wrong and sometimes, that's what I say you do, you do unconsciously think, you're making links as well with some of the story that they tell it, and that's how particularly I would have behaved. ...* (Participant 2: 998–1014)

Several of the participants mentioned the prison gate as a psychological and physical boundary between the world inside and outside. Most thought that it was helpful to try to keep the two separate.

> *A very old PO once told me when you come in the gate in the morning, you pick your keys up and you hang your personality on the key hook. You do your bits and pieces, on the way out you throw your keys in you pick your personality up and you walk back out the gate. And that's a lovely way to look at it. You've got two separate lives, one inside the wall one outside the wall. And if you can hang your personality up to a certain extent then you'll be all right.* (Participant 3: 766–776)

However, participants also suggested that it was difficult to maintain such a clear distinction. It is noteworthy that participants' struggle with this issue was apparent in the difficulty in articulating the processes that might be involved.

> *I was aware that I wasn't leaving the gate like I usually do at other prisons and drive home looking forward to the weekend, that it was still ... Instead of thinking about Saturday's events and meeting friends and going out for a drink ... I was thinking 'what are you doing?' You're still thinking about how you're going to plan out Monday. So after about a year I was aware that it was coming out of the gates more than it should do.* (Participant 2: 1027–1039)

Theme 3.2 Sharing the load

All participants highlighted the importance they placed on sharing emotional reactions to, and thoughts about, the work with each other. It has been a consistent finding in research regarding occupational stress that social support from colleagues and friends and family relates to reduced job strain (Moore & Cooper, 1996).

> *It's about not holding it in, and it's what we encourage the lads to do, we encourage them to voice how it's made them feel and if we don't get the opportunity to do that feedback and to voice it we're holding onto it and it will just come out sideways. The same way as it's done for the lads.* (Participant 6: 650–656)

All of the participants reported feeling supported by their colleagues and all stated that they could approach several of their colleagues to discuss work-related or personal issues.

> *Being able to talk is the thing that saves me in reality ... and having a staff team around me that I know will contain me. So that's the big difference actually, I can talk about anything whether it's work related or not, I'm in a position where I am able to talk and people will listen and try to help really.* (Participant 4: 1808–1820)

Participant 3 described an attempt at this prison to challenge an expectation that a prison officer should be able to handle any situation without demonstrating emotion.

> *When I joined* [the prison service] *five years ago, it was a case of you don't show emotions – these are the words that were used at the time – 'these are the scum that we have to deal with, you don't let them under your skin, if you do they've got you ...' I suppose it's dropping an image in a way, cos you get the sort of feeling in this job that you need a hard sort of character, that nothing*

gets to you, and that's not the case. You can let that go, and it's just encouraging people to do that if they're feeling down. (Participant 3: 614–620; 602–609)

Theme 3.3 Developing self-care

Participants highlighted the importance of managing their own workload, developing a sense of when they were overworked and taking preventative action. This relates to the need for therapists to be aware of the potential impact of their work and to develop a self-care plan (Saakvitne & Pearlman, 1996). In addition to talking to colleagues, several participants discussed the benefits of taking time alone to process the events of the day as a way of managing stress.

Normally I use the journey from work to process what's happened. It's only 20 minutes, but it's 20 minutes on your own in peace and quiet. And if I can't get through whatever I'm thinking by the time I get home then I'll know I'm in for a crap night. (Participant 1: 1312–1328)

Several of the participants highlighted the importance of monitoring their workload and managing their own stress levels.

Yes you can become overloaded by it. Erm, and as I alluded earlier then people see you more and so they expect more of you. And it's just a case of you enforce the boundaries, you say no I'm not prepared to do that and refer them to their personal officer or what have you. I mean a clichéd term we use in the prison service is to slope shoulders on this one. But you don't you don't overload yourself [...] you just set that level. (Participant 7: 446–460)

Conclusions

This study describes the experience of working in a therapeutic community prison from the perspective of the staff. Previous literature has commented on the seemingly conflicting purposes of a therapeutic community and a prison (Genders & Player, 1995) and this study has provided a description of how this conflict impacts on staff working in such an institution. The study has provided further evidence that hearing distressing material can have a lasting impact on therapists, including experiencing intrusive images, changing perceptions of risk and mood and health changes, as predicted by theories of vicarious traumatisation and secondary traumatic stress. The findings have also provided an understanding of the ways in which participants justified their work, to themselves and others, and some of the personal benefits and rewards they obtained from the role.

When listening to vivid descriptions of traumatic events, therapists are faced with the challenge of remaining empathic and supportive while attempting to overcome their own distressing reactions to witnessing human vulnerability and the capacity for violence and abuse in human behaviour (Herman, 1992). It is important that members of staff and organisations are aware of the potential for these effects and that means of reducing the sources and impact of the contributory factors are implemented and evaluated. Participants did describe the rewards and benefits associated with their work and these positive attributes should be considered when formulating the impact of working as a therapist on an individual.

It is important that the effects highlighted in this study continue to receive attention in future research and in organisations employing staff in a therapeutic role so that appropriate support systems may be implemented. It is also important that staff themselves are aware of the potential consequences of their work and develop ways of mediating these.

> The challenge lies in the fact that wellness is a concept that we as counsellors often focus on more readily for our clients than ourselves. Counsellors who are trained to care for others often overlook the need for personal self-care and do not apply to themselves the techniques prescribed for their clients. (O'Halloran & Linton, 2000, p. 354)

Acknowledgement

Martina Mueller, for supervision and stimulating an interest in this area of research.

References

American Psychiatric Association (2000). *Diagnostic and Statistical Manual of Mental Disorders – Text Revision (DSM-IV-TR)*. Washington, DC: APA.

Crawley, E. (2004). *Doing Prison Work: The Public and Private Lives of Prison Officers*. Cullompton: Willan Publishing.

Festinger, L. (1957). *A Theory of Cognitive Dissonance*. New York: Harper & Row.

Figley, C.R. (1995). Compassion fatigue: towards a new understanding of the costs of caring. In B.H. Stamm (Ed.) *Secondary Traumatic Stress: Self-care Issues for Clinicians, Researchers and Educators*. Lutherville, MD: Sidran Press.

Genders, E. & Player, E. (1995). *Grendon: A Study of a Therapeutic Prison*. Oxford: Oxford University Press.

Herman, J. (1992). *Trauma and Recovery: The Aftermath of Violence – From Domestic Abuse to Political Terror*. New York: Basic Books.

McLean, S., Wade, T.D. & Encel, J.S. (2003). The contribution of therapist beliefs to psychological distress in therapists: an investigation of vicarious traumatisation, burnout and symptoms of avoidance and intrusion. *Behavioural and Cognitive Psychotherapy*, *31*, 417–428.

Moore, K.A. & Cooper, C. (1996). Stress in mental health professionals: a theoretical overview. *International Journal of Social Psychiatry*, *42*(2), 82–89.

O'Halloran, T. & Linton, J. (2000). Stress on the job: self-care resources for counsellors. *Journal of Mental Health Counselling*, *22*, 354–364.

Pearlman, L.A., MacIan, P.S., Johnson, G. & Mas, K. (1992). *Understanding Cognitive Schemas across Groups: Empirical Findings and their Implications*. Paper presented at the Eighth Annual Meeting of the International Society for Traumatic Studies, Los Angeles, CA.

Pearlman, L.A. & Saakvitne, K.W. (1995). *Trauma and the Therapist: Countertransference and Vicarious Traumatisation in Psychotherapy with Incest Survivors*. London: Norton.

Reid, K., Flowers, P. & Larkin, M. (2005). Exploring lived experience. *The Psychologist*, *18*(1), 20–23.

Saakvitne, K.W. & Pearlman, L.A. (1996). *Transforming the Pain: A Workbook on Vicarious Traumatisation*. New York: Norton.

Sabin-Farrell, R. & Turpin, G. (2003). Vicarious traumatisation: implications for the mental health of health workers? *Clinical Psychology Review*, *23*, 449–480.

Schauben, L.J. & Frazier, P.A. (1995). Vicarious trauma: the effects on female counsellors of working with sexual violence survivors. *Psychology of Women Quarterly*, *19*, 49–64.

Smith, J.A. (1996). Beyond the divide between cognition and discourse: using interpretative phenomenological analysis in health psychology. *Psychology and Health*, *11*, 261–271.

Steed, L. & Bicknell, J. (2001). Trauma and the therapist: the experience of therapists working with the perpetrators of sexual abuse. *Australasian Journal of Disaster and Trauma Studies*, *5*(1). Retrieved 13 April 2005 from www.massey.ac.nz/~trauma/issues/2001-1/steed.htm

Steed, L.G. & Downing, R. (1998). A phenomenological study of vicarious traumatisation amongst psychologists and professional counsellors working in the field of sexual abuse/assault. *Australasian Journal of Disaster and Trauma Studies*, *2*. Retrieved 21 January 2005 from www.massey.ac.nz/~trauma/issues/1998-2/steed.htm

Watkins, C.E. (1989). Countertransference: its impact on the counselling session. In W. Dryden (Ed.) *Key Issues for Counselling in Action*. London: Sage.

Way, I., VanDeusen, K.M., Martin, G., Applegate, B. & Jandle, D. (2004). Vicarious trauma: A comparison of clinicians who treat survivors of sexual abuse and sexual offenders. *Journal of Interpersonal Violence*, *19*(1), 49–71.

Yalom, I.D. (2002). *The Gift of Therapy: Reflections on Being a Therapist*. London: Piatkus.

Chapter 14

Emotional Influence and Empathy in Prison-Based Therapeutic Communities

Karen Niven, David Holman and Peter Totterdell

Introduction

> Wherever human beings spend long periods of time together in intimate settings they are drawn into emotional engagement with each other. Crawley (2004, p. 415)

In therapeutic communities (TCs), it is typical for individuals to spend a great deal of time in the company of fellow TC members. This is particularly true of prison-based TCs, where staff members and inmates work and live in close quarters. The amount of time spent with fellow TC members produces a large amount of interactions, which are often emotional in nature. As Crawley maintains in the quote above, emotional interactions and engagements are inevitable in such environments.

An important type of emotional interaction that occurs between members of TCs is *emotional influence*. The term emotional influence describes the deliberate regulation of another person's feelings. Research into emotional influence indicates that this process may be used constructively, for example to help oneself and others cope with strain and to build and maintain positive relationships (e.g. Francis *et al.*, 1999). Emotional influence may also be used in a more destructive manner, acting as a source of strain and giving rise to poor quality relationships.

Grendon and the Emergence of Forensic Therapeutic Communities: Developments in Research and Practice
Edited by Richard Shuker and Elizabeth Sullivan
© 2010 John Wiley & Sons, Ltd.

However, the factors that affect how emotional influence is used have yet to be identified.

This chapter argues that the individual characteristic of empathy may play a key role in terms of affecting individuals' use of emotional influence in TCs. Empathy concerns the cognitive and emotional responses an individual has to another person's experiences. Broadly speaking, it is proposed that individuals with higher levels of empathy are more likely to use emotional influence constructively. It is further proposed that an individual's empathy will grow with time spent in a TC. These propositions were tested in a research study, which was conducted with the participation of staff members and prisoners from three of the TCs at Grendon prison.

Emotions in Prison TCs

Emotions form an important part of everyday prison life. The detention of individuals for punitive reasons fosters emotions such as sadness, anger, frustration, regret and resentment (Greer, 2002). Imprisoned individuals may also be dangerous and unpredictable, producing fear and anxiety amongst both inmates and staff members (Crawley, 2004). In therapeutic prisons, such as HMP Grendon, the emotional nature of the prison environment is further compounded by emotion-rich discussions between the therapist and client (in this case the prisoners) (e.g. Cooke & Kipnis, 1986), and between fellow group members during group therapy (e.g. Francis, 1997). The TC context adds yet another layer of emotions to this type of prison setting, as TCs are designed to encourage both inmates and staff members to discuss their emotions and emotion-relevant matters on a daily basis (Greenall, 2004; Parker, 2003).

It is clear then that emotions are likely to be both frequent and intense within prison-based TCs. Some researchers have therefore begun to examine the emotion management methods that individuals use to deal with their emotions in such settings. For example, Greer's (2002) interview-based research into a women's prison in America described the metaphorical 'emotional tightrope' (p. 125) of prison life, highlighting a number of strategies that inmates used to regulate their own emotions, including diversion, spiritual pursuits, self-reflection and humour. A three-year ethnographic observation study across six UK prisons also highlighted the everyday management of emotions performed by uniformed prison officers in efforts to cope with their emotionally demanding job roles, using the strategies of inmate depersonalisation, detachment, and humour (Crawley, 2004).

However, the more interpersonal aspects of emotional life in such environments have yet to be explored. Not only are prison wings, and especially prison-based TCs, inherently emotional places, but they also require the individuals who live and work there to spend a great deal of time in each other's company. Staff members and inmates are expected to live and work in close quarters, and there may be few opportunities for interactions with anyone outside the prison wing or TC. Coupled with the emotional nature of the setting, this close proximity results in staff members and inmates being frequently drawn into emotional engagements (Crawley, 2004). Whilst we know that emotional interactions and engagements occur in prison-based TCs, to date there has been a lack of research aimed towards understanding and specifying the nature of these interactions.

Emotional Influence

One important type of emotional interaction that may occur between members of prison-based TCs is emotional influence. Emotional influence is an interpersonal form of emotion management, and refers to any deliberate attempt to regulate or manage the emotions or moods of another person. So, for example, if a male inmate felt anxious about an upcoming probation meeting, a staff member might try to make the inmate feel calmer by getting him to discuss his worries, or pointing out the upsides to his situation. Given this example, it is important to note that emotional influence is distinct from the concept of social support. Whilst individuals may regulate others' affect with the intention of support, emotional influence may also be performed to worsen others' affect. For instance, if an inmate was irritating a fellow community member, the community member might try to upset the inmate, by shouting at him, or ignoring him.

The topic of emotional influence has attracted interest in recent years, largely due to evidence of the occurrence of this process, in a variety of settings. Emotional influence has been reported between family members in research concerning guilt induction (Vangelisti *et al.*, 1991), between peers in research concerning bullying (Sutton *et al.*, 1999), and even between relative strangers, in a study examining how wheelchair users deal with others' reactions to them (Cahill & Eggleston, 1994). Emotional influence also occurs in organisational contexts. For instance emotional influence has been reported between colleagues in medical settings (Francis *et al.*, 1999), social care agencies (Kahn, 1993), legal firms (Lively, 2000) and debt collection agencies (Sutton, 1991). Frequently, employees also use emotional influence towards their customers or clients, for example in medical (Francis *et al.*, 1999) and retail settings (Lee & Dubinsky, 2003).

Research suggests that emotional influence may have implications for individuals' emotions and moods (Niven *et al.*, 2007), and also longer-term consequences. In particular, using emotional influence to improve others' affect can impact positively on the general well-being of both the person whose emotions are being regulated and the person performing the regulation, and promote positive relationships between these individuals. For example, Williams (2007) argues that using strategies to improve others' emotions can be an effective means of reducing threat and promoting trust in relationships, especially those relationships that span boundaries (e.g. between organisations). In contrast, using emotional influence to worsen others' affect can result in negative well-being, and relationships between individuals characterised by distrust and a lack of respect. For instance, Kahn's research in social care agencies indicates that behaviours that display a lack of care towards colleagues can result in those colleagues experiencing emotional exhaustion and depersonalisation (Kahn, 1993).

Given that emotional influence has important implications for people's affect, well-being and relationships, understanding the factors that affect the use of emotional influence is a key concern. This is especially true in prison-based TCs, where such outcomes have extra resonance. Both staff members and inmates have reported high levels of strain and poor well-being in past research (e.g. Koo & Kim, 2006), meaning that it is important to understand causes and means of coping with strain. Additionally, relationships between prisoners and staff members are seen as central to therapeutic efficacy in prison-based TCs (Genders & Player, 1995).

Empathy and Emotional Influence

Empathy is one particular factor that may affect individuals' use of emotional influence. Empathy refers to 'the reactions of one individual to the observed experiences of another' (Davis, 1983, p. 113). It is a multidimensional construct, comprising cognitive and emotional elements (Davis, 1980). The main cognitive aspect to empathy is perspective taking, the tendency to adopt the point of view of others (Davis, 1983). The main emotional aspects to empathy are empathic concern (also referred to as reactive empathy) and personal distress (or parallel empathy) (Stephan & Finlay, 1999). These emotional elements regard other- and self-oriented feelings, respectively. Empathic concern refers to feelings of sympathy or concern for others, whereas personal distress relates to self-experienced feelings of anxiety and unease in tense interpersonal situations (Davis, 1983).

It is proposed that an individual's level of empathy may relate to his or her tendency to use emotional influence constructively (i.e. to use strategies to improve others' affect) or destructively (i.e. to use strategies to worsen others' affect). Previously, there have been theoretical links made between empathy and positive interpersonal behaviours, including altruism (Hoffman, 1984), and a review by Eisenberg and Miller (1987) concluded that empirical evidence provided support for a relationship between empathy and helping. Studies that look more closely at the cognitive and emotional aspects to empathy indicate that perspective taking and empathic concern are positively related to pro-social behaviours and social functioning (Litvack-Miller *et al.*, 1997; Oswald, 1996), whereas personal distress is negatively related (Davis, 1983; Eisenberg & Fabes, 1990).

Associations have also been theorised between empathy and negative interpersonal behaviours, with researchers proposing that empathy may inhibit antisocial types of behaviour (Feshbach & Feshbach, 1982). These associations have been supported in reviews (e.g. Miller & Eisenberg, 1988) and empirical studies (e.g. Richardson *et al.*, 1994), which have reported empathy to be negatively related to aggression and antisocial behaviours. Moreover, a lack of empathy may be linked with bullying behaviours (Ireland, 1999) and other antisocial behaviours (Eysenck, 1981). Looking at the different elements of empathy, these studies suggest that perspective taking and in particular empathic concern are negatively related to negative behaviours. However, the links between personal distress and such behaviours are less clear.

Following from the discussions above, the first research question sought to explore: *is empathy related to constructive emotional influence?*

Empathy is a particularly interesting individual characteristic to examine, due to the ongoing debate about whether or not empathy can be taught (Davis, 1990). A number of studies have demonstrated that it may be possible to increase people's levels of empathy through training (e.g. Erera, 1997; Pacala *et al.*, 1995). Although some researchers maintain that empathy cannot be forced to occur, most allow that it can be facilitated, for example through increasing individuals' self-awareness, improving listening skills, and encouraging respect for and tolerance of others, for example by being exposed to relevant behaviours modelled by others (Davis, 1990).

The teaching of empathy is particularly relevant in a prison like Grendon. Inmates in general have been reported to have lower levels of empathy (Jolliffe & Farrington, 2004), especially those inmates who have committed sexual offences (Covell & Scalora, 2002). Recipients of childhood abuse, like many of Grendon's inmates, have also been found to have low levels of empathy (Miller & Eisenberg, 1988). Moreover, the TC model followed by Grendon strives to create an environment that increases individuals' awareness of their own actions and the effects these have on others, which fosters respect and tolerance (Parker, 2003) – qualities that are claimed to facilitate empathy (Davis, 1990). The longer individuals spend at Grendon, the more opportunity they will have to model their behaviours on the empathic behaviours of others, and the greater their awareness of the effects of their actions should be. Thus, time spent at the prison should facilitate empathy.

The Current Research

Based on these assertions, the second research question asked: *do individuals who have been at HMP Grendon longer report higher levels of empathy?*

To explore these research questions, a social network questionnaire approach (e.g. Tichy *et al.*, 1979) was used amongst three TCs at HMP Grendon, referred to as TC1, TC2 and TC3. This approach involved asking individuals from each TC about their interactions with other members of that TC, in order to map out the networks of emotional influence within the TCs. A questionnaire was distributed amongst staff members and inmates from the three TCs, and was completed by a total of 60 participants. There were 12 participants from TC1, 22 participants from TC2, and 26 from TC3 and 49 of the participants were inmates, aged between 21 and 71 (mean age = 37 years), who had been at the prison for an average of 18 months. The remaining 11 participants were staff members, including uniformed prison officers, wing psychologists and wing therapists, who had been at the prison for an average of seven years. These included 7 female staff members and 4 males, aged between 28 and 60 (mean age = 45 years).

The questionnaire measured the extent to which individuals had used emotional influence behaviours towards other members of their TC. Each participant was given a list of the names of all other participating members of their own TC[1], and was asked to place a tick next to the names of all those individuals who they had used particular emotional influence strategies towards, during the previous two weeks. The use of ten different emotional influence behaviours was assessed. These included five strategies

---

[1]Only those people who had actively agreed to participate in the research were included in the questionnaire.

that typically have constructive effects on well-being and relationships (complimenting, listening, joking, using soothing tones or words, pointing out the upsides) and five strategies that typically have destructive effects on well-being and relationships (criticising, ignoring, mocking, using aggressive tones or words, pointing out the downsides). All of the strategies were derived from a previous study by the authors, concerning the ways in which people try to influence others' emotions (Niven *et al.*, 2009).

The questionnaire also assessed individuals' empathy. Empathic concern, perspective taking and personal distress were all measured using the Interpersonal Reactivity Index (IRI; Davis, 1983). Each construct comprised seven items, for example 'I often have tender, concerned feelings for people less fortunate than me' (empathic concern), 'I believe that there are two sides to every question and try to look at them both' (perspective taking), and 'Being in a tense emotional situation scares me' (personal distress). Participants were required to indicate how well each item described them, on a five-point scale ranging from 'does not describe me well' to 'describes me very well'.

Empathy and the Use of Emotional Influence Strategies

Mean levels of emotional influence use and empathy

Looking at the usage of each of the emotional influence strategies, a greater proportion of the total emotional influence within the TCs studied was constructive as opposed to destructive (see figure 14.1). The most reported behaviour was joking, which was used towards around 40 per cent of fellow TC members. This corroborates previous research highlighting the central role of humour in organisations and communities where members are forced to deal with difficult issues, for example in medical and social work settings (Francis *et al.*, 1999; Sullivan, 2000). Listening was the second most frequently reported strategy, used towards around 25 per cent of fellow TC members. Aggressive tones or words and then mocking were the least reported strategies.

Differences were found between staff members and inmates regarding the use of emotional influence, such that inmates used less constructive emotional influence and more destructive emotional influence, compared to staff members. Specifically, staff members reported complimenting ($t = 2.02$, $p < .05$), using soothing tones or words towards ($t = 4.63$, $p < .01$) and listening to more fellow TC members ($t = 2.81$, $p < .01$) than did inmates. In contrast, inmates reported mocking ($t = -2.86$,

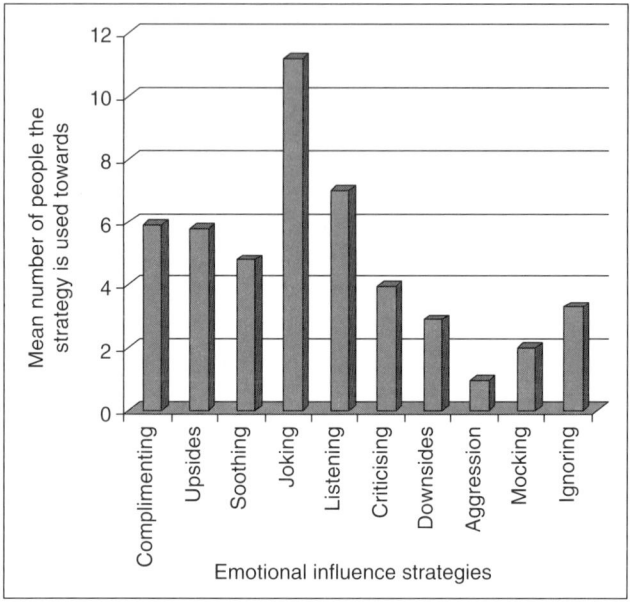

Figure 14.1   Mean usage of each of the emotional influence strategies

$p < .01$) and ignoring ($t = -3.43$, $p < .01$) more fellow TC members than did staff members. These differences could be due to a number of factors other than reasons of incarceration, including the amount of time spent in the research context (since staff members are able to leave the TC, they can deal with negative feelings outside of this context) and the fact that emotional influence may be an implicit role requirement for staff members.

Participants' mean scores on the three aspects of empathy measured were also examined, and compared to data available regarding empathy scores from two sources. The first was data regarding the mean IRI scores of medical interns, provided in Bellini *et al.* (2002). The second was normative data for the IRI estimated by Bellini *et al.* (2002). The mean scores for the current sample and the comparison data are shown in table 14.1. As can be seen in the table, staff members' scores on perspective taking and empathic concern closely resembled those from the normative data. Staff members' personal distress scores were lower than those of the normative sample, but resembled those of the medical interns. This could reflect the need for individuals to become less emotionally reactive in such occupations where distressing events occur relatively frequently. In contrast, inmates displayed slightly lower perspective taking and empathic concern compared to the normative data, the medical interns and the TC staff members. This is in line with previous studies suggesting that inmates have lower levels of empathy than the general adult population (Jolliffe & Farrington, 2004). However, inmates' levels of personal distress were

Table 14.1 Mean levels of empathy for current sample and comparison samples

	Staff members	Inmates	Norm data	Medical intern data
Perspective taking	18.00	15.51	17.37	20.25
Empathic concern	20.78	19.39	20.36	22.00
Personal distress	8.31	12.41	10.87	8.78

* The total possible score for any of the aspects of empathy was 35 indicating high empathy, as constructs were measured using seven items, each scored between 1 and 5.

higher than those of the comparison groups, and were significantly higher than those of the TC staff members ($t = -3.11, p < .01$). This result may be related to the fact that many of Grendon's inmates have Dangerous and Severe Personality Disorders (DSPDs). Personal distress is a self-directed form of responding to others, and individuals with DSPDs commonly have a self-focused, self-centred nature (Trediget, 2001).

Relationships between empathy and emotional influence

The first research question concerned potential links between individuals' levels of empathy and their use of emotional influence. Correlation analyses were conducted between the three aspects of empathy examined and the number of fellow TC members that participants reported using each of the ten emotional influence strategies towards. The results, presented in table 14.2, demonstrate three clear patterns.

The first pattern is that, for both inmates and staff members, perspective taking was positively related to the use of constructive emotional influence strategies such as listening (inmates $r = .33, p < .05$; staff members $r = .72, p < .05$). Those with higher levels of perspective taking are able to adopt others' points of view, and are therefore more likely to interact in a positive manner with other people, as supported by previous research concerning behaviours such as helping (e.g. Oswald, 1996). The second pattern is that, for staff members only, empathic concern was also positively related to the use of constructive emotional influence strategies including joking ($r = .75, p < .01$). Those with higher empathic concern have greater feelings such as sympathy towards others, and so are more likely to want to improve others' affect. However, this pattern only applied to staff members, suggesting inmates' level of concern about fellow TC members did not affect their use of these emotional influence behaviours.

Table 14.2   Significant correlations between empathy and use of emotional influence strategies

	Inmates (N = 49)			Staff members (N = 11)		
	Perspective taking	Empathic concern	Personal distress	Perspective taking	Empathic concern	Personal distress
Complimenting	.24~			.70*	.71*	
Pointing out the upsides	.26~			.78**	.68*	
Using soothing tones or words	.30*			.79**	.65*	
Joking	.29*			.67*	.75**	
Listening	.33*			.72*	.67*	
Criticising			.29*			
Pointing out the downsides			.31*			
Using aggressive tones or words			.30*			
Mocking			.31*			
Ignoring			.41**			

~ = $p < .1$, * = $p < .05$, ** = $p < .01$

The third and final pattern is that inmates' personal distress was positively related to the use of destructive emotional influence behaviours like ignoring ($r = .41$, $p < .01$). Those with higher personal distress tend to experience fairly self-orientated emotions in interpersonal situations. They are therefore less aware of their effects on others, which might mean that their use of antisocial behaviours, such as mocking and ignoring, is less inhibited. This last pattern might have bearing on inmates' higher use of negative emotional influence behaviours compared to staff members, as discussed above. Since personal distress was positively associated with the use of such behaviours, inmates' higher levels of personal distress compared to staff members might in part explain their higher use of these behaviours.

Can Empathy be Learned?

The second research question concerned whether empathy could be learned through spending time in a TC environment. To explore this research question, correlation analyses were conducted between the length of time that participants had spent in the prison and participants' levels of empathy. There were no relationships found between length of time at the prison and empathy for staff members. However, for inmates, length of time at the prison was positively related to perspective taking ($r = .29, p < .05$). This suggests that spending time in a prison-based TC can help inmates to develop their perspective-taking skills. The TC environment, and also the therapy offered at Grendon, is designed to enhance awareness of one's effects on others. Thus, the longer that an individual spends there, the greater his tendency to take others' perspectives should be. Length of time at the prison was also negatively related to inmates' personal distress ($r = -.26, p < .05$). Spending time in a prison-based TC therefore appeared to reduce the amount of self-focused emotion that inmates experienced in tense situations, perhaps due to habituation to the highly emotional environment.

These changes in inmates' empathy, as a result of spending time in the TC environment, are important due to the demonstrated links between empathy and emotional influence. It may then be that the learning of empathy in the TC environment could impact on TC members' use of emotional influence behaviours. However, further analyses showed that length of time at Grendon was only associated with the use of one emotional influence strategy; the longer inmates had been at Grendon, the more they used soothing tones or words ($r = .32, p < .05$).

Implications

The findings indicate that empathy may indeed be an important factor in terms of affecting whether individuals use emotional influence in a constructive manner. More specifically, perspective taking is associated with the use of constructive emotional influence strategies, whilst personal distress is associated with destructive behaviours. Perspective taking was found to be higher, and personal distress lower, with time spent in the prison. However, the length of time inmates had been at Grendon had little impact on their emotional influence behaviours. These findings suggest that in the TC environment, empathy may be learned or even taught, but evidence that this leads to improvements in the use of emotional influence strategies is limited.

Other research conducted by the authors in this context has indicated important effects of emotional influence for individuals' moods, well-being and the quality of their relationships (e.g. Niven *et al.*, 2007). Clearly then, if the empathic benefits of spending time in the TC environment could be translated into changes in the use of emotional influence, this could have desirable effects for the well-being and social functioning of those living and working in TCs.

One way that more constructive emotional influence could be encouraged at Grendon would be to use the therapy that is already practiced as a forum for exploring the use and effects of emotional influence. Emotional influence strategies are at present not explicitly taught in the TCs. However, the small group therapy sessions in particular may provide a good environment within which to discuss the use of specific emotional influence strategies. The social nature of this setting would also allow community members to hear about the effects of their behaviours on those towards whom they had used emotional influence.

Another possible route of intervention, which concentrates on changing the use of emotional influence outside of therapy, is diary-keeping. Diary-keeping might, for example, take the form of semi-structured daily diary entries requiring inmates to reflect on incidents and experiences concerning the use of emotional influence behaviours. Such interventions are increasingly seen as 'writing cures' (Lepore & Smyth, 2002), as they can increase awareness of one's interpersonal behaviours and the effects these have on oneself and others. Diary-keeping would provide individuals with the opportunity to enact change on a more personal level, but could also be used as a means of stimulating group discussions about emotional influence during therapy.

References

Bellini, L.M., Baime, M. & Shea, J.A. (2002). Variation of mood and empathy during internship. *Journal of the American Medical Association, 287*, 3143–3146.

Cahill, S.E. & Eggleston, R. (1994). Managing emotions in public: The case of wheelchair users. *Social Psychology Quarterly, 57*, 300–312.

Cooke, M. & Kipnis, D. (1986). Influence tactics in psychotherapy. *Journal of Consulting and Clinical Psychology, 54*, 22–26.

Covell, C.N. & Scalora, M.J. (2002). Empathic deficits in sexual offenders – An integration of affective, social, and cognitive constructs. *Aggression and Violent Behavior, 7*, 251–270.

Crawley, E.M. (2004). Emotion and performance: Prison officers and the presentation of staff in prisons. *Punishment and Society, 6*, 411–427.

Davis, M.H. (1980). A multidimensional approach to individual differences in empathy. *JSAS Catalog of Selected Documents in Psychology, 10*, 85.

Davis, M.H. (1983). Measuring individual differences in empathy: Evidence for a multidimensional approach. *Journal of Personality and Social Psychology, 44,* 113–126.

Davis, M.H. (1990). What is empathy, and can empathy be taught? *Physical Therapy, 70,* 32–40.

Eisenberg, N. & Fabes, R.A. (1990). Empathy: Conceptualisation, measurement, and relation to pro-social behaviour. *Motivation and Emotion, 14,* 131–149.

Eisenberg, N. & Miller, P.A. (1987). The relation of empathy to pro-social and related behaviours. *Psychological Bulletin, 101,* 91–119.

Erera, P.I. (1997). Empathy training for helping professionals: Model and evaluation. *Journal of Social Work Education, 33,* 245–260.

Eysenck, S.B.G. (1981). Impulsive and antisocial behaviour in children. *Current Psychological Research, 1,* 31–37.

Feshbach, N.D. & Feshbach, S. (1982). Empathy training and the regulation of aggression: Potentialities and limitations. *Academic Psychology Bulletin, 4,* 399–413.

Francis, L.E. (1997). Ideology and interpersonal emotion management: Redefining identity in two support groups. *Social Psychology Quarterly, 60,* 153–171.

Francis, L.E., Monahan, K. & Berger, C. (1999). A laughing matter? The uses of humor in medical interactions. *Motivation and Emotion, 23,* 154–177.

Genders, E. & Player, E. (1995). *Grendon: A Study of a Therapeutic Prison.* Oxford: Clarendon Press.

Greenall, P. (2004). Life in a prison-based therapeutic community: One man's experience. *British Journal of Forensic Practice, 6,* 33–38.

Greer, K. (2002). Walking an emotional tightrope: Managing emotions in a women's prison. *Symbolic Interaction, 25,* 117–139.

Hoffman, M.L. (1984). Interaction of affect and cognition in empathy. In C.E. Izard, J. Kagan & R.B. Zajonc (Eds) *Emotions, Cognitions, and Behaviour* (pp. 103–131). Cambridge, UK: Cambridge University Press,.

Ireland, J.L. (1999). Provictim attitudes and empathy in relation to bullying behaviour among prisoners. *Legal and Criminological Psychology, 4,* 51–66.

Jolliffe, D. & Farrington, D.P. (2004). Empathy and offending: A systematic review and meta-analysis. *Aggression and Violent Behavior, 9,* 441–476.

Kahn, W.A. (1993). Caring for the caregivers: Patterns of organisational caregiving. *Administrative Science Quarterly, 38,* 539–563.

Koo, J.W. & Kim, H.J. (2006). The factor affecting job stress and psychosocial well-being of prison officers. *International Congress Series, 1294,* 175–178.

Lee, S. & Dubinsky, A.J. (2003). Influence of salesperson characteristics and customer emotion on retail dyadic relationships. *International Review of Retail, Distribution and Consumer Research, 13,* 21–36.

Lepore, S.J. & Smyth, J.M. (2002). *The Writing Cure: How Expressive Writing Promotes Health and Emotional Well-being.* Washington, DC: American Psychological Association.

Litvack-Miller, W., McDougall, D. & Romney, D.M. (1997). The structure of empathy during middle childhood and its relationship to pro-social behaviour. *Genetic, Social, and General Psychology Monographs, 123,* 303–324.

Lively, K.J. (2000). Reciprocal emotion management: Working together to maintain stratification in private law firms. *Work and Occupations, 27*, 32–63.

Miller, P.A. & Eisenberg, N. (1988). The relation of empathy to aggressive and externalizing/antisocial behaviour. *Psychological Bulletin, 103*, 324–344.

Niven, K., Totterdell, P. & Holman, D. (2007). Changing moods and influencing people: The use and effects of emotional influence behaviours at HMP Grendon. *The Prison Service Journal, 172*, 39–45.

Niven, K., Totterdell, P. & Holman, D. (2009). A classification of controlled interpersonal affect regulation strategies. *Emotion, 9*, 498–509.

Oswald, P.A. (1996). The effects of cognitive and affective perspective taking on empathic concern and altruistic helping. *Journal of Social Psychology, 136*, 613–623.

Pacala, J.T., Boult, C., Bland, C. & O'Brien, J. (1995). Aging game improves medical students caring for elders. *Gerontology and Geriatrics Education, 15*, 45–57.

Parker, M. (2003). Doing time: A group-analytic perspective on the emotional experience of time in a men's prison. *Group Analysis, 36*, 169–181.

Richardson, D.R., Hammock, G.S. & Smith, S.M. (1994). Empathy as a cognitive inhibitor of interpersonal aggression. *Aggressive Behaviour, 20*, 275–289.

Stephan, G. & Finlay, K. (1999). The role of empathy in improving intergroup relations. *Journal of Social Issues, 55*, 729–743.

Sullivan, E.L. (2000). Gallows humour in social work: An issue for supervision and reflective practice. *Practice, 12*, 45–54.

Sutton, J., Smith, P.K. & Swettenham, J. (1999). Social cognition and bullying: Social inadequacy or skilled manipulation? *British Journal of Developmental Psychology, 17*, 435–450.

Sutton, R.I. (1991). Maintaining norms about expressed emotions: The case of bill collectors. *Administrative Science Quarterly, 36*, 245–268.

Tichy, N.M., Tushman, M.L. & Fombrun, C. (1979). Social network analysis for organisations. *Academy of Management Review, 4*, 507–519.

Trediget, J.E. (2001). The aetiology, presentation and treatment of personality disorders. *Journal of Psychiatric and Mental Health Nursing, 8*, 347–356.

Vangelisti, A.L., Daly, J.A. & Rudnick, J.R. (1991). Making people feel guilty in conversations: Techniques and correlates. *Human Communication Research, 18*, 3–39.

Williams, M. (2007). Building genuine trust through interpersonal emotion management: A threat regulation model of trust and collaboration across boundaries. *Academy of Management Review, 32*, 595–621.

Chapter 15

The Quality of Life of Prisoners and Staff at HMP Grendon

Guy Shefer

Introduction

The aim of this chapter is to introduce and analyse the findings of two surveys that were conducted in Grendon with the purpose of measuring the quality of life of prisoners and staff in this prison. The surveys, both developed by the Prisons Research Centre at the Institute of Criminology in Cambridge University, are the MQPL (Measuring the Quality of Prison Life) and the SQL (Staff Quality of Life) surveys. The findings from Grendon are compared with the findings of these surveys in other prisons, in order to assess to what extent, and in what ways, the quality of life of prisoners and staff is different in Grendon from other prisons. The MQPL data is taken from a survey that was conducted by the Standards Audit Unit in Grendon during February 2007. The SQL data is taken from research conducted by the author in Grendon during October 2006.

Why Focus on the Quality of Life?

The reasons for dedicating a chapter to the discussion of the quality of life of prisoners in Grendon (and even more so to discuss the quality of life

Grendon and the Emergence of Forensic Therapeutic Communities: Developments in Research and Practice
Edited by Richard Shuker and Elizabeth Sullivan
© 2010 John Wiley & Sons, Ltd.

of staff) deserve some explanation. The tendency with rehabilitation institutions like Grendon is to focus on their reformative, 'post-release' goals,
and on the efforts to achieve them. Most research attention is directed at
the attempts to change the perceptions, lifestyles and patterns of criminal
behaviour of each participant in the programme and the conditions that
enable this intervention to be successful. This is particularly so in the
current prison system in England and Wales with its strong 'effectiveness'
orientation (Liebling, 2004) and more generally in the current penal climate
where 'treatment programmes and rehabilitative interventions are targeted
not at the needs of the offending individual and his or her social conditions,
but at safeguarding the public' (Crewe, 2009: 16; Garland, 2001). However,
the role of prison research is not only to assess whether a prison is *'effective'*
but also (some would say primarily) to explain what prison, or what
imprisonment *is*. Record numbers of prisoners currently take part in rehabilitation and offending behaviour programmes throughout the prison
system in England and Wales, which makes it particularly important to
understand how prisoners experience imprisonment in the most intense
and radical programme in the prison system – the therapeutic community.
Even if it does not add much to our knowledge about how successful
Grendon is in transforming people's lives in the long term, answering these
types of questions of how prisoners experience their imprisonment in
Grendon can significantly increase our knowledge about what imprisonment is and what imprisonment can be. It might reveal some of the difficulties, dilemmas and problems involved in this type of work and also some
of the advantages, innovations and alternative approaches to various
aspects of imprisonment that this programme brings with it. Of course,
this should not be interpreted as implying that the nature of the therapeutic climate has no impact on the effectiveness of TCs. To the contrary,
different aspects that are referred to in this chapter as dimensions of the
quality of life of prisoners and staff, particularly safety and good relationships, are widely regarded as key factors in treatment outcome. The focus
of this chapter, however, is on the perceptions of prisoners about Grendon
as a prison.

Prisoners are not the only 'actors' in the prison scene however, and
understanding life in Grendon requires attention to the experiences and
perceptions of staff. In recent years a growing body of research about
prison officers has emerged and a growing consensus has been formed that
'the profile of staff is important in understanding "what goes on" in prisons'
(Liebling & Price, 2001, p. 35; see also Arnold, 2005; Arnold *et al.*, 2007;
Bennett *et al.*, 2008; Crawley, 2004). Studying both prisoners and staff
using a similar (although not identical) survey tool, as is done in this
research, also provides an opportunity to explore differences in the ways
both groups perceive similar areas of life in the prison (for example, staff–

prisoner relationships). Comparing the Grendon findings to those of staff and prisoners in other prisons where the same surveys were used, suggests ways in which 'doing time' and working in Grendon is different from other prisons.

Issues that are related to the quality of life of prisoners or staff have not been totally ignored in the literature about Grendon. Some of the aspects of managing Grendon and other prison-based democratic therapeutic communities and the conflicting priorities that are sometimes involved in it (for example, formal against 'dynamic' security measures) were recently discussed (Bennett, 2006; Bennett, 2007; Leggett & Hirons, 2007; Woodward, 2007). In some of these works, the author referred to the highly humane nature of the regime and to the very good prisoner–staff relationships (e.g. Bennett, 2006). Over the years, collections of interviews with prisoners and staff have been published in which both parties talk, among other things, about their experiences in Grendon (Parker, 1970; Smartt, 2001). Aspects of everyday life and prison culture in Grendon have also been discussed by Morris (2004) and by Genders and Player (1995) who discussed the improved relationships between prisoners and staff. Genders and Player described the transformation of prison culture, and traced the gradual replacement of the 'inmate code' by a value system that was linked to the therapeutic community ethos. None of these studies, however, used systematic measurement scales that would provide a comprehensive picture of the experience of living or working in Grendon. The purpose of this chapter is to present such scales and to discuss initial findings from administering them in Grendon.

Methodology and Context of the Research

The surveys – general

Both the MQPL and the SQL originate in a research project led by Professor Alison Liebling together with Helen Arnold entitled 'Measuring the Quality of Prison Life and Locating the Energy for Change' that was conducted in 2000–2001 (Liebling, 2004). Liebling and Arnold used Appreciative Inquiry (AI) methodology, which involved conducting a series of workshops and interviews with prisoners and staff in five prisons. Their aim was to identify 'what matters most' in prisons, to assess their 'moral performance' and to capture the 'softer' aspects of the quality of life in prison, like trust, respect and humanity. Based on this inquiry, they developed surveys that were used, in that and later research projects, to capture the life quality for both prisoners and staff.

The prisoners' survey – the MQPL

As part of their study, Liebling and Arnold divided their life quality measures into three main areas: relationships, the prison regime and social structures. The 'relationships' section included dimensions (or factors) like 'relationships', 'respect' and 'humanity'. The 'regime' section included dimensions like 'fairness', 'well-being', 'order' and 'safety'. The 'social structures' included dimensions like 'power' and 'prisoners' social life'. Each dimension was comprised of a list of between 3 and 22 statements. Prisoners were asked to circle whether they *strongly disagreed, disagreed, neither agreed nor disagreed, agreed* or *highly agreed* with each of them. Some modifications were made using information from a pilot in one prison, statistical analysis and consultation with prisoners and staff. At the end of the project the survey was handed over to the Prison Service and is administered by the Standards Audit Unit (SAU) on a regular basis (at least once every two years) in all prisons in England and Wales. The SAU, in consultation with the Prisons Research Centre at Cambridge, has modified the MQPL several times, added some items and dimensions, and re-clustered others according to the changing policies and priorities of the Prison Service. The most recent version, from which the data that is presented in this chapter is taken, comprises 109 items clustered into the following 17 dimensions: 'relationships with staff 1', 'relationships with staff 2', 'inclusion', 'fairness', 'order', 'decency', 'supporting safety', 'feeling safe', 'drug culture, 'well-being', 'entry into custody', 'specialist support', 'healthcare', 'offending behaviour programmes', 'rehabilitation', 'outside relationships' and 'race equality'. Prisoners were also asked to circle, on a scale of 1–10, their level of overall quality of life. The questionnaire also included two qualitative questions where prisoners were asked to list the three most negative and three most positive aspects of life in the prison (Liebling, 2004). Finally, prisoners were asked to provide some demographic details: age, length of time in the prison, number of times they have been in prison before, etc.

The staff survey – the SQL

In 2005 the Prison Service contracted the Prisons Research Centre to formally develop a valid and reliable measure of the quality of prison life for staff, based on a staff survey that was developed by Liebling and Arnold in the same study. The project of developing the survey lasted six months. In the beginning of the process, the questionnaire covered five main areas:

relationships with different working circles (peers, line management, senior management and the Prison Service); relationships with prisoners; staff commitment and involvement in work; some other general dimensions (e.g. 'safety/security/control', 'communication', 'stress') and finally, professional orientation dimensions which were adopted (with modifications) from the Klofas and Toch survey (Klofas & Toch, 1982; Whitehead *et al.*, 1987). The professional orientation dimensions were slightly different from the other dimensions, as they were intended to measure level of punitive orientation, style of authority maintenance and inclination to be involved in rehabilitation work. Factor analysis and reliability tests were conducted twice (after three prisons had been surveyed and again after six prisons) before the final version was developed. The final version of the questionnaire consisted of 117 items grouped into the following dimensions: 'treatment by senior management', 'attitudes towards senior management', 'perception of the Prison Service', 'relationships with peers', 'relationships with line management', 'treatment by line management', 'commitment', 'safety/security/control', 'recognition and personal efficacy', 'involvement in prison', 'involvement in work', 'stress', 'relationships with prisoners', 'professional support', 'social distance', 'authority maintenance' and 'views on punishment and control'. The survey also asked staff for demographic details and for assessment of their overall quality of working life and overall level of stress on a scale of 1–10. Respondents were also asked to list the three most satisfying aspects and the three most stressful aspects of their job.

The Administration of the Surveys

The MQPL was administered in Grendon by the Standards Audit Unit on February 2007. This was part of the regular annual (or bi-annual) MQPL administration that was taking place in all prisons. The sample consisted of 86 residents that were selected randomly from all the wings, including the induction unit. Prisoners completed the survey in groups of between 10 and 17. The SQL survey was administered in Grendon four months earlier, during five consecutive days in October 2006. The SQL survey was part of a PhD study whose focus was relationships between prisoners and staff in prison-based therapeutic communities. Ideally, the staff survey should be administered in a full staff meeting. However, at the time when this survey was conducted in Grendon, this was not possible. Instead, staff on all wings were approached personally by the author and asked to complete the questionnaire. In order to include as many staff members as possible, each wing was visited every day at different times. Most completed questionnaires were collected personally by the author but some were later sent by mail. The target sample was all the staff working in Grendon: 102 members were personally requested to complete the questionnaire; 57 completed it and returned it to the author.

Reading the Data

The scores of the dimensions below are presented on a range from 1 to 5, and are coded so that higher scores indicate a better result. For example, if the score of the dimension 'relationships with staff' is 5, it means that prisoners are extremely and uniformly positive about their relationship with staff. If the score of the same dimension is 1 it means prisoners are very negative about their relationships with staff. Scores of 5 or 1 are extremely rare however, and the range of scores is usually between 2 and 4. A score which is higher than 3 is generally interpreted as positive and a score which is lower than 3 is generally interpreted as negative. The score of a dimension represents the mean score of all the items in that dimension. This means that if the dimension score is 3, it can be assumed that many staff members were neutral about most of the items of that dimension but it can also mean that some staff were positive about the items and some were more negative about them so the score reflects the average of the two. With regard to some specific items, the percentage of agreement or disagreement is presented below. It is important to note that, despite using terms like 'scores', the surveys are not measuring any type of performance but rather the subjective perceptions of prisoners and staff about their quality of life.

Findings

The MQPL

The scores of the MQPL survey completed in Grendon show that prisoners generally held a highly positive perception of their quality of life. Out of 14 dimensions, 3 had scores of 4 or higher; 8 had scored 3.5 or more and the other 3 dimensions scored 3.4 or higher. Figure 15.1 and table 15.1 illustrate how the findings of Grendon compare to other institutions.

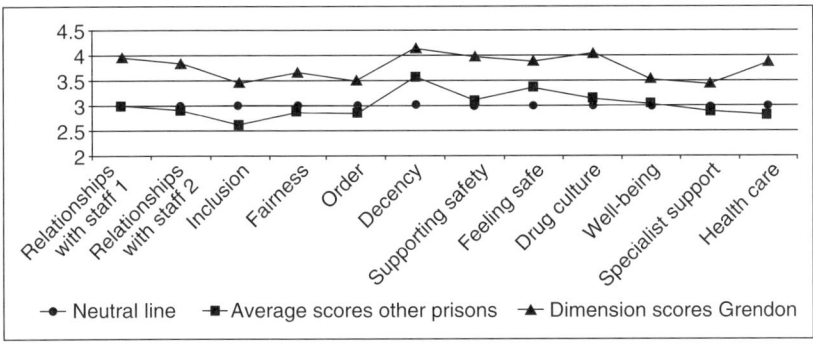

Figure 15.1 Dimension mean scores of the MQPL at Grendon compared with the average dimension mean scores in eight other Cat B male prisons

Table 15.1 Comparing the scores of Grendon with the highest scores of other establishments

Dimension	Grendon score	The highest scoring prison of all other prisons for that specific dimension
Relationships with staff 1	3.96***	3.53
Relationships with staff 2	3.83*	3.56
Inclusion	3.47*	3.19
Fairness	3.66**	3.37
Order	3.49	3.58
Decency	4.16**	3.96
Supporting safety	3.98***	3.64
Feeling safe	3.90	3.91
Drug culture	4.04	4.01
Well-being	3.52	3.56
Specialist support	3.46	3.42
Healthcare	3.86	3.75
Rehabilitation	4.29***	3.39
Outside relationships	3.86	3.81

$* = p < .1$, $** = p < .01$, $*** = p < .001$

Figure 15.1 compares the scores on the dimensions in Grendon to the average dimension score in the other 8 category B training prisons in which the survey was conducted by the Standards Audit Unit in the years 2005–2006 and 2006–2007. As this figure shows, the scores of all the dimensions of Grendon are higher than the average in other prisons.

Table 15.1 compares the scores of Grendon to the best scores that were received for each of the dimensions in any of the 87 non-open male prisons of various categories (dispersal, B or C) that were surveyed during the years 2005–2007. It can be seen that for all the dimensions but three, Grendon's score was *higher than the highest* of all other institutions and in seven it was significantly higher. This is particularly impressive given the fact that these highest scores are spread between different prisons, with no prison (other than Grendon) holding more than three of the (second) highest scores.

Predictably, 'rehabilitation' is the dimension where the difference between Grendon and other prisons is the highest. Of the Grendon prisoners, 88 per cent agreed and only 1 disagreed that Grendon helped them to lead a law-abiding life on release into the community, and 91 per cent felt they were encouraged to work towards goals/targets in Grendon. The 2 'relationships with staff' dimensions also had exceptionally high scores, where 86 per cent of prisoners agreed or highly agreed and only 2 per cent disagreed with the statement 'relationships between staff and prisoners in this prison are good'. Furthermore, 85 per cent felt they were 'treated as a human being' in Grendon, and 80 per cent thought that most staff in Grendon showed concern and understanding towards them.

This is not to suggest that there were unanimous positive views about all aspects of life or even about all aspects of staff–prisoner relationships. 'Order' was one dimension for which prisoners in Grendon scored just below 3.5 and slightly lower than another prison (although still high overall); 30 per cent of prisoners did not think that Grendon was good at delivering a structured and predictable regime and 46 per cent of prisoners did not think Grendon was well organised.

Although the above indicates that many prisoners in Grendon believe they have a better quality of life than prisoners in other prisons, the stay in Grendon is not an 'easy ride': 52 per cent found the experience of imprisonment in Grendon stressful and 42 per cent found the experience of Grendon painful.

Interestingly, there was not a significant correlation between the length of stay in Grendon and the scores of the different dimensions. The meaning of this fact will be discussed below.

Finally, the mean score of the last item of the questionnaire, where prisoners were asked to assess their overall quality of life on a scale of 1–10 (where 1 represents poor quality of life and 10 high quality of life), was 6.99. This again is the highest score of all the 97 male adult prisons that were surveyed in the years 2005–2007 and one of only 3 prisons where this score was above 6.

The SQL

The picture of the scores of the staff survey in Grendon is more varied than that of the MQPL. Seven dimensions had a score of 3.5 or higher, the scores of 3 dimensions were between 3 and 3.5 and the scores of the other 7 dimensions were between 2.5 and 3.0. Figure 15.2 presents the scores of selected SQL dimensions compared to the average score of the same dimensions in 9 category B prisons in which the survey has been conducted during the last two years. For the sake of unity, all the results presented here include only discipline staff, unless explicitly noted.

As can be seen from figure 15.2, the scores of most of the dimensions in Grendon are close to the average scores in other category B prisons. The main areas where the scores of officers in Grendon were lower (that is, more negative) are perceptions of senior management and the Prison Service (the scores in the left side of the chart) and levels of stress. The areas where the scores of staff in Grendon were higher were their perceptions of the level of safety, security and control, and the professional orientation dimensions (the scores in the right side of the chart). In particular, officers at Grendon had higher scores than other prisons for the dimensions 'authority maintenance' and 'views on punishment and control'.

Starting with the lower scores first, it should be said that the dimensions, which refer to senior management and the Prison Service, are typically low in all establishments. The results in Grendon are even lower than in other prisons, however. There are several plausible explanations for this. First,

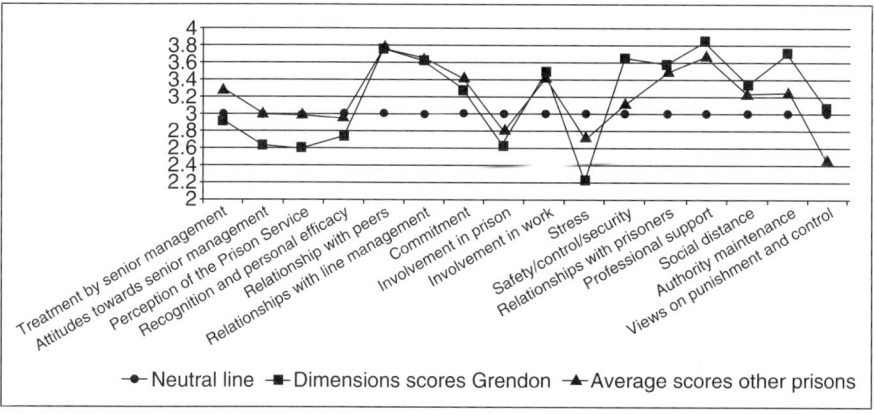

Figure 15.2   Mean scores for selected dimensions of the SQL at Grendon and the average dimension scores in nine other Cat B male prisons (discipline staff only)

there are some indications that this might have to do with the different method of administration of the survey in Grendon and in the other prisons. In most other prisons the survey was conducted in a full staff meeting with a response rate of above 95 per cent. In one other prison where the method of administration was similar to the one used in Grendon, the scores of the working circles dimensions were almost as low as in Grendon (but the other trends that will be discussed below were not similar). There might be other reasons, however, for this low score. It could be, for example, a reflection of the historical tension between what junior staff believe to be the 'real therapeutic work' which they are involved in, and the focus of senior management on the more mundane aspects of prison management (which staff sometimes see as detrimental to the therapeutic process), such as security and performance management (see Bennett, 2006). In some small units which have followed the TC model, there are periods when prisoners and junior staff within the community share a strong sense of a united community vis-à-vis the outside world and higher ranks. This is how the atmosphere in the early days of the famous Barlinnie Unit was described by some of the people who stayed there (in particular Boyle, 1984). However, the scores of some of the items suggest that such an explanation is less plausible in Grendon. Like most other prisons, the lowest scoring item in these two dimensions is the item 'There are times where Governors in here fail to support staff in dealing with prisoners': 70 per cent of staff agreed or strongly agreed with this statement. This implies that many staff members see the Governors as taking the prisoners' side (a very common argument in mainstream prisons) which is less consistent with a united prisoner–staff partnership against the rest of the system. A better explanation may concern staff dissatisfaction with the level of recognition and support they receive. Only 38 per cent of staff were happy with the level of recognition for their achievements in Grendon.

As in other prisons, staff in Grendon perceived their relationships with peers and line managers as very positive. Like prisoners, officers were happy with the level of safety in the prison: 97 per cent of staff thought assaults by prisoners on staff were rare in Grendon and 82 per cent felt safe. These scores are even more impressive given the high percentage of prisoners with a volatile background in Grendon compared to other category B prisons.

Despite the multidisciplinary nature of the staff team, 56 per cent rarely felt they are involved in the decision-making process and 42 per cent did not feel part of the bigger picture in Grendon. This again is a typical result. Seventy-four per cent of officers in Grendon thought they had good relationships with prisoners. Staff in many prisons perceive their relationships with prisoners positively but this is not always the view of prisoners. In Grendon this positive perception of staff is supported by prisoner accounts.

The two dimensions where the scores of Grendon officers stood out compared to other prisons were the dimensions 'authority maintenance' and 'views on punishment and control'. Higher scores on these dimensions represent a more informal style of maintaining authority and a lower level of punitive orientation. Scores for 'views on punishment and control' are typically low across establishments and Grendon was the only prison in which officers scored above 3 on this dimension. For example, only 27 per cent of the officers in Grendon thought that 'Grendon was too comfortable for prisoners' and 46 per cent disagreed or strongly disagreed with this statement. In other category B prisons, the trend was the opposite with an average of 43 per cent agreeing or strongly agreeing with this statement and only 25 per cent disagreeing or strongly disagreeing with it. Similarly, 38 per cent of the officers in Grendon agreed that 'most prisoners are decent people'. In the other category B prisons that were surveyed, only an average of 15 per cent agreed with the same statement.

Despite (or maybe because of) working in a rehabilitation institution, officers in Grendon were disillusioned about the prospect of rehabilitation for most offenders. The percentage of staff in agreement with the statement 'Most prisoners can be rehabilitated' was distributed almost evenly between those who agree or strongly agree (35 per cent), those who neither agree nor disagree (35 per cent) and those who disagree or strongly disagree (30 per cent).

When asked to assess their overall quality of life on a scale of 1–10 (where 1 represents poor and 10 represents high quality of life) the mean score in Grendon was 6.3. This is the second highest score (that is, the second most positive) among the category B prisons in which the survey has been conducted. However, when asked to assess their level of stress on a scale of 1–10 (where 1 represents low level of stress and 10 high level of stress) the mean score of staff in Grendon was 6.6, which is the highest (that is, representing the highest level of stress) of all the category B prisons that were surveyed. The scores of other items that form the dimension 'stress' tell a similar story: 91 per cent of staff thought that the work in Grendon was highly emotionally demanding and 55 per cent reported that many of the stressful aspects of the work stayed with them when they were at home. The same number also reported that the stress levels of their job caused them concern. Typically, the scores of non-discipline staff in Grendon were slightly more positive for all the dimensions, but followed the same patterns as the discipline staff.

Discussion

The findings of the MQPL and SQL teach us that both staff and prisoners in Grendon enjoy, overall, a good quality of life but also find some aspects of their experience stressful or, in the case of some prisoners, painful. There is a distinct difference between the two groups however, which becomes evident when comparing Grendon's results to those of other, similar prisons. While the scores of the staff survey fall overall within the range of results in other prisons, with some areas where staff have more positive perceptions and some areas where they have more negative perceptions, the scores of prisoners in Grendon are significantly higher than in other prisons across the board.

The meaning of these findings, both for prisoners and for staff, is far from straightforward, however. The first question raised by the prisoner findings is the extent to which the high level of satisfaction reported by prisoners represents improvement of 'objective' factors which constitute the different aspects of life in the prison (e.g. different aspects of the regime, the attitudes of staff, the level of violence, the style of management, the routines, the structure, the balance of power, etc.) rather than a change in their state of mind. As Crewe (2009: 4) notes, the early prison sociology literature (Berk, 1966; Grusky, 1959; Street *et al.*, 1966) demonstrated that 'where prisons were treatment-oriented rather than custody-oriented, the values and behaviour of prisoners were less "oppositional"'. There may be several reasons for such a change of perception, not all related to changes in the objective conditions of imprisonment. It could, for instance, be a result of conceiving the stay at a place like Grendon as a progress and a step forward rather than the non-purposeful wasted stay in the mainstream prison. It could also be linked to the high motivation, enthusiasm and wish to turn a new page, which are all associated with taking part in an ambitious rehabilitation programme. Prisoner perceptions might also be affected by the rolling or 'slow open' (Morris, 2004) method which is used in Grendon for introducing new prisoners, in which they join an already existing group of experienced residents who are highly committed to the therapeutic community ethos and are convinced of its benefits. This can have some impact on the responses of prisoners who take part in the survey. It could also be argued that the referral process is selective and aimed to ensure that only motivated people with some level of readiness to participate in such a demanding programme are admitted to Grendon. This might suggest that Grendon has a population of prisoners who are more content than prisoners in other prisons, either because of their personality traits or maturation to a less anti-authoritarian life-stage.

Interpreting the scores of the staff survey also presents some difficulties. Focusing, for example, on high levels of stress, it could be argued that this is a result of the very demanding nature of both the prison work and the therapy. Alternatively, it could be argued that this reflects greater willingness of staff to admit that their job is emotionally demanding, admissions that may be less acceptable in the more 'macho' staff cultures of non-therapeutic prisons.

Another challenge is distinguishing between cause and effect in Grendon. For example, are the less punitive attitudes of staff influenced by the positive attitudes of prisoners, or are the less oppositional views of prisoners shaped by staff attitudes? Which of the two groups start this feedback loop and can a 'starting point' in this process even be identified?

Finally, which of the differences in prisoners' perceptions should be attributed to the impact of therapy and to long-term processes of change, and which should be attributed to more 'immediate' factors in the regime? This question is important, not only for Grendon but for the rest of the prison system. If such immediate factors (e.g. informality and using first name terms) provide part of the answer, it might be easier to extend them to the rest of the prison system.

Some Initial Explanations: Safety, Inclusion, Staff Attitudes

A general survey about the quality of life cannot answer all the above questions. This would require further specific quantitative and qualitative research. However the data that comes out of the survey does allow for initial discussion about what the findings represent and what their causes are.

First, it would be unrealistic to assume that the perceptions of prisoners about their quality of life in Grendon are not affected at all by their subjective awareness that they are staying in a purposeful, therapy-oriented environment in which they volunteered to participate. The fact that many prisoners are very positive about the strong rehabilitation orientation is reflected in the very high score of the 'rehabilitation' dimension compared with other prisons. At the same time, there are some strong indications that this cannot be the only or even the dominant factor that accounts for these positive scores. For example, the fact that there are no significant differences in the level of overall quality of life between newcomers, people who are halfway through their therapy and more experienced residents indicates that this cannot be passed off as initial enthusiasm about the programme or as a result of changes of values or perceptions which are an outcome of deep involvement in the therapy. Although the current data does not include details about psychological personality traits, research conducted in Grendon has found that its population was comprised of 'damaged, disturbed and dangerous' offenders with severe personality disorders (Shine & Newton, 2000). Grendon receptions were above average of either the general male adult population or other prisoners, in terms of neuroticism, criminality and addictiveness, with additional tendencies towards impulsivity, risk taking, solitary and disturbed behaviour (Cullen, 1997; similar findings were also reported by Marshall, 1997). Therefore it cannot be assumed that this population come to Grendon with more 'pro-system' values than others.

In addition, some of the survey dimensions seem to suggest something beyond a change of mindset. This is, for instance, the case of the dimension 'safety/security/control'. As mentioned above, both staff and residents had high scores on dimensions related to safety, with 98 per cent of prisoners agreeing and no one disagreeing that violence between prisoners in Grendon was rare. Furthermore, 97 per cent of staff thought that assaults by prisoners on staff were rare. Such scores regarding the level of violence are unlikely to be a result of subjective state of mind. If actual violence took place in Grendon, prisoners and staff would find it hard to ignore, even if their motivation, or expectations from the programme, predisposed them to have a very positive perception of the place.

The impact of violence and lack of safety in prison should not be under-estimated (see Edgar *et al.*, 2003). A violent incident has an impact beyond the people directly involved in it. People staying or working in a violent atmosphere must constantly be alert and 'watch their back'. Prisoners in other prisons often report needing to 'put on a mask' of toughness, and show willingness to fight if they are challenged. In prison-based therapeutic communities, prisoners often report a strong sense of relief at being able to take off this mask and 'be themselves'. This is also the case with staff, who can be less worried about 'watching their back' and can therefore develop relationships with prisoners more freely.

One of the dimensions for which the prisoners in Grendon reported significantly higher scores than other prisons was 'inclusion'. The dimension refers mainly to how much officers treat prisoners as individuals, provide them with feedback and explain the reasons for decisions that concern them. The high score for this dimension in Grendon is not surprising. The communal nature of the therapeutic community and the sense of belonging, together with increased attention to individuals, is part of the essence of the life of residents and staff in a therapeutic community. This attention to each individual can at times be very demanding, especially where the behaviour of each individual is constantly assessed and challenged, and it can reinforce at times a wish to be left alone. However, communal life also provides a sense of support. This is a big contrast to the more alienated, atomised 'everyone for himself' atmosphere that is associated with contemporary mainstream prison culture (see Crewe, 2009). In conversations with Grendon residents, many of them refer back to their impressions from their first days in the place – the warm personal welcome, the offers of support from both staff and residents, and the informality. All this contributes (usually after an initial suspiciousness and a period of familiarisation) to a sense of inclusion.

The sense of inclusion is also enhanced by less punitive staff attitudes. It should be noted that staff attitudes in most prisons have gone through significant changes in recent years (Crawley, 2004; Liebling & Price, 2001). Violence of staff against prisoners is rare and there is growing awareness of the need to deal with prisoners using a respectful and fair approach. At the same time, however, the growing punitive rhetoric in the general population together with some traditional negative cultural legacies, leave their mark on staff views in other prisons. In Grendon, it seems that many staff members are able to stay immune to this general anti-offender rhetoric. This is reflected in the scores of the dimension 'views on punishment and control': 39 per cent of discipline staff in the other category B prisons, but only a third of this number (13 per cent) in Grendon, thought that 'prisoners spend too much of their time out of their cell'. Almost two thirds (66 per cent) of discipline staff in the category B prisons thought that their prison is too comfortable for prisoners; only slightly more than a third (39 per cent) thought so in Grendon. Prisoners can easily sense these differences in views. It makes it easier for them to see beyond the officers' uniforms and not to identify them with the more punitive parts of the society. It enables them to co-operate with staff and start building relationships of trust and support.

Safety, inclusion, and less punitive staff attitudes do not explain the whole picture of quality of life in Grendon and, again, there is a strong case to argue that they are partly the result of (rather than the causes for) the better overall atmosphere in Grendon. Nonetheless, as a starting point, they can usefully be considered as independent variables, and may generate further thought about the pains of imprisonment in a non-therapeutic environment.

Conclusion

Prisoners in Grendon do not only discuss their pasts and are not only working on their futures. They also live there in the present, some of them for long periods. Staying in such an environment with its 'highly incongruous co-habitees' (Genders & Player, 1995, p. 120) – the custodial and the rehabilitation roles – can be confusing, intense and stressful, not only for prisoners but also for the staff who work there. This chapter has presented and discussed some of the aspects of life in Grendon as they are reflected in the findings of the MQPL and the SQL surveys. The focus has been on the more positive results which suggested that, overall, prisoners perceive their quality of life more positively than in other prisons of the same category. More research is needed in order to further explore these findings and identify which factors could be applied in mainstream prisons as well. Some of the more disturbing aspects of the surveys – the level of staff stress, and those aspects that make the stay of the prisoners painful – should also be further explored.

It has to be remembered that one of the reasons behind the original initiative to establish a prison like Grendon was the need to provide solutions 'for the offender who proved quite unable to adapt himself to ordinary social conditions but for whom reformative measure, however specialised, seemed useless [...]' (Newell & Healey, 2007, p. 62, citing East & de Hubert, 1939). It is arguable that, today, the experimental nature of the work in Grendon could be extended, beyond this original task, to learning about how prison cultures could be transformed and how a different experience of imprisonment could be created, not just for 'hard copers' but for the benefit of the prison system as a whole.

References

Arnold, H. (2005). The effects of prison work. In A. Liebling & S. Maruna (Eds) *The Effects of Imprisonment*. Cullompton: Willan.

Arnold, H., Liebling, A. & Tait, S. (2007). Prison officers and prison culture. In Y. Jewkes (Ed.) *Handbook on Prisons*. Cullompton: Willan.

Bennett, J., Crewe, B. & Wahidin, A. (Eds) (2008). *Understanding Prison Staff*. Cullompton: Willan.

Bennett, P. (2006). Governing a humane prison. In D. Jones (Ed.) *Humane Prisons*. Oxford: Radcliffe.

Bennett, P. (2007). Governing Grendon Prison's therapeutic communities: The big spin. In M. Parker (Ed.) *Dynamic Security – The Democratic Therapeutic Community in Prison*. London: Jessica Kingsley.

Berk, B. (1966). Organizational goals and inmate organization. *American Journal of Sociology, 71*, 522–524.

Boyle, J. (1984). *The Pain of Confinement: Prison Diaries*. Edinburgh: Canongate.

Crawley, E. (2004). *Doing Prison Work: The Public and Private Lives of Prison Officers*. Cullompton: Willan.

Crewe, B. (2009). *The Prisoner Society: Power, Adaptation, and Social Life in an English Prison*. Oxford: Oxford University Press.

Cullen, E. (1997). Can a prison be a therapeutic community: The Grendon template. In E. Cullen, L. Jones & R. Woodward (Eds) *Therapeutic Communities for Offenders*. Chichester: Wiley.

Edgar, K., O'Donnell, I. & Martic, C. (2003). *Prison Violence: The Dynamics of Conflict, Fear and Power*. Cullompton: Willan.

Garland, D. (2001). *The Culture of Control, Crime and Social Order in Contemporary Society*. Oxford: Oxford University Press.

Genders, E. & Player, E. (1995). *Grendon: A Study of a Therapeutic Prison*. Oxford: Clarendon Press.

Grusky, O. (1959). Organizational goals and the behaviour of informal leaders. *American Journal of Sociology*, 65, 59–67.

Klofas, J. & Toch, H. (1982). Alienation and desire for job enrichment among correction officers. *Federal Probation*, 46(1), 35–47.

Leggett, K. & Hirons, B. (2007) Security and dynamic security in a therapeutic community prison. In M. Parker (Ed.) *Dynamic Security – The Democratic Therapeutic Community in Prison*. London: Jessica Kingsley.

Liebling, A. (assisted by H. Arnold) (2004). *Prisons and Their Moral Performance: A Study of Values, Quality, and Prison Life*. Oxford: Clarendon Press.

Liebling, A. & Price, D. (2001). *The Prison Officer*. Winchester: Waterside Press.

Marshall, P. (1997). *Reduction in Reconviction of Prisoners at HMP Grendon*. Home Office Research Bulletins 61. (Reprinted in Shine, J. (Ed.) (2000). *A Compilation of Grendon Research*. Leyhill Press. Available from Psychology Unit, HMP Grendon, Grendon Underwood, Aylesbury, HP18 OTL.)

Morris, M. (2004). *Dangerous and Severe – Process, Programme and Person*. London: Jessica Kingsley.

Newell, T. & Healey, B. (2007). The historical development of the UK democratic therapeutic community. In M. Parker (Ed.) *Dynamic Security – The Democratic Therapeutic Community in Prison*. London: Jessica Kingsley.

Parker, T. (1970). *The Frying-Pan: A Prison and its Prisoners*. London: Panther Books.

Shine, J. & Newton, M. (2000) Damaged, disturbed and dangerous: A profile of receptions to Grendon therapeutic prison 1995–2000. In J. Shine (Ed.) *A Compilation of Grendon Research*. Leyhill Press. Available from Psychology Unit, HMP Grendon, Grendon Underwood, Aylesbury, HP18 OTL.

Smartt, U. (2001). *Grendon Tales: Stories from a Therapeutic Community*. Winchester: Waterside Press.

Street, D., Vinter, R. & Perrow, C. (1966). *Organization for Treatment*. New York: The Free Press.

Whitehead, J., Lindquist, C. & Klofas, J. (1987). Correctional officer orientation: A replication of the Klofas-Toch Measure. *Criminal Justice and Behaviour*, 14(4), 468–486.

Woodward, R. (2007). Symbiosis: Therapeutic communities within non-therapeutic community organizations. In M. Parker (Ed.) *Dynamic Security – The Democratic Therapeutic Community in Prison*. London: Jessica Kingsley.

Chapter 16

Suicide and Self-injurious Behaviours at HMP Grendon

Adrienne Rivlin

Introduction

Every year in prisons in England and Wales there are approximately 60 to 90 suicides (Fazel & Benning, 2006). A recent study found that between 1978 and 2003 the suicide rate in male prisoners was five times higher than in men in the general population of similar age (Fazel *et al.*, 2005). For women and younger offenders this proportional excess is even larger (Fazel *et al.*, 2005; Kariminia *et al.*, 2007). Of the total male prison population, 5 to 6 per cent attempt suicide or self-harm every year resulting in approximately 9500 incidents of self-injurious behaviours (SIB) that do not lead to death (Safer Custody Group, 2006). These rates are so disproportionately high compared to the general population that reducing the number of suicides and SIBs by prisoners has become both a prison service (HM Prison Service, 2002) and a public health priority (Department of Health, 2002). However, despite expensive initiatives to reduce suicide and SIB in prisons, recent evidence suggests that they are continuing to rise (Blud, 1997; Howard League for Penal Reform, 2005; Paton & Jenkins, 2005; Safer Custody Group, 2006).

There is a puzzle in the Home Office statistics on suicide and SIB. HMP Grendon is a category B prison housing some of the country's most

Grendon and the Emergence of Forensic Therapeutic Communities: Developments in Research and Practice
Edited by Richard Shuker and Elizabeth Sullivan
© 2010 John Wiley & Sons, Ltd.

dangerous violent and sexual offenders. By all accounts Grendon *should* have a high level of suicide and SIB; a large proportion of its inmates match statistical profiles of suicide and SIB victims, and many have prolific biographies of self-destructive behaviours (Rivlin, 2006). Yet rates of suicide and SIB are remarkably low at Grendon compared with other prison establishments. For example, Grendon's rate of SIB is approximately 29 incidents per 1000 prisoners per year, compared to a rate in the mainstream prison service of between 130 and 137 incidents per 1000 prisoners per year. There is no evidence that these low rates can be explained by selection effects into, or out of, the prison (Rivlin, 2006).

This chapter details the qualitative results of a 10-week period of participant observation combined with 56 semi-structured and open-ended interviews with staff and inmates which sought to investigate the range of possible protective factors for SIB associated with incarceration at Grendon. (For more information regarding the methodology, please see Rivlin, 2006; Rivlin, 2007.) In this research SIB refers to 'any intentional self-inflicted injury irrespective of the apparent purpose of the act' (Hawton & Catalâan, 1987, p. 5). Several factors identified by staff and prisoners, and unique to Grendon (when compared to prisons in general), had resulted in a qualitatively less distressing prison environment. These included improved contact with family and friends and a concurrent reduction in loneliness, reduced levels of bullying and victimisation, and improved levels of constructive activity (therapy, education classes, work) and hence less boredom. In addition, Grendon's inmates benefit from a reduced sense of hopelessness, and more optimistic beliefs about the future, improved self-esteem and self-worth, reduced anger and frustration, a reduced sense of powerlessness and increased feelings of control over one's life-path, and much improved relationships with staff and other inmates which provide a source of social support.

Accounting for Grendon's Rates of Self-injurious Behaviours

Some 'distressing' factors are implicit in any prison regime and cannot be removed. These include restrictions on movement, removal from a familiar environment and deprivation of liberty, autonomy and heterosexual relationships (see, for example, Sykes, 1958). However, many potentially distressing factors vary with the type of prison establishment, for example, contact with family and friends, bullying and victimisation, loneliness, lack of activity and boredom and prison facilities such as access to exercise equipment or education.

Contact with family, friends and 'the outside'

The relationship between an inmate and his family and friends is complex. Many inmates have experienced physical or sexual abuse in the home or by a close relative. Alternatively, the victims of his offence may have been his family or friends. Nevertheless, incarceration removes an individual from his primary support group and prisoners may have to forfeit visits from family and friends if they are transferred to prisons far from where they live. Some prisoners are lucky in that their family provides both financial and emotional support throughout their stay in prison but others are less so if their relationships with family and friends are non-existent. However, there can be no doubt that even for those prisoners whose family and friends are generally supportive, being imprisoned adds an enormous burden to those relationships. Suicide attempts and SIB in prison have been linked to problems with relatives and friends, homesickness and a general lack of social support from 'the outside' (Blaauw *et al.*, 2002; Borrill *et al.*, 2005; Liebling & Krarup, 1993).

The attitude of the prison and its governor is thus very important in helping to facilitate better relationships between inmates and family or friends, for example in the nature of the visiting policy. All prisons offer visiting times and facilities to their inmates but Grendon also offers additional services almost unique within the prison system. Family days and children's days allow an inmate a full day (10am–4pm) with his visitors. These each occur twice a year. Social evenings held every six months on each wing are chances for members of the public to visit Grendon and socialise with the inmates. 'Conferences' are held from time to time and are chances for Grendon's prisoners to socialise, or be involved with various outside groups.

Not all inmates at Grendon had positive relationships with family and friends outside but it was clear that the prison's visiting policy had helped those inmates, for whom it was possible, to work on their relationships:

If there's one thing that I'm grateful for to Grendon it's bringing me a lot closer to my relatives … we have good conversations … they see the change in me. I would have loved to have had a better relationship with me Dad 'cause being at Grendon it's helped me do that. And I think out of all the things I've done since I've been here that's been the most positive thing that I've done. Even thinking about all the courses, the exams that I've passed – that doesn't come close. (P26)

Bullying, victimisation and violence

Bullying is a risk factor for suicide and self-injury in prison (Beck, 1992; Blaauw *et al.*, 2001; Blaauw *et al.*, 2002; Borrill *et al.*, 2005; Power & Spencer, 1987; Towl, 1997), an association well understood by prisoners and staff at Grendon: '*There are a lot of suicides through bullying – that's a fact*' (P4). Inmates described the '*bullying, torment and personal abuse*' (P15) that they had suffered, or perpetrated, in the 'system'[1] and compared it with the '*safer environment and close-knit community*' (S46) in Grendon which afforded much reduced rates of bullying and victimisation. A particularly interesting account of the low incidence of bullying came from P1 who has spent over 20 years in prison including time at a Dangerous and Severe Personality Disorder unit. P1 is serving a life sentence for murdering a sex offender and five years concurrent for GBH and attempted murder, acts all committed on other inmates whilst in prison. He made a point of commenting on how little violent behaviour there was in Grendon compared with the 'system':

> *Prisoners … the way they act here don't act like that in dispersals. There ain't been one fight since I've been here in six weeks. And that's – for the prison system – I'd say you usually get about two or three a week at least.*

Bullying was not completely absent from Grendon. Staff and inmates appreciated that it was '*an issue that could raise its head now and again*' (S44) but agreed that if bullying did occur, it tended to be in '*mild forms*' (S44), rather than '*the way it was in the system*'. There was a common consensus that bullying was dealt with promptly and effectively by initiating anti-bullying procedures and by addressing the issue in therapy groups and on the wing: '[Bullying is] *going to be exposed and it's going to be dealt with either on the small groups or through the community*' (S46). '*Here, if you're a bully you're challenged on the wing. If you don't change you're out, you're gone*' (P4).

Loneliness

Feelings of loneliness, isolation or abandonment are commonly found to be associated with prisoner suicide (Liebling, 1992; Liebling & Krarup,

---

[1]'System': the term used to refer to the prison system outside of Grendon.

1993; Sykes, 1958). At Grendon, prisoners frequently cited an overwhelming sense of loneliness as a precipitating factor behind their past suicide attempts and self-injurious acts: *'It's like I'm feeling fucking lonely, I need to talk'* (P38). P23 made sense of his wrist-cutting in terms of a similar sense of isolation and abandonment: *'I felt really lost. Lonely. I was really missing my family'.*

Grendon's inmates found prison to be an extremely lonely place. Almost every inmate reported that he had no friends in prison: *'I never get close friends. I've never tried to. You can't get friends'* (P1), although most inmates admitted that they did know *'acquaintances'* (P15), *'friendly people'* (P1) or those that they could *'get on with a bit better'* (P9). In fact, the inmates did not appear to have close friends that they could confide in anywhere, inside prison or out: *'I wouldn't say I had close friends anywhere'* (P5). P8 for instance, told me that he *'ain't been out [of prison] long enough to form proper friendships'*, stating: *'I don't like to have friendships. And if I'm honest I've never really had true friends'.*

Prisoners tried to avoid forming close relationships with other inmates for a number of reasons. A rigid prison hierarchy left some inmates feeling a sense of superiority over 'lesser' criminals, especially if they found themselves at the top of the pecking order (for example, armed robbers). Prisoners who have committed certain types of act – usually sex offenders or murderers of young children – are at the *'bottom of the pile'* (P9) and are universally ignored by other inmates. Friendships between different strata in the hierarchy are unlikely to develop.

Second, inmates commonly stayed clear of close friendships in order to avoid the *'transmission of criminal values'*, especially if they were trying to *'come good'* (P15). P15 explained that *'a lot of people who are inside you don't really want to meet on the outside'*. He had *'resolved not to lead a criminal lifestyle'* and the last thing he wanted was to meet a person outside prison that he had known inside and get into *'confrontations or conflicts'* with him or have him *'pull [me] down'.*

Whilst friendship seemed a closely guarded term rarely, if ever, used by Grendon's inmates, the prisoners did express that at Grendon they had formed *'positive relationships'* with the other men on their wing even if they *'obviously don't get on with everyone'* (P4 and P15). The men acknowledged *'there were personality clashes'* (P2) but stated that they did *'get on with the majority of people'* (P15). If a problem with another inmate arose they felt *'compelled to sort it out, to go and talk and make an effort which you wouldn't do in a normal prison'* (P2). They believed they had to form positive relationships with other inmates in order to 'do' therapy. P29, for instance, described that he was *'very very close'* to the inmates on his therapy group and felt *'an emotional attachment'* to them because *'you talk to your core* group about things that you wouldn't even say to your family … things that my Mum doesn't even know about'. He stated 'we're helping each other, we need each other'.

Lack of activity and boredom

Leese *et al.* (2006) found that in prisons where there was a high level of purposeful activity and less boredom the rate of suicide was lower. A number of Grendon's inmates saw their SIB as the result of a boring prison day: '*I had nothing to do so I used to cut meself and that would cheer me up really*' (P26).

Inmates at Grendon were, for the most part, kept constructively occupied through therapy, paid work, 'rep' jobs, education and exercise. Therapy sessions form the backbone of the day at Grendon but prisoners also have limited paid work and 'rep' jobs (for instance DVD rep, social rep, health and hygiene rep), which are not financially rewarded but are therapeutically motivated to '*show your commitment to the wing – what you're giving back to the wing*' (P29). Additionally, inmates can attend educational classes.

Work and education programmes are limited at Grendon so that inmates concentrate primarily on their therapy rather than on other activities. P9 described how inmates '*tend to escape through education and take themselves away*' rather than '*engaging in therapy*'. He was adamant that an inmate needed '*time for reflection out of groups*' instead of '*keeping busy, keeping yourself occupied … not facing things*'. The lack of opportunity for work or other activity frustrated some men who wanted '*something constructive to keep occupied*' (P39) to fill their free time instead of '*watching mid-morning TV*' (P39) or '*playing pool or darts*' (P29).

Hopelessness and the future

Hopelessness, characterised by pessimism about the future and a belief that life's circumstances will not improve (Towl, 1997), has been repeatedly associated with an increased risk of suicide (Beck *et al.*, 1989; Beck *et al.*, 1974; Snow, 2002). Liebling has argued that lifers who are racked with guilt for their offence and see no future for themselves comprise between 5 and 20 per cent of the total prison suicide population (Liebling, 1992; Liebling & Krarup, 1993). Grendon's inmates often made sense of their SIBs in these terms. P29, serving a life sentence, described how the guilt that he felt for his arson attack, which left three people dead, and his lack of hope for the future, contributed to his suicide attempt when he first came to prison:

> *When I was still on remand for my offence I wasn't in my right mind to be honest … it was the guilt … just thinking about it – the guilt about my crimes. I couldn't deal with what I'd done. And I just thought 'I don't want to live. There's nothing to live for'. It's that hopelessness where you think I'm better off out of here.*

Grendon's inmates described their futures in overwhelmingly positive terms. P17 told me that he '*used to believe that nothing was at the end – that there was nothing to help [him], nothing to look forward to. The only thing I had to look forward to was people abusing me in some shape or form*'. Since being in Grendon however he '*know[s] that there is a light at the end of that tunnel. I'm not saying I've solved all my problems but I know that there is a light at the end*'. P29 credited Grendon with giving him 'hope', making him appreciate that:

> *This isn't the end of the road … this isn't as good as it's going to get. It's going to get better. I will always know that it will get better. I will always know that it can … that I can have a decent life, I can do things with my family and that. It's not all hopeless.*

P08 similarly commented: '*It's all about the future innit? Do you know what I mean? The past is the past. I can't keep living in the past. I have got a future*'.

Inmates at Grendon saw a point to their prison sentence, in sharp contrast to their experiences at previous prisons. P23 asked: '*why should I want to live?*' when '*there's no help and I'm not making no progress and nothing's getting sorted out*'. He '*felt stuck*' which was '*probably the worst thing for me*'. Prisoners viewed the therapeutic process at Grendon as '*pointful*' and '*meaningful*':

> *I'm finally doing something that's worthwhile towards me sentence. After four years of doing bugger all, I'm now doing something that could really help me get out, understand meself, give people the answers they need, give me the answers I need and that's the best thing. (P5)*

Those inmates who had perceptions of their futures that were positive and clearly goal-orientated were the most likely to report a reduction in their SIBs. P22, a chronic self-harmer who had self-injured on a daily basis since the age of 12 but who had not self-harmed for 15 months since arriving at Grendon, described looking forward to getting married when he left prison and jokingly stated: '*My life's finished at 24! No I'm really, really happy about it – about the way things worked out. We're going to get a place of our own, go to college, work*'. Having self-harmed regularly since the age of 15 when he was first sent to prison, P23 described his reduction in self-harm as being directly related to his new-found positive attitude: '*I haven't really thought about self-harm [since my arrival at Grendon]. I wasn't ever put in a situation where I've felt like that … I've started being positive you know in the last couple of years*'.

Improved self-esteem and self-worth

A lack of self-esteem and low self-worth has been recognised as a risk factor for suicide and SIB (Babiker & Arnold, 1997). Liebling's study of young offenders highlighted low self-esteem as being particularly important for repeated self-injury (Liebling, 1992). Grendon's inmates also often explained their suicide attempts and SIB in terms of feelings of worthlessness and low self-confidence. P40 who self-harmed at Grendon by beating himself across the back with electrical cord explains that he self-injured because a therapy session '*made me feel worthless … I was angry at myself … so I stripped a cord off and I strapped meself really bad on me back*'. P25 described his two suicide attempts and three self-harming episodes in one year as being the result of '*no feeling of self-worth … and low self-esteem*'. P19 who saw his prostitution to men when he was 13 years old as being a form of SIB commented: '*I saw myself as worthless … to be used. I just let men abuse me*'.

Staff at Grendon also highlighted feelings of low self-worth as being a serious risk factor for suicide and SIB in prison. S44, in explaining why an inmate had attempted suicide at Grendon, commented that the young prisoner

> '*had the most appalling childhood. He used to suffer nightmares and he just felt that he was worthless and couldn't live with all the negative, all the horror, that people had put into him*'.

Inmates whose SIBs had decreased since arriving at Grendon explained this trend as being associated with increases in their levels of confidence and self-esteem. P22 was a particularly clear example of this. In describing why he no longer self-harms he stated:

> *Self-confidence – that's gone up. More confidence. I've got more confidence in myself. I care about myself more. I care about people out there. I care about me*

missus and me Mum and sisters and Grandma you know. I think about what effect it has on them when I self-harm. The effect self-harm has on other people not just myself.

Reduced anger and frustration

Studies have shown that SIBs are often carried out by individuals in search of psychological relief from emotions such as anger and frustration (Dear *et al.*, 2000; Snow, 2002). Some inmates at Grendon clearly saw their SIB as being related to their anger: '*When I first came here I was a very angry person. I was self-harming a lot*' (P17). Self-harming was a way to '*get rid of all that anger*' (P38), '*feel a hell of a lot better … to me I was getting me anger out in some way*' (P12) and relieve the '*build-up of frustration and anger*' (S45). In one suicide attempt P25 swallowed two four-inch screws and half a battery. He asserted '*it was done in anger. I did a very dangerous thing taking out my frustration and anger inappropriately on myself*'.

Staff perceived self-harming as a method by which inmates could exorcise '*frustration, anger, hurt. Rather than talking about it and getting it out that way they can't and they threaten to hang themselves. They don't know any other way*' (S49). Staff commonly saw SIB as an alternative to violence directed towards others. S45 had to manage the aftermath of an inmate at Grendon who had burnt his forehead '*because he had a massive build-up of frustration and anger and he couldn't get it out in any other way*'. The staff member observed that the inmate '*didn't want to hurt other people but he had to get the anger out of himself and his way of doing that would be to harm himself*'. S41 remarked that inmates frequently self-injured '*rather than taking the anger out on someone else*' whilst S44 saw inmate SIB as '*pre-empting hostility that's gonna hurt people by directing the hostility back in on themselves and hurting themselves first*'. Prisoners too saw their SIB as a redirection of anger that could otherwise have been levelled at another inmate or member of staff:

> *Why do I think I punch the walls and burn myself? Because for me it's safe. If I inflict that anger and anxiety on somebody else's chin or face and if I hit somebody as hard as I'm hitting the walls I would really hurt them and I can't afford for that to happen. And plus it's nobody else's fault that I'm feeling the way I'm feeling.* (P39)

Inmates believed that therapy had helped them reduce their levels of anger. P38 recounted how he was able to '*pretty much leave the violence behind*' whilst P17 stressed that his therapy:

... has come on a long way in the last 12 months ... definitely I've been on a far better level of anger for me as a person. Before it, I used to be up there, down there, up there, down there whereas now it's really levelled out ... so therapy has been working and I've been working at therapy.

Powerlessness and a sense of control

An overwhelming sense of powerlessness and of total dependency on others as a result of an impersonal decision-making process has been associated with an increased risk of suicide and SIB (Bowker, 1980; Johnson, 1976; Kerkhof & Bernasco, 1990). Feeling as though one has no control over one's life direction is frightening, traumatic and, in some cases, completely debilitating. Grendon attempts, in line with therapeutic philosophy, and as far as is possible within a prison, to assuage that sense of powerlessness and of a loss of control. One of the key principles of a therapeutic community is that participants are empowered, through a democratic enfranchisement process, to run parts of the therapeutic wing. Prisoners elect a chairman of the wing and other members of the community to perform certain jobs for which they are held accountable at wing meetings twice a week. Wing members can vote each other off the wing if a breach of the wing rules has occurred. The outcome of these policies is that prisoners feel that they have some power over the direction their life is taking as P4 explained: *'I'm getting control of my life. Not thinking about drink and drugs and self-harm when I'm struggling'.*

Staff/inmate relationships

For those inmates who had been able to reduce their SIB, the most commonly cited reason was the high level of emotional support that they received from staff on their wing. Recognition of these close relationships was often juxtaposed with a 'system' comparison whereby the *'vast majority of staff'* in other establishments *'don't give a toss, they don't care about you'* (P4) and inmates similarly *'go out of their way to antagonise people'* (P1).

Although there are only a few studies investigating the effects of staff/inmate relationships on suicidal behaviours, the evidence from the literature that is available indicates that good relationships with prison officers play an important part in reducing suicide and SIB amongst inmates (Paton & Jenkins, 2005). Biggam and Power (1997) in a study of Scottish young offenders, reported that levels of hopelessness and suicidal thoughts were correlated with the level of social and emotional support received by the inmates from family and friends but also, importantly, from staff. The quality of an inmate's relationship with his Personal Officer was found to be the best predictor of hopelessness. It is implied by the authors that poor relationships with staff lead the inmates to believe that there are no adequate social support mechanisms to deal with their problems, thus increasing suicidal tendencies.

The importance of good staff/prisoner relationships has been recognised by prison services around the world. In Australia, for example, with the aim of reducing suicide, prisons have introduced the concept of 'unit management' which involves the creation of small and manageable offender units which facilitate better interaction between staff and prisoners (McArthur *et al.*, 1999). Similarly, the USA's suicide prevention strategy has included 'unit management' which Hayes (1995) suggests has been important in improving prison staff's relationships with inmates and thus reducing prison suicide. A similar strategy is in place at Grendon. With wings of only 40 men, Grendon's staff are able to cultivate close relationships with their inmates. Prisoners felt that staff '*are approachable*' (P8), '*are always ready to really listen*' (P23) and '*will do things for ya*' (P22). This is in contrast with the 'system' which is '*totally different*' because staff '*do not listen to you*' (P26).

Communication between inmates and staff was seen as the first step towards a meaningful relationship and was an intimate process perceived as 'care', a term which was repeatedly mentioned by the inmates and staff in the context of SIB. A lack of 'care' from close relatives or friends appeared to motivate some SIB. P8 commented that prisoners who self-harmed or attempted suicide '*had a shite upbringing, no family members in contact, they're on their own*'. He explained that they '*wanted love or they wanted care or they just wanted someone to listen to them*'. P26, who had grown up in children's homes and who had self-injured since the age of eight, described how his SIB was motivated by the 'care' that he would receive from staff at the children's homes. He believed that he was '*looking for care and attention*'.

Staff at Grendon see their role both as 'care' providers as well as security officers: '*We sit down and show them care*' (S46). In explaining why suicide and SIB was lower at Grendon than other prisons, S44 stated that it was because '*you actually care for them as human beings*'. Staff '*cared about the lads*' (S44) and were willing to '*give something of themselves to what they do here*' (S46). Inmates saw the largest difference between Grendon's officers and 'system' staff in terms of their ability to listen and 'show care'. Staff in mainstream prisons were portrayed by the inmates as '*screws*[2]

---

[2]'Screws': a derogatory term used by prisoners to describe uniformed prison officers.

who don't care' (P4) but staff at Grendon were universally seen as *'more caring'* (P17):

> *The staff are very different here 'cause they actually care about the inmates – they don't just want to bang you up, they want to see why you've got your problems or how to overcome your problems and support you.*

Staff 'cared' for inmates and, in return, prisoners 'trusted' staff, a term, much like friendship, which is not used lightly or flippantly by inmates: *'Grendon is a good place to trust staff'* (P2). 'Trust' facilitates therapy and lubricates relationships on the wing; its power is illustrated by P22 who cited a lack of trust in staff and inmates as the sole reason explaining why he removed himself from therapy groups:

> *What cemented my decision not to be on groups was 'cause I didn't trust 'em. I didn't trust the people, I didn't trust the wing. Basically that's what it was. It was the wing … the wing in general. I lost all faith in them.*

The outcome of caring and trusting relationships between staff and inmates is that prisoners feel able to talk openly and honestly about their past and present issues: *'You build up a relationship with the staff and trust them and start discussing your problems'* (P9). Being able to talk about problems within the context of a 'safe' environment and 'safe' relationships for many of the inmates was a significant motivating factor behind the reduction in their SIB, especially because for most prisoners, staff often represented violently hated figures of authority such as fathers who physically or sexually abused them. P9 described why he has not self-harmed at Grendon: *'It's talking isn't it? It's support, knowing that people do care. You don't get that a lot in the system'*. Similarly, 'talking' enabled P22, a young arsonist, to dramatically reduce his chronic self-injury:

> *Why don't I self-harm? Because I can talk about it. That's what it is – it's all about talking innit? It is just talking. People are there to talk to you. People I can talk to. It's all about talking with me. That's the only thing that will stop me doing anything – it's talking you know. That's what it is with me – I need to talk.*

Talking appeared to engender a cathartic effect that most inmates found difficult to explain. There seemed to be an element of empowerment associated with talking through one's problems on the wing and in therapy. P8 was able to describe how through talking about his issues he was able to assuage his SIB:

Talking helps doesn't it? Because I used to suppress me feelings and me anger and that. I suppressed me abuse. I suppressed all the anger towards me Dad about him beating me. I suppressed all that a lot. And when you're not talking about it, it just went boom – the lid come off. [After talking] I feel relieved. I feel like I'm carrying a burden and I'm sharing it and getting advice and looking at things different and all that sort of stuff. Just talking helps – I never used to talk to people but now I try and talk to different people as often as I can. I never really talked about myself to anyone before.

Inmate/inmate relationships

Previous research has noted that inmates who self-harm or attempt suicide are likely to have minimal social support networks (Biggam & Power, 1997). Although prisoners did not make 'friends' at Grendon, they did form close relationships with other men. Whilst inmates at other prisons find it difficult to ask for help and guidance from their peers (Borrill et al., 2005), or from staff (Hobbs & Dear, 2001), Grendon's inmates provided each other with a source of emotional support to make the painful disclosures necessary to engage fully with the therapy programme. They encouraged one another, taking comfort in the fact that many inmates had experienced similar problems, abuses and betrayals. P23 remarked that:

There's always inmates that I can go and talk to and they can help me. Cause a lot of stuff has happened to a lot of the boys in here. And they run into a lot of similar problems to me, to what I've come up against. There's always someone who's had that problem and dealt with it so I actually listen to them, to what they did to get through it. That helped me.

Those inmates whose SIB failed to be reduced in severity or frequency at Grendon often did not feel that they had developed meaningful relationships with other inmates. P39 had '*no faith in anybody in here because of the disgusting things that we're all in here for*'. He could see

… no benefit in trying to establish any form of relationship with any inmate in here because we're all very devious and manipulative and acted like animals and any relationship that I would or could build in here I wouldn't.

Conclusion

This chapter drew attention to a puzzle in the Home Office statistics on suicide and SIB: that Grendon's rates of SIB are lower than would be expected given the incarcerated population. Previous research (most notably, for example, Liebling, 1992; Liebling, 1999) has identified the importance of environmental, situational and relational aspects in an individual's decision to self-harm or attempt suicide. In particular, the distressing nature of the prison environment – bullying, violence and victimisation, guilt, boredom and the deprivation of liberty, for instance – has been highlighted. By interviewing men with a wide variety of SIBs it has been possible to show that the prison environment itself can contribute both to the cause, and alleviation, of SIB. In discussing their SIB, inmates identified several factors that had contributed to the cessation or diminution of their behaviours whilst at Grendon. The prison's unique therapeutic environment makes the extrapolation of these results to other prisons difficult, but it is hoped that prison governors and the Home Office take notice of the factors that prisoners and staff argue both trigger and assuage the self-destructive actions that cause so much misery to inmates, their families and prison staff.

References

Babiker, G. & Arnold, L. (1997). *The Language of Injury*. Leicester: Blackwell.

Beck, A., Brown, G. & Steer, R. (1989). Prediction of eventual suicide in psychiatric inpatients by clinical ratings of hopelessness. *Journal of Clinical and Consulting Psychology, 57*, 309–310.

Beck, A.T., Weissman, A., Lester, D. & Trexler, L. (1974). The measurement of pessimism: The Hopelessness Scale. *Journal of Clinical and Consulting Psychology, 42*, 861–865.

Beck, G. (1992). *Bullying, Suicide and Self-injury*. Paper presented at Her Majesty's Young Offender Institute Thorn Cross.

Biggam, F. & Power, K. (1997). Social support and psychological distress in a group of incarcerated young offenders. *International Journal of Offender Therapy and Comparative Criminology, 41*, 213–230.

Blaauw, E., Kraij, V., Arensman, E. *et al.* (2002). Traumatic life events and suicidal risk among jail inmates: the influence of types of events, time period and significant others. *Journal of Traumatic Stress, 15*, 9–16.

Blaauw, E., Winkel, F. & Kerkhof, A. (2001). Bullying and suicidal behaviour in jails. *Criminal Justice and Behaviour, 28*, 279–299.

Blud, L. (1997). Screening for suicide risk in young offenders. *Inside Psychology*, *3*, 115–120.

Borrill, J., Snow, L., Medlicott, D. *et al.* (2005). Learning from near misses: interviews with women who survived an incident of severe self-harm. *Howard League Journal*, *44*, 57–69.

Bowker, L.H. (1980). *Prison Victimisation*. New York: Elsevier.

Dear, G.E., Thomson, D.M. & Hills, A.M. (2000). Self-harm in prison: manipulators can also be suicide attempters. *Criminal Justice and Behaviour*, *27*, 160–175.

Department of Health (2002). *National Suicide Prevention Strategy for England and Wales*. London: Department of Health.

Fazel, S. & Benning, R. (2006). Natural deaths in male prisoners: a 20-year mortality study. *European Journal of Public Health*, *16*, 441–444.

Fazel, S., Benning, R. & Danesh, J. (2005). Suicides in male prisoners in England and Wales, 1978–2003. *Lancet*, *366*, 1301–1302.

Hawton, K. & Catalâan, J. (1987). *Attempted Suicide: A Practical Guide to its Nature and Management*. Oxford: Oxford University Press.

Hayes, L. (1995). *Prison Suicide: An Overview and Guide to Prevention*. US Department of Justice, National Institute of Corrections.

HM Prison Service (2002). *Suicide and Self-harm Prevention. Prison Orders*. London: HM Prison Service.

Hobbs, G. & Dear, G. (2001). Prisoners' perceptions of prison officers as sources of support. *Journal of Offender Rehabilitation*, *31*, 127–142.

Howard League for Penal Reform (2005). *Briefing Paper on Prison Overcrowding and Suicide*. London: The Howard League for Penal Reform.

Johnson, R. (1976). *Culture and Crisis in Confinement*. Lexington: Heath.

Kariminia, A., Butler, T.G., Corben, S.P. *et al.* (2007). Extreme cause-specific mortality in a cohort of adult prisoners – 1988 to 2002: a data-linkage study. *International Journal of Epidemiology*, *36*, 310–316.

Kerkhof, A. & Bernasco, W. (1990). Suicide behaviour in jails and prisons in the Netherlands. *Suicide and Life-Threatening Behaviour*, *20*, 123–137.

Leese, M., Thomas, S. & Snow L. (2006). An ecological study of factors associated with rates of self-inflicted death in prisons in England and Wales. *International Journal of Law and Psychiatry*, *29*, 355–360.

Liebling, A. (1992). *Suicides in Prison*. London: Routledge.

Liebling, A. (1999). Prisoner suicide and prisoner coping. *Crime and Justice*, *26*, 283–359.

Liebling, A. & Krarup, H. (1993). *Suicide Attempts and Self-injury in Male Prisons*. London: Home Office.

McArthur, M., Camilleri, P. & Webb, H. (1999). Strategies for managing suicide and self-harm in prison. *Trends and Issues in Crime and Justice, no. 125*.

Paton, J. & Jenkins, R. (2005). Suicide and suicide attempts in prisons. In K. Hawton (Ed.) *Prevention and Treatment of Suicidal Behaviour: From Science to Practice*. Oxford: Oxford University Press.

Power, K.G. & Spencer, A.G. (1987). Parasuicidal behaviour of detained Scottish young offenders. *International Journal of Offender Therapy and Comparative Criminology, 31*, 227–235.

Rivlin, A. (2006). *Suicide and Parasuicide at a Therapeutic Community Prison for Men.* Unpublished master's thesis, Brasenose College, University of Oxford.

Rivlin, A. (2007). Self-harm and suicide at Grendon Therapeutic Community Prison. *Prison Service Journal*, 34–38.

Safer Custody Group (2006). *Recorded Self-harm in the Prison Service 2003–2005.* London: Safer Custody Group, Research and Development Network.

Snow, L. (2002). Prisoners' motives for self-injury and attempted suicide. *British Journal of Forensic Practise, 4*, 18–29.

Sykes, G. (1958). *Society of Captives: A Study of a Maximum Security Prison.* New Jersey: Princeton University Press.

Towl, G.J. (1997). *Suicide and Self-injury in Prisons: Research Directions in the 1990s.* Leicester: British Psychological Society.

Chapter 17

Changes in Prison Offending Among Residents of a Prison-Based Therapeutic Community

Margaret Newton

Abstract

Grendon has a very low rate of prison adjudications, though residents have a substantial history of offences in their previous prisons, suggesting that the Grendon regime facilitates the safe and effective management of a difficult group of prisoners. For those men who move on to other prisons from Grendon, the adjudication rate then increases to a level that is still significantly lower than the initial rate, and this may reflect a degree of therapeutic success. Data for non-Grendon prisoners suggests that the Grendon pattern is not just a consequence of maturation or the stage men are at in their sentences. As initial adjudication rate is related to reconviction, it is suggested that it may make a useful additional variable in studies matching for risk of reconviction. In addition, further work should explore empirically whether change in adjudication rate indicates change in risk of reconviction.

Grendon and the Emergence of Forensic Therapeutic Communities: Developments in Research and Practice
Edited by Richard Shuker and Elizabeth Sullivan
© 2010 John Wiley & Sons, Ltd.

Introduction

Inmates of any prison in England are bound by a series of rules, and if they break these, they are liable to be placed on report and adjudicated by the Governor. Examples of rules include assaults on staff or other prisoners, disobeying lawful orders, testing positive on mandatory drug tests and failure to comply with prison good order and discipline. Prison offending at Grendon is of interest for two reasons. One is as a measure of the successful management of a difficult section of the long-term prison population. Does Grendon work well as a prison, providing an orderly and safe environment within which the therapeutic communities can function? The other relates to the long-term goal of reducing re-offending. This has been, and continues to be, the subject of direct research reported elsewhere (Marshall, 1997; Newton, 1971; Robertson & Gunn, 1987; Taylor, 2000). However, it seems reasonable to assume that if residence in the therapeutic communities is to make a sufficient impact on some of the men for them to desist from re-offending after eventual release, then it should be possible to record some short and longer-term changes in behaviour, while they are still at Grendon or in other prisons. Previous research has shown that men certainly *say* different things about themselves after a period at Grendon (Newton, 1998), but do they also *behave* differently?

This research focuses on analysis of prison adjudications, i.e. the official prison procedure for dealing with prisoners who have broken prison rules. The reason for this is that any claim that an aspect of behaviour is different at Grendon, and represents an improvement, has to be backed up by equivalent observations of the same men before they arrived, otherwise any apparent differences may be the result of selective attention or a policy of admitting men who have previously been well-behaved in prison. The system of prison adjudications provides a service-wide process for monitoring rule breaking that is consistently recorded and is now accessible within prisons through an electronic database of prisoner information (IIS).

Cullen (1994) reported that Grendon had one of the lowest rates of Governor's Reports (i.e. adjudications) of any prison of its category in the country, and it had been consistent over the previous three decades. That did not seem to be because Grendon had selected a particularly well-behaved group of prisoners: Grendon men then had an average number of reports in the six months *prior* to arrival at Grendon that was nearly seven times higher than the average number of reports in the first six months *at* Grendon. Again, this phenomenon had first been noticed decades earlier (Newton, 1971). In a different setting, Taylor (2003) reported a rather similar analysis of violent incident rates in the Dangerous Severe Personality Disorder Unit at HMP Whitemoor. He found that 55 prisoners who had volunteered for the pilot programme (of assessment in a therapeutic environment) recorded 10 violent incidents over the 16-week assessment period, compared to the 37 which would have been expected on the basis of their records prior to admission to the unit. Cook (1989) carried out a similar analysis of the Barlinnie Special Unit. However, none of those studies followed the men up after they had left the units in question. A comparison with the subsequent adjudication records of men who have moved on from Grendon to other prisons should indicate how far any apparent change endures or is situation-specific. Comparison with the adjudication records of a similar, non-Grendon sample of men at an equivalent stage in their sentences should show whether changes are due to maturation or the stage a man is at in his sentence. Analysis of change in relation to length of residence should indicate whether any effect is dependent on the time a man spends in the TC, in parallel with changes in psychological test scores (Newton 1998) and differences in reconviction rates (Marshall, 1997). Finally, the relationship between initial level of prison offending and reconviction should throw light on the significance of prison offending as a predictive factor for re-offending, and its possible value as an indicator of dynamic risk.

One objection to using total adjudication rate as a universal index of prison offending is that for less serious offences, prison officers are less likely to put a man on report at Grendon than in other prisons. It is therapeutic community policy to deal with everyday transgressions by making men accountable to the community and dealing with them in group therapy, so it follows that some infractions will not appear on the adjudication record at Grendon. However, if a man behaves violently, he will be put on report at Grendon the same as in any other prison, and if he has a positive mandatory drugs test or is found to possess drugs, he will be put on report just as in any other prison. Therefore, comparing adjudication rates for violent, and possibly also drugs-related offences, should give a true indication of between-prison differences in prisoner behaviour, cutting out the effect of dealing with some relatively minor offences in different ways at Grendon, and also acknowledging the possibility that some kinds of minor rule-breaking in the prison world might not necessarily be regarded as examples of antisocial behaviour.

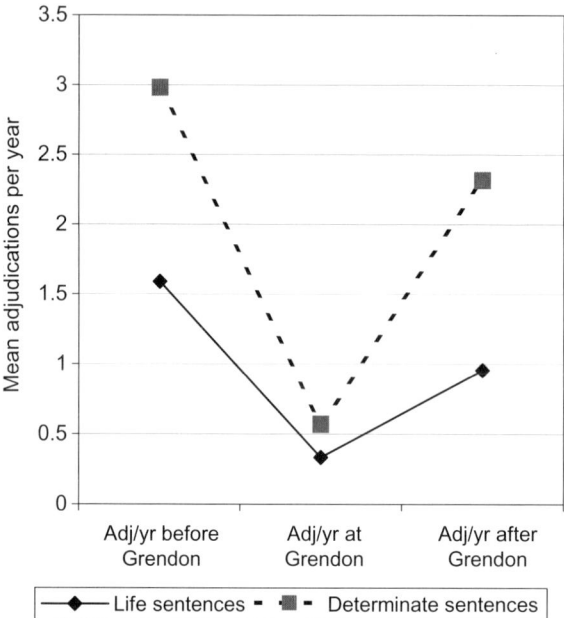

Figure 17.1   Mean adjudication rates before admission to Grendon, at Grendon, and after transfer to other prisons

Method and Results

The number of prison adjudications per 100 population in 2002 was calculated from Grendon adjudication records and compared with published figures (Prison Statistics, 2002) for all male closed training prisons. Including all offences, the training prison adjudication rate (109) was five times as high as Grendon's (22), and for violent offences, the training prison rate (7) was seven times as high as Grendon's (1).

The rate of prison adjudications per 100 men per year at Grendon was compared with the adjudication rate for the same men on the same sentence before transfer to Grendon. The rate for all offences was eight times higher prior to Grendon (167 compared to 22), staff assaults were ten times higher (5 to 0.5), prisoner assaults were twelve times higher (6 to 0.5) and drug-related offences were twelve times higher (24 to 2).

Using IIS as the source for all data[2], average adjudication rates at Grendon were compared with the pre-Grendon rate and, for men who went on to other prisons from Grendon, with the post-Grendon rate. Figure 17.1

[2]For this and all subsequent analyses.

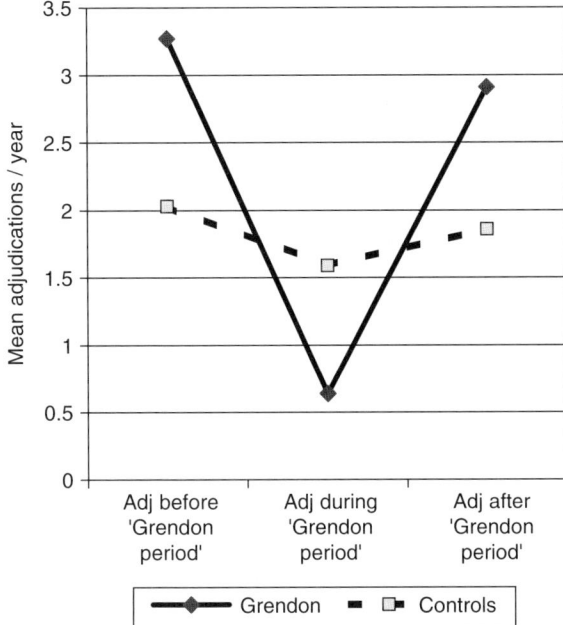

Figure 17.2   Mean adjudication rates for Grendon men serving determinate sentences, and a control group of non-Grendon men

shows the adjudication rates for men transferred to other prisons at the end of their time at Grendon. (Values for pre-Grendon and Grendon adjudications of men released *directly* from Grendon are not shown but are similar to those for men serving life sentences.)

For the men released directly from Grendon (not shown), the reduction in adjudication rate, from 1.65 before Grendon to 0.23 at Grendon, is statistically significant ($N = 26$, paired samples $t = 2.9$, $p = .08$). For men who went on to other prisons after leaving Grendon, adjudication rates in the periods before and *following* residence at Grendon were also significantly different (for men serving life sentences, $N = 120$, $t = 4.6$, $p = .000$ and for men serving determinate sentences, $N = 181$, $t = 2.4$, $p = .015$), the magnitude of the mean difference being similar for men serving life or determinate sentences.

From the sample of men serving determinate sentences and transferred to other prisons on leaving Grendon, 93 men were matched one-to-one on criminological variables with men from the prisoners index released in the same year. Data on adjudication rates was obtained for each man in the control group, for the period before, during and after the relevant dates and compared with his 'matched pair' at Grendon. Figure 17.2 shows that

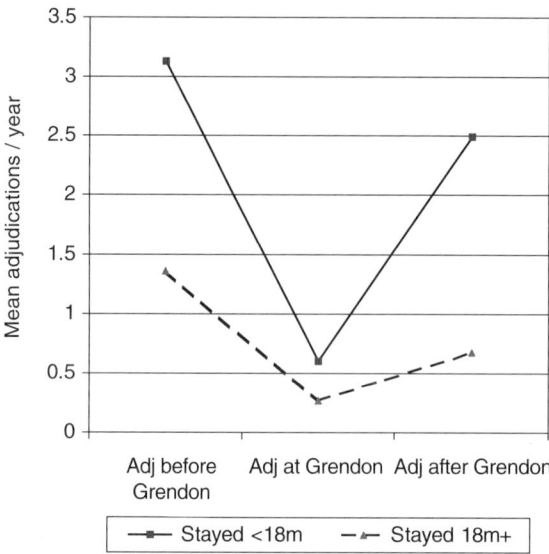

Figure 17.3   Mean adjudication rates according to length of stay at Grendon

the marked reduction in adjudication rates in the Grendon sample is not paralleled by a similar reduction in the control group at an equivalent point in sentence (the reductions in mean adjudication rate for the control group were not statistically significant). Similarly, for the sample of 26 men released directly from Grendon, the significant reduction in adjudication rates at Grendon was not paralleled by a significant reduction in its control group. Adjudication rates for the Grendon and control groups are significantly different from each other at each of the three points.

While Grendon does not have a fixed programme or 'treatment length', research (Genders & Player, 1995; Marshall, 1997) has suggested 18 months as the minimum period necessary for Grendon to make an impact on risk of reconviction. The sample of men who had gone on to other prisons was divided into 182 men who had stayed at Grendon for under 18 months and 119 men who had stayed at least 18 months. Mean adjudication rates are shown in figure 17.3. The difference between mean pre-Grendon and post-Grendon adjudication rates was statistically significant and similar for both groups.

For 224 Grendon men, and separately for 158 men taken from the control group, mean initial adjudication rates for men reconvicted within four years were compared with those for men not reconvicted in four years. For both Grendon and non-Grendon samples, the initial adjudication rate was significantly higher for reconvicted men.

Discussion

First of all, this study confirms Cullen's (1994) results and shows that the total adjudication rate at Grendon is one fifth of the rate for prisons of a similar category (closed training prisons), and that the overall adjudication rate for Grendon men was eight times higher before they came to Grendon. If attention is restricted to prison offences involving violence, staff or prisoner assaults or drugs-related offences, the difference between the Grendon rates and those with which it is being compared are even greater. As the *overall* adjudication rate is not exaggerating those differences, it should provide an appropriate index for comparisons of prison offending. The study also highlights that mean adjudication rate falls at Grendon, reaching a fairly similar low level whether it started off very high (men serving determinate sentences who were subsequently transferred from Grendon to other prisons) or not so high (men serving life sentences and men released directly from Grendon). After transfer from Grendon back into the rest of the prison system, adjudication rate rises again to a level that is proportional to, but significantly lower than, the original level. That the same pattern is observed in men serving determinate as well as life sentences, suggests that the changes are not just a consequence of life sentenced men's desire to get a good report when their progress is reviewed.

Is the improvement in adjudication rates something to do with Grendon, or can it be attributed to maturation, or perhaps a tendency for long-term prisoners to get into trouble early in their sentences, settle down to a quiet life in the middle and then get into trouble again as release approaches? The results suggest that we are not looking at a general pattern for prisoners, as the changes in the control group's adjudication rate are neither statistically significant nor substantial. Something else which might at least partly explain away the Grendon results is the phenomenon of statistical regression. As Taylor (2003) points out in relation to his own study, high pre-test scores can often be lower at the post-test stage simply because the pre-test scores are so extreme. This may apply in the present study, though the magnitude of the change for Grendon men and the absence of similar, significant results for the non-Grendon men suggest that even if statistical regression can account for some of the change, some other process must surely also be at work. It therefore seems reasonable to conclude that the low adjudication rate at Grendon shows that residents are being managed more successfully than at other prisons, and that a suitable environment has been created for the therapeutic work. The low adjudication rate at Grendon would in addition be compatible both with a treatment effect and with a temporary, situational adaptation. However, the improvement in *pre-post* adjudication rates suggests that relatively enduring change has occurred in some residents, and this may provide better evidence of therapeutic success.

The high levels of the pre-Grendon adjudication rates in figure 17.1 show that the reason for Grendon's low adjudication rates in relation to other prisons is not because it selects particularly well-behaved men. On the contrary, the high adjudication rate is compatible with, and may be related to, the high level of psychopathy among men at Grendon, where rate of adjudications has already been shown to be significantly related to psychopathy (Shine & Hobson, 2000), as it is elsewhere (Clark, 2000). Figure 17.2 suggests that even when Grendon men are compared to prisoners who are similar in terms of sentence, criminal histories, age, offence prediction scores and the like, the Grendon men have a significantly higher initial adjudication rate. However, one cannot simply extrapolate the comparative data in figure 17.2 to include *all* Grendon receptions, as this sample does not include men released directly from Grendon (about a quarter of men who started therapy, with a prior adjudication rate which was not significantly different from their controls[3]) or men serving life sentences (about a third of men starting therapy, and for whom this study had no comparison group). Considering the Grendon population as a whole, the best interpretation of the data may be that for men serving determinate sentences, Grendon residents have a prior adjudication rate that is higher than one would expect on the basis of criminal history, (though not as high as in figure 17.2), and there is no reason to expect the situation to be different for residents serving life sentences.

Research generally suggests that there may be more evidence of change, especially in criminogenic risk, in men who have been resident at Grendon for over a year or 18 months, although some improvement, in variables such as emotional stability, can be observed in a shorter period (Newton, 1998; Shuker & Newton, 2008). This study shows that both short-term increase in conformity (at Grendon) and long-term improvement (at subsequent prisons) are apparent in men who stay under 18 months as well as those who stay longer. This suggests that Grendon starts to makes an impact on prison behaviour quite quickly, which you would expect if the change were situational, but there is also an enduring element of behaviour change in shorter-stay as well as longer-stay residents. Such a change would be consistent with therapeutic goals such as reduced impulsiveness, aggressive behaviour and anti-authority attitudes, which are generally regarded as dynamic risk factors for offending.

Would rate of prison offending make a useful addition to factors included in risk prediction? Figure 17.4 demonstrates that initial adjudication rates

---

[3]Grendon mean 1.7 compared to control mean 2.1, $N = 26$.

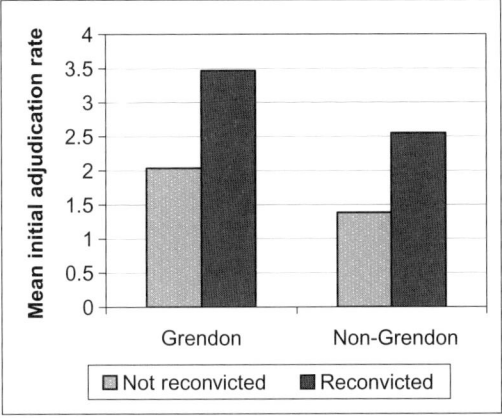

Figure 17.4   Mean initial adjudication rate by reconviction in four years

are predictive of reconviction in both the Grendon and non-Grendon samples and also highlights that adjudication rates differ significantly between Grendon and non-Grendon samples that have already been carefully matched for actuarial risk. Perhaps this reflects levels of psychopathy, which are high in the Grendon population, and which are known to predict both reconviction and prison adjudications (Clark, 2000). It is possible that the inclusion of adjudication rates would improve the accuracy of risk prediction equations, and particularly of matching exercises in reconviction studies with this kind of population.

It is also possible that adjudication rates might sometimes provide a useful measure of change following interventions in the course of imprisonment. As discussed earlier, there are problems interpreting change when a prisoner has moved from an ordinary prison into a therapeutic environment, but they can be overcome by recording *post-treatment* rates after return to normal prisons. Of course, not all prisoners start off with high adjudication rates (for example, sex offenders as a group, and paedophiles in particular, tend to have low mean adjudication rates[4]), and some residents may readily become institutionalised, without any increase in their ability to cope with the pressures of their environment outside. One can also imagine individuals (possibly some psychopaths) who have the ability to conform when necessary as part of a long-term strategy to get parole. Despite that, as initial adjudication rates predict reconviction for the

---

[4]From the Grendon database, paedophiles have a significantly lower prior adjudication rate of 1.0 per year ($N = 104$), compared to the non-sex-offenders' 2.6 per year, ($N = 926$) $t = 7.429$, $p = .000$.

population as a whole, it might be appropriate to consider changes in adjudication rates in an outcome study as an indicator of changes in risk. However, before that could be done with confidence, it would be necessary to demonstrate empirically whether *changes* in adjudication rates are indeed linked to changes in risk.

Conclusion

- Adjudication rates at Grendon are much lower than in prisons of a similar type and much lower than you would expect on the basis of the men's adjudication histories, suggesting that a difficult section of the prison population is being managed successfully.
- Post-Grendon adjudication rates are lower than pre-Grendon rates, so ex-residents continue to be rather easier to manage after transfer to other prisons.
- As a measure of therapeutic progress, reduction in adjudication rates at Grendon may provide behavioural confirmation of reduction in criminogenic factors such as impulsiveness, aggression and anti-authority attitudes, which have already been indicated by research using test scores and interviews.
- Pre-Grendon to post-Grendon differences, though smaller, suggest that some degree of enduring change has occurred in residents, rather than just an immediate reaction to a changed environment.
- As (initial) adjudication rate is predictive of reconviction, and seems not to be completely accounted for by the usual actuarial variables, it may provide a useful additional factor to improve prediction or matching for risk.
- As adjudication rate predicts reconviction, change in adjudication rate might indicate change in risk, and further work should be directed towards testing this hypothesis.

Acknowledgements

Matt Erickson of the Home Office Research, Development and Statistics Directorate, who supplied the reconviction data, and members of the Research and Development Unit at Grendon, particularly Natalie Ker Watson and Kim Liddiard.

References

Clark, D. (2000). The use of the Hare Psychopathy Checklist Revised to predict offending and institutional misconduct in the English penal system. *Prison Research and Development Bulletin 9*, 10–14. London: Home Office.

Cook, D.J. (1989). Containing violent prisoners; an analysis of the Barlinnie Special Unit. *British Journal of Criminology, 29* (2), 129–143.

Cullen, J.E. (1994). Grendon: the therapeutic community that works. *Therapeutic Communities for Offenders, 15*, 301–311.

Genders, E. & Player, E. (1995). *Grendon: A Study of a Therapeutic Prison.* Oxford: Clarendon Press.

Marshall, P. (1997). *A reconviction study of HMP Grendon therapeutic community. Research Findings, 53.* London: Home Office Research, Development & Statistics Directorate.

Newton, M. (1971). Reconviction after treatment at Grendon. *Chief Psychologist Report Series B, 1.* Prison Department, Home Office. (Abridged version in Shine, J. (Ed.) (2000). *A Compilation of Grendon Research.* Leyhill Press. Available from Psychology Unit, HMP Grendon, Grendon Underwood, Aylesbury, HP18 0TL.)

Newton, M. (1998). Changes in measures of personality, hostility and locus of control during residence in a prison therapeutic community. *Legal and Criminological Psychology, 3*, 209–223.

Prison Statistics England and Wales (2002). London: HM Stationery Office.

Robertson, G. & Gunn, J. (1987). A ten-year follow-up of men discharged from Grendon prison. *British Journal of Psychiatry, 151*, 674–678.

Shine, J. & Hobson, J. (2000). Institutional behaviour and time in treatment among psychopaths admitted to a prison-based therapeutic community. *Medicine, Science and Law, 40* (4), 327–335.

Shuker, R. & Newton, M. (2008). Treatment outcome following intervention in a prison-based therapeutic community: a study of the relationship between reduction in risk and improved psychological wellbeing. *British Journal of Forensic Practice, 10* (3), 33–44.

Taylor, R. (2000). *A seven-year reconviction study of HMP Grendon therapeutic community. Research Findings, 115.* London: Home Office Research, Development & Statistics Directorate.

Taylor, R. (2003). *An assessment of violent incident rates in the dangerous severe personality disorder unit at HMP Whitemoor. Research Findings, 210.* London: Home Office Research, Development & Statistics Directorate.

Chapter 18

Changes in Interpersonal Relating Following Therapeutic Community Treatment at HMP Grendon[1]

Richard Shuker and Michelle Newberry

Abstract

Although prison-based therapeutic communities have conceptualised their treatment model as one incorporating social learning and interpersonal approaches, little research has been conducted to evaluate how far they are effective in modifying maladaptive interpersonal styles. This study aimed to evaluate the efficacy in promoting adaptive styles of interpersonal relating. Changes in relating style were measured over an 18-month period during treatment at Grendon. The third version of the *Person's Relating to Others Questionnaire* (PROQ3; Birtchnell *et al.*, submitted), a measure of interpersonal relating styles, was administered to 130 prisoners on arrival at Grendon, after 9 months and after 18 months. Significant improvements in relating styles were demonstrated after 9 months and improvement was maintained between the 9 and 18-month intervals. Twenty-two per cent of participants showed statistically reliable improvement in terms

[1]The research presented in this chapter is part of a larger study reported in Birtchnell, J., Shuker, R., Newberry, M. & Duggan, C. (2008). An assessment of change in negative relating in two male forensic therapy samples using the Person's Relating to Others Questionnaire (PROQ) [Electronic version]. *Journal of Forensic Psychiatry and Psychology*, 1–21. DOI: 10.1080/14789940802542840 Reproduced by permission of the publisher (Taylor & Francis Ltd, http://www.tandf.co.uk/journals). Article available at http://www.informaworld.com

Grendon and the Emergence of Forensic Therapeutic Communities: Developments in Research and Practice
Edited by Richard Shuker and Elizabeth Sullivan
© 2010 John Wiley & Sons, Ltd.

of their PROQ3 total score after 18 months. It is concluded that the therapeutic community treatment model at HMP Grendon is effective in producing positive changes in interpersonal relating in personality disordered offenders.

Introduction

Prison-based therapeutic communities (TCs) have consistently shown that men who participate in interventions demonstrate improvements in mental health and psychological well-being, whilst at the same time showing reductions in antisocial attitudes, hostility and impulsivity (Gunn & Robertson, 1982; Newton, 1998; Shuker & Newton, 2008). The efficacy of democratic TCs has also been demonstrated in non-secure settings for personality-disordered patients (Chiesa & Fonagy, 2000; Dolan *et al.*, 1992; Warren *et al.*, 2006), where reductions in psychological distress, anxiety, impulsivity and self-harm have consistently been reported.

Prison-based TCs have also demonstrated improvements in behaviour. Lees *et al.* (1999) reported fewer assaults and serious incidents than were expected and Newton (2006) illustrated significant improvements in behaviour compared with behaviour exhibited prior to joining, with improvements in behaviour being maintained following transfer from the TC to a mainstream prison. Newton (2006) also demonstrated significant reductions in self-harm and drug use during intervention in a prison-based TC.

Whilst therapeutic communities have conceptualised their treatment model as one incorporating cognitive and interpersonal approaches, little research has been conducted to evaluate how far they are effective in modifying and adapting interpersonal styles or promoting competence in relationships. This study aimed to evaluate the interpersonal dimension of therapeutic community intervention and the extent to which the treatment model adopted can be considered applicable when targeting deficits in interpersonal relating.

Personality disorder and interpersonal relating

Therapeutic communities have demonstrated their efficacy in promoting improved psychological and social functioning with people with personality disorder, and Warren *et al.* (2003) suggests that TCs hold the most promise in the development of interventions for personality-disordered people, especially where they are able to incorporate components from different treatment modalities. A number of theorists have suggested that personality disorder can be construed in interpersonal terms (Blackburn, 1998; Kiesler, 1996), and whilst TCs have evaluated cognitive, attitudinal and behavioural change, the interpersonal model which underpins the work with personality-disordered offenders is yet to be fully evaluated.

Interpersonal theory and personality disorder

Interpersonal theory deals with an individual's characteristic patterns of interaction, which vary along the dimensions of dominance/submission and hostility/friendliness. The two dimensions on which interpersonal behaviour is classified form part of the five-factor model of personality (McCrae & Costa, 1990), which suggests that each person has a preferred pattern of interpersonal behaviour, with pathological and maladaptive behaviour seen as an over-rigid and extreme style of relating. The theory suggests that in general, people with rigid, inflexible personalities have more problems and that personality disorder can be construed as an extreme variation of the person's preferred interpersonal style.

An alternative theory that attempts to make sense of deficits in interpersonal relating is relating theory (Birtchnell, 1996). This theory proposes that humans have an innate tendency to strive towards four principal relating objectives, with each particular relating objective having advantages under certain circumstances. Birtchnell proposed that people relate to achieve interpersonal objectives (which he considers to represent basic needs) along the dimensions of *upperness* (relating from a position of authority or power) and *lowerness* (relating from a position of neediness or subordination) on one dimension, and closeness and distance on the other. Relating theory proposes that these dimensions represent the fundamental axis of relating. In relating theory (as in interpersonal theory) intermediate positions are present. For example, upper relating can also consist of upper *distant* and upper *close* (in addition to upper *neutral*). Figure 18.1 represents the theoretical structure known as the interpersonal octagon, consisting of the eight relating positions which are possible within the two intersecting axes (where the distant close axis is represented by a horizontal axis and the upper lower axis by a vertical axis).

Birtchnell considers that each relating style carries, under certain circumstances, its advantages (see figure 18.2), and relating theory suggests that positive relating reflects competence in achieving relating objectives, whereas negative relating reflects incompetence. Disorders in relating arise

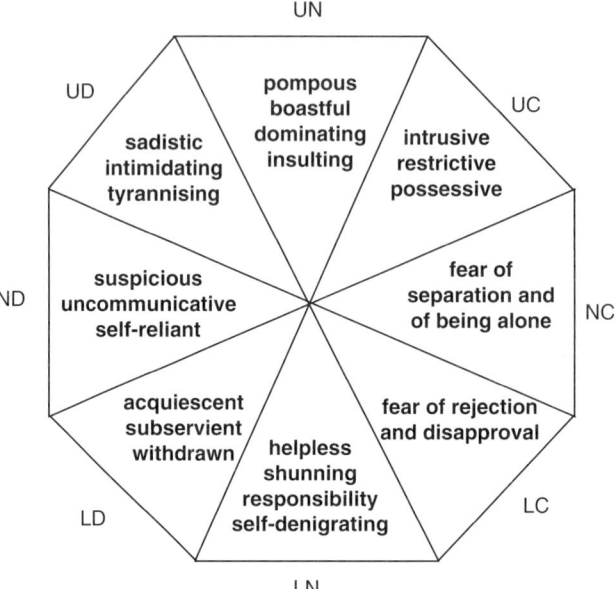

UN

UD

pompous
boastful
dominating
insulting

UC

sadistic
intimidating
tyrannising

intrusive
restrictive
possessive

ND

suspicious
uncommunicative
self-reliant

fear of
separation and
of being alone

NC

acquiescent
subservient
withdrawn

helpless
shunning
responsibility
self-denigrating

fear of rejection
and disapproval

LD

LC

LN

Figure 18.1   Negative forms of relating. The pairs of initial letters are abbreviations for the full names of the octants. The diagram first appeared in Birtchnell, J. (1994). The interpersonal octagon: an alternative to the interpersonal circle. *Human Relations, 47*(5), pp. 518 and 524. © The Tavistock Institute. Reprinted by Permission of SAGE

Relating style	Advantages
Closeness	Involvement, co-operation, sharing
Distance	Separation, development of own ideas
Upperness	Success, leadership, knowledge
Lowerness	Accepting advice, support, protection

Figure 18.2   Advantages of different relating styles

where an individual lacks competence in one or more relating objectives either by avoiding a particular relating style or by attempting to achieve the objective using inappropriate means, for example, attempting to achieve closeness through being domineering or controlling.

An incompetent relater will avoid certain types of relating. Incompetence is also indicated where an individual attempts to achieve relating objectives using counterproductive means, for example where the objective of getting close is attempted by being forceful and domineering. To be a competent relater an individual needs to possess the skills to relate effectively in all positions. The *Person's Relating to Others Questionnaire* (PROQ) was designed as a measure of negative relating with its items corresponding to the eight areas within the interpersonal octagon.

Personality disorder and negative relating

Personality disorders can be construed as disorders of relating (Blackburn, 1998; Kiesler, 1996 – see Shuker, chapter 7 this edition). This has implications for the understanding of the development of particular disorders and, more importantly implications for treatment where specific deficits can form the focus for intervention, and where particular methods can be used to address affective, social and interpersonal needs. Research has suggested that PROQ scores have strong correlations with DSM-IV personality disorders, particularly avoidant, dependent, schizoid, histrionic and dependent personality disorder (Birtchnell & Shine, 2000). Whilst this suggests a significant association between negative relating and personality disorder, further work remains necessary to assess the extent to which particular areas of relating incompetence tend to be focused upon in therapy.

Aims of the Study

The main aims of the present study were to explore: a) whether the PROQ3 scores of prisoners who were returned prematurely from the therapeutic community to their prison of origin differed from prisoners who were not, and b) whether scores registered significant improvement over the course of therapy. The study also examined whether prisoners received higher mean PROQ3 scores than a non-prisoner population sample and a different prison therapeutic community sample. It was hypothesised that the mean scores of prisoners would be higher than those of non-prisoners and that they would reduce significantly over the course of therapy.

Method

Participants

Participants of the study were 410 prisoners who completed the PROQ3 upon admission to Grendon therapeutic community prison. The age range of the sample was 21 to 65 (M = 34.4, SD = 8.2). Following admission, prisoners were transferred to one of five therapy wings where they completed the PROQ3 again after 9 months and 18 months. Permission to conduct the research was obtained from the Prison Research Advisory Group and participants were informed of the nature of the research before being asked to give their written consent to participate.

At Grendon, non-compliant or unsuitable prisoners are returned prematurely to their place of referral. There were 172 prisoners tested on admission and at 9 months, 141 prisoners tested on admission and at 18 months, and 130 prisoners tested on all three occasions. The present sample was compared with a population sample of English men (n = 59) who completed the PROQ3 for the purposes of an earlier study (Birtchnell *et al.*, submitted) as well as a sample of men (n = 234) who were admitted to another prison therapeutic community.

Measures

The third version of the PROQ – the PROQ3 (Birtchnell *et al.*, submitted) – was used to assess the relating styles of prisoners in the present study. The PROQ3 has fewer items than the PROQ2 (Birtchnell & Evans, 2004 – 48 items compared to 96 items). The PROQ3 items were derived from the PROQ2 items that loaded most heavily on the extracted factors and that loaded only on one factor. Like the PROQ2, the PROQ3 has 8 scales that are based upon the 8 negative octants of the interpersonal octagon, as illustrated in figure 18.1. Each scale includes unscored, positive items which serve to increase motivation and each item has 4 response options: *Nearly always true, Quite often true, Sometimes true* and *Rarely true,* which yield a score of 3, 2, 1 and 0, respectively. The maximum score for each scale is 15. The higher the total score indicated by the PROQ3, the more relating deficits the respondent has. Computer software is used to score the PROQ3 (obtained from the instrument's developer), which provides a numerical printout of scores as well as a visual representation of scores in the form of shaded areas of the octants of the octagon.

There is factor analytic support for most of the 8 scales of the PROQ3 and they are reported to have good internal reliabilities (Birtchnell *et al.*, submitted). In addition, correlations between the PROQ3 scales are consistent with underlying theory and they correlate positively and meaningfully with scales of measures based upon the interpersonal circle (Birtchnell *et al.*, submitted). Furthermore, the mean scores for psychotherapy patients have been found to be significantly higher (indicative of more problems) than those for non-patients, and scores on most scales have been found to improve significantly during the course of therapy (Birtchnell, 2002).

In an attempt to support the validity of the PROQ3, another measure was administered to prisoners on admission and discharge. The measure selected for this purpose was the *Hostility and Direction of Hostility Questionnaire* (HDHQ; Caine *et al.*, 1967), which is the measure administered to prisoners at Grendon that comes closest to being a measure of negative relating. It has five subscales: AH (urge to Act out Hostility), CO (Criticism of Others), PH (Projected Delusional or Paranoid Hostility), SC (Self Criticism) and DG (Delusional Guilt). There are also scales of outwardly directed and inwardly directed hostility. The HDHQ was administered to 56 prisoners on admission and discharge.

Procedure

The PROQ3 was administered to prisoners on admission, after 9 months and after 18 months. Mean scores and standard deviations were calculated for the sample at all stages. Independent samples *t*-tests were performed to compare PROQ3 scores between samples, and paired-samples *t*-tests were conducted to compare PROQ3 scores of the samples at different times. The *reliable change index* (RCI; Jacobson & Truax, 1991) was used to calculate statistically reliable changes in PROQ3 scores over time. All analyses were performed using SPSS version 12.0.

Results

The mean PROQ3 scores for the total sample were compared with those for a male population sample of English men ($n = 59$, from Birtchnell *et al.*, submitted). The prisoners had a significantly higher mean score on LC and ND and a significantly lower mean score on UN, although the samples did not differ significantly in terms of total mean score.

The mean PROQ3 scores for prisoners who were returned to their prison of origin as being unsuitable for treatment were compared with those who stayed the full 18 months. The prisoners who were returned prematurely received significantly higher UD scores, indicative of a greater number of relating deficits (8.1 compared with 7.0; $t = 2.04$, $p < .05$) and significantly lower LD scores, reflecting fewer deficits (5.0 compared with 6.3; $t = -3.02$, $p < .01$).

There were 172 prisoners who were tested on admission and after 9 months. As shown in table 18.1, there were significant reductions in mean scores on 7 of the 8 scales as well as the total score. The one scale on which there was no significant reduction (UN) was the one on which prisoners did not receive a higher mean score than the male population sample.

At both 9 months and 18 months, 130 prisoners completed the PROQ3. As shown in table 18.2, there were further significant reductions on 3 scales (UC, LC and LN) and on the total score. Thus, although most improvement occurred during the first 9 months, further improvement occurred during the second 9-month period.

There were 141 prisoners who completed the PROQ3 at both admission and at 18 months. As shown in table 18.3, there were significant reductions

Table 18.1   Mean PROQ3 scores on admission and nine months post-admission ($n = 172$)

	UN	UC	NC	LC	LN	LD	ND	UD	Total
Admission	5.9	4.6	4.8	8.1	5.8	6.3	8.6	7.4	51.7
9 months	5.8	3.0	3.7	6.7	4.9	5.2	7.2	6.5	42.9
t	.5	5.2	4.0	4.3	3.5	3.7	4.5	2.9	5.9
p	.64	.00	.00	.00	.00	.00	.00	.00	.00

Table 18.2   Mean PROQ3 scores at nine months and at eighteen months ($n = 130$)

	UN	UC	NC	LC	LN	LD	ND	UD	Total
9 months	5.8	3.2	3.7	6.6	4.8	5.2	6.9	6.4	42.6
18 months	5.7	2.6	3.4	5.5	4.1	5.1	6.6	6.5	38.8
t	.4	2.2	1.0	3.2	2.4	.4	.4	.4	2.6
p	.66	.03	.31	.00	.02	.72	.72	.66	.01

Table 18.3   Mean PROQ3 scores at admission and at eighteen months ($n = 141$)

	UN	UC	NC	LC	LN	LD	ND	UD	Total
Admission	5.7	4.8	5.0	8.0	5.8	6.3	8.5	7.0	51.2
18 months	5.7	2.7	3.4	5.7	4.2	5.1	6.7	6.5	39.6
t	.2	6.2	4.8	6.5	4.6	3.5	2.5	1.6	6.9
p	.86	.00	.00	.00	.00	.00	.01	.12	.00

in mean scores on 6 scales. The 2 scales on which there was no significant improvement were UN and UD. Interestingly, no significant improvement was demonstrated on the UN scale for any of the comparisons, although the UD scale showed significant improvements over the first 9 months.

Using the *reliable change index* (RCI; Jacobson & Truax, 1991), it was found that after 18 months, using each prisoner's total PROQ3 score as the criterion, 31 prisoners (22.0 per cent) showed reliable improvement (indicated by a total score that decreased by 27 or more), 108 (76.6 per cent) showed no reliable change, and 2 (1.4 per cent) demonstrated deterioration (indicated by a total score that increased by 27 or more). The 31 reliably improved prisoners showed significant reductions on all of the scales. These prisoners also showed significant reductions on all of the scales after nine months.

The 56 prisoners who completed the HDHQ on admission and at discharge demonstrated significant improvements on all of the scales as well as the total score. Using the RCI and each prisoner's HDHQ total score as the criterion, it was found that 23 prisoners (41.1 per cent) showed reliable improvement (indicated by a total score that decreased by 11 or more), 32 (57.1 per cent) showed no reliable change and 1 (1.8 per cent) showed deterioration (indicated by a total score than increased by 11 or more).

Discussion

The findings of the present study suggest that following treatment at Grendon, prisoners experience significant improvement in the ability to relate effectively to others. Significant improvements were seen in virtually all relating styles and over a fifth of the sample showed statistically reliable improvement in total score on the PROQ3. The study supports the hypothesis that therapeutic communities are effective in promoting more competent and adaptive relating.

The only scale on which there was no improvement was upper neutral, which is characterised by a domineering, controlling and self-important interpersonal style. It is interesting to note that this relating style is resistant to treatment in non-forensic therapy populations as well as forensic groups. Given that the defining traits of the upper neutral octagon are not dissimilar to a narcissistic or psychopathic interpersonal presentation, this has implications for assessing participants for suitability for treatment in a therapeutic community. The finding that those showing deficits in lower distance (characterised by an acquiescent, subservient and withdrawn interpersonal style) deselect or are deselected from treatment prematurely may indicate that the presence, or at least recognition, of deficits in this area is a factor which is associated with readiness for treatment.

The relationship between time in treatment and improvement in relating reveals interesting patterns and merits exploration. Whilst upper neutral (domineering, self-important) scores remain unchanged during treatment, upper distant (intimidating and callous) show significant changes throughout the first nine months of treatment. However no significant differences are found between pre-treatment scores and scores at the 18-month stage of treatment. Upper neutral and upper distant were the only areas not to show significant change at the 18-month stage of treatment. This provides further support for the suggestion that personality styles characterised by a domineering, un-empathic and callous interpersonal style are resistant to change (Barbaree, 2005; Hart & Hare, 1997; Rice & Harris, 1997). More recently Shuker and Newton (2008) found that aggressive, antisocial and tough-minded personality features are more resistant to change than disorders characterised by a lack of self-esteem, personal distress and personal inadequacy.

The present study indicates that the progress seen in some relating styles (upper close, lower close and lower neutral) within the first nine months continues up until the 18-month period. This may indicate that prisoners with deficits in competence in achieving closeness may need greater time in therapy in order for major improvement to be made. It may also suggest that deficits concerning helplessness and personal inadequacy in relationships continue to occur throughout the therapeutic process rather than just in the first nine months.

The study also suggests that a sizeable proportion of the sample made significant changes during treatment. It also indicated that those with very high PROQ3 scores on admission demonstrated that they were capable of considerable improvement. There was also a small cohort of the sample who demonstrated no reliable change (and even some who demonstrated deterioration), suggesting that there are some prisoners, particularly those who score highly on the upper scales, who do not respond well to treatment in a TC.

The finding that changes in the HDHQ corresponded with changes in the PROQ3 provided a further indication that treatment was effective in promoting more adaptive interpersonal beliefs and attitudes. The HDHQ is a measure of hostility that closely reflects some of the interpersonal characteristics assessed by the PROQ3. The finding that there was an overlap between prisoners who demonstrated reliable change on the HDHQ and those who reported reliable change on the PROQ3 provides support for the conclusion that therapeutic communities are effective in promoting greater competence in interpersonal relating. The results lend support to the validation of the therapeutic community treatment model as one that impacts upon interpersonal processes and promotes more adaptive interpersonal styles and beliefs.

References

Barbaree, H. (2005). Psychopathy, treatment behavior and recidivism: An extended follow-up of Seto and Barbaree. *Journal of Interpersonal Violence, 20*(9), 1115–1131.

Birtchnell, J. (1996). *How Humans Relate: A New Interpersonal Theory*. Hove: Psychology Press.

Birtchnell, J. (2002). *Relating in Psychotherapy: The Application of a New Theory*. Hove: Brunner-Routledge.

Birtchnell, J. & Evans, C. (2004). The Person's Relating to Others Questionnaire (PROQ2). *Personality and Individual Differences, 36*, 125–140.

Birtchnell, J., Hammond, S., Horn, E. & De Jong, C. (submitted). *A Shorter Version of the Person's Relating to Others Questionnaire (PROQ3)*.

Birtchnell, J. & Shine, J. (2000). Personality disorders and the interpersonal octagon. *British Journal of Medical Psychology, 73*, 433–448.

Blackburn, R. (1998). Psychopathy and the contribution of personality to violence. In T. Millon, E. Simonsen, M. Birket-Smith & R. Davis (Eds) *Psychopathy: Antisocial, Criminal and Violent Behaviour* (pp. 50–68). New York: Guilford Press.

Caine, T., Foulds, G. & Hope, K. (1967). *Manual of the Hostility and Direction of Hostility Questionnaire (HDHQ)*. London: University of London Press.

Chiesa, M. & Fonagy, P. (2000). Cassel personality disorder study. Methodology and treatment effects. *British Journal of Psychiatry, 176*, 485–491.

Dolan, B., Evans, C. & Wilson, J. (1992). Therapeutic community treatment for personality disordered adults: Changes in neurotic symptomatology on follow-up. *International Journal of Social Psychiatry, 38*, 243–250.

Gunn, J. & Robertson, G. (1982). An evaluation of Grendon prison. In J. Gunn & D. Farrington (Eds) *Abnormal Offenders, Delinquency and the Criminal Justice System* (pp. 285–305). Chichester: Wiley.

Hart, S. & Hare, R. (1997). Psychopathy: Assessment and association with criminal conduct. In D. Stoff, J. Breiling & J. Maser (Eds) *Handbook of Antisocial Behavior* (pp. 22–35). New York: Wiley.

Jacobson, N. & Truax, P. (1991). Clinical significance: A statistical approach to defining meaningful change in psychotherapy research. *Journal of Consulting and Clinical Psychology, 59*, 12–19.

Kiesler, D. (1996). *Contemporary Interpersonal Theory and Research: Personality, Psychopathology and Psychotherapy*. New York: Wiley.

Lees, J., Manning, N. & Rawlings, B. (1999). *Therapeutic Community Effectiveness: A Systematic International Review of Therapeutic Community Treatment for*

People with Personality Disorders and Mentally Disordered Offenders. University of York: NHS Centre for Reviews and Dissemination.

McCrae, R. & Costa, P. (1990). *Personality in Adulthood.* New York: Guilford Press.

Newton, M. (1998). Changes in measures of personality, hostility and locus of control during residence in a prison therapeutic community. *Legal and Criminological Psychology, 3,* 209–223.

Newton, M. (2006). Evaluating Grendon as a prison: Research into quality of life at Grendon. *Prison Service Journal, 164,* 18–22.

Rice, M. & Harris, G. (1997). The treatment of adult offenders. In D. Stoff, J. Breiling & J. Maser (Eds) *Handbook of Antisocial Behaviour* (pp. 425–435). New York: Wiley.

Shuker, R. & Newton, M. (2008). Treatment outcome following intervention in a prison-based therapeutic community: A study of the relationship between reduction in criminogenic risk and improved psychological well-being. *British Journal of Forensic Practice, 10*(3), 33–44.

Warren, F., Evans, C., Dolan, B. *et al.* (2006). Impulsivity and self-damaging behaviour in severe personality disorder: The impact of democratic therapeutic community treatment. *Therapeutic Communities: The International Journal of Therapeutic Communities and Supportive Organisations, 25,* 55–71.

Warren, F., McGauley, G., Norton, K., Dolan, B., Preedy-Fayers, K., Pickering, A. *et al.* (2003). *Review of Treatments for Severe Personality Disorder.* Home Office Online Report 30/03.

Chapter 19

The Experiences of Black and Minority Ethnic (BME) Prisoners in a Therapeutic Community Prison

Michelle Newberry

Introduction

Research has indicated that black and minority ethnic (BME) sex offenders in England and Wales are less likely to participate in the Prison Service Sex Offender Treatment Programme (SOTP) than non-BME sex offenders (Cowburn *et al.*, 2008), and that BME men who complete the SOTP feel that group facilitators treat them differently to white group members. Specifically, some prisoners reported that they felt victimised, patronised or stereotyped and that cultural factors relating to their offence were overlooked (Patel, 1997). In addition, Wakama (2005) found that BME sex offenders and white SOTP facilitators both reported difficulties in understanding the impact of cultural values on offending behaviour. However, because the majority of studies have focused on BME offenders in the wider prison system, there is a paucity of research concerning the experiences of BME offenders in therapeutic community (TC) prisons.

This chapter will focus on discussing themes that have emerged from empirical research conducted with BME prisoners at Grendon therapeutic prison. Research that has investigated the number of BME admissions to Grendon and the length of time BME prisoners spend in therapy will be reported, as well as possible reasons why some BME men might not apply

Grendon and the Emergence of Forensic Therapeutic Communities: Developments in Research and Practice
Edited by Richard Shuker and Elizabeth Sullivan
© 2010 John Wiley & Sons, Ltd.

to Grendon. Recent research conducted at Grendòn into the views of BME prisoners in relation to the therapeutic process will also be discussed.

Admissions of BME Prisoners to Grendon

The number of BME prisoners admitted to Grendon is low compared to the number of BME prisoners in the wider prison system. For example, the percentage of receptions to Grendon from ethnic minorities increased to 6–7 per cent in 1993–1995 and peaked at 16 per cent in 1997 (Newton, 2000), although this is still low when compared to the national figure of 21 per cent for adult male prisoners serving sentences of over four years (Prison Statistics England and Wales, 1997, cited in Newton, 2000). A number of potential reasons have been suggested as to why fewer BME men have been admitted to Grendon in recent years. Peter Bennett, the Governor of Grendon, suggests that the imbalance raises important questions about prisoners' and staff perceptions of Grendon and asks, 'Are there aspects of Grendon which appeal to some cultural groups less than others?' (Bennett, 2007, p. 6). Research carried out by Sullivan (2007) suggests that this may well be the case. She interviewed five BME men about their experiences of applying to Grendon and identified seven themes surrounding why men from BME communities might not choose to apply. These were:

- **Stigma** – which was primarily related to the fact that potential residents would be required to engage in therapy alongside sex offenders. Comments from the men highlighted that relationships with family, especially female family members, are particularly important, and that values surrounding domestic or sexual abuse result in intensely negative feelings for sex offenders. Stigma was also related to the belief that Grendon is about naming others as wrongdoers or 'grasses' (Sullivan, 2007). Although prisoners in general tend to avoid grassing on others due to concerns for their safety, this may be more of a concern for BME men who associate feelings of 'honour' with belonging to a group (e.g. a gang).
- **Communication** – this referred to the fact that some prisoners may not be fluent in English, which may make them less comfortable about engaging in the therapeutic community process. In addition, comments made by one of the men (a traveller) suggest that travellers tend to keep themselves to themselves due to experiences of discrimination in the past. This might mean that these individuals are less likely to engage in a TC environment.

- **Stereotyping** – which concerned the notion that prison staff may hold inaccurate beliefs about which prisoners would be suitable for referral to Grendon, either because of their race or culture, or offending behaviour. The men felt that violent and drug-related gang crime was particularly prevalent among BME offenders and that staff tend to perceive this type of crime as an indicator that an individual is not suitable for referral. As Sullivan notes, if this were true, or believed to be true, this may help to explain why less BME men apply to Grendon.
- **Cultural values** – which alluded to the idea that beliefs about crime differ across cultures, and was another factor which was considered relevant to whether or not a BME prisoner would apply to Grendon. For example, honour killings are perceived as socially acceptable in some cultures, and would therefore not be amenable to therapy designed to promote recognition of criminal behaviour.
- **Not being a good (criminal) career move** – which referred to the belief expressed by respondents that a proportion of the BME criminal population commit profitable offences such as drug dealing and trafficking, which may continue whilst in prison. These men may find Grendon less appealing because of its strict no drugs policy (Sullivan, 2007). Although these activities are not specific to BME offenders, this theme offers a potential explanation as to why BME prisoners might be less likely to apply to Grendon, as one man quoted by Sullivan suggests:

Well, if you look at the nature of crime that black men and white men come in for, there's a stark difference (…) black men predominantly come to jail for stuff like drug dealing, importation, sometimes murder, homicides, (…) a lot of white people (…) their crime is normally different, shoplifting, burglary, you know, domestic violence, (…) you can't do domestic violence in jail so it's not easy for them to further their crime in jail (…) don't get me wrong, I think there are white people who do that as well but I think predominantly it's people from BME backgrounds because that's what they've done and that's what's got them in jail in the first place.

- **The importance of belonging** – this was considered to be a crucial factor contributing to why some BME prisoners might not apply to Grendon. As Cowburn *et al.* (2008) note, most prisoners have links with communities outside of prison from which their sense of identity originates and is maintained during their sentence. BME prisoners might be less likely to apply to Grendon as opportunities to relate to others who share one's cultural heritage are more likely to exist in prisons where there are larger populations of BME men.
- **Fear** – which might arise in response to anticipation of stigma, stereotyping or victimisation (Sullivan, 2007).

Other research has also identified themes that may be relevant in attempting to understand why BME prisoners might be less likely to apply to Grendon. For example, Gilligan and Akhtar (2006) suggest that the concepts of *sharam* (shame/embarrassment), *izzat* (honour/respect) and *haya* (modesty) inhibit discussion about sexual matters in many Asian communities, which might mean that some Asian prisoners may be less comfortable talking about certain aspects of their offending behaviour.

Whilst the research conducted by Sullivan highlights a number of possible explanations as to why BME prisoners might be less likely to apply to Grendon than non-BME prisoners, it is important to note that once accepted onto one of the therapeutic communities, BME men tend to progress positively. For instance, research conducted by Newton (2000) found that ethnic minority prisoners admitted to Grendon between 1995 and 1999 were just as likely as white prisoners to progress onto one of the therapeutic communities and were no more likely to leave prematurely. Furthermore, the research found that 62 per cent of ethnic minority prisoners remained in therapy for at least 18 months compared to 55 per cent of white prisoners (18 months in therapy is equated with treatment completion at Grendon). These findings indicate that the TC model is appropriate for members of ethnic minorities (Newton, 2000).

So far, this chapter has highlighted that the majority of research surrounding BME prisoners in the therapeutic community context has focused on attempting to understand why BME men might not apply to Grendon in the first place, or has examined how many prisoners remain in therapy once accepted. It is equally important, however, to explore the perceptions of BME prisoners who are accepted to Grendon and who engage in therapy. Research surrounding the quality of prison life has provided insight into the perceptions of BME men at Grendon, and has informed subsequent research in this area.

BME Prisoners and Quality of Prison Life

The *Measuring the Quality of Prison Life* (MQPL) survey was developed at the Prisons Research Centre at the University of Cambridge in an attempt to capture prisoners' perceptions of their quality of life in individual establishments. It was developed through a process of consulting prisoners and staff and was adopted by the Prison Service in 2002 to become part of formal audit visits. The MQPL survey conducted at Grendon between February and March 2007 provided insight into the views of BME prisoners in relation to the therapeutic process. Although the *Race Equality* score produced by white prisoners was higher than that produced by BME prisoners, BME prisoners had positive perceptions on average (Goodall & Imbert, 2007). However, comments made during group discussions regarding race equality at Grendon suggested that some BME prisoners felt that therapy did not suit them to the extent that it suited white prisoners and that staff did not make enough effort to accommodate therapy to their needs. These findings parallel those reported by Patel (1997) in relation to BME sex offenders who completed the SOTP.

In response to the findings of the MQPL survey, Newberry (2008) carried out a survey to explore the views of BME prisoners at Grendon in relation to the therapeutic process, from which a number of themes emerged which impacted upon their experience of therapy.

Treatment expectations

Prisoners were asked to describe their initial perceptions of Grendon, including where their information about therapy came from prior to their arrival and whether their experiences of therapy matched their expectations. The majority of respondents reported that their information came from either a prisoner or a member of staff at another prison and felt that their expectations of therapy were mainly accurate. However, some men claimed that they found Grendon a 'culture shock' and unlike anything they had experienced before, as the following quotations illustrate:

> *I didn't know what to fully expect. Grendon is very different from any prison I have ever been to.* (Black Caribbean prisoner)
> *I didn't realise it would be so in depth and that it would take years for me to have an understanding of myself.* (Black Caribbean prisoner)

These comments support the suggestion of Sullivan (2006), that access to better information about Grendon prior to arrival may be warranted and that the right message about therapy at Grendon is portrayed.

Newberry (2008) describes a BME prisoner who felt that his experience of therapy at Grendon did not match his expectations because he thought that more residents would genuinely want to change. He felt that Grendon does not always work for those who want to change as 'it only supports devious, manipulative actors who are just playing the parole game' (Asian Indian prisoner, p. 9). It is not possible to say whether this respondent was referring to other BME prisoners or prisoners in general, although it is likely that there will always be offenders who give the impression that they want to change even if they genuinely do not, regardless of their ethnicity. Other examples of therapeutic expectations which BME men considered had not been met in fellow BME prisoners include a respondent who claimed that even though he was a BME prisoner himself, he felt that other men from ethnic minorities sometimes use their race or cultural background in an attempt to obtain preferential treatment. Another BME prisoner stated that:

> We can commit the same crimes as non-BME [men]. I don't agree that we should be given preferential treatment in any way, shape or form. Therapy targets the mind, not the skin/religion or any other differences. (Asian Indian prisoner)

It is interesting that this prisoner implies that his mind is distinct, and independent from his 'skin/religion', whereas other prisoners feel that their race, religion and/or cultural background are integral to the way they think. Therapy facilitators must therefore consider the relevance of these factors on a case-by-case basis as one approach is unlikely to fit all.

Awareness of cultural background

In respect of the treatment of BME prisoners by staff, Newberry (2008) found that the majority of BME prisoners reported that staff at Grendon treat them better compared to staff at other prisons because staff respect them and do not tolerate racial discrimination. However, not all BME respondents felt that therapy at Grendon addressed their cultural needs, and a large proportion of the men stated that it would improve their experience of therapy if staff from a similar cultural background to their own were present. Furthermore, some BME prisoners stated that there is a need for therapy facilitators who have a genuine belief in the therapeutic process, as opposed to 'just doing their job' (Newberry, 2008, p. 17). This has important implications because if members of a therapy group trust and perceive the facilitator positively, the group is more likely to have positive therapeutic outcomes. As Sue and Sue (1977) note, therapy may be terminated early if there is miscommunication between the client and therapist due to 'cultural variations in communication [which may]… lead to alienation and/or an inability to develop trust and rapport' (p. 420). In a similar vein, Mandikate (2007) claims that:

> There is danger in a therapeutic relationship, where the therapist is white
> and the patient from a minority ethnic group, that the therapist may 'inter-
> pret away' the patient's culturally bound material and assume that therapy
> has been successful when there is less evidence of resistance to therapy from
> the patient ... what's left is the patient's compliance with the therapist's
> norms of being. (p. 15)

Interestingly, BME prisoners at Grendon have reported that therapy
facilitators sometimes encourage them to 'let go' of their cultural background (Newberry, 2008, p. 18). In addition, some men feel that their
expression of emotions during therapy is sometimes misinterpreted as
aggression as they often express themselves in ways that are perceived as
aggressive in western culture (Newberry, 2008). This illustrates how culturally specific behaviours might be misinterpreted or disregarded altogether
and leads to the question posed by Bennett (2007): '... what people say,
believe, describe and express ... varies from culture to culture. Surely this
diversity is relevant when seeking to understand how different participants
in therapy describe their childhood experiences?' (p. 7). One prisoner who
responded to the survey conducted by Newberry (2008) stated that therapy
facilitators need to 'appreciate the cultural differences and the way we
speak, act and interact' (mixed white and black Caribbean prisoner, p. 14).

Beliefs about BME prisoners

A number of black prisoners at Grendon reported that they feel misunderstood with respect to their upbringing. For example, one man described
by Newberry (2008) claimed that therapy facilitators think that 'black
people are strong people and that their needs are not as important as non-
BME residents who they see as weak and vulnerable and a "victim" of
circumstance' (black African prisoner, p. 14). If staff perceive black men
to be 'strong' in comparison to men from other ethnic groups then this
may influence an individual's progression through therapy; an individual
who feels that they have to portray themselves as 'tough' and 'masculine'
may find it more difficult to engage in therapy and talk about their personal
experiences. The belief that staff tend to 'foster' non-BME prisoners suggests that it would be interesting for future research to explore how therapy
facilitators perceive prisoners from different cultural backgrounds.

Of concern is research that reports black prisoners at Grendon having
more experiences of being the victim of racist attitudes, body language or
comments from other prisoners than members of other minority groups

(Newberry, 2008). However, whilst overt racist comments are difficult to misinterpret, more subtle manifestations of prejudice may be confused with body language, which could be misconstrued as such. As Boyd-Franklin (1989) suggests, some prisoners might be more sensitive during interactions with others due to differences in cultural upbringing:

> Black people, because of the often extremely subtle ways in which racism manifests itself socially, are particularly attuned to very fine distinctions among such variables in all interactions... Because of this, many black people have been socialized to pay attention to all of the nuances of behaviour and not just to the verbal message. The term most often applied to this multilevel perception of black culture is 'vibes'. (p. 97)

Dealing with racism within the therapeutic setting

Although Boyd-Franklin (1989) refers specifically to black individuals, therapy facilitators need to be aware that individuals from any ethnic minority group may be more attuned to subtleties in behaviour such as respect and sincerity than non-BME prisoners. Although some facilitators may, as Mandikate (2007) suggests, 'interpret away' an individual's culturally bound material, it is likely that facilitators sometimes find it difficult to address racism in the therapeutic context. As Lee (2005) notes: 'Therapists are placed in a double bind whether they choose to speak up or remain silent about racism' (p. 98). He illustrates this by providing an example of the 'slippery slope' of addressing racism in therapy, which he reconstructed from memory based on a conversation he had with a client:[1]

Client:	You know, you have to watch them Mexicans. They'll steal the rug out from under you if you let them.
Therapist:	What do you mean by that?
Client:	(Immediately getting defensive) Hey, don't get me wrong, I'm not racist or anything like that. I work with a lot of them. I have just had some negative experiences with them that make me suspicious.
Therapist:	Do you think that all Mexicans steal and can't be trusted?
Client:	(Defensive and hurt) Hey, man, are you saying I'm a racist for what I said? You're a therapist and you're making me feel like a bad person.

[1]*Note:* Excerpt taken from Lee, L. (2005). Taking off the mask: Breaking the silence – The art of naming racism in the therapy room. In M. Rastogi & E. Wieling (Eds) *Voices of Color: First-person accounts of ethnic minority therapists* (pp. 91–115). Thousand Oaks, CA: Sage Publications. Reproduced with permission from SAGE publications.

Because a therapy facilitator may be accused of being judgemental if they take an active role in addressing prejudice, they may decide to ignore it. They may also fail to acknowledge the influence they have on an individual in the therapeutic context, as Lee (2005) states:

> … I, as a male therapist, have to be conscious of what I embody purely based on the context of my gender when sitting in a therapy room with a woman who has been sexually or physically abused or both. Most white clinicians have absolutely no problem accepting this as ethical and responsible practice. However, when … working with a person of color who has experienced repeated trauma by white people, or who had been the victim of a hate crime, white clinicians defensively respond that they are not racist or responsible for this client's victimization. (p. 97)

Therapist response and background

It is important that facilitators are cognisant of their influence on individuals who engage in therapy. A challenge for the facilitator is to understand personal and ethnic transference as well as countertransference, and to determine culturally suitable goals and therapeutic techniques while examining whether these choices reflect personal values or the individual's needs (Tseng, 2001). A number of BME prisoners at Grendon have reported that it would improve their experience of therapy if there were more facilitators from diverse backgrounds or if therapy facilitators received more diversity training (Newberry, 2008). In particular, one prisoner claimed that he would like:

> *Just someone to relate to or someone who can see things from my perspective. A mindful approach from any person of any race would work if correct training were given.* (Mixed white and black Caribbean prisoner)

Such an objective has been implemented elsewhere. For example, in response to research which indicated that black prisoners in the wider prison system who took part in the SOTP experienced a 'lack of facilitator awareness and poor communication' (Patel & Lord, 2001), the SOTP, led by a Multi-Racial Advisory Group (MRAG), implemented a number of changes to its initial facilitator training and developed an additional specialised *Working with Black Sex Offenders* training course for facilitators and supervisors. These measures aimed to improve the experiences of black sex offenders in treatment. Grendon may benefit from similar action with respect to working with BME prisoners.

Conclusion

This chapter has highlighted that the number of BME prisoners admitted to Grendon is low compared to the number of BME prisoners in the wider prison system. In the hope of attracting more BME prisoners, Grendon has reviewed and updated its recruitment literature by including photographs of BME staff and prisoners along with comments made from named prisoners about their positive experiences in therapy. However, it is too early to assess whether or not this has made a difference and it is perhaps over simplistic to assume that more BME prisoners will put themselves forward on the basis of changes to the recruitment literature (Bennett, 2007). Rather, in light of the findings of Sullivan (2007) discussed in this chapter, it is possible that prisoners' perceptions of therapy at Grendon conflict with their cultural beliefs. For example, the notion of 'therapy' in the western sense has no equivalent in traditional Asian conceptual frameworks, which means that there is limited understanding of its meaning and purpose (Sullivan, 2007). Although research conducted by Newberry (2008) has indicated that, overall, BME prisoners who are referred to Grendon tend to have positive views of therapy because they believe that staff treat them with respect and do not tolerate racial discrimination, not all BME prisoners feel that their cultural backgrounds are taken into consideration during therapy. Given that diversity is such a sensitive topic, it is possible that white therapy facilitators may have fears about acknowledging and encouraging discussion about the cultural backgrounds of BME prisoners, and so a challenge is for diversity training to instil confidence in facilitators to do so. Most importantly, however, therapy facilitators must strive to *understand* the cultural backgrounds of BME prisoners, as one prisoner at Grendon has stated:

> At Grendon we're taught links to childhood and my childhood was typical of a first-generation British-Indian. Understand that and understand my link to that …

References

Bennett, P. (2007). Why do relatively few BME residents choose to come to Grendon? Introduction to the third Grendon Winter Seminar, 23 January 2007. *Prison Service Journal, 173,* 5–8.

Boyd-Franklin, N. (1989). *Black Families in Therapy: A Multisystems Approach.* New York: Guilford Press.

Cowburn, M., Lavis, V. & Walker, T. (2008). Black and minority ethnic sex offenders. *Prison Service Journal, 178,* 44–49.

Gilligan, P. & Akhtar, S. (2006). Cultural barriers to the disclosure of child sexual abuse in Asian communities: Listening to what women say. *British Journal of Social Work, 36,* 1361–1377.

Goodall, P. & Imbert, D. (2007). *MQPL Survey Research Carried out at HMP Grendon 26th February to 1st March 2007.* London: HM Prison Service Report.

Lee, L. (2005). Taking off the mask: Breaking the silence – The art of naming racism in the therapy room. In M. Rastogi & E. Wieling (Eds). *Voices of Color: First-person Accounts of Ethnic Minority Therapists* (pp. 91–115). Thousand Oaks, CA: Sage Publications.

Mandikate, P. (2007). Culture and psychotherapy. *Prison Service Journal, 173,* 15–20.

Newberry, M. (2008). *The Needs of Black and Minority Ethnic (BME) Prisoners at HMP Grendon in Relation to the Therapeutic Process.* Unpublished Prison Service Report.

Newton, M. (2000). Ethnic minorities at Grendon: Trends in admission and length of stay. In J. Shine (Ed.). *A Compilation of Grendon Research* (pp. 37–44). Leyhill Press. Available from Psychology Unit, HMP Grendon, Grendon Underwood, Aylesbury, HP18 OTL.

Patel, K. (1997). *Evaluating the Sex Offender Treatment Programme: Does it Meet the Needs of Ethnic Minorities?* London: Unpublished Prison Service Report.

Patel, K. & Lord, A. (2001). Ethnic minority sex offenders' experiences of treatment. *Journal of Sexual Aggression, 7,* 40–51.

Prison Statistics England and Wales (1997). Home Office. London: Stationery Office Ltd.

Sue, D. & Sue, D. (1977). Barriers to effective cross-cultural counselling. *Journal of Counselling Psychology, 24,* 420–429.

Sullivan, E. (2006). Moving on: Exit interviews in a therapeutic community prison. *Therapeutic Communities, 27*(3), 359–372.

Sullivan, E. (2007). Straight from the horse's mouth. *Prison Service Journal, 173,* 9–14.

Tseng, W. (2001). Culture and psychotherapy: An overview. In W. Tseng. & J. Streltzer (Eds) *Culture and Psychotherapy: A Guide to Clinical Practice* (pp. 3–12). Washington: American Psychiatric Press.

Wakama, S. (2005). *The impact of race and culture on the sex offender treatment programme: From the perspective of ethnic minority prisoners and white facilitators.* Unpublished MSc dissertation, University of Leicester, UK.

Chapter 20

Research in Prison

Martin J. Fisher, Carol Ireland and Elizabeth Sullivan

Research can be a rewarding experience, yet one which requires careful and realistic planning. Completing a piece of research from the initial idea to publication can be challenging if a reasonable period of time is not spent considering the research idea and how its potential can be realised. Possible pitfalls should be considered in advance, with a clear plan of management to mitigate them. This chapter aims to consider the practical and logistical aspects of carrying out research in a prison setting such as HMP Grendon. It will present in brief some suggestions about how both qualitative and quantitative research can be undertaken, and consider some potential pitfalls along the way. While this chapter does not give detailed advice on research methods, which can be found in numerous textbooks, it does consider the implications for the prison researcher of the choices they might make.

Developing the Research Idea

When planning prison research problems can arise if the research context is not properly considered. The National Offender Management Service (NOMS) is the agency of the Ministry of Justice (MoJ) in England and

Grendon and the Emergence of Forensic Therapeutic Communities: Developments in Research and Practice
Edited by Richard Shuker and Elizabeth Sullivan
© 2010 John Wiley & Sons, Ltd.

Wales responsible for the delivery of custodial and community services to offenders. As such, NOMS' broad research aims are directed at assessing the impact of central policy on reducing reoffending and other connected outcomes. Thus, when planning to undertake research in prisons such as HMP Grendon consideration needs to be given to how the proposal might interface with the broader research aims of both NOMS and the prison itself. Practical considerations such as limiting duplication of effort across the prison estate and ensuring that research proposals meet the criteria and protocols applicable to carrying out research in a custodial environment, must be taken into account by the researcher and will be considered by the decision-making body. In addition, the topic should be something that increases current knowledge and which the researcher(s) intend to disseminate by publication.

At HMP Grendon there is a strong tradition of research undertaken by both internal and external researchers. The democratic environment at the prison extends to research and is evidenced in the participation of prisoners and staff together in deciding what the research priorities for Grendon should be. These are described in the Grendon Research Topic List, which is designed to help prospective researchers align their proposals to Grendon's own agenda.

The protocols for seeking to undertake research in prisons (including HMP Grendon), as an external researcher, are contained within Prison Service Order (PSO) 7035 (www.hmprisonservice.gov.uk/resourcecentre/research/) and are overseen by the National Research Committee (NRC) of the Prison Service. In seeking to carry out research in a public sector prison setting, it is essential from the outset to develop the idea with the requirements of the potential host organisation in mind. The most effective means of accomplishing this is to organise information under some standard headings such as are suggested here:

1. Identify the research question(s) that will be investigated.
2. Give a general introduction to the theoretical background and previous research in the area, showing how and why the research question(s) and hypotheses have been generated. The research methodology should be described here with a rationale for its choice. For example, will the research be qualitative, quantitative, or use mixed methods?
3. Give a brief overview and review of key literature, including how key texts have shaped the proposal.
4. Describe the research design, including time line, and the proposed methods of data collection, demonstrating how they are the most effective methods for the research. Detail any equipment that will be

used on prison premises and for which permission will be required, such as recording devices, data sticks, laptops etc.

5. Include some preliminary discussion of the proposed methods of analysis, for example, if the research is quantitative, discuss the numbers of participants required and what statistical analyses are likely to be used, or if the research is qualitative, will thematic analysis be employed and will 'inter-rater reliability' need to be established?

6. Ethical implications will need to be discussed. If required, how will informed consent be obtained? It is useful to develop an information and consent sheet for the decision-making body to see. If confidentiality is an issue how will it be dealt with? Could participating in the research disadvantage or potentially harm participants, if so, what measures would you put in place to protect them?

7. Describe how the results of the research could benefit the prison, the prison population in general, or add to current knowledge in the area.

8. Give an indication of how and where the results are likely to be disseminated and how the individual participants or the prison will obtain feedback.

A failure to consider these aspects of a proposal at an early stage can be risky, as often the researcher is then faced with a range of difficulties, from analysis to successful completion. For example, the nature of the study may require substantial participant numbers to obtain meaningful data, which may not be practically possible in the custodial environment, or may require access to a population that is not feasible. For example, the population size at HMP Grendon is relatively small and is atypical (Shine & Newton, 2000), making it difficult to draw conclusions that can be generalised to other forensic populations. If the intention is to interview or otherwise involve prisoners, consideration must be given to their daily routine. At Grendon for instance, it can be very difficult to find times for groups of men to be available because of the busy timetable of therapy, community responsibilities and other routines. Access to prison-based participants needs careful consideration, and may require prior discussion with the prison concerned. At Grendon, it often takes much longer to collect data than the researcher originally imagined!

Developing the Research Question or Hypothesis

There are a number of issues that should be taken into account when developing a research question. Firstly, it is important that the question or hypothesis should indicate the necessary research tools rather than the available research tools dictating what the hypothesis will be. This can be one of the first pitfalls in research, where researchers initially identify a psychometric they have *available* to use, and administer it without having a clear understanding of what the research question will be. Secondly, research should be informed and directed by existing theory and, where relevant, previous findings (Bryman & Cramer, 1990). New research normally relates closely to existing literature in two ways:

a)   it may look to examine alternative explanations for particular observations other than those offered in similar research; or
b)   it may consider questions that arise from existing findings in research but that have not been answered by them (Lewis & Habeshaw, 2001).

It appears to be a truism that the research question should be *practically possible* to research, however, unless proper consideration is given to the time it will take to gather and analyse the data, the size and nature of the population to be studied and the impact of the research on them, the extra burden on prison staff who will be required to support the activities of external researchers and so on, the proposal will not be accepted.

Seeking Approval

This brings us to the question of gaining access. Once the proposal has been finalised, it is imperative to consider the process by which such research can be agreed through the organisation, as well as the ethical process by which such research can be approved. As far as access to HMP Grendon, for example, is concerned, the process is covered in the PSO referred to above: figure 20.1 shows the subsequent consideration process. It is imperative that the research is provided with clear consideration of ethical issues following the relevant professional code of conduct (e.g. British Psychological Society, 2009; Health Professions Council, 2009). Most organisations have some formal process for this and in the case of HM Prison Service it is the Regional Medical Research Ethics Council (MREC). The proposal must show how the informed consent of the participants will be sought, how data will be kept secure, and give a clear undertaking about the intended use of the data to be collected. For example if a participant in a forensic setting agreed to undertake a risk assessment or personality assessment as part of the research, their data could not be used to clinically inform on their progress if they did not initially sign up to this as part of the informed consent process.

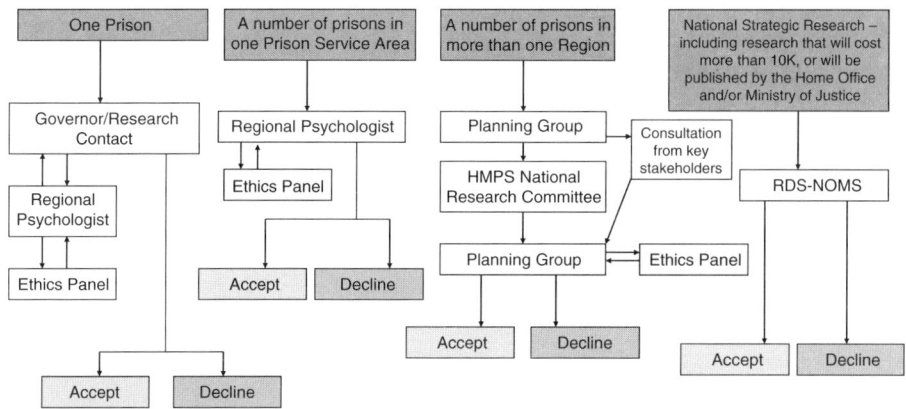

Figure 20.1   Process for consideration of research applications made to HM Prison Service

The general process at HMP Grendon is as shown in figure 20.1 (for one prison), however, there are additional local arrangements, which are shown in figure 20.2. The democratic nature of therapeutic communities (TCs) demands a more inclusive approach to decisions about research than might be generally found. At Grendon each wing or TC is invited to nominate a research representative who is the interface between the TC and Grendon's Research Advisory Group (GRAG). The research reps are trained by the Research Officer to read and understand research proposals and to obtain the views of their own TC on them. The TC views are then taken to GRAG by the Research Officer and considered along with the views of other GRAG members. In this way the people most affected by research – the prisoners – are involved in the decision-making process. The research reps also have other research-related duties such as being responsible for smoothing the researcher's access to communities by raising forthcoming data-collection visits at community meetings, greeting researchers and introducing them to the community, helping to make sure that participants are reminded of time and place, and helping to disseminate results.

The issue of consent for incarcerated offenders taking part in research can be one of much debate and it is critical that the individual participant understands the purpose of the research. Similarly, they should be made aware that irrespective of their decision to participate or not, their choice will have no impact on decisions about their future progress (Koocher & Keith-Spiegel, 1998). HMP Grendon's internal research team are familiar

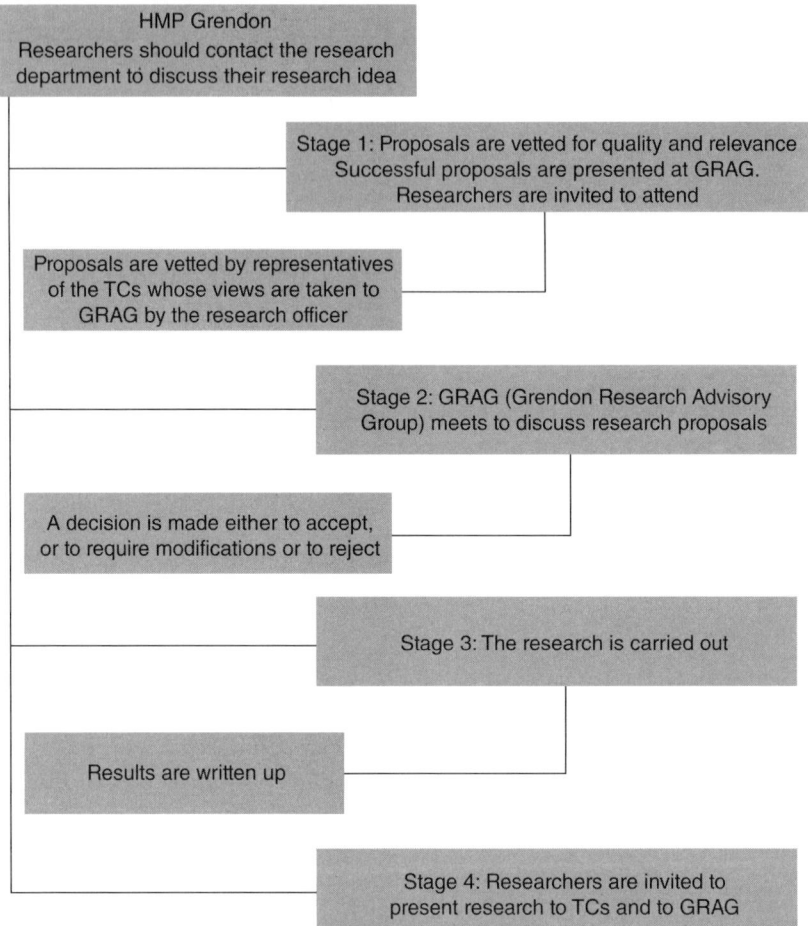

Figure 20.2   Showing the approval process at HMP Grendon

with this set of issues, which is clearly advantageous in planning research in the TCs as the researchers are not only familiar with the relevant protocols, but also with the context of the research environment. Thus, potential external researchers would be wise to consult the team at the outset.

Generally, data collected for research should be kept separate from that which is used to inform clinical judgement. However, if the same set of data-collection tools, such as psychometric tests for example, is to be used later for clinical work, and the earlier completion of these for research might have an undesirable impact (potentially being seen as, or operating as, contaminating factors) judgement must be used, and consent must be obtained from the participant. Such difficulties need to be considered prior to collecting research data and should form part of the informed consent.

Lewis and Habeshaw (2001) suggest three helpful ethical questions to consider when developing research. These are:

- What are the main ethical issues that arise in your area of research? Describe these.
- What ethical issues do you think may arise in your research in the future? Describe these.
- Are there any general ethical issues that surround research in your discipline? Do these have any impact on your area of research/current research projects?

As such, research in a custodial setting requires careful consideration, planning and attention to relevant organisational, ethical and professional protocols and considerations. Without this triangulation of features it is likely that any proposal for research in a custodial setting will fall at the access hurdle.

Data Collection and Considering Data Analysis

Once approval has been gained and access has been negotiated and arranged, the collection of the information on which the research is reliant can commence. Depending on the approach used this may be either quantitative (e.g. Marshall, 1997), using methods such as survey or questionnaire, or qualitative (e.g. Webster & Beech, 2000) using methods such as interviews, focus groups, observations and so on. It is important to allow time for adequate data collection and to build in contingency plans for the inevitable delays caused by unforeseen events. The collection time for data should not be underestimated. During the data collection period time can be spent considering in more detail how it will be analysed. A helpful approach to this can be the composition of a one to two page summary recording the proposed steps to be taken and the reasons why. It is important to consider the basis of the analyses and the underlying interpretative models, as this can help direct and explore the form of analysis that will be undertaken, whether statistical or otherwise (Willig & Stainton-Rogers, 2008).

Generally, statistical analysis will consider how data sets will be screened for missing data and how it will be managed, as well as exploring for outliers in the data set, which may need further consideration. Following this, methods of statistical analysis in line with each hypothesis should be considered. One of the best recommendations at this stage can be to ensure that the researcher's knowledge of statistics is always kept up to date. This can mean investing in a good book of multivariate analysis (e.g. Kinnear & Gray, 2004). Importantly though, no researcher is fully knowledgeable in all areas of statistics; all researchers have their own preferences based on their experiences. Yet, learning about new methods of statistical analysis can be helpful for a researcher and a real opportunity to learn and develop as professionals.

The analysis of qualitative data will depend on how it was collected. Transcription of tape recordings is very time consuming and can begin immediately, without waiting until all the data has been collected. A rule of thumb is that every hour of recording will take a moderately competent typist three hours to transcribe before analysis can begin. If a typist is to be employed to transcribe, consideration has to be given to issues of confidentiality and this information should be included in the proposal. It should also be noted that bringing equipment such as recorders, data sticks and laptops into prison requires special permission that can take some time to obtain, so including this information in the proposal is important.

Dissemination of Results and Writing for Publication

Research that has carefully followed the steps above is likely to be of a standard that would satisfy a professional peer-reviewed journal. If a researcher is to encourage a participant to engage in, and give their time to participate in research, the research should be of a high enough standard for publication. In any case, it is good practice to share a report of the findings with the host organisations. HMP Grendon encourages researchers to present their findings in person, and although this may not be possible or relevant in other settings, it is desirable to provide a summary of the results for information.

Whilst the research may have been commissioned by an organisation or prison to meet its own needs, it is still important to consider writing it up for publication in a journal in order to disseminate the findings as widely as possible. Careful consideration of which journal would be the most appropriate to submit to can be facilitated by reading the 'notes for authors' provided by each journal. This information helps the researcher to focus their writing in the most appropriate way and maximises the chance of being accepted. A write-up of research must follow a number of core principles. It should offer the reader a short abstract containing the main purpose of the study and its core findings. Next, the introduction should clearly link to the literature, appropriate theoretical models and previous research. The method section should be clear and concise, written in a manner by which the reader could easily replicate the approach should they wish to do so. Finally, the discussion section should identify the key findings of the research, discuss these in relation to the literature and previous research, as well as focus on the limitations and implications of such findings. Most journals also encourage writers to provide a list of key words that can be used to facilitate literature searches.

Conclusion

Through a relatively short descriptive process this chapter has sought to offer initial and summary guidance on the principles and protocols of carrying out a piece of research in a custodial setting. Critically, the balance between an effective research methodology and the organisational requirements needs to be measured carefully such that the former is not adversely affected by the latter, whilst bearing in mind that without gaining access to the setting, the research cannot proceed.

References

British Psychological Society (2009). *Code of Ethics and Conduct*. Leicester: BPS.

Bryman, A. & Cramer, D. (1990). *Quantitative Data Analysis for Social Scientists*. London: Routledge.

Health Professions Council (2009) *Standards of Proficiency: Practitioner Psychologists*. Kennington, London: Health Professions Council.

Kinnear, P. R. & Gray, C. D. (2004). *SPSS 12 Made Simple*. New York: Psychology Press.

Koocher, G. P. & Keith-Spiegel, P. (1998). *Ethics in Psychology: Professional Standards and Cases* (2nd edn). Oxford: Oxford University Press.

Lewis, V. & Habeshaw, S. (2001). *Interesting Ways to Supervise Student Projects, Dissertations and Theses*. London: The Cromwell Press.

Marshall, P. (1997). *A reconviction study of HMP Grendon Therapeutic Community. Research Finding 53*. Research & Statistics Directorate, London: Home Office.

Shine, J. & Newton, M. (2000). Damaged, disturbed and dangerous: a profile of receptions to Grendon therapeutic prison 1995–2000. In J. Shine (Ed.) *A Compilation of Grendon Research*. Leyhill Press. Available from Psychology Unit, HMP Grendon, Grendon Underwood, Aylesbury, HP18 OTL.

Webster, S. D. & Beech, A. R. (2000). The nature of sexual offenders' affective empathy: a grounded theory analysis. *Sexual Abuse: A Journal of Research and Treatment, 12*(4), 249–261.

Willig, C. & Stainton-Rogers, W. (Eds) (2008) *The Sage Handbook of Qualitative Research in Psychology*. London: Sage.

Index

*Grendon and the Emergence of Forensic Therapeutic Communities: Developments in
Research and Practice*
Edited by Richard Shuker and Elizabeth Sullivan
© 2010 John Wiley & Sons, Ltd.